Industrial Violence and the Legal Origins of Child Labor

Industrial Violence and the Legal Origins of Child Labor disturbs settled understandings of child labor by tracing how law altered the meanings of work for young people in the United States between the Revolution and the Great Depression. Rather than locating these shifts in statutory reform or economic development, it finds the origin in litigations that occurred in the wake of industrial accidents incurred by young workers. Drawing on archival case records from the Appalachian South between the 1880s and the 1920s, the book argues that young workers and their families envisioned an industrial childhood that rested on negotiating safe workplaces, a vision at odds with child labor reform. Local court battles over industrial violence confronted working people with a legal language of childhood incapacity and slowly moved them to accept the lexicon of child labor. In this way, the law fashioned the broad social relations of modern industrial childhood.

James D. Schmidt is associate professor of history at Northern Illinois University. His first book, *Free to Work* (1998), examined the relationship between labor law and the meanings of freedom during the age of emancipation. He teaches courses on the history of law, capitalism, childhood, and the United States in the long nineteenth century.

Cambridge Historical Studies in American Law and Society

SERIES EDITOR

Christopher Tomlins, *University of California, Irvine*

PREVIOUSLY PUBLISHED IN THE SERIES

Andrew Wender Cohen, *The Racketeer's Progress: Chicago and the Struggle for the Modern American Economy, 1900–1940*

Davison Douglas, *Jim Crow Moves North: The Battle over Northern School Segregation: 1865–1954*

Tony A. Freyer, *Antitrust and Global Capitalism, 1930–2004*

Michael Grossberg, *A Judgment for Solomon: The d'Hauteville Case and Legal Experience in the Antebellum South*

Rebecca M. McLennan, *The Crisis of Imprisonment: Protest, Politics, and the Making of the American Penal State, 1776–1941*

David M. Rabban, *Free Speech in Its Forgotten Years*

Robert J. Steinfeld, *Coercion, Contract, and Free Labor in the Nineteenth Century*

Michael Vorenberg, *Final Freedom: The Civil War, the Abolition of Slavery, and the Thirteenth Amendment*

Jenny Wahl, *The Bondsman's Burden: An Economic Analysis of the Common Law of Southern Slavery*

Barbara Young Welke, *Recasting American Liberty: Gender, Race, Law, and the Railroad Revolution, 1865–1920*

Michael Willrich, *City of Courts: Socializing Justice in Progressive Era Chicago*

Industrial Violence and the Legal Origins of Child Labor

JAMES D. SCHMIDT

Northern Illinois University

CAMBRIDGE
UNIVERSITY PRESS

32 Avenue of the Americas, New York NY 10013-2473, USA

Cambridge University Press is part of the University of Cambridge.

It furthers the University's mission by disseminating knowledge in the pursuit of
education, learning and research at the highest international levels of excellence.

www.cambridge.org
Information on this title: www.cambridge.org/9780521155052

© James D. Schmidt 2010

This publication is in copyright. Subject to statutory exception
and to the provisions of relevant collective licensing agreements,
no reproduction of any part may take place without the written
permission of Cambridge University Press.

First published 2010

A catalogue record for this publication is available from the British Library

Library of Congress Cataloguing in Publication data
Schmidt, James D.
Industrial violence and the legal origins of child labor / James D. Schmidt.
p.   cm. – (Cambridge historical studies in American law and society)
Includes bibliographical references and index.
ISBN 978-0-521-19865-3 – ISBN 978-0-521-15505-2 (pbk.)
1. Child labor – Law and legislation – United States – History.   2. Workers
compensation – Law and legislation – United States – History.   3. Industrial
safety – Law and legislation – United States – History.   4. Child labor – United
States – History.   I. Title.   II. Series.
KF3552.S36 2010
344.7301'31–dc22   2010000033

ISBN 978-0-521-19865-3 Hardback
ISBN 978-0-521-15505-2 Paperback

Cambridge University Press has no responsibility for the persistence or accuracy
of URLs for external or third-party internet websites referred to in this publication,
and does not guarantee that any content on such websites is, or will remain,
accurate or appropriate.

for Ted, Bruce, and the rest
and
for Andrea, who listened

Contents

Illustrations

Acknowledgments

This book would not have been possible without the tireless assistance of staff at state archives. Thanks to everyone who helped me at the Georgia Archives, the Kentucky Department for Libraries and Archives, the Library of Virginia, the North Carolina State Archives, the Tennessee State Library and Archives, and the West Virginia State Archives, Charleston, West Virginia. I have benefited from comments and discussions with numerous fellow historians, especially Eric Arnesen, Patricia Cooper, Laura Edwards, Howard Erlanger, Leon Fink, Hendrik Hartog, Mark Lause, Kriste Lindenmeyer, Susan Pearson, and Jennifer Ritterhouse. Christopher Tomlins has aided and supported this project at two stages, first as editor of an article that appeared in *Law and History Review* and now as editor of the Cambridge Historical Studies in American Law and Society series. His insightful criticisms and helpful suggestions have sharpened my analysis immensely. Thanks to the anonymous readers in *LHR* who provided valuable points on what constitutes Chapter 4 of this book. Thanks also to *LHR* for permission to reprint sections of that article. The anonymous readers for Cambridge dramatically improved the subtlety of my argument. Eric Crahan at Cambridge has been a generous advocate of the book, and Emily Spangler and Jason Przybylski are due thanks for helping the book through the production process.

Northern Illinois University supported this project with summer research money and a semester-long sabbatical. My colleagues at NIU have endured the accident stories with good grace and great insight. Thanks especially to Sean Farrell, Rosemary Feurer, and Beatrix Hoffman, who commented on drafts of chapters. Emily Lowe and Bill Reck assisted with research via NIU's Undergraduate Research Apprenticeship Program. My graduate students have heard about the book much more than they probably desired. Special thanks to students in my Fall 2008 law and society research seminar who read and commented on the book in draft form. Sean Cadagin, Melissa Hayes, and Michael Spires supplied particularly useful criticisms. Melissa Hayes also served as a research assistant, and our countless conversations about each other's research have sharpened my thinking about interactions between law and society.

Low-paid child labor was crucial to this project's timely completion. Thanks to Mike and Drew for lawn mowing, barn cleaning, and garden weeding, and for enduring my other attempts to instill producer values. Once again I salute my parents for all their support and for teaching me how to work. Andrea Smalley should practically be credited as a co-author. She helped with research during a time-constrained archival trip; listened and talked endlessly about the book's organization, argument, and title; and read it all with cheer. She is the brightest and the best.

Prologue

The Job

Around four in the afternoon on March 31, 1969, a welder's spark touched off a grain dust explosion at Circle E Ranch, a large-scale cattle feeding company near the town of Potwin in south-central Kansas. The force of the blast lifted the concrete roof on the lot's grain elevator and twisted the steel buildings that housed the feed mill at the heart of the operation. The accident injured four workers, three of them moderately. The fourth, Ted Pope, worked in the elevator that had borne the brunt. Fire shot up the lift that raised employees to the top of the structure, engulfing Pope in flames and leaving him with third-degree burns over 80 percent of his body. The only places not burned were those protected by leather: his hands, his feet, and his waistline. Twenty-one years old at the time, Ted lay in an El Dorado, Kansas, hospital for months, undergoing repeated surgeries to reconstruct his body, especially the facial features that had been removed by the conflagration. After he recovered from his injuries, Pope returned to the feedlot, working a few years before crashing his motorcycle on a curve near town, a final accident that ended his short life.[1]

I had not known Ted before the explosion. I met him in the summer of 1972, when I worked at Circle E, as I would most summers growing up on the Kansas plains. Ted sat across the table from me at lunch, and his disfigured face provided my most vivid introduction to the violence of modern industry. That summer, I spent most of my time at Circle E,

[1] I have reconstructed this story from my own memory and that of my father, Dean Schmidt. The only public records are newspaper accounts, which are not wholly accurate. See "Three Injured in Blast," *El Dorado Times* April 1, 1969. For Ted Pope's obituary, see *El Dorado Times*, May 31, 1973.

helping my dad and the others lay the groundwork for a quarter-mile-long confinement barn on the property. I was eleven at the time. Oblivious to the state's child labor laws, I was happy to make the five dollars a day my dad paid me to be an all-purpose helper. No one at the feedlot seemed to care that I was there, so long as I stayed out of the way. In any case, since the company had not hired me directly, I was not technically illegal.

By the time I returned to the place as a law-abiding laborer at sixteen, work at the feedlot dominated my three months away from school. At fifty-four hours a week with time-and-a-half for the last fourteen, "the job" supplied ready cash for college and a source of worry for my mother. An amalgam of industry and agriculture, a modern cattle feeding operation offers a multitude of dangers. I had been warned. Growing up, I listened to my dad's stories of men ground up in hay mills or sliced in half by dump trucks, and I had seen him and others endure countless minor and not-so-minor injuries. Still, I had my share of mishaps and close calls. In the record-breaking heat of July 1980, we pulled long shifts refitting the mill. Stumbling across the top of the plant one night, my leg suddenly dropped. Someone had left the cover off of a processed grain bin. Had I been unlucky enough to fall in, I would have plunged thirty feet onto a spiked breaker bar. I was more careful after that, but paying attention only goes so far. For working people, death and injury are part of daily life. That lesson came home to my family in December 1983 when the counterweights of an oil field pump crushed one of my older cousins to death.

A career in the academic realm removed me from the world of industrial violence until I ran into Bruce Holt. I met Bruce at the North Carolina State Archives in Raleigh. As I listened to him and his mother, Cora, talk about Bruce's accident, their experiences sounded familiar. Bruce was hurt at Oval Oak Furniture in Siler City on July 5, 1917, when a wood-working machine slammed a board into his midsection. Unconscious for four weeks after the accident, the young worker endured months of agonizing treatment and rehabilitation, efforts that saved his life but left him debilitated. One of the millions hurt during the grand era of U.S. industrialization, Bruce's calamity did not make headlines in his own time. Its only record lies in the neatly organized archives of the Supreme Court of North Carolina. Bruce's story has survived because he, like many of his fellow young workers, took the company to court.

I had looked up Bruce in the first place because I intended to write a book about young workers and the law during the nineteenth century. I thought that following the archival trail of high court cases, as historians were beginning to do, might provide some good details to liven up a potentially lifeless tale. The more I encountered people like Bruce, the more I realized that the history of their encounters with the violence of modern industry deserved to be told on its own terms. This book is theirs, but it is still the story of how law changed the meaning of work for young people in the United States between the Revolution and the Great Depression. As such, it is a book about what people nowadays call "child labor." Unknown at the turn of the nineteenth century, that moniker for the labors of young people arose after the U.S. Civil War and came to dominate public discussion of youthful labor during the era that historians used to call Progressive. By the mid-twentieth century, child labor had become a symbol for childhood lost, its practice considered a violation of human rights. Knowing what I did about working people in the nineteenth century, I wondered how that momentous change came about. I think part of the answer to that question can be found in the stories of young people such as Bruce Holt, particularly in the ways their industrial accidents brought them and their families into contact with new definitions of childhood via the avenue of the courts.[2]

The main characters that populate my recounting of that story hail from the Appalachian South. I chose to center on Appalachia in order to situate the narrative in a social context that would keep some specificity in view, a valuable part of historical inquiry that gets lost in "national" histories. Too often, the history of the United States has been told from the viewpoint of its northeastern corridor and its other urban centers. The recent rush to transnational storytelling, while a laudable effort to combat American exceptionalism, has further diminished the attention to time and place that should undergird our efforts to read the past. Beyond these general motivations, I have focused much of the story on Appalachia

---

[2] Barbara Young Welke's work first showed me how the archival trail of appellate cases offered a middle ground between the top-down view of doctrinal analysis and the usually time-consuming and ultimately less-than-fruitful approach initiated entirely from below by using local records. While studies based in local records can have great potential, they are confined by the nature of record-keeping in a particular place, and they often lead to an overemphasis on large, urban centers. Using state high court records provides a much broader source base, supplying examples from cities to hamlets. More importantly, by the late nineteenth century, the appeals process guaranteed that some sort of transcript would be generated from the court stenographer's notes, creating a record that (if it survived) is simply not available in other places on such a consistent basis. See *Recasting American Liberty: Gender, Race, Law, and the Railroad Revolution, 1865–1920* (New York, 2001). On the potential difficulties of local sources, see Stephen Robertson "What's Law Got to Do with It?: Legal Records and Sexual Histories," *Journal of the History of Sexuality* 14 (2005): 161–185.

for reasons arising from the historical record itself. Unlike the long transition to industrial capitalism that occurred in the so-called North, the transformation of the Southern countryside was quick and intensive. The very rapidity of the region's industrialization between 1880 and 1920 means that the changes I seek to illuminate are somewhat easier to see there than in locales where the same process took longer. Looking at that relatively condensed process over about a forty-year period allows us to witness the encounter between young people and industrial life within one or two generations, offering the opportunity for careful investigation while avoiding the pitfalls of supposedly "local" studies. More important, the eastern parts of the South became a center of child labor reform activity in the Progressive period. In the late nineteenth and early twentieth centuries, child labor reformers focused much of their attention on the southeast and its seemingly "backwards" expansion of youthful labor. For this reason as well, it is a social context where the workings of law in culture can be seen more clearly. For many reform-minded people, the mills, mines, and workshops of Appalachia were *the* battleground, for in their estimation, matters in the "North" were well in hand. The South, however, represented a locale squarely in the sights of the Progressive era reformers who fashioned the language of child labor. Hence, Appalachia provides the best place to examine the central questions that prompted my curiosity about young workers and the law.[3]

Attention to place is vital to any meaningful account of the past, but I do not intend to tell a strictly Southern story. Rather, this book is an

[3] As historical geographer D.W. Meinig famously remarked, "history takes place." For a recent reflection on Meinig's views, see Graeme Wynn, "D.W. Meinig and the Shaping of America," *Journal of Historical Geography* 31 (2005): 610–633. Place has always mattered to those who study the U.S. South, but the struggle to get others to see its importance continues. For recent statements, see Melvin Patrick Ely, *Israel on the Appomattox: A Southern Experiment in Black Freedom from the 1790s Through the Civil War* (New York, 2004), esp. 14–15; and Erskine Clarke, *Dwelling Place: A Plantation Epic* (New Haven, 2005), ix–xi and *passim*. For an excellent example of a legal study that pays attention to local context while not losing sight of the so-called big picture, see Karl Jacoby, *Crimes against Nature: Squatters, Poachers, Thieves, and the Hidden History of American Conservation* (Berkeley, 2001).

Most recently, Laura Edwards has made a powerful case for the centrality of the southern story to U.S. legal history. See *The People and Their Peace: Legal Culture and the Transformation of Inequality in the Post-Revolutionary South* (Chapel Hill, 2009), 10–16, 223–227. Additionally, she argues convincingly that law and society studies must pay attention to the divergences between what she terms "localized law" and "state law." *The People and Their Peace*, esp. 3–10, 26–53. While *The People and Their Peace* appeared too late for full incorporation into what follows, my account confirms and extends Edwards's suggestion that localized law persisted after the rise of state-centered legal systems. *The People and Their Peace*, 287–289.

American story with a Southern accent. While events south of the Mason-Dixon Line figure prominently, the history of young workers, industrial violence, and the law is not confined to the South. Over the course of the nineteenth century, legal developments dramatically altered the way people understood youthful labor. As we shall see, these changes took place as often in Massachusetts or Minnesota as they did in North Carolina. Certainly, those northern and western locales generated their own dialects, but those tongues are no more or less normal and national than the ones spoken in warmer climes.

On a wider scale, the transformation of youthful wage work into a social injustice is something that occurred across the whole of the industrializing world. My discussion of the broader changes in law and the language of child labor is framed as a conceptual question that concerns a long transition in modern life: from childhood as a time of preparation for economic production to a stage of life that centers on play and formal schooling, a form of socialization more fitted for the "consumer society" of advanced capitalism. My account illuminates a part of that transformation, one bounded by historical circumstance yet crucial to the larger linguistic reformulation necessary to imagine child labor. Anchoring this tale in other places would no doubt alter the circumstantial evidence, but it likely would not fundamentally reshape the outcome. As a variety of peoples came into the industrial world, they found themselves forced to confront the conundrums about young people and work generated by industrial capitalism. Whether in Appalachia, the Midlands of England, northern Germany, or places farther away from the industrial core, the quandaries of young workers came to the fore in the late nineteenth and early twentieth centuries. In the early twenty-first, we are still trying to sort out the consequences of the fundamental shifts these changes produced.[4]

At the core of my story, then, is a large shift in the cultural imagination of youthful labor that occurred between the late nineteenth and early twentieth centuries. That shift originated in a conflict over how young people would fit into the increasingly dangerous nature of work in modern societies. On one side stood young workers and their families who sought an industrial childhood, one that found a safe place for young people in the world of work. Against this outlook, reformers conjured

---

[4] I have hence followed the insight of Richard White that there is no "right" scale for historical study. Rather, the scale must fit the questions being posed. Richard White, "The Nationalization of Nature" *Journal of American History* 86 (1999): 976–986.

a different vision, one that resolved the dilemmas of modern capitalism and youth by excluding younger people from productive life. The legal system – from high courts to local law offices – provided a central arena for this conflict to play out.

The timing of this long transition in youthful labor cannot be easily attached to a particularly dramatic reform tract or a signal piece of legislation. No particular high court decision can be said to have significantly altered the lives of young workers in its own right. Still, much had changed by the second decade of the twentieth century. By that time, young workers and their families had spent more than four decades bringing their stories of death and disfigurement to local courthouses. Over that same period, the nation's legal system had resolved the necessary paradoxes that youthful labor presented to a capitalist legal culture based on the fiction of autonomous adulthood. The interaction between these two ends of the legal process, and all the parts in between, encouraged young workers and their families to speak the language of modern childhood. This process slowly edged working people toward a revised understanding of growing up, one that shifted value away from work and toward school and play.

At the end of the American Revolution, a very different understanding of young workers prevailed. Slavery expanded; indentured servitude and apprenticeship, though under stress, remained normal. Young people worked, and many toiled away from their parents. These social arrangements continued into the late nineteenth century as industrialization proceeded at a more intensive pace. Given this long and uneven process of change, this book is organized topically rather than chronologically. I start by outlining the ways through which working people sought to integrate the young into industrial production. They did so not merely because of economic necessity or because they lacked feeling for the younger members of the household. Rather, they had their own vision about the place of young people in industrial society. Shared by young and old alike, that outlook expected people to contribute to their own livelihoods as soon as they possessed the physical capacity to do so. Those abilities could be measured by size and experience much easier than they could by calendar age. Learning to work was a slow process, one not distinctly removed from play. Shop floor antics introduced young workers, especially boys, to the world of production.

By the turn of the twentieth century, this view was under siege as reform writers took up the cause of "child labor." Their efforts produced a genre of "protective legislation" that prohibited work under certain ages and regulated it for others. In doing so, they imagined the source of "the child labor problem" inside working households, particularly in the dereliction of "lazy fathers." In their efforts to remedy this social ill, they articulated a new definition of childhood itself, one that located young people's legitimate activities in the schoolroom and at the playground, not on the shop floor. In the gaze of reformers, young workers lost their capacities to produce and to influence their own futures. They became instead "little sufferers" who needed to be protected from their employers, their parents, and the world's work. Silenced by this literary amelioration, young people obtained "the divine right to do nothing."

Resolution of this conflict over the meaning of youthful labor turned on a number of broad changes in Western society, changes that altered schooling, socialization, and sexuality – almost every conceivable corner of growing up. As with other areas of modern life, violence propelled the pace of change. In the middle chapters, I consider how working people encountered that violence and how jurists who heard claims for redress outlined a legal language of childhood and youth.

Certainly, machine production is inherently dangerous, yet the industrial violence of mines and factories originated in social conflict as much as it did in technological improvement. Young workers and their families hoped to enter the industrial world with producer-oriented values intact, but they did not do so haphazardly. Instead, they struggled to control the terms of labor for young people, aiming to make bargains that would ensure safety at work. The daily cupidity of specific employers and the systemic hierarchies of industrial capitalism undermined the pains they took to protect the young. In the place of a relatively safe workplace that eased young people into their laboring lives, they got injury and death. The horrors of those experiences and the wrenching dislocations of extended recoveries motivated young workers and their families to seek redress.

Violence by itself did not force working people to relinquish their desire for a different industrial childhood, for the understandings people assign to pain, injury, and death change over time. What these events meant to young workers and their families originated in how they viewed labor, youth, and the connection between the two, but they also came from sources outside working households: the language of child labor created by reformers, and especially, the definition of childhood authored by the nineteenth-century legal system. While much of the discussion about youth in nineteenth-century courts revolved around the "best interests of the child" in domestic law, judges around the country also talked about young workers and their families. Early in the century, they sealed off apprenticeship as a bound relationship, ensuring the split between work and education that would became the hallmark of Western growing-up. At the same time, they released young people from strict parental control, authorizing the work arrangements that these laborers made on their own initiative.

Having conceived of young workers as independent agents, judicial minds initially wrote them into the legal regime for adults who incurred workplace accidents. As the nineteenth century wore on, however, the courts slowly crafted a new understanding of young people and industrial violence, one that placed them outside the law for older workers. This new vision incorporated ideas about childhood that developed as a result of mishaps in nonindustrial settings. In thinking about those deaths and injuries, judges concluded that the causes lay in the natural instincts of children. By the late nineteenth century, they incorporated these notions of incapacity into their thinking about youthful labor, stamping it as illegitimate. By the turn of the twentieth century, courts began to interpret child labor statutes through this lens, often reaching the proposition that illegal employment of young people was automatic grounds for compensation. These changes opened the courthouse doors to working families, turning a sprinkling of suits into a deluge.

These shifts in the judicial imagination of youth provided the backdrop against which Progressive era families would seek to deal with industrial violence. The book's final chapters take up this part of the tale to illuminate how the commonplace legal interactions of young people and industrial violence contributed to the foundations of modern childhood. These interactions of law and society occurred because coming to court compelled young workers and their families to confront the growing challenge presented by reformers. Statutory prohibition of child labor threatened to end once and for all the quest for an industrial childhood. Those enactments sought to replace a dynamic process of learning governed by natural markers of capacity and with a simplified legislative assertion of incapacity. Often uncertain about calendar age, young workers and their families reacted to these new rules in a variety of ways, sometimes complying, sometimes breaking the law outright, sometimes evading it or using it to their benefit.

If uncertain about the law as proclaimed from the statehouses, working people possessed more confidence about their chances in the courts. There, they hoped to make employers pay for their broken promises. In these fights, they were not alone. Kinfolk, neighbors, fellow workers, and of course, employers encamped on court days to talk about young people, work, and violence. Less dramatic than the street battles of the union movement, legal confrontations involved no less vital issues for laboring people. In these struggles for power, workers often won the battles, even if they lost the war in the end.

These courtroom conversations brought laboring people into contact with ideas about childhood and work that diverged from their own. Looking to enforce their own ideas that the job could be organized to protect youth, they retold their tales of violence and reenacted their injuries. Talking about family tragedies in the witness box, however, was not like stories relayed on the porch, at the general store, or in church. In court, the language of the law channeled the ways working people could make their claims. With childish impulse as its leitmotif, the law's script encouraged the assembled court to fill in the pictures sketched by reform writers. Playing at work became a sign not of industrial learning but of the natural incapacity to coexist with hazardous equipment. School marked the proper place for youngsters. Completing more than a century of contestation, the courtroom encounter between industrial violence and the law prompted laboring people to re-vision young workers as child labor.

Big Enough to Work

I never told Williams when he was talking to me about playing with the
machine, that it was none of his damn business. I don't use that sort of
language. (Jimmie Taylor, 1894)

Jim Kendrick was late for work. Truth be told, the whole family had
overslept. Now, the household hurried to make it to their places on
time. J.P. Butler, Jim's stepfather, ran a blacksmith shop in the mill
town connected to High Shoals Manufacturing Company in Walton
County, North Carolina. The rest of the Butler clan, including Jim,
a son from Mrs. Butler's previous marriage, worked in the mills and
knew they would be in trouble if they showed up late. Jim's brothers
and sisters headed for work without eating breakfast, but he stayed
behind. "Mama had got breakfast and the whistle blowed and I was
hungry and I waited and she fixed me a lunch," Jim, age thirteen, later
recalled. Biscuit in hand, Jim hightailed it for the mill, passing his
father's shop on the way.[1]

Perhaps Joe Pettit liked trains. At age eleven, Joe tried several odd jobs
in and around South Rocky Mount, North Carolina, but he kept coming
back to the rail yards of the Atlantic Coast Line, dodging locomotives
to ferry messages between the men working in the depot. The work was
arduous: twelve-hour shifts, seven days a week. But Joe liked to work.
He had helped out at Clarence Miller's bakery as an order boy, clearly
meeting the man's approval. "I knew the boy and learned to love him,"

---

[1] *Record in Kendrick*, 51, 61, 89. In order to save space and needless repetition in notes to
the archival record of cases, I have adopted a shortened form throughout. For an explanation and the full citations, see "Note on Sources" following the Epilogue.

Miller remembered. "When I told him to do anything it was a pleasure for him to do it." When Joe met J.R. Jones, another boy who had been working as a messenger, J.R. recruited Joe to work in the yards. J.R. described their negotiations: "I was working night and day and I couldn't get anybody to help me out and I asked him if he would help me, and if he would come back I would give him the day job and I would take the night job." Joe agreed, collecting his wages and bringing them home to his mother Sallie: a poor, illiterate, widowed mother of eight, who was wholly unaware of what Joe was doing. "He told me he was a messenger boy, but I didn't know anything about it," she disclosed.[2]

Jim Kendrick and Joe Pettit present two quite different faces of youthful labor in the industrializing South. Kendrick embodies the family labor system. Common in textile manufacturing but also present in many other industries, family labor dominated the mill villages that dotted the Southern landscape after the Civil War. Male-headed households took their broods to the mills to find work when crops and fortunes failed. For several decades, these mill villages and the culture they fostered formed a vital center of Southern working life. Joe Pettit's brief life, however, paints a different picture. Although Sallie Pettit later remarried, when Joe worked for the Atlantic Coast Line, he lived in a female-headed household on the margins of the Southern economy. Partially due to this fact, he possessed a great deal of autonomy to come and go as he pleased, making his own work arrangements and receiving his own pay. Yet, he also acted as the man of the house, bringing wages back to the family purse.[3]

A century later, people know that Jim and Joe should not have been at work. This understanding of young people's work derives from a middle-class rendition of childhood that triumphed over the course of the nineteenth century. Centered on involuntary schooling and voluntary play, this lexicon imagined wage work for young people below a statutorily regulated age as fundamentally illegitimate. Its traditions about youthful

---

[2] *Record in Pettit 1911*, 9–10; *Record in Pettit 1923*, 22, 25–26.
[3] Jacquelyn Down Hall et al., *Like a Family: The Making of a Southern Cotton Mill World* (Chapel Hill, 1987); Douglass Flamming, *Creating the Modern South: Millhands and Managers in Dalton, Georgia, 1884–1984* (Chapel Hill, 1992), esp. Ch. 5; Cathy L. McHugh, *Mill Family: The Labor System in the Southern Cotton Textile Industry, 1880–1915* (New York, 1988). Perhaps the best treatment of young workers in the New South can be found in I.A. Newby, *Plain Folk in the New South: Social Change and Cultural Resistance, 1880–1915* (Baton Rouge, 1989), 132–140. My evidence confirms much of Newby's analysis of textile mill children and extends that analysis to other areas of work.

work have come down to us as "child labor." This convention refashioned a wide range of day-to-day experiences into the unitary construction of the child, a powerful image that obscures the ways in which young workers and their families thought about what they were doing.[4]

For much of the period of industrialization, working people articulated their own outlook for young persons in industrial society, a vision of industrial childhood that put them at odds with the middle-class project. Young workers like Joe Pettit entered the workforce with a degree of autonomy, whereas those like Jim Kendrick began their working lives under the guidance of parents. In both instances, however, young people expected to abide by a common set of values, a worldview that historians usually call producer ideology. Drawing on roots in agrarian life, young workers and their families brought producer values from the countryside into the mills, mines, and shops. Those values placed a premium on the physical production of the world's goods and asserted that those who made them comprised the true citizenry of a republic. As such, working people envisioned childhood not as a special time devoted to education and leisure, but as a slow transition into an adult identity bound up in the world's work. This commitment to a useable industrial childhood did not preclude time for merriment. Tinkering with technology often ended tragically, but it did not originate in the uncontrollable impulses of childhood, the view taken by outside observers. In fact, play on the shop floor

---

[4] On the rise of middle-class childhood, see among many others, Harvey Graff, *Conflicting Paths: Growing Up in America* (Cambridge, 1995); Steven Mintz, *Huck's Raft: A History of American Childhood* (Cambridge, 2004), esp. Ch. 5.; and Daniel Thomas Cook, *The Commodification of Childhood: The Children's Clothing Industry and the Rise of the Child Consumer* (Durham, 2004). For a critique, see Olga Nieuwenhuys, "Child Labor and the Paradox of Anthropology," *Annual Review of Anthropology*, 25 (1996): 237–251.

My argument here and throughout proceeds from the assumption that we can and should use age as a category of analysis. On this matter, the best introduction to date is the inaugural edition of *Journal of the History of Childhood and Youth*, 1 (2008). In particular, see articles by Peter Stearns, "Challenges in the History of Childhood" (35–42); Joseph Hawes and N. Ray Hiner, "Hidden in Plain View, The History of Children and Childhood in the Twenty-First Century" (43–49); and Steven Mintz, "Reflections on Age as a Category of Historical Analysis" (91–94). Howard Chudacoff pioneered the subject of age analysis as opposed to the history of childhood. See *How Old Are You? Age Consciousness in American Culture* (Princeton, 1989). For the concept in practice, see Mintz, *Huck's Raft*; Stephen Robertson, *Crimes against Children: Sexual Violence and Legal Culture in New York City, 1880–1960* (Chapel Hill, 2005); Stephen Lassonde, *Learning to Forget: Schooling and Family Life in New Haven's Working Class, 1870–1940* (New Haven, 2005); Holly Brewer, *By Birth or Consent: Children, Law, and the Anglo-American Revolution in Authority* (Chapel Hill, 2005); and Karen Sanchez-Eppler, *Dependent States: The Child's Part in Nineteenth-Century American Culture* (Chicago, 2005).

formed a vital part of growing up as a worker. In one of the central conflicts of the progressive era, it was this vision of childhood that reformers
sought to eradicate.[5]

HELP WANTED

Young Southerners who embarked on industrial labor hailed from a wide
variety of backgrounds. They spanned a range of ages, from children as
young as eight to incipient adults in their late teens, but the prototypical
younger worker was between twelve and sixteen. Some were from failing yeoman families migrating to the mills. Others came from single-
parent abodes or from households under stress for a range of reasons.
Some found work with their parents or with siblings, but many joined
the workforce on their own accord, often without their parents' consent
or knowledge, sometimes in open defiance. Moreover, they often demonstrated keen knowledge of how the labor market functioned, contradict-
ing notions that they were simple-minded innocents abroad.

   Of course not every working family left the countryside in the late
nineteenth century. In fact, the majority remained, and young people in
these households continued to do productive labor, sometimes within the
family economy and sometimes outside of it. Up and down the eastern
seaboard, young people worked in truck gardening and berry farming.
On the Gulf Coast, they did stints in canneries and other food processing

---

[5] The history of "child labor" has most often been written from the reform tradition and
from reformers' sources. With the exception of a few industry or job-specific treatments,
the lives of young workers are practically unstudied in labor history. They occupy the
place that women and people of color once did: relegated to a place "outside" of the
field. I think that can be explained by the hegemony of the cultural trope I seek to decon-
struct in this book: child labor. The best recent example of this approach to the topic is
Hugh D. Hindman, *Child Labor: An American History* (Armonk, 2002). The issue of child
labor reform sometimes populates stories of the labor movement. See Gary M. Fink, *The
Fulton Bag and Cotton Mill Strike of 1914–1915: Espionage Labor, Conflict, and New
South Industrial Relations* (Ithaca, 1993), esp. 51–58 and Shelley Sallee, *The Whiteness
of Child Labor Reform in the New South* (Athens, 2004), esp. Ch. 2. Only occasionally
have historians placed age at the center of that story. For examples, see Ava Baron, "An
'Other' Side of Gender Antagonism at Work: Men, Boys, and the Remasculinization of
Printers' Work, 1830–1920," in *Work Engendered: Toward a New History of American
Labor*, ed. Ava Baron (Ithaca, 1991): 47–69; and Jacquelyn Dowd Hall, "Disorderly
Women: Gender and Labor Militancy in the Appalachian South," *Journal of American
History* 73 (1986): 354–382. Perhaps, the single best account of young workers involves
the coal industry in Canada. See Robert McIntosh, *Boys in the Pits: Child Labour in the
Coal Mines* (Montreal, 2000). McIntosh's sensitive and subtle account of young colliers
aligns with much of what I argue here.

concerns. For freed families, the place of young people's labor became a central hallmark of liberty, as parents and other family members gained the authority to direct young workers. Still, young freedpeople themselves often asserted control over the fruits of their labors. In most agrarian families, whatever their regional location, young people participated in productive households early on, taking over small chores in gardens and farmyards. In doing so, they helped reproduce the economic culture of country life.[6]

For all of this work on the farm, agricultural labor for young people was something different from work in the industrial world to come. It is important to bear in mind that much of "child farm labor" in both the past and present is nothing of the sort. It is actually industrial labor for agricultural production. Nonetheless, such labor in the progressive era was largely handwork, not tied to the dangers of mechanization that took center stage in textiles, woodshops, and mines. For actual work in the fields, the industrial relationships of factory work did not apply. Young people in these situations had both more and less autonomy: more in the sense of not being under an unrelated boss, less in the sense of being more thoroughly under the watchful eye of their parents. Moreover, farm mechanization in the late nineteenth and early twentieth centuries did not produce the harrowing threats presented by the behemoths of twentieth-century farm technology. Nor did it rival the forces unleashed by industrial mechanization. A horse-drawn hay rake could hurt somebody, but it simply did not have the destructive power of a woodworking machine. Working families would encounter industrial life primarily in factories, not on farms.[7]

Although the family labor system was by no means the only way that young Southern workers entered the labor market, it nonetheless held sway in large parts of the South. As the agricultural crisis of the late nineteenth century swept across the region, dislocated Southern families sought work in burgeoning mill towns, often on the fall line where mountains and hills gave way to more gentle coastal plains. In this region,

---

[6] Hindman, *Child Labor*, 248–290; Cindy Hahamovitch, *The Fruits of Their Labors: Atlantic Coast Farmworkers and the Making of Migrant Poverty, 1870–1945* (Chapel Hill, 1997), 39–45, 51–52; Dylan C. Penningroth, *The Claims of the Kinfolk: African American Property and Community in the Nineteenth-Century South* (Chapel Hill, 2003), 164–170; Jane Addams, *The Transformation of Rural Life: Southern Illinois, 1890–1990* (Chapel Hill, 1994), 100–105.

[7] Canneries present a prime example of industrialized agricultural processing. See Hindman, *Child Labor*, 263–274. On the power of industrial machines and a further discussion of farm mechanization, see Chapter 3.

often called the Piedmont, Southern entrepreneurs financed the erection of cotton factories, woodworking plants, and a wide variety of other small manufacturing concerns. In other parts of the South, iron and coal production dominated local economies. Outside of these core industries, growing Southern mercantile towns hosted small metal shops; canneries, confectionaries, bottling plants, and other food production facilities; steam laundries; and, of course, hotels, restaurants, and other small businesses. Across the region, the expanding rail network required ever more labor. In the communities that grew around these centers of production, Southern families found a place to earn cash in the increasingly market-driven Southern economy.[8]

The transition to industrial work took a considerable amount of time, often leaving parents back on the farm with little idea about what their children were doing at work. Families came to mills and mines only to return a season later, as hope remained that next year would bring the good crop that would guarantee life in the countryside. Southern farmers such as William Starnes brought wives and children to the mills in an attempt to escape the vagaries of the Southern economy. Starnes confided to a fellow worker that "he was working his chaps now, and he was going to try to come out of debt." Poverty clearly played a role in the Starnes family's decision to move. "Mr. Starnes came to pick my cotton and then went to the mill," a neighbor reported. "He had nowhere else to go." Going back and forth between farm and industry was not confined to textiles. A West Virginia mine foreman maintained that Charley Daniels hired his son in the mines, saying that "I am trying to make a crop and I need all me and the boy can make." All of this moving around meant that parents often remained in the dark about what went on in mills, mines, and factories. G.W. Harris, whose son Jim worked for Union Cotton Mills in Georgia, put the matter simply: "I do not know anything about cotton mill work, I never worked in one."[9]

Family labor normally meant that fathers found work for their children, either singly or as a group. Columbus Barnes wrote to the Augusta Company in 1881, seeking work for his children. Receiving a request "to bring them on," he sent Anna Elizabeth, his oldest daughter, to the factory with a family associate two weeks before he moved the rest of

---

[8] For introductions to Southern economic change in this era, see Gavin Wright, *Old South, New South: Revolutions in the Southern Economy Since the Civil War* (New York, 1986); and Edward L. Ayers, *The Promise of the New South: Life After Reconstruction* (New York, 1992), Chs. 1–5.

[9] *Record in Starnes*, 33, 26; Record in *Harris*, n.p.; *Record in Daniels*, 127.

the Barnes clan. More often, negotiations took place face to face. Walter Affleck, fifteen, and his brother William, sixteen, worked for Powhatan Lime, one of several lime manufacturing firms near Strasburg, Virginia. "Me and papa went down there and we seen Mr. Richards, and he told him that he would like to get us a job, and he said all right," Walter relayed. The elder Affleck then inquired about what sort of work the boys would be doing. "Well I can give them a job nailing barrels," their prospective employer replied. If they did not do that, they would unload coal or "pick up a little lime." Negotiations might be this straightforward, or hiring might simply evolve out of informal arrangements. A fellow worker at Lynchburg Cotton Mills recalled that Tom McDaniel "used to come with his father, and then he came all the time after he could work." Such evolutions might grow out of something closer to daycare than to child labor. Eight-year-old Willie McGowan accompanied his parents to work at Ivanhoe Manufacturing so they could keep an eye on him. "My father and mother were both working in the mill and there was no one left at home," Willie remembered. Tagging along with Mom and Dad, he found himself doing "various little jobs" with "free access to mill and machinery."[10]

While fathers frequently took the lead in finding work, mothers also served as labor agents. Sometimes they played this role well into their offsprings' adulthood. In early 1907, Georgia Starnes traveled to Mountain Island, North Carolina, to get work for her married daughter. More commonly, mothers acted in ways similar to fathers, finding work for younger children entering the labor market. When the Ward family left the farm for the factory in the autumn of 1893, Mrs. Ward came to the mills first with children in tow. According to W.R. Odell, the mill's secretary-treasurer, "she came in the office and told us what hands she had … and I told her that she did not have a sufficient family to make a living. That her children were too young." Mrs. Ward pressed the mill to employ her family, for she planned to rent the family farm and supplement her children's income with sewing. If Odell is to be believed, Mrs. Ward slowly wore down the mill's resistance. "She cried and seemed to be very much in earnest, and we finally consented to take them in the mill," he averred. The exact cause of Mrs. Ward's distress remains a mystery, but her husband, S.P., corroborated the notion that finding employment for eight-year-old Ebby and the others was her doing. "My wife put him

[10] *Record in Augusta Factory*, 3; *Record in Powhatan Lime Co.*, 138; *Record in McDaniel*, 63; *Record in McGowan*, 14, 4.

there," S.P. stated bluntly. "He brought the money home, and we generally put the money in my wife's care."[11]

Then as now, family connections proved important in getting work. Young workers often started their careers by accompanying older siblings. Willie Bartley, for example, went to work in a Kentucky mine to help out his older brother. Fitz Stanley assisted his older brother in a Virginia textile plant, receiving no wages for his tasks. Siblings also communicated vital information about open positions. Eleven-year-old Luther Green heard about an opening at Ornamental Iron and Wire in Chattanooga, Tennessee, from his brother. "My brother told me that they had a boy there that they was giving $2.50 a week and that they would give me a job at 25 cents a day," Luther reported, "and the Boss asked Will if I wanted a job of work." Extended family connections worked equally well in small mill and mine communities. Sam Honaker's uncle hired him to work in a West Virginia mine as a trapper and then as an assistant brakeman. Irene Davis described how her daughter, Kate, got work at The Augusta Factory, through a sister-in-law who planned to quit.[12]

Parental supervision, working with kinfolk, using family connections to find work all represent part of the family labor system. All were widespread practices in the industrializing South, but other young workers belonged to different kinds of households and entered the labor market in a variety of ways. Households or marriages under stress meant something different from fatherly control. Unemployment, criminality, and injury all changed the family dynamic when it came to younger members looking for and finding work. Single-parent households, especially those headed by women, pushed younger members, especially boys, into the labor market sooner than they probably would have done in two-parent settings. Finally, orphans and younger children who lived with relatives created a set of relationships that often pitted relatives against each other for influence, if not control, of a younger worker's labor.[13]

Not surprisingly, the legendary patriarchal households of the New South were no more free of conflict that those of any other period. Intrafamily strife often played a role in the decision to work outside the household. Mattie Cooper relayed how fights between her two sons led

---

[11] *Record in Ward*, n.p. Mrs. Ward's first name does not appear in the record.
[12] *Record in Bartley*, 14–16; *Record in Lynchburg Cotton Mills*, 2; *Record in Ornamental Iron and Wire Co.*, 18; *Record in Honaker*, 14; *Record in Davis*, n.p.
[13] For a similar account of young workers seeking jobs on their own, see McIntosh, *Boys in the Pits*, 160–164.

to one leaving. Her boys "had a fuss about work on the farm" that ended in a knife fight with biblical overtones. "I saw they couldn't get along together, that the other one would kill Tom," she disclosed, "so I took him to Mr. Bud Newton's and got him to keep him." Conflicts need not be this dramatic to push young workers into a job. J. B. Ensley secured a position for his son because the sixteen-year-old was thinking about leaving home and "his mother was very much troubled about it."[14]

If internal pressures stressed Southern working families, external shocks weighed even heavier. Many Southern fathers were anything but upstanding role models. Luther Green's father was in jail for counterfeiting when the lad got himself a job. With his mother home sick, Luther no doubt saw both the opportunity and responsibility to earn his keep. Unemployment also prompted families to put more reliance on the efforts of their younger members. Ralph Girvin ended up working at Georgia Veneer and Package Company after family fortunes tumbled. "Mr. Girvin was running a bicycle shop, but he failed a few months before that, and that is why we got a position for the boy," Ralph's mother, Kate, reported. "We could hardly live at that time." Work accidents themselves also played a decisive role in the employment of young workers. "My mother sent me to see Mr. McArthur and try to get a job because my brother who is older than I am and had been working in the mines had his arm broke," Johnnie Queen reported. When Elliot Smith got mashed up in a Kentucky coal mine, his young son Bentley took his father's place. "He come to me and said to me, 'Pa, I want to work in the mine, you are mashed up and our house rent is to pay and we have got to live,'" the elder Smith recalled.[15]

Injuries also diminished parental authority, leading to the disappearance of children into the world of work. Elliot Smith had tried to stop Bentley, but the boy sneaked off to the mine, purloined his old man's check number, and went to work with his older brother, Pitman. "I was mashed up and he slipped off from me that morning and went ahead anyway," Elliot noted. When Joseph Woodruff got hurt on the Central Railroad in Georgia, he, too, lost more than his ability to work. His boys fought with each other and, perhaps, with their new stepmother.

---

[14] *Record in Newton,* 1–2; *Record in Ensley,* 14. In fact, Gary Freeze has argued that the decline of patriarchy helps explain mill village paternalism. Gary R. Freeze, "Patriarchy Lost: The Preconditions for Paternalism in the Odell Cotton Mills of North Carolina, 1882–1900," in *Race, Class, and Community in Southern Labor History,* ed. Gary M. Fink and Merl E. Reed (Tuscaloosa, 1994), 27–40.

[15] *Record in Ornamental Iron and Wire Co.,* 19; *Record in Girvin,* 9; *Record in Moore (Kentucky),* 4; *Record in Queen,* 22–23.

Then, William just got up and left, running away to work on the railroads in Alabama. His father guessed that William had headed for an uncle's place in Knoxville, but he could not hunt for him "on account of being crippled up." In fact, Joseph attributed William's desertion to his own injury and the loss of authority it caused. "He was a very dutiful boy ... until I got crippled up so," Joseph figured. "He went off after I got crippled up when he had no parent to look over him like other boys; they get wild mighty quick."[16]

Stressed families such as the Woodruffs reveal households where male-directed labor forces were not the norm. Another such family type was the single-parent household. Divorce, abandonment, and death took their toll on many marriages, leaving men and women to fend alone, often with many children. Such households were often headed by men. Charley Daniels looked after his children as well as he could after his wife's murder. Charley stuck it out on the farm in Kentucky, while his boys went across the Tug Fork of the Big Sandy River into West Virginia to live with a brother-in-law and work for Thacker Fuel in their coal mines. While Daniels's misfortune was dramatic, some Southern men really did live out the stereotype of the legendary ne'er-do-well. B.E. Raines fit the model so well as to almost be a caricature. B.E., a self-described "rambler," scratched out an existence however he could after his wife died, leaving him with six children. With a hint of pride, B.E. described his survival strategies: "I make a living the best way I can. Sometimes I work and make it, sometimes I peddle and make it, and sometimes I farm and make it." Even the farming was tenuous. B.E. owned about five and a half acres and "a little log cabbin." Although B.E. also farmed some rented land, the home place toted up to not more than fifty dollars. "It ain't worth what I can get out of it," he concluded. As a result, part of B.E.'s meager income came from the labor of his son Bub, on the rails. For B.E., though, this was nothing to be embarrassed about. He firmly denied that he "relied" on Bub for his support.[17]

While such male-headed households appeared frequently, families overseen by women were more common. If divorce was relatively rare, abandonment was rife. The penchant of Southern working men to

---

[16] *Record in Moore (Kentucky)*, 4; *Record in Davis*, n.p.; *Record in Woodruff*, 7–9.

[17] *Record in Raines*, 16; *Record in Daniels*, 92. B.E. Raines "dual tenancy" arrangement resembles the household economy that Sharon Ann Holt found among freedpeople in Granville County, North Carolina. *Making Freedom Pay: North Carolina Freedpeople Working for Themselves, 1865–1900* (Athens, 2000).

"ramble" often left women to fend for themselves, sometimes temporarily, sometimes indefinitely. Nancy Queen ran an African-American family by herself in Morgantown, Tennessee, after her husband vanished. "I have been married but my husband don't live with me now," she noted. "I don't know where he is." Sabina Allen, a West Virginian, found herself in a similar predicament. Abandoned by her husband, she tried to keep hearth and home together as a single mother. In this arrangement, her older son Russell took over as head of household, providing the main family income.[18]

Abandonment left some hope of return, but the relentless rounds of death in an industrializing economy meant that many Southern women suddenly had to figure out how to cope with the task of raising children on their own. Surviving often involved collecting the wages of younger members of the family, but just as often it meant losing control, either voluntarily or inadvertently. After Charles Giebell's father died, his mother simply let the sixteen-year-old keep the money he made in a woodworking plant. "Yes, she let it be mine," a somewhat surprised Giebell acknowledged. "She didn't try to take it away from me or anything. After I paid my board it was mine what was left." Of course, giving Charles his wages was a kind of survival strategy: His independence reduced his reliance on the family exchequer. But many such partings were not so amicable. As with male-headed households, families headed by single mothers afforded young workers more autonomy in the labor market and at work. Mary Honaker lost her husband, and she had a hard time keeping track of her son Sam. The fourteen-year-old brought home about twenty dollars a month from the mines, but that's about all she knew about it. She claimed she paid "very little attention" to Sam's job, knowing little about the nature of it or about his wages.[19]

Single-parent households presented a complex set of motivations for work, especially from the perspective of the parent. Another sort of Southern family arrangement created complicated pressures from the point of view of younger workers. Orphans and children sent to live with relatives found their labor directed not only by household heads but also by concerned relations. From an economic outlook, boarding a younger sibling was a losing proposition, and older brothers and sisters expected youngsters to earn their keep. Gus Stanley, for example, apparently found work for his little brother Fitz in order to offset the boy's

[18] *Record in Queen, 24–25; Record in Allen, 21.*
[19] *Record in Giebell, 24; Record in Honaker, 43–47.*

expenses. According to company officials, the older Stanley "wanted regular employment for him as he had his board to pay and clothes to buy." Relatives keeping children might also find work for them simply to make sure they were under a watchful eye. Frank Rhodes's step-grandfather took him to the mines in West Virginia for this purpose. "Frank worked with me," H. Marshall admitted. "I could take care of Frank as well as any man could, and I would rather he work with me than to go in and undertake to be floater around the mines." When children boarded with relations while their parents still lived, things could get even more complicated. J.W. Baldwin of Garland Pocahontas Coal described such a conflict between Phillip Waldron's father and H.S. Short, his step-grandfather, with whom the sixteen-year-old was living: "Mr. Short intimated to me that he wanted the boy to go to school, and his father wanted him to work on, and I kind of interpreted Mr. Short as meaning that if I got him away from there, it would relieve him of the burden; that he didn't want any friction with his father."[20]

Southern working families came in many flavors, and many of those allowed considerable discretion for young workers in making decisions about how and when to enter the labor market. In many instances, however, young workers exercised even greater autonomy, finding work on their own and making their own decisions about what to do with the proceeds. They evinced an understanding of the workings of the Southern labor market and responded to the growing temptations of consumer products. All of this is not to say that young workers possessed the same level of "freedom" attained by adult workers. Rather, it is to point out that enough young workers enjoyed enough control over their own decisions as to constitute a distinct slice of the labor force. Young workers were not simply an extension of their parents; they frequently acted on their own.

For many young workers, finding a job often meant venturing out into the world of mines and mills by themselves or with other young laborers. Arthur Burnett, an orphan of fourteen, was hired at a North Carolina cotton mill in 1906. Myrtice Ransom had an active imagination about her own age, but she claimed to be twelve when she secured a position in 1918 without the permission of her parents, working as a caramel chopper at the Nunnally Company, a confectionary in Atlanta. Clarence Broyles was eleven when he asked for a spot at Keystone Coal and Coke

<hr>

[20] *Record in Lynchburg Cotton Mills*, 85–86; *Record in Rhodes*, 131; *Record in Waldron*, 98.

in McDowell County, West Virginia. As T.F. Smith, the mine foreman recalled, Broyles "just come and asked me for work." William Fitzgerald, age ten, supplied a lengthy description of getting work on his own: "[I] had never before worked in a factory," he conceded. With his father out of town, he headed for the factory bright and early on Monday morning and asked for a position. "Mr. Grissom, the Foreman of the factory, said he could give me 25¢ a day," William remembered. "I hired to him and he put me to 'tailing the molder' and pulling saw-dust to the furnace." As these examples should make clear, children sought and found work at quite young ages without the involvement of their parents.[21]

Younger children also got jobs on their own by tagging along with older siblings. Fourteen-year-old Mary Michels's experience at Casperson's laundry in Louisville, Kentucky, was typical. Mary had been waiting tables at the Business Woman's Club when she decided to go along with her older sisters, Florence and Josephine, to their jobs at Portland Laundry, owned by L.C. Casperson. Her parents knew she was working there, but they were apparently uninvolved in her decision. "Neither of them told me I could go," Mary acknowledged. "I just went with my sisters." In fact, her sisters and her fellow young workers were the prime movers in her decision to switch jobs. "I was short of help," L.C. Casperson recalled, "and I asked some of the girls if they knew of any girl who wanted work and one of the girls said that I had two of the Michel [*sic*] girls there and said another one of the Michel girls wanted to work and I told them to bring her along."[22]

Mary Michels's interaction with other young workers in securing employment was not unusual. Boys and girls often recruited other boys and girls to work alongside them or to take their places as they departed for other jobs. As we saw earlier, Joe Pettit ended up as a messenger boy at the behest of another message carrier. Mike Hatfield took up a paper route for the Owensboro, Kentucky, *Daily Inquirer* by first accompanying Leon Marian on his route. When Leon fell sick, he asked Mike to take over the task. "Jobs" might also come up simply by following friends around. There was considerable dispute about whether Ellis Crosby was ever employed at a Waycross, Georgia, bottling plant, but adult workers at the facility mainly recalled him "working" with a friend, David Salzman, whom they insisted on referring to as the "Jew

---

[21] *Record in Burnett*, 13–14; *Record in Ransom*, 1; *Record in Swope*, 21; *Record in Fitzgerald*, 9.

[22] *Record in Casperson*, 1–6, 17, 49.

Boy." Tillman Rogers, who ran a bottler, reckoned that Ellis initially did not work "two days out of three" but that he "followed the Jew Boy around." H.D. Adams, another Waycross resident who had worked at the facility, viewed the situation similarly: "The Jew Boy was working for Mr. Keen. Ellis worked there only what time he was hanging around the Jew Boy." Clearly, Ellis and David were pals. "Ellis and I are right good friends," David proclaimed. He also maintained that the plant's owner, D.L. Keen had made a deal with the two youngsters: "Mr. Keen told us both if we would go ahead and work like we ought to we would have a job for all the season."[23]

While young workers formed employment networks, they also responded to businesses that actively sought their labor. Leander Hendrix worked at Cooleemee Mills after the company came to him. Sam Carter, a worker in the plant, visited the Hendrix abode at the behest of the overseer in the weaving room. "I told Carter to go out and find me a sweeper," the overseer stated. "The only thing I said to the boy when he come on was to ask him if he was a smart boy." A similar, but more complicated, arrangement prevailed in mining districts. In many mines, adult "miners" worked as independent contractors, having the power to hire and fire their own helpers. Henry Lavier, superintendent at North-East Coal in Kentucky, explained how this worked: "Well, we have a custom over there, an accommodation to the men, to allow them to draw on the man they work for; then at the end of the week we give this man credit, and it is deducted from the man's wages that hired the boy."[24]

Young workers who entered the Southern labor market occasionally did not know what to expect, but just as often they acted in ways similar to adult laborers. Sometimes that meant conforming to the racial ideologies of adult workers. When Charles Turner applied for work with the Richmond and Rappahannock Railway Company, racism figured heavily in his decision. E.W. Thomas, who hired him, remembered an exchange with Turner about laboring in a mixed-race group. "I told Mr. Turner I had a gang of men cutting wood this side of the Chickahominy River, colored men and white men mixed up together, and that he could go down there and work if he wanted to," Thomas said. "That didn't seem to suit him." Turner's aversion conformed to the racial ideologies of the Jim Crow era. The notion that hard, dangerous work was "Negro labor"

---

[23] *Record in Pettit (1911)*, 9–10; *Record in Hatfield*, 52; *Record in Keen*, 12, 16, 21.
[24] *Record in Hendrix*, 2; *Record in North-East Coal Co.*, 107. See also *Record in Smith*, 16–30.

persisted throughout the period. At a Georgia woodworking plant, for example, white workers recognized a racial dimension to the highly treacherous work that took place around open vats of boiling water. "I always saw men, colored men, working out there," Blair Latham, a young white worker reported. "They always had colored men and not boys working around these vats." Learning the subtle (and not so subtle) racial signals of the Southern working world came with age, and at least in some instances, cross-racial friendships were not unheard of. Twelve-year-old Gaines Leathers maintained a friendship with Cephas Thompson, a black fellow worker, at Blackwell Durham Tobacco. "Cephas and I were friendly," Leathers recalled. "He had given me a banana." In other words, racial thinking figured in the response of young workers to the Southern industrial landscape, but young workers also found ways around the stifling atmosphere of the Jim Crow South.[25]

The most common way that young workers evinced an understanding of the labor market appeared in their efforts to increase their wages. After a while, Gaines Leathers sought to work at a higher-paying job at Blackwell Durham. Originally hired to pack boxes going out of the factory, he quickly learned that tying tobacco sacks netted better pay because it paid by the piece. "It was my purpose to try to learn to tie and make more money," he acknowledged. Similar wage practices occurred throughout the Southern textile industry. As W.H. Hobby, a worker at Tifton Cotton Mills in Georgia, explained there were "two sides in these spinning frames, and if a child could keep up both sides they would get 12 1/2 cents to 15 cents to a side." In mining, working for subcontractors instead of directly for the company might pay higher dividends. Phil Waldron apparently understood this fact and switched work in order to get fifty cents more a shift. Mining and other industries also rewarded certain dangerous jobs more than others. Such "opportunities" might lead young workers to deceive parents who thought their children were working at relatively safe places. Sam Honaker's mother could not have been too pleased when she heard that he had labored for ten months as a pigtailer when she thought he had been working as a trapper. A somewhat chagrined Sam had to answer for telling tales to keep his Mom from knowing what he was up to. Why had he deceived her? "Because

---

[25] *Record in Turner*, 74; *Record in Girvin*, 9; *Record in Leathers*, 19; Daniel Letwin, "Interracial Unionism, Gender, and 'Social Equality' in the Alabama Coalfields, 1878–1908," *Journal of Southern History* 61 (1995): 519–554. On how children interacted across racial lines, see Jennifer Ritterhouse, *Growing Up Jim Crow: How Black and White Children Learned Race* (Chapel Hill, 2006), esp. Ch. 4.

there was more money in pigtailing," he revealed. Perhaps Sam Honaker's storytelling can be put down as youthful naïveté, but it is more likely that he had learned quite a bit about how mining worked during his thirteen years. Certainly, plenty of young workers had little notion about the value of their labor or about the meaning of its conditions. Still, without the ideological and institutional underpinnings of innocence, they figured out how the world worked fairly well.[26]

The desire to increase wages arose from two seemingly contradictory desires. On the one hand, young workers, especially older ones, sought to contribute to family economies. On the other, they strove for independence from the economic control exerted by their parents or guardians. Numerous young workers sallied forth and found jobs on their own, only to turn over the proceeds to the family purse. Carl King got a job in an Atlanta shop at the suggestion of a boarder in the King household, but he had an eye on making a contribution. "I went and got that job myself," he admitted. "I carried the money home and gave it to my mother." Katie Davis did something similar with her pay from The Augusta Factory. With Katie's dad out of work and her fifteenth birthday past, she must have felt the burdens of economic necessity when she found work and brought the money home. "She drew it and gave it to me herself," her mother, Irene, explained. "She earned from 60 to 65 cents a day which was a contribution to my support which I was mostly dependent upon." According to B.E. Raines, Bub plainly saw his work as helping out the family. Leaving home at around age thirteen, Bub lived with his brother, Lewis, worked on the rails, and "paid for his clothes with his own money." Still, he kept contact with his roving father. "He gave me a little bit more than $1.00 a month," B.E. recalled. The elder Raines could not recall how often Bub pitched in, but he reckoned that the boy dropped something off on almost every visit home. "He would hand me a little bit of money and would say 'I'll give you this to help you out with the children'," B.E. remembered. Clearly, gender and age relations in the Raines household were in flux. With B.E. in his late forties and down on his luck, young Bub assumed a provider role, at least on a temporary basis. Such was often the case in single-parent households or other families under stress.[27]

Still, Bub's desire to buy some clothes and pay for them with his own money revealed a different set of motivations. Getting and spending

[26] *Record in Leathers*, 17; *Record in Gibbs*, 4; *Record in Waldron*, 89; *Record in Honaker*, 22.
[27] *Record in King*, 11; *Record in Davis*, n.p.; *Record in Raines*, printed case record, 15.

money outside parental management indicated an important step toward adulthood. Then as now, such transitions frequently took time. Young workers could be dependent one day, independent the next. A.L. Mills was a West Virginia farmer, whose son James Allen, worked on the railroads. Like the Raines clan, economic relationships shifted back and forth. A.L. Mills recalled that James Allen gave him "the substance" of his pay to buy livestock or clothes for the boy, but sometimes the younger Mills "bought his clothes, something he needed." In the mixed-up world of mines and mills, however, economic power was not so easy for parents to maintain. At age ten, Charley Burke, Jr. worked as a trapper in a West Virginia mine, and much to the consternation of his father, Charles, Sr., he asserted more than a little economic independence. Asked about the disposition of Charley's wages, the elder Burke tersely replied: "I suppose he received them himself or took it up in scrip and fooled it away. I never got it." In fact, fooling away wages on consumer goods appealed to many a young worker. William Woodruff had a keen eye on "holding up his corner" with his mates. If he had three hundred dollars a year, he would spend it, and he knew how. "I would drink soda water and beer and things of that kind," the worldly wise William declared.[28]

Seeing how and why young Southerners gained employment reveals a world of work in which young people had considerable autonomy yet also contributed to the family economy. People as young as ten actively sought employment, oftentimes on their own, without the knowledge or consent of their parents. More typically, youngsters in their early teens joined the workforce, sometimes at the behest of their elders, sometimes on their own, often in some combination of the two. That should not be surprising if we realize that young people in a world of production wanted to work, both for the economic rewards and as a part of growing up.

AT PUBLIC WORK

The desire to be productive, to exercise a modicum of adult independence, met an industrial world of work constructed by divisions based on age. Southern working people reserved some kinds of labor for children and youth, especially boys. Certain work remained "boys' work,"

---

[28] *Record in Mills,* 77; *Record in Burke,* 62; *Record in Woodruff,* 49. The entrance of children into consumer activities before the mid-twentieth century has been rarely addressed, but see Miriam Formanek-Brunell, *Made to Play House: Dolls and the Commercialization of Girl Culture* (Baltimore, 1998); Cook, *Commodification of Childhood,* 22–40; and James Marten, *The Children's Civil War* (Chapel Hill, 1998), 177–185.

not normally performed by men. Other jobs were "men's work," tasks not normally assigned to boys under sixteen or thereabouts. Generally speaking, boys' work (and girls' work) was supposed to be easier, both in skill level and physical difficulty. Nonetheless, it sometimes called for considerable responsibility and judgment. At the same time, many young workers occupied the ambiguous position of "general help." In this case, they were not unlike older laborers hired in that position, yet as children and young people, they were subject to the dictates of adults, be they bosses or fellow adult workers. Being a younger worker, then, seemed both clear-cut and nebulous.[29]

This age-structured workplace did not correspond cleanly to reckoning by the calendar. Especially early in the period, size and physical ability counted for more than formal age. Indeed, many Southern workers, both young and old, did not know their exact ages. Referring to a young person as a "big boy" or a "big girl" was a plain descriptor that might or might not relate to the number of birthdays that had passed. In addition to the physical dimensions of being "big enough to work," capacity with machines meant something as well. Encountering the factory brought young workers face to face with captivating and dreadful equipment that had to be learned and mastered, or at least accommodated. With little formal training, young working people gained knowledge of the mysteries of technology from fellow laborers, young and old. Acquiring the skills of factory life formed part of the vision of Southern working people. Wanting to work went hand in hand with learning labor's ways.

Southern workplaces maintained semiformal divisions based on age. These customary lines can be difficult to see from a distant perspective, but Southern working people held common, if sometimes contested, notions about what constituted proper tasks for adults and young people. In part, these divisions arose from the ways factories organized the work environment. Textile plants and other factories often promulgated internal rules about where young workers could and could not go. According to Jarvis Stow, a carder at Albion Manufacturing, "all the hands in the carding room were grown men." These rules built upon management directives that confined workers to "their rooms." While such regulations structured Southern work spaces by age and gender, they drew upon a language already known to working people. In cotton mills, for instance, carrying waste out was usually considered a boys' work, while oiling the machinery was "a man's job." In woodworking, taking away the finished

[29] For a brief economic analysis of this issue, see McHugh, *Mill Family*, 44–46.

product was almost universally done by young workers. Although the categories remained constant, workers frequently disputed the precise definitions of who belonged in what job. "The work of stripping cards was a man's job, was work that men did everywhere," James Harris, a young Georgia textile worker, insisted. Fellow worker D.E. Dunwoody saw the matter differently. "I had seen lots of boys at it, in fact had done it myself," he maintained.[30]

Certain jobs, then, became more or less the exclusive province of young workers. Images of child labor passed down over the years have left an indelible memory of one particular role taken by young working people: the bobbin boy (or girl). Indeed, removing filled bobbins was a common sort of boy and girl labor throughout the industrializing South. Clearing bobbins fit into the more general category of "doffing," which might be used in the strict sense of removing full bobbins from spinning frames, or in more general sense of taking care of finished work. Often, such work was combined with sweeping, one of the first jobs young workers usually performed. Fitzhugh Stanley's experience was typical. He started out at Lynchburg Cotton Mills in spring of 1902 as a sweeper in the carding room. About three weeks later, he moved to the bagging room where he worked as doffer. Sweeping was probably the most universal of all employment for younger children, and it intermingled with other jobs around factories. Willie Rolin performed an array of tasks at RJR Tobacco, including weighing tobacco and cutting lumps, but this work was interspersed with sweeping.[31]

Beyond doffing and sweeping, younger workers labored at various small chores. All jobs required the regular watering of parched employees, and water carrying remained a ubiquitous task for boys well into the twentieth century. Gray Haynie toted water three-quarters of a mile to men building a railroad grade. Earl Butner worked as a water carrier at Brown Brothers Lumber Company, drifting in and out of the job, as did other boys in the town attached to the woodworking factory. Woodworking plants also considered taking away finished work to be boys' labor, though generally somewhat older lads were used in this position. In the numerous plants that punctuated the Piedmont and upcountry regions of the Appalachian South, young workers who applied for a job often found themselves "tailing" a molder, planer, or cross-cut saw.

[30] *Record in Starnes*, 14; *Record in Elk Cotton Mills, passim; Record in Eagle and Phenix Mills*, 22, 60; *Record in Fitzgerald*, 14; *Record in Harris*, n.p.
[31] *Record in Lynchburg Cotton Mills*, 2; *Record in Rolin*, 18.

FIGURE 1. Woodworking provided a common source of employment for boys and young men in the industrializing South. "Tail boys," such as the one on the left removed finished work from the machinery. Lewis Hine, 1913. Library of Congress, Prints & Photographs Division, National Child Labor Committee Collection, LC-DIG-nclc-05546.

Tailing drew upon and fed circulating images of child labor. As companies saw it, tailing required "quickness and not strength or endurance."[32]

Another common position for younger workers was trapping in mines. Daniel M. Woody of Big Sandy Coal supplied a description of a trapper's duties: "A trapper is a boy whose duties are to tend to a door used for ventilating the mines and turning the air into different parts of the mines," Woody noted. "He has to open the door; as soon as the cars go through, he has to close the door." For Woody and others, a trapper was a boy, pure and simple. A general notion prevailed in mining communities that trapping required little skill and so was a fitting job for young workers just entering the mines. Still, trapping could easily turn into signaling, or "flagging," as Woody indicated, and such tasks presented trappers with critical decisions. David Lang, a miner at Ewing and Lanark Fuel in West Virginia, outlined the trapper's role in coordinating the movements

[32] *Record in Haynie,* 14–15, 19; *Record in Butner,* 27; *Record in Miller Mfg. Co.,* 6. On tailing, see also *Record in Fitzgerald,* 14; *Record in Standard Red Cedar Chest Co.,* 31–33.

of mine cars. "It was his duty when both drivers come together to hold one of them; flag him by moving his light across the track," Lang stated, "and if there was no [one] he waved it up and down that it was clear and for him to come on, and when the driver got to the parting with his load, he would hitch to his empty and take it back." Such operations required close coordination between trapper and hauler. "When the hauler got to the parting, he would generally holler to the boy if it was clear and the trapper had the habit of hollering that everything was allright [*sic*] or waving his light up and down." As with specific tasks in the mills, trapping could easily turn into something else. Because trappers were low-skilled workers, they appeared to bosses as general labor. James Hastings, mine foreman for Sabine Colleries, maintained that Elbert Byrd had been hired for "several purposes; trapping, braking, and road cleaning. You know when you employ a boy or a man as a day laborer in the mines he is supposed to do any kind of labor he is asked to do."[33]

Hastings captured the ambiguous nature of much of the work performed by younger workers. While some did work for long periods at the same job, most moved positions frequently, a central facet of getting a job as "general help." Such work went by a variety of monikers in the industrializing South. H.B. Owen, who ran a blind and sash factory in Virginia, referred to them as "lacky boys," claiming that they did not do anything other than "sweep, bring ice water, &c." Of course, that "&c" was the trick. Being a "Jim Hand" or doing "little jim" work, as it was sometimes dubbed, meant being at the beck and call of the boss man. General help was not a category of work confined to boys or men. Betty Evans recalled her time at Josephine Mills as an all-purpose helper. "I did anything and everything," she said. "I just went around hunting something to do." The ambiguity of such positions enticed companies to move young workers around at will to meet the demands of production. When the mill was "short of help in the room," Wesley Howard reported, "they would put the sweeper on another job anywhere they wanted to." Howard, who worked at Eagle and Phenix Mills in Georgia, maintained that such repositioning of young workers was regular practice. If older hands failed to show up for work, younger ones might be put in their place in order to "make the time."[34]

---

[33] *Record in Burke*, 100; *Record in Ewing*, 78; *Record in Byrd*, 62.
[34] *Record in Jones*, 111; *Record in Evans (Georgia)*, 5; *Record in Eagle and Phenix Mills*, 22–23. On the "Jim Hand" and "little jim" references, see *Record in Ewing*, 33; and *Record in Roberts*, 77.

Work for younger people constituted a multifaceted and often contradictory experience. Some children and youth did fit the model of lint-covered textile workers or soot-encased miners, but their tasks in those workplaces varied considerably from the legends of constant drudgery. Moreover, they often possessed considerable autonomy in getting work and keeping it. Once on the job, their occupations might change rapidly within a single day. For all this diversity, however, Southern working people maintained relatively constant expectations about the economic roles of younger folk. Before exploring those expectations, it is important to understand that "Southern working people" included workers of all ages. While workplaces themselves might be structured by age, expectations about youthful labor were not neatly divided into those of "adults" and those of "children," with the older folk wanting to exploit their family's labor and the younger ones wanting the carefree life of a middle-class child. Social expectations, obviously, are something learned organically, starting with observations made at a very young age. Moreover, they are defined in historical context, subject to variation over time and place. Finally, they are often contested, as they were in the industrializing South where school and popular culture presented working people with a different conception of what a youngster's life should be.[35]

The expectations of Southern working people drew deeply on the long tradition of producer values embedded in the life of the agrarian South. Those traditions defined a household as an economic unit to which all members contributed. While such arrangements have been sometimes seen as hierarchical and exploitative, this view misses the collective nature of such enterprises. In a literal sense, if anyone was exploiting economic resources in such settings, it was small children, who contributed little and demanded much. But such seemingly silly assessments only serve to illustrate the point that understanding Southern households from a modern, middle-class perspective sheds little light on their actual dynamics. Producer ideology placed slight worth on those who did not work in some capacity. Most children learned this core value rapidly.[36]

Throughout the period of Southern industrialization, Southern working families clung to some values of agrarian life while altering others. Most importantly, they hewed to the notion that children's capacities

[35] Hall et al., *Like a Family*, Chs. 1–3; Newby, *Plain Folk*, Chs. 4–7, 17.

[36] On the household, see Elizabeth Fox-Genovese, *Within the Plantation Household: Black and White Women of the Old South* (Chapel Hill, 1988), Ch. 1; and Stephanie McCburry, *Masters of Small Worlds: Yeoman Households, Gender Relations, Band the Political Culture of the Antebellum South Carolina Low Country* (New York, 1997), Chs. 1–3.

should be measured not by their calendar age but by their physical size and ability, and their actual life experience. Being "big enough to work" was not a metaphor about having reached a certain birthday. Rather, it was a literal truth. A twelve-year-old boy weighing 140 pounds might be more ready to work than a 90-pound fifteen-year-old. A thirteen-year-old girl who had been in and around the mills since she was seven might be much more ready to take on the responsibilities of a more complicated machine than a seventeen-year-old who had just entered the factory from the farm. Such a view evinced a natural understanding of the manifest differences in human development, something that rigid statutory requirements did not. Had these views met a thoroughly middle-class world in the mines, mills, and factories, they would have faded far more rapidly than they did. For several decades, however, the developing Southern labor market incorporated and reinforced working people's perspective of the capacities of young workers. Hiring practices and wage structures constantly reinforced the conviction that size mattered.

The producer values of the farm, however, did not enter the industrial world unchanged. Commencing labor at any age meant learning about work: its tools, its techniques, its folkways. Craft apprenticeship had never been widespread in the South, nor had industrial schools caught on (with some notable exceptions, of course). Consequently, learning to work required interactions with other workers, young and old. It also meant gaining an appreciation of machines themselves, of their potentialities and perils. Like Henry Adams's marvels at the Corliss steam engine, Southern working people of all ages displayed a keen fascination with the raw power exerted by machines. They wanted to touch them, to feel their muscles, to grasp the huge expansion of human facility they portended. For younger workers, getting in touch with machines meant entering the adult world. In a time before bourgeois childhood became the universal model of human fulfillment, children wanted to grow up. In the industrializing South, part of that process involved reckoning with machines.[37]

Throughout the several decades of Southern industrialization a competing vision of childhood struggled with the outlook of working people. We shall explore that vision in detail later on, but for now it is enough

[37] Although apprenticeship was unusual, historians are finding more and more free labor in the slave South. See Michelle Gillespie, *Free Labor in an Unfree World: White Artisans in Slaveholding Georgia, 1789–1860* (Athens, 1999); and L. Diane Barnes, *Artisan Workers in the Upper South: Petersburg, Virginia, 1820–1865* (Baton Rouge, 2008).

to note that its main institutional manifestation – the school – offered a counterbalance to the producerist vision. On a day-to-day basis, it presented working people with a choice: work or school. In fact, most young people and their families made that decision on a daily basis. While some young workers attended school consistently into their early or middle teenage years, most went sometime to school and sometime to work. After about age ten, however, the labor market always lurked as a better and perhaps more exciting place than the often violent Southern school room, where the lash was applied frequently. Many working parents must have felt the frustration that Charles Burke did with his son Charley. "I had him in school as much as I could keep him in it," Charles, Sr. maintained. "He seemed to get along very well at school until Mr. Woody told him that he had a job for him." At age eleven, Charles, Jr. followed the route many of his peers chose: to chance it with the boss instead of the schoolmaster.[38]

That decision was informed by widely held ideas about how to judge when a young person was ready to take on work. Parental assessments of their progeny's strength and capacity helped create these assumptions. When asked about age, working people often responded that their youngster was "old enough to work in the mills" or "old enough to trap." Such language blended easily with "big enough" because physical size remained the primary marker of age. When J.C. Shortt, mine foreman, reckoned Charley Burke's age, he based his judgment on the boy's size, guessing him at between twelve and fourteen. "He was big enough for a boy of that age," Shortt recalled. Jim Castle, a West Virginia miner, echoed such language, saying he had been in the mines "ever since I was big enough to get in one." Wesley Howard declared that he had known young Edward Moncrief "ever since he was just big enough to sweep."[39]

The melding of age, size, and capacity that informed the thinking of Southern working people rendered the simple question "how old are you?" into a potentially confusing inquiry. J.D. Floyd ran the spinning room at Elk Cotton Mills, with Charley Grant's father under him as assistant foreman. The room needed "a boy to make bands," so Floyd asked Charley's dad about his boy's abilities. "He said Charley was old enough to make bands," Floyd recalled. "Charley's father had told me that Charley had made bands before and he made bands without having to be learned." L. Massey had a similar conversation with Jesse

---

[38] *Record in Burke*, 62. On the interplay between work and school, see McHugh, *Mill Family*, Ch. 4.

[39] *Record in Starnes*, 25–26; *Record in Burke*, 149; *Record in North-East Coal Co.*, 140; *Record in Eagle and Phenix Mills*, 21.

Taylor about his ambiguously aged son, Jimmie. Jesse had gotten fired, and he wanted a job for Jimmie. "I told him that I didn't want him that he looked too small," Massey disclosed, "and he says he is 13 going on 14 years old, and I says, 'he cannot reach the work'." Met with Massey's stonewalling, Jesse proceeded to show him that Jimmie could do the work. "He brought him upstairs and showed me that he was tall enough to reach the top of the frames," Massey continued, noting that he hired Jimmie about a week later. In the latter case, the elder Taylor might simply have been trying to deceive Massey, but even this deception rested on a work culture that recognized size and physical capacity as more important than calendar age. Charley Grant's dad simply measured his son's "age" by his capacity. He was "old enough to make bands." It did not really matter how many candles were on the cake on his last birthday.[40]

Judgments about capacity worked in the negative as well. Young workers might even be deemed "too light to sweep," the usual first job in mills and other workplaces. In mining, where physical strength was crucial, judgments about size controlled the assignment of tasks. Before motorized trams with their electric brakes became commonplace, stopping a moving coal car required healthy force applied to a mechanical brake. Miners sized each other up as to whether they were up to it. E.O. Pendeleton, for instance, deemed Harlie (a.k.a. Holly) Daniels to be "too light for the car, a loaded car especially." Sixteen-year-old H.E. Kinder heard a similar line from fellow mine workers. "Several men told me I was too light for the work," he recalled. The same kind of judgments applied in metal shops. Willis Wynne described his son, W.H., as "a good chunk of a little boy," but he still did not think he was suited for work on tin shears. "It would take a man to run that," Willis Wynne estimated. "It is hard and the legs are too high for a boy. It would take too much strength in the knees and the joints for a boy of his size to work." The elder Wynne's judgment reflected the common practice of centering employability on physical development.[41]

Young workers and their families carried these ideas to and from work. Like the sign at the entrance to the roller coaster, their notion that "you must be *this* big to work here" shaped the wage structures of the Southern

[40] *Record in Elk Cotton Mills*, 40; *Record in Bibb Manufacturing Co.*, 28; *Record in Kinder*, 65.
[41] *Record in Lynchburg Cotton Mills*, 78–79; *Record in Daniels*, 106; *Record in Kinder*, 65.

labor market. In turn, those wage structures sustained working people's ideas about age, size, and capacity. The idea that a certain sized worker was "worth" more persisted into the early twentieth century. Grady Loftin of Standard Red Cedar Chest Company in Virginia recalled a conversation with Johnson C. Monroe's stepfather, who paid a visit to inform Mr. Loftin that "he did not think these boys were getting enough money." Loftin tried to put off the older man with talk of prevailing wage rates at the plant, but James Monroe would have none of it. According to Loftin, Monroe argued that since his boys were older and "so much larger ... that they ought to be worth more money." Loftin responded with a raise to seventy-five cents a day. This interplay of size, capacity, and wages harkened back to days before the Civil War when the institution of chattel slavery created an elaborate language of "fractional hands." Sometimes, this language persisted in direct form. I.L. Affleck considered his son, William, to be "small for his age, he could not make half a hand in a heap of work." Or worth might be measured in the number of men a job required. A Kentucky mine was described as having "two boys do and perform the work of at least three men, or, two men and one boy."[42]

Wage rates often reflected these assessments, sending signals that melded physical size, the ability to work, and the legitimacy of industrial labor for young workers. Being stout meant a great deal in a labor market heavy with manual jobs. Wesley Smith discovered this fact when he went looking for work in an Atlanta planing mill in 1893. Wesley had little idea what wages to demand, so the boss man looked him over and said, "you are a pretty good-sized boy, I will give you what I give the rest of the hands." R.R. Hairston, the superintendent of the plant, was quite blunt about why he hired Smith. "I did not care whether he had any knowledge or experience in running machinery," Hairston declared. "Muscle was what I was looking for." Even if "muscle" was not required, size might still determine wage rates. Daniel M. Woody, superintendent of a West Virginia coal company, laid out one relationship between wage rates, age, and size. "We only paid 75 cents and one dollar for trappers, according to the size of the trapper," Woody stated. "Some of the trappers have two doors to attend but they were boys from 18 to 20 years old, and we gave them $2 a day." Here as elsewhere, age was size, and size was age. It mattered less how old somebody was according to the calendar, and a great deal more how much they could do.[43]

<hr/>

[42] *Record in Standard Red Cedar Chest Co.*, 33–34; *Record in Powhatan Lime Co*, 166; *Record in Stearns Coal & Lumber Co.*, Appellant's Brief, 25–26.
[43] *Record in Burke*, 135; *Record in May & Co.*, 12, 32.

Of course, the capacity for labor depended on more than physical ability. Developing a facility with machines and with industrial work, in general, formed a central experience for young workers. In fact, they often shared this occurrence with other members of their families, at least in settings that fit the label of family labor. As Southern households moved from farm to factory, all hands could become "learners." When William Starnes moved his family into Mt. Holly, North Carolina, to work at Albion Manufacturing, a cotton plant was new to all. The family's teenage daughters came first, followed by their father, mother, and the rest of the younger children. "They all had to learn" was how Superintendent J.S. Downum saw it. "Hadn't worked in a mill before." Once in the industrial workforce, families still moved from town to town and job to job, a fact that required workers, young and old, to get acclimated to new work sites. Besides moving from town to town, workers changed positions frequently on the job, especially in textiles. This, too, meant that young workers often found themselves laboring with others who had little experience or training.[44]

Only rarely was the process of learning formalized in Southern workplaces. Older workers sometimes recalled their days coming up as a young apprentice, but by the late nineteenth century, that institution remained in place only in certain skilled trades such as railroad shop machinists and, later, electricians. The workplaces that did practice apprenticeship retained considerably stricter rules about where young workers could and could not be. Young apprentices in the Memphis and Charleston Railroad's shops, for instance, were not normally placed at dangerous work without the supervision of a journeyman or skilled machinist.[45]

Even if such rules were honored more in the breach, they created a more highly structured work environment than the freewheeling world of the mills and mines. There, learning took place in a variety of ways: by going to work with parents or siblings; by being trained by other workers, young and old; by personal observation and experimentation. In some instances, being a "learner" bore some resemblance to apprenticeship, reaching the distinction of being a semiformal status. U.S. Leather Company, for example, kept an internal policy that young workers would not be given charge of machinery until after they had worked as

---

[44] *Record in Starnes*, 27–28; *Record in Kinder*, 57; *Record in Sanitary Laundry Co.*, 34; *Record in Elk Cotton Mills*, 28; *Record in Pelham Manufacturing Co.*, 66–68.
[45] *Record in Ballard*, 3; *Wilson v. Valley Improvement Co.* 69 W. Va. 778 (1911);*Whitelaw v. Memphis and Charleston RR Co.*, 84 Tenn. 391 (1886).

a "helper." Occupying a semiformal status as a beginner was especially the case for railroad brakemen, where "cubbing" was the common term for learning the job. Many railroads, however, maintained their own age regulations about such positions, often restricting them to young men over the age of twenty-one.[46]

More often, young workers simply went to work in the mills and learned by doing or by training each other. Willie McGowan worked around his father for a good while, so much so that it remained unclear as to whether the mill actually had employed him or not. When Jackson Ewing was asked how he learned to couple cars in the West Virginia mines, he gave the common sense answer: "I just noticed the way other people coupled them." Such interactions with fellow workers, often fellow young workers, were probably the most common way initiates got to know the ropes. Will McNally reported a typical "training session" at Crown Cotton Mills. Moved from the weave shop to the carding room, McNally got no more than verbal instructions from the foreman, a Mr. Fallis. Another boy, who Will estimated to be about sixteen, "pretended to show me ... but he never did tell me nothing about the machine," he insisted. "I just watched him."[47]

Will McNally's consternation was not an insolated incident. Neither was his compliance with seemingly unreasonable demands. Indeed, the necessity of learning how to run machines in order to keep a job played into the decisions of young workers to learn by doing. Thirteen-year-old Edward Moncrief recalled how he and Joe Coggins, a fellow worker close to his own age, struggled to master a lap-winder at Eagle and Phenix Cotton Mills. Edward was not exactly the man for the job, having little idea what he was doing himself. "The foreman told me – he says, 'When you get through getting your floors cleaned, every time you get your floors cleaned, go help and show Joe Coggins how to run it'," Edward remembered. "I told him I didn't know much about running it ... . I didn't know exactly how to do it; I done it the best I could." Ed and Joe soldiered on in a general state of confusion. Joe "didn't know much about it and I didn't either – only I knew how to run it from seeing other people." Wesley Howard revealed more about Edward's quandary. Ed had swept and doffed, but when asked to work on other machines, he had little choice in the matter, Howard declared. After a

[46] *Record in Louisville and Nashville R.R. Co.*, *passim*; *Record in United States Leather Co.*, 96.
[47] *Record in McGowan*, 16; *Record in Ewing*, 55; *Record in Crown Cotton Mills*, n.p.

FIGURE 2. This scene from Tennessee textile mill depicts the typical case of young laborers training each other on the job. The boys are working at a warping machine. Lewis Hine, 1910. Library of Congress, Prints & Photographs Division, National Child Labor Committee Collection, LC-DIG-nclc-05391.

few years of sweeping and doffing, Ed "gradually tried to learn about machinery, and when they put him on a job he tried to do it," Howard reported. "If he didn't they didn't want him."[48]

Young workers such as Edward Moncrief and Will McNally learned their jobs on the fly. In the broad sense, they ended up in such tight spots because of the power relations of industrial capitalism, but in a narrower sense, their older, fellow workers put them there. Especially in the early years of Southern industrialization, the "bosses" had come up through the ranks of workers. Like many adults, when it was time to teach a younger person how something worked, they assumed that it was all just "common sense." T.F. Smith, foreman at Keystone Coal, simply could not see how riding or braking mine cars might not be as natural as falling off a log. "Anybody would know how to ride on a car if he was on it," a somewhat incredulous Smith declared. When pressed about the tricky business of stopping a speeding car laden with coal, Smith stuck to his guns. "Well, he knowed how to put on the brakes," the foreman maintained about

[48] *Record in Eagle and Phenix Mills*, 22–23, 26–30.

eleven-year-old Clarence Broyles. "Anybody knows how to set a brake on a car. All you have got to do is to tell him that he has got that to do."[49]

If young workers did not always possess the "common sense" it took to get the hang of a particular machine, it did not mean that they universally sought to avoid them. In fact, they often displayed an intense curiosity about how machines worked, and as we shall see momentarily, they often sought to operate them on their own volition, an activity that companies called "meddling" but which should more rightly be seen as a part of learning. An even clearer indication of the desire to learn industrial work was a certain pride in their skills that young workers displayed. Sometimes this came out in competitions between young workers to see who could do the most work. Benny Laverty recalled such a contest taking place in a West Virginia keg factory, although he sought to deny the implications. "We weren't racing to see which could cut the most staves," he explained. "We were cutting fast. What I call racing." Pressed about whether the boys were "seeing which one could cut the most," Benny had to admit that, in fact, that was the long and short of it. This intermixture of work and leisure drew on old traditions in the South, such as corn shucking contests. Piece rates fostered such practices, engendering pride in skill and affording bragging rights on the shop floor, not to mention preventing the unseemly event of getting docked in pay. Gaines Leathers intimated that tying tobacco sacks was a competitive activity at Blackwell Durham. "There were boys there who could beat me tying a good deal, and others who could not tie as fast as I," Leathers reckoned. Of course, the ever-present threat of having pay cut for making mistakes while speeding focused Leathers's attention and left him with a sense of pride for avoiding the inspector's watchful eye. "I was never 'docked' that I know of. My tying is all right," Leathers declared, with a hint of forced modesty.[50]

Learning the job, then, was no easy undertaking, but it could pay off, both in wages earned and in competencies gained. Consequently, young Southern workers faced the industrial workplace with both trepidation and anticipation, but mostly they carried with them the producer values of their culture. Those values made wanting to help into an economically, culturally, and socially rewarding behavior. This milieu led young workers toward their own decisions about entering the labor force and about how they would operate in it. Mary Evans recalled how her daughter, Betty, decided to go to work for Josephine Mills. "We didn't go exactly to

[49] *Record in Swope*, 25.
[50] *Record in Laverty*, 62; *Record in Leathers*, 17, 20; Eugene Genovese, *Roll, Jordan, Roll: The World the Slaves Made* (New York, 1974), 319.

get her a job, but went with another person to get a job, and Betty took a notion that she wanted to work," the elder Evans explained. At age eleven, Betty had already worked a little in other mills, so she knew what working at textiles was about. Now, she had begun to see herself as capable of making the decision to enter employment for herself. Countless of her fellow young workers took similar steps. While the labor market they joined was certainly cruel and exploitative, they acted in accord with the culture of Southern working people when they started public work. That culture told them that to be helpful, to aid in the production that carried human life forward, was a positive and rewarding activity. Once on the shop floor, they continued to act in accordance with those values. J.W. Williams, who worked in card room No. 2 at Eagle and Phenix, observed Ed Moncrief and other young workers around the plant helping out on their own volition. "Nobody told him to help as I know of. He came up with his own accord I guess," Williams figured. "Not only him but nearly every kid around there will help on nearly all the frames."[51]

This desire to help, to do something productive, to be a grown-up, formed the core value for young Southern workers and their families. It meant that being "big enough to work" implied many changes in one's life. In many cases, it portended making a contribution to the family economy, either at the dictates or request of older people, or on one's own accord. It also meant getting cash for clothes, amusements, or just "beer and soda water." All of this is not to say that young Southern workers embraced factory labor wholeheartedly or without fear, but it does suggest a modicum of legitimacy for the decisions they made in a bewildering period of economic change. Before we think time in the factory was all work, however, we must examine a topic seemingly at odds with producerist values: play.

MESSING WITH THE MACHINERY

One morning in 1914, young Conley Robinson prepared for work as a doffer boy in a North Carolina textile mill. Bending over a bobbin box, Conley remained unaware as his companions in the mill snuck up from behind to goose him with an air hose. Unknown to the other boys, the regulator on the air compressor had been set to the full 120 pounds per square inch. The result for Conley was ruptured intestines and permanent disability. Conley's mishap came from what was routinely described as a

---

[51] *Record in Evans (Georgia)*, 10; *Record in Eagle and Phenix Mills*, 46.

"childish prank," but it was by no means an isolated incident. Looking carefully at these incidents can tell us more about what it meant to be a young worker in a producer culture.[52]

In many circumstances, the nature of work, especially young boys' work, left considerable time for play in and around Southern workplaces. Play in such instances served many purposes. For one, it complemented family labor, as parents could watch younger children at work and at play in the mills, making mill life more akin to the agrarian world these folks had recently left behind. From a child's point of view, such play broke the routine of factory labor, rendering it more familiar and acceptable. But play, especially among boys, also became a critical part in the formation of gendered work identities. While youthful inquisitiveness certainly figured in boys' activities, play on the shop floor constituted an important part of gender construction for young male workers in at least two crucial ways. First, "playing with machines" introduced them to the powers and dangers of industrial work. By going "beyond their duties" to operate machines on their own accord, young workers simultaneously staked a claim to adulthood and to their own agency as producers of economic value. Second, play between workers, especially pranks and other kinds of horseplay, evinced the acquisition of behaviors particular to working-class constructions of gender. Horseplay on the shop floor constituted a central facet of working-class manhood in the early twentieth century. For young male workers, pranks were not simply the product of "childish impulses." Rather, they were a part of acting like an adult worker.[53]

Evidence is scant to investigate girls' play, but that which does exist suggests that play for girls, especially pranks and horseplay, was not as common as it was for boys. Girls sometimes reported reading books or

---

[52] *Record in Robinson*, 15–16.

[53] Steve Meyer, "Rough Manhood: The Aggressive and Confrontational Shop Culture of U.S. Auto Workers during World War II," *Journal of Social History* 36 (2002): 125–147. On working-class masculinity generally, see especially Steven Maynard, "Rough Work and Rugged Men: The Social Construction of Masculinity in Working-Class History," *Labour* 1989 (23): 159–169; Paul Michael, "What We Want Is Good, Sober Men: Masculinity, Respectability, and Temperance in the Railroad Brotherhoods, c. 1870–1910," *Journal of Social History* 36 (2002): 319–338; Gregory L. Kaster, "Labour's True Man: Organised Workingmen and the Language of Manliness in the USA, 1827–1877," *Gender & History* 13 (2001): 24–64; Stephen Norwood, *Strikebreaking and Intimidation: Mercenaries and Masculinity in Twentieth-Century America* (Chapel Hill, 2002). On the gendering of boys, see particularly Julia Grant, "A 'Real Boy' and Not a Sissy: Gender, Childhood, and Masculinity, 1890–1940," *Journal of Social History* 37 (2004): 829–851; and Kathleen W. Jones, *Taming the Troublesome Child: American Families, Child Guidance, and the Limits of Psychiatric Authority* (Cambridge, 1999), esp. 156–165.

newspapers while tending machines, a common practice since the earliest days of textile factories. They also played to pass the time while waiting to leave the workplace. A particularly good example of the latter type of play comes from a Georgia cotton mill in the early 1880s. The plant had worked into the wee hours of a Sunday morning, leaving a group of early teenage girls alone in the factory, save for the night watchman. Waiting for dawn and a safe trip home, some slept, but others took up a game of "hide and seek." In part, the lower incidence of girls' play may have been because girls' work demanded more constant attention, but it also constituted part of the gendering of the workplace. Walter Duncan, an employee in a Virginia textile mill, acknowledged as much. Duncan reported in 1902 that while he had seen boys and men frequently playing with the belts of a carding machine, he had "never seen little girls playing with them."[54]

Whether for boys or girls, many industrial settings allowed considerable time for play between tasks. Southern children seemed to recognize this and noted the lack of time for play when work was constant. Eleven-year-old Betty Evans recalled work routines in a Georgia mill as all work and no play. "It was pretty hard to stay there and work all day," she reported. "We did not play any." While Betty's testimony evokes Dickensian imagery, it also illuminates her expectation that play was a normal part of factory life. Indeed, other Southern working children described a fluid work environment where play and work freely intermingled. For young boys, sweeping or doffing did not require their full attention. Nine-year-old Harry Starnes's experience in Mt. Holly, North Carolina, was typical of this type of job. "When I would catch up with my work I would go outside and play – out around the mill," Harry noted in his 1908 case against Albion Manufacturing. This sort of play carried rural life into the factories. White Southern children, unaccustomed to constant employment, often found an environment not unlike the yeoman households they had left, an environment where work and leisure intermixed as demands to complete tasks waxed and waned.[55]

Play and work also intermixed because early factory life in the South did not necessarily lead to strict policing of the factory gates. In many Southern communities, siblings, parents, relatives, and community members came and went during working hours almost at will. Children played

---

[54] *Record in Lynchburg Cotton Mills*, 78; *Record in Vinson*, 3; *Record in Atlanta Cotton Factory Co.*, 39–40, 96; Hindman, *Child Labor*, Ch. 6; Hall et al., *Like a Family*, 56.
[55] *Record in Evans (Georgia)*, 5; *Record in Starnes*, 10; Hindman, *Child Labor*, 161.

in and around factories, sometimes having jobs there, sometimes not. Young Ellis Crosby was one of many boys who frequented the vicinity of a bottling plant in Waycross, Georgia. Willie Broach, an employee, described the plant as "a pretty big hang-out for loafing boys." Another employee, H.D. Adams, had seen Ellis and "a bunch of little boys" playing in the street in front of the plant, "always wanting to hang around and drink a bottle of soda water every chance they got," Adams related. The situation at Brown Brothers Lumber, a wood processing plant in North Carolina, was similar. Earl Butner, a boy who lived in the town connected to the plant, said that he and neighborhood boys made the factory a regular play place. "I went into the mill about every day and had done so ever since I had been there," Earl noted. "There were nearly 40 boys who lived around there and they played on the docks and in the mill." Garrett Honeycutt, a mill employee, described the factory as a place where children "would go most any place they wanted to." Mill foreman Arthur Brown confirmed that "nearly every day boys were fooling around the mill and I had to chase them out." Here, too, play slid easily into work as the boys occasionally took jobs as water carriers in the factory.[56]

Children played in Southern workplaces for many reasons, but two important patterns dominated, and both were particularly common for boys. First, boys fiddled with the machinery and tools, sometimes directly emulating older men or boys, sometimes simply experimenting with what was available. This sort of activity represented a typical pattern for play described by modern social scientists: the need for competency and mastery and the desire to participate in the creation of economic value. It had important gendered meanings as well. Producer values supplied a bridge between the culture of rural, yeoman households and working-class life. Knowledge and skill with machines came to define a central facet of Southern working-class manhood. When boys played with machines, however dangerous, they performed their emerging roles as working-class men. A second type of play also indicated working-class masculinity, but in a more complex fashion. Pranks and horseplay on the shop floor were not confined to children. Indeed, horseplay took a central part in marking male gender identities. When Southern working boys pulled tricks on each other, their actions evinced a complex mixture of child-centered play and adult-focused gender development.[57]

[56] *Record in Keen*, 19, 12; *Record in Butner (1920)*, 25; *Record in Butner (1921)*, 27.
[57] Nieuwenhuys, "Child Labor and the Paradox of Anthropology," 237–251; Meyer, "Rough Manhood."

Messing with the machinery could take many forms. One was simply to appropriate company tools. The Odell Manufacturing Company in North Carolina saw boys frequently "take the tools and other things and carry them off." Ebbirt Ward, a young operative at Odell, found himself accused of using a punch during break-time for his own purposes. A similar event occurred in Atlanta when W.H. "Hamp" Wynne tried to use a mechanical tin shears to make a picture frame out of a piece of scrap metal. "The other boys were making them, and I thought I would make one," Hamp later noted. Hamp's actions are particularly telling for they reflect a mixture of adult and youthful desires. On the one hand, Hamp wanted to keep up with his peers, but on another he did so by appropriating the company's tools, a practice he certainly must have witnessed in adults. In either case, he asserted his right to use the technology of industrial life for his own independent goals, a common facet of working-class manhood.[58]

While boys might use machines strictly for their own purposes, they frequently interfered with machinery in ways considerably more ambiguous. Whirling belts and gears provided a peculiar fascination, perhaps because they combined elements of both work and play. Fitz Stanley's experience in a Virginia textile mill is revealing. Fitz was hurt when playing with the belts on a carding machine. As the family's lawyer put it, the appeal of such machines was almost universal. "A carding machine with its swiftly moving pulleys and gliding noiseless belts is an attractive object to grown people," he averred. "The fascination of such a machine for a child is well nigh irresistible – it almost speaks to him in audible voice, saying come play with me." Fitz said that he had seen boys "throwing the belt off and putting it on." He apparently wanted to do the same, as described by Willie Duncan, another boy in the plant. "Me and Walter Duncan went to the water closet and was coming on back, and Lee Duncan and Fitzhugh were standing there fooling with the belt," Willie disclosed. The boys took turns pulling the belt off and letting it slap back on. Willie tried to dissuade Fitz to no avail. "I said, 'Fitz, come on, let us go on back,' and he said nothing, but pulled the belt off again and started to throw it back on and got his arm caught." In playing with the belt, Fitz modeled his peers, but he also appears to have imitated behavior he saw in the adult men who worked at the plant. "Men are just as liable to fool with the belts as the boys," one employee reported. "I have seen men play with them, as far as that goes."[59]

---

[58] *Record in Ward*, n.p.; *Record in Wynne*, 16.
[59] *Record in Lynchburg Cotton Mills*, 44–45, 70, 95. For a similar case, see *Record in Haynie*.

Fitzhugh Stanley's accident arose from something closer to pure play, but other incidents started when boys experimented with machines in normal use. Such was the case with Johnson C. Monroe at the Standard Red Cedar Chest Company in Virginia. Employees at the plant had frequently witnessed Johnson messing with a planer. "He would go around and try to start it up and put a plank in it," one employee recalled. "Looked like he wanted to learn how to run the machine and often when I would step away and come back he would be trying to operate it." Willie Rolin was hurt in a processor at RJR Tobacco when he was cleaning the machine on his own accord at the end of the day. "No one told me to clean up the machine," Willie testified. "I saw others cleaning up the machine and I did so." Judge Connor of the North Carolina Supreme Court in reviewing the case described Willie's actions as "a boy seeking to discharge his duty to his employer" and as illustrating "the alertness and desire of children to be useful." Both of Connor's perspectives point to the gendered meanings of Willie's actions and to the fluid state of Southern working-class manhood. A "desire to be useful" located Willie's actions in producer ideology, yet discharging his "duty" to his employer evinced newer lines of gendered authority present in factory settings.[60]

Willie Rolin's story spanned lines in other ways as well, for he was injured as a result of a prank. Another boy in the factory threw a chunk of tobacco into the stopped machine and then turned it on as Willie reached in to remove the plug. Pranks with compressed air, such as the one that injured Conley Robinson, were not unusual. A nearly identical incident happened in Kentucky. Conley himself witnessed other doffers playing with the air hose, while Ralph Mitchell saw boys "just shooting each other's faces and blowing hats off, such as that." Frank Thornburg, second boss of the spinning room where Conley was injured, confirmed that the incident was a prank: "I walked down there and says 'What the devil you boys doing?'; Conley was lying down there just gasping, I thought he was putting on."[61]

Horseplay in the factory often occurred between boys, but it sometimes took place between boys and adults. One such case from a Virginia cotton mill details this point and illustrates how boys acted out the gender identity of Southern white working-class men. Twelve-year old Tom McDaniel, described by one observer as "a powerfully fat boy," was big for his age and precocious in many ways. Tom's life ended when he fell

---

[60] *Record in Standard Red Cedar Chest Co.*, 40, 49; *Record in Rolin*, 19.
[61] *Record in Rolin*, 19–20; *Record in Ballard*, Complaint, 2.

to his death in an elevator shaft, so what we know of him comes from his co-workers. They described a boy seeking to take the part of an independent-minded man, all the while acting the childish cut-up. George Daniel remembered Tom as "a joking fellow" and relayed some of his antics around the factory's elevator. Tom had a penchant for dancing in the lift when the overseer was not looking. "He would just try to instruct me how to dance a certain kind of dance which he called Possumala, and he would get on there and dance that dance, and try to show me how," Daniel recollected. "He was so funny I used to laugh at him." Tom apparently performed this and other tricks regularly, testing the lines of authority in the factory. After a near miss with the elevator, George Daniel scolded Tom. "I says, 'Tom you are going to get killed unless you keep off of there,' and he says, 'I don't give a dam[n],' or something like that. He used bad words," George recalled.[62]

Indeed, "bad words" were part of Tom's regular vocabulary, but he used them with a view to the listener. A bevy of adults cautioned Tom about his actions. Mrs. R.E. Womack caught Tom using the elevator shaft to hurl bobbins at another worker. He met her rebuke by telling her to "take care of yourself." When Miss Cora Robinson warned him about swinging on the elevator rods, Tom dismissed her concern. "He would say he wasn't afraid or it wasn't dangerous, and what in the devil did I have to do with it," she reported. Another female operative described a similar incident: "Mr. Brooks … told him he had better stop jumping through there, he would get his damn neck broke, and he told Mr. Brooks he didn't give a damn, he had but one time to die." Still, Tom's foul mouth was not constant, and he knew whom to respect. Mr. George Roberson, the overseer, had also surprised Tom on the elevator, but he met with a different reaction. "I told him if he didn't stay away from there I would discharge him," Roberson recounted. "He didn't say anything. He was not a boy that made any back talk."[63]

Tom's actions provide a fitting summary for the many elements of boys' play in Southern factories. By age twelve, Tom had developed a sense of industrial authority. The boss, Mr. Roberson, was to be respected and obeyed, at least when a direct confrontation occurred. But interactions with fellow workers were suffused with different class-based gender identities. Tom's "bad words" clearly mimicked those of his elders,

---

[62] *Record in McDaniel*, 63, 27, 29. For other examples of play on elevators, see *Record in Kendrick*, 2–3, 51, 57, 60, 65, 70, 78, 89, 94; *Record in Hauser*, 2, 19, 27, 39.
[63] *Record in McDaniel*, 30, 45, 49.

especially the male ones. His constant taking of the prankster role also evinced a common element of working-class masculinity. His life and his death reveal a world where work and play freely intermingled, at least for younger boys.

The complexity of Tom's life points to a common problem in trying to get at the meaning of play on the part of young workers. Play often defies clear definition or analysis. For psychologists, it is a natural element of cognitive development; for sociologists, it is central to the socially circumscribed functions of socialization; for anthropologists, it is part of the culturally defined process of enculturation. For historians, the study of play has often been as much about the material culture of middle-class childhood as about children's actual experience. Studies that have investigated the meanings of play often carry the underlying assumption that an activity is "play" primarily because it is not work. Play, or at least its "appreciation," is sometimes seen as emerging with modern definitions of childhood, and it is usually confined to pre-teen years. Yet the rise of leisure culture and the commodification of adult leisure complicate these definitions. In modern, consumption-driven America, adulthood is organized around play nearly as much as is childhood, at least in cultural iconography. Still, play is what happens after work. These assumptions about the oppositional relationship between work and play can obscure our ability to understand the role of play in the past, when the divisions were not as stark as they are today.[64]

---

[64] Peter K. Smith and Ralph Vollstedt, "On Defining Play: An Empirical Study of the Relationship between Play and Various Play Criteria," *Child Development* 56 (August 1985): 1042–1050; A.D. Pellegrini and Peter K. Smith, "Physical Activity Play: The Nature and Function of a Neglected Aspect of Play," *Child Development* 69 (June 1998): 577–589; Douglas P. Fry, "'Respect for the Rights of Others Is Peace': Learning Aggression versus Non-Aggression Among the Zapotec," *American Anthropologist* N.S. 94 (Sept. 1992): 621–639; Gerald Handel, "Revising Socialization Theory," *American Sociological Review* 55 (June 1990): 463–466; Jeffrey Jensen Arnett, "Broad and Narrow Socialization: The Family in the Context of a Cultural Theory," *Journal of Marriage and the Family* 57 (August 1995): 617–628; Gary Cross, *Kids' Stuff: Toys and the Changing World of American Childhood* (Cambridge, 1997); Formanek-Brunell, *Made to Play House*; Karen Calvert, *Children in the House: The Material Culture of Early Childhood, 1600–1900* (Boston, 1992), 47–52, 79–82, 110–119; Priscilla Ferguson Clement, *Growing Pains: Children in the Industrial Age, 1850–1890* (New York, 1997), Ch. 6; David E. McCleod, *The Age of the Child: Children in America, 1890–1920* (New York, 1998), 65–71, 120–131; David Nassaw, *Children of the City: At Work and At Play* (Garden City, 1985), 17–38.Much of this literature draws a distinct line between work and play. Play, in Wilma King's words, is "the antithesis of work." Wilma King, *Stolen Childhood: Slave Youth in Nineteenth Century America* (Bloomington, 1995), Ch. 3. A notable exception to this trend is the fine treatment of play in Elliott West, *Growing Up*

In Southern workplaces at the turn of the twentieth century, play and work often intermingled even after the onset of "industrialization." Young Southern workers, especially male ones, did not envision the shop floor as a place where "work" must take precedence over all. Southern children played at work: with peers, with adults, and with machines. For boys in particular, play at the workplace formed a central part of identity creation both in class and gender terms. To "fiddle with the machines" was a part of learning what it meant to be a Southern working man. To pull practical jokes on co-workers was an entrée to the culture of working-class manhood. Understanding the gendered meanings of play on the shop floor in this fashion adds a final element to the reconstruction of young workers in the industrializing South.

The folkways of that time and place defied easy characterizations about what was "childish" or the result of "natural instincts," whether in play or at work. From little on up, Southern youngsters came of age in a social setting that valued production, a place that had not yet completed the modern divisions that put work on one side of a chasm and home, school, and play on the other. As a result. young workers often entered "public work" as soon as they were big enough, either at the behest of their elders or just to take a shot at being grown up. For decades, Southern industrial life authorized their actions. Yet for anyone who cared to look, that modern, middle-class world of separations could be found in the better parts of town, and more importantly, on every news stand.

---

with the Country: Childhood on the Far Western Frontier (Albuquerque, 1989), 101–117. West explores a range of ways in which work and play intermingled in the lives of rural children, and hence his treatment is particularly applicable to my argument here. Although West is talking about the West, his story could work equally as well in the rural South. This view of play provides the immediate backdrop for yeoman families recently removed to mill towns, and more important, it clarifies that work and play need not be separated.

The Divine Right to Do Nothing

When your children romp around the Christmas tree, think of two million little wage slaves. (*Cosmopolitan*, 1906)

Like young workers in the South, Stanny Mattcvitcz entered the Pennsylvania coal mines at a young age. There, he loaded coal cars, heaping up the hard anthracite that a growing U.S. economy prized. Stanny's work was hard. "In de morning awful easy," he recalled, "but in de night awful hard." By age twelve, Stanny had attended the local Polish school a total of three years. He found the drudgery of the classroom little better than the toil of the coal face. "Me no like school," he confided, "radder play baseball and chase de cows." Though he wished for an airy, playful childhood, Stanny's overbearing father dashed his hopes. Although Pennsylvania law prohibited boys of his age from working in the mines, his father dragged him there nonetheless. "Me been going on twelve and me go to the mines to help mine fadder," he revealed. "He take me in every day when de work been goin' on." Resisting the elder Mattcvitcz's unreasonable demands was not a possibility. "Wen de fadder say, 'Get up and put on yer mine clothes,' me got to get up or he lick me," the boy disclosed. Stanny had paid dearly for his father's lawbreaking, ending up with a crushed leg that doctors told him would "take a long time to get good."[1]

Stanny's poignant story likely moved the hearts of listeners to pity and perhaps to action, but was it real? Stanny's words might have been his own, but his dialogue reached his auditors via the pen of Scott Nearing,

[1] Scott Nearing, "Stanny Mattcvitcz," *The Independent*, Sept. 26, 1907, 746–747.

a member of the Pennsylvania Child Labor Committee. Nearing wrote "from observation," *The Independent* magazine assured its readers when the piece appeared in September 1907. Later the patron saint of the back-to-the-land movement, Nearing occupied a prominent position as an economics professor at the University of Pennsylvania. He employed his prestige to agitate against the evils of child labor until the trustees unkindly told him in 1915 that his services were no longer needed. Until then, Nearing tirelessly cranked out magazine articles, pamphlets, speeches, and one book about "the child labor problem." Some of his work read as one would expect from a social scientist, all statistics and logic, but Nearing displayed his literary side as well. In stories such as "Stanny Mattcvitcz," he blurred the lines between "fact" and "fiction," fashioning personalized tales that authenticated the narratives about young people and work being spun by other Progressive-era writers.[2]

As such, Nearing joined a social and literary movement that had emerged in the decades after the U.S. Civil War, a drive for reform that would dramatically alter the cultural environment in which young workers and their families could operate and in which the legal language of childhood capacity and incapacity would be interpreted. Drawing on an organizational model pioneered by reformers in New York City, societies for the protection of children began to spring up in urban areas around the country. The "child savers" who populated these groups coalesced into a powerful new force for "children's rights" by the time Ellen Key declared in 1900 that the coming era would be the "Century of the Child." These men and women passed down to later generations what became known as child labor laws: statutes that prohibited or restricted wage work by young people. As we shall see later, the outcome of this legislative agenda was not as straightforward as reformers hoped, but it was not their exertions in state capitals or in Washington, D.C. that would have the most influence on young workers. Instead, the power of child labor reform lay in narratives such as Nearing's. Tied to reformers across the Atlantic, U.S. authors told tales that constructed a new language for

---

[2] For some other literary efforts by Nearing, see "On the Trail of the Pittsburgh Stogie," *The Independent*, July 2, 1908, 22–24; and "One District Messenger," *The Independent*, Feb. 22, 1912, 412–413. He wrote about these issues at great length in *The Solution to the Child Labor Problem* (New York: Moffat, Yard, 1911). For a contemporary rendition of Nearing's dismissal from Penn, see "The Burning Issue of Free Speech at Western as Well as Eastern Universities," *Current Opinion*, August 1915, 111. Nearing's early work is also outlined in his autobiography, *The Making of a Radical* (New York: Harper and Row, 1972). For a modern biography, see John Saltmarsh, *Scott Nearing: An Intellectual Biography* (Philadelphia, 1991).

talking about young workers, their families, and their employers. While these conventions drew upon images available since the dawn of the nineteenth century, they gained new power as that century drew to a close. In part, this occurred simply because the means of dissemination allowed greater access to an increasingly literate public. Mass-market newspapers and magazines, along with the ever-popular reform pamphlet, enabled transmission of photos, sketches, and word pictures that constructed an iconography of "child labor" in ways that antebellum reform writing, with its treatise-like quality, did not.[3]

Still, the message was more than the medium. The power of the new language lay in its distillation of the complicated transition to capitalism for young workers to a set of images about "child labor." As in any effective reform discourse, enemies were needed. Contrary to what later historic memory might imagine, factory owners did not provide an uncomplicated foil. While greedy capitalists supplied one partner in crime, the real antagonists were parents. Lazy, drunken fathers and their hapless or vain wives carried the story along, forcing their progeny into factories to satisfy their own selfish desires. In the stories reformers narrated about themselves, they arrayed their armies against these malignant forces and stood as defenders – of the worker, the race, the nation, and ultimately, the child on whom all depended. In doing so, reform writers birthed a new and powerful figure that would grow and mature throughout the twentieth century: the helpless child. At times, that child seemed more troubled than tamed, and writers fretted that vice and criminality lay down the road. For the most part, though, those narrating its

---

[3] It is not my intention here to recount the history of "child labor reform." That story has been deftly told by numerous historians, and it can be found in many a U.S. survey textbook. For standard scholarly treatments, see Jeremy P. Felt, *Hostages of Fortune: Child Labor Reform in New York State* (Syracuse, 1965); Walter Trattner, *Crusade for the Children: A History of the National Child Labor Committee and Child Labor Reform in America* (Chicago, 1970); Viviana A. Zelizer, *Pricing the Priceless Child: The Changing Social Value of Children* (New York, 1985), Ch. 3; Joseph M. Hawes, *The Children's Rights Movement: A History of Advocacy and Protection* (Boston, 1991), Ch. 4; and most recently, Hugh D. Hindman, *Child Labor: An American History* (Armonk, 2002), Ch. 3. On the U.S. South specifically, see Dewey Grantham, *Southern Progressivism: The Reconciliation of Progress and Tradition* (Knoxville, 1983), 178–199; William A. Link, *The Paradox of Southern Progressivism, 1880–1930* (Chapel Hill, 1992), 161–182; and Shelley Sallee, *The Whiteness of Child Labor Reform in the New South* (Athens, 2004). Instead of recounting the reform movement, this chapter traces part of what Michael Grossberg has called the "public narrative" that informs "legal experience." Chapter 4 continues that discussion. See Michael Grossberg, *A Judgment for Solomon: The d'Hauteville Case and Legal Experience in Antebellum America* (New York, 1996), xiv.

story knew where the child belonged: at play and in school, not at work. When the latter calamity befell, decay ensued. In portraying the worlds of young workers, reformers reduced a myriad of jobs and circumstances to images of "little prisoners," toiling away in dingy, dark, and dangerous factories. Gone were the rosy cheeks of childhood, replaced with the wizened appearance of the "little pygmies." In this narrative, accidents occasionally took fingers and lives, but too much work and too little play made girls and boys dull indeed. Whether physically deformed or just dog-tired, these "little sufferers" could do nothing for themselves. Nor should they. In opposition to the vision of industrial childhood common among working people, reformer writers envisioned a childhood based in homebound dependence and passivity rather than slow inculcation into workplace production and growing capacity. By the time World War I approached, reformers had elevated incapacity to a divine right.[4]

THE EMPLOYMENT OF CHILDREN

Before the late nineteenth century in the United States, child labor had little iconic power. In fact, the term seldom appeared in print culture. More often, reform writers and others referred to the "employment of children," if they discussed the matter at all. That is not to say that work for younger people went entirely unnoticed in the popular imagination. For instance, the lives of slave children sometimes appeared in antislavery discourse, especially in autobiographical narratives such as Frederick Douglass's *Narrative of a Life* or Harriet Jacobs's *Incidents in the Life of a Slave Girl*. In the free-labor North, the decline of apprenticeship as a common institution and the rise of the binding-out of poor children occupied reform tracts and state government reports. The famous Lowell System of textile manufacturing occasioned impassioned debates about labor rights and wrongs, often carried out in the pages of the Lowell *Offering*, one of the first publications in U.S. history run primarily by younger people.[5]

---

[4] For brief discussions of child labor reformers similar to the one presented here, see Link, *Paradox of Southern Progressivism*, 161–163; David L. Carlton, *Mill and Town in South Carolina, 1880–1920* (Baton Rouge, 1982), 174–183; and especially I.A. Newby, *Plain Folk in the New South: Social Change and Cultural Resistance, 1880–1915* (Baton Rouge, 1989), 494–503.

[5] Frederick Douglass, *Narrative of the Life of Frederick Douglass*; Harriet Jacobs, *Incidents in the Life of a Slave Girl*. For examples of state reports, see *Report of Select Committee Appointed to Visit Charitable Institutions Supported by the State and All City and County Poor and Work Houses and Jails: New York Sen. Doc. 8, 1856* (New York, Arno

If child labor had yet to gain widespread currency, an incipient language that led in that direction began to appear. The English debates over the factory system and the eventual passages of the Factory Acts provided U.S. writers with the opportunity to ornament the growing edifice of American exceptionalism, while at the same time sounding a warning bell about the progress of labor degradation on the shores of the New World. American writers kept track of goings-on across the Atlantic, reprinting British publications whole-cloth (as was common in that era). These publications introduced U.S. audiences to what would become the common language of child labor, but they came accompanied with breezy suggestions that all would be well. Reviewing the state of the working classes in Britain, the *New England Family Magazine* bemoaned the state of "the degraded and miserable poor of Great Britain." Being so distant from the wretchedness of industrialism, Americans could only sympathize and pray. "We have ample cause for gratitude that in our own land we are not as yet pained with the sight and sound of such misery and destitution," the editors assured their readers. "May that evil day be far hence."[6]

It took a Herculean act of imagination to render New England into a laborer's paradise by the time these words appeared in 1845. The facts of life in U.S. manufactories made it increasingly difficult to imagine the horrors of industrialism as an Old World calamity that had luckily passed by the United States. At the same time, the antebellum labor movement had begun to notice the employment of children, providing a second source for talking about child labor. Importantly, however, labor writers included the work of young people inside the story of labor's overall diminution of rights and power. Children working for wages presented an indictment of wage-labor capitalism, one that called for resistance to the

Press, 1976); *Report of the Commissioners ... on the Subject of the Pauper System of the Commonwealth of Massachusetts* (New York: Arno Press, 1971 [repr. Boston: Dutton and Wentworth, 1833]); and "Legal Provision Respecting the Education and Employment of Children," *Connecticut Common School Journal*, July 1, 1842, 141–142. On Lowell, see Thomas Dublin, *Women at Work: The Transformation of Work and Community in Lowell, Massachusetts, 1826–1860* (New York, 1979).

[6] "Employment of Children in British Cotton Factories," *New England Family Magazine*, Sept. 1, 1845, 93–95; "First Report of the Children's Employment Commission," *Campbell's Foreign Monthly Magazine*, Sept.–Dec., 1842, 159–184; "Legal Provision Respecting the Education and Employment of Children," *Connecticut Common School Journal*, July 1, 1842, 142–157. On exceptionalism and its rejection by Progressive era reformers, see Daniel T. Rodgers, *Atlantic Crossings: Social Politics in a Progressive Age* (Cambridge, 2000).

whole rather than efforts simply to remove those most affected. In 1832, for instance, the *Workingman's Advocate* warned U.S. operatives about the dangers of "The Factory System." By that system and the machinery that powered it, "a small company of men, possessing a large stock of money, and sometimes aided by legislative enactments, are enabled to avail themselves of the labor of hundreds and frequently thousands of men, women, and children," the editors revealed. Those laborers were "generally worked to the utmost possible number of hours a day, and paid for their work the smallest possible compensation which will enable them to keep life in the body in sufficient strength to return to their daily task." Here, children simply occupied one part of a labor force abused by avaricious capitalists. Commenting on the passage of the 1844 British Factory Act, the *Subterranean* noted its protection of young workers. "No such protection is offered to the children of American operatives," the editor declared, "the capitalist may work them as young and as many hours as he pleases."[7]

A third location for the lexicon of child labor, and perhaps the most important one, came from education reform writers. From Thomas Jefferson, Judith Sargent Murray, and Benjamin Rush onward, political thinkers in the early Republic and antebellum eras connected learning to liberty. A republican citizenry had to be brought up correctly if it was to pick the "best men" to lead. By the 1820s, state governments in the Northeast increasingly concerned themselves with public education, initiating the long American tradition of the educational jeremiad. Those reports, with their ever-lengthening statistical tables, attributed Johnny's inability to read and cipher to his frequent attendance in the mills (and grogshops). Enacted in the 1820s and 1830s, the first child labor laws in U.S. history formed part of the movement to compel school attendance, if not education. In the language that reformers fashioned to undergird these efforts at state-building, they began to enunciate many of the arguments that would come to the fore in the late nineteenth century: The state has an interest in the child; factory work, and perhaps all labor, debilitates young people both mentally and physically; time spent at work unfits young people for citizenship and threatens the republic; factory life deprives children of sunshine and play time. Commenting on the ten-hour movement in 1849, a New Jersey paper called for good wages for working men, wages that would allow wives to stay home and children to

---

[7] "The Factory System," *Workingman's Advocate*, March 24, 1832, 3; "The Factory System," *Subterranean*, Nov. 16, 1844, 3.

remain at school or "at play in the open air invigorating their bodies, and strengthening their constitutions for a healthful and happy existence."[8]

The foremost voice to arise from these antebellum efforts was Horace Mann. "No greater calamity can befall us as a nation than that our children should grow up without knowledge and cultivation," Mann wrote in a declaration often quoted later. "If we do not prepare them to become good citizens, develop their capacities, enrich their minds with knowledge, imbue their hearts with a love of truth and all things holy, then our republic must go down to destruction as others have gone before it." Children of ten to fourteen who worked in factories, Mann feared, would undo the nation when they became adults. "When they go, blunted in morals, blind in intellect, from the sphere of childhood to full political sovereignty," he predicted, "there will come a terrible retribution." Missing from all of this, however, was the heightened sentimentalism of decades later and the notion of childhood as a time strictly cordoned off from adulthood.[9]

If school reformers led the way towards childhood innocence and rights, another group of writers took a somewhat less rosy view. In Western thought and culture, young people had long occupied a conflicted space between good and evil. Original sin must be forgiven and wills must be broken if angels are to emerge. By the early nineteenth century, these images were all the more in flux as a result of two centuries of philosophical theorizing about the younger sort. In particular, popularized versions of Jean-Jacques Rousseau's *Emile* broadened a romantic notion of children who discovered the wonders of the natural world and the wonders of the natural order. Underneath these balloons of innocence, however, lurked the fear that children might not be so nice after all. In the antebellum United States, these niggling doubts took on the cast of class, spawning alarmed calls to "do something" about child vagrancy and juvenile delinquency. As young people left the countryside in the wake of the market revolution, they encountered tractarians with a pamphlet for every occasion. As working families made their way in the growing slums of the country's largest urban centers, their progeny

---

[8] The Ten Hour Law," *N.J. State Gazette*, reprinted in *The Friend*, Sept. 15, 1849, 415; "Educate the Children of the Poor," *Subterranean*, July 18, 1846, 2; Carl. F. Kaestle, *Pillars of the Republic: Common Schools and American Society, 1780–1860* (New York, 1983), 96–98; Steven Mintz, *Huck's Raft: A History of American Childhood* (Cambridge, 2004), 71–74.

[9] "Children Who Work," *Scribner's Monthly*, April 1871, 615; Leonora Beck Ellis, "Child Operatives in Southern Cotton Mills," *The Independent*, Nov. 7, 1901, 2644.

used the streets in ways they had done for centuries, only to be met by Children's Aid Society agents intent on saving them from their own parents. Girls who wandered too close to the era's masculine sporting culture and its fascination with youthful sexuality might end up in a home for the wayward. All of this activity left a legacy quite different from the emancipatory impulse of factory reformers, labor leaders, and school writers. Instead of being freed, young people needed the rod, if only institutionally.[10]

By the end of the Civil War era, many elements in the language of child labor had already appeared. In particular, educational reformers had begun to shift the places where young people could be expected to spend their time. Play and school had begun to take the place of work and home. Utilizing the agitation in England, reform writers had also begun to make child labor a potent symbol for the dangers of industrialization. Throughout much of the antebellum era, however, that indictment remained focused on working families as a whole. Poor conditions for young people formed part of degraded life for all. As a result, "child labor" had not yet appeared, for in its maturity this notion would separate young workers from their elders, making the latter culpable for their fate rather than a part of it.

NOBLE CAPITALISTS AND LAZY FATHERS

The reformers who turned their attention to the employment of children in the first several decades of the nineteenth century had laid the foundation for what would follow. Finishing the house of child labor, however, fell to their descendants, who took up the cause after the Civil War. Those women and men formed an interconnected corps of writers, legislators, and activists who comprised what historians once called the "Progressive era." Attached to kindred in Europe, they articulated ways of understanding modern, industrial life, and not infrequently backed up their imaginations with the force of law. Their causes were many: trusts and other monopolies; pure food and pure drugs; votes for women; good roads, good genes, and good government. Those who took up the cause of youthful

---

[10] Charles Loring Brace, "What Is the Best Method for Care of Poor and Vicious Children?," *Journal of Social Science*, May 1880, 93–102; Mintz, *Huck's Raft*, 154–184; Christine Stansell, *City of Women: Sex and Class in New York, 1789–1860* (Urbana, 1982), 193–216. For a particularly perceptive view of the work of child savers and child saving in the postbellum era, see Linda Gordon, *The Great Arizona Orphan Abduction* (Cambridge, 1999), 8–13 and *passim*.

wage work sometimes came from these movements and the organizations they spawned, and sometimes not. Some outlived their era to become household historical names, such as Jane Addams, Felix Adler, or Samuel Gompers. Others only starred in their own movements in their own time. Anyone connected to child labor reform would have known the names of Alexander McKelway and Edgar Gardner Murphy of the National Child Labor Committee, and Indiana Senator Albert J. Beveridge, congressional patron of the group's program. Minor poets such as Elbert Hubbard or Marion Delcomyn fell into disuse in later years, even if minor socialists such as Scott Nearing experienced a renaissance. Behind these luminaries marched a throng of authors, important only for their words, not their deeds. And there was no shortage of words. As Owen R. Lovejoy proudly reported in 1911, the National Child Labor Committee by itself in one year issued more than 3.3 million pages of "child labor publications." But it was those words that began to articulate new ways of talking about young workers. Circulating in the nation's rapidly growing press, it mattered less who said what than whether it was said at all. As unknown writers picked up the lingo, it became all the more powerful. During the years between 1890 and 1920, these voices authored what became standard ways of making meaning for young people who worked.[11]

Reform writers narrated tales of morality, and if those stories needed villains, then the obvious choice in the Progressive era would seem to be the avaricious capitalist. Indeed, factory owners and businessmen in general often appeared as the root of the child-labor evil. At times, capitalism or industrialism itself stood in for the captains of industry. In

---

[11] "National Child Labor," *New York Observer and Chronicle*, Nov. 30, 1911, 707. As Lovejoy's report indicates, there is no shortage of sources for studying the language of "child labor." I have chosen to focus primarily on reform-oriented pieces that appeared in magazines, partly on the assumption that these reached a wider audience than did pamphlets, speeches, or even items in daily, local newspapers. That said, I am less interested in tracing out the actual "origins" of these ideas with any one person or figuring out which pieces might be "representative" as I am with what Gail Bederman has called "the process of articulation." While Bederman chose to study this process by looking carefully at four important voices, it can also be done with a body of writing. For Bederman's statement, see *Manliness and Civilization: A Cultural History of Gender and Race in the United States, 1880–1917* (Chicago, 1995), 23–24. I have also followed the lead of cultural historians who have examined the emergence of language. In particular, James W. Cook, *The Arts of Deception: Playing with Fraud in the Age of Barnum* (Cambridge, 2001); Michael Sappol, *A Traffic in Dead Bodies: Anatomy and Embodied Social Identity in Nineteenth-Century America* (Princeton, 2004); and T.J. Jackson Lears, *No Place of Grace: Anti-modernism and the Transformation of American Culture, 1880–1920* (New York, 1983); Daniel Wickberg, "Heterosexual White Male: Some Recent Inversions in American Cultural History," *Journal of American History* 92 (2005): 136–157.

1913, Illinois factory inspector Helen Todd folded young workers into the general dehumanization of machine production. "All that is needed to make an iron and steel machine perfect in its money-making power is the addition of the human cog," Todd wrote. "A child will do as well for this human cog as a man, and so a use has been found for the children of the working people." Visual images in particular drove home the iconography of avarice. A 1911 cartoon in *Life* magazine depicted an enormous, bloated businessman reposing in front of a "child labor factory." The man's height and girth required a ladder to scale. At the top of eleven steps, representing eleven hours a day, a small child dumped a bucket of "profits" into the man's gaping maw. So that the irony should not be missed, the cartoonist, Arthur Young, labeled the drawing: "And a Little Child Shall Feed Them ... The Biblical Law as Interpreted by Employers of Child Labor."[12]

While factory owners appeared as modern Molochs, their countenance was not always foreboding. For one thing, welfare capitalism clouded the picture of capitalists as perpetrators. Reform writers revealed the softer side of businessmen, sometimes portraying them as good-hearted paternalists doing their best for the youngsters (and oldsters) in their employ. In 1910, *The Independent* featured the model mill village established by Caesar Cone near Greensboro, North Carolina. The good Mr. Cone, the magazine relayed with no apparent irony, "treats his operatives as good as he does his machinery." Southern reformer Leonora Beck Ellis let a young mill mother do the talking about her well-meaning employer. "There's good wages, an' good cottages, an' Mr. Moring treats us right," the North Carolina resident supposedly told Ellis. The best of such treatment meant voluntary avoidance of child labor altogether, with beneficial effects. In mill towns without child labor, Ellis opined in another piece, "you would find such pleasing evidence as better homes, more domesticity and thrift among the women and girls, well-filled schools and good standards of scholarship, ruddy cheeks and spring steps among the youthful."[13]

---

[12] Helen M. Todd, "Why Children Work," *McClure's Magazine*, April 1913, 71; Elbert Hubbard, "White Slavery in the South," *The Philistine*, May 1902, 173; Arthur Young, "A Little Child Shall Feed Them," *Life*, Feb. 16, 1911, 341. The image of a fat cat businessman appeared frequently in *Life*. See April 17, 1913, 778; April 10, 1913, 726; Feb. 19, 1914, 314, 315; Sep. 19, 1914, 435.

[13] Truman S. Vance, "How a Man Went to Meet His Labor Troubles," *The Independent*, May 17, 1910, 563; Leonora Beck Ellis, "A New Class of Labor in the South," *Forum*, May 1901, 310; Leonora Beck Ellis, "Child Operatives in Southern Cotton Mills," *The Independent*, Nov. 7, 1901, 2644. On such arrangements, which are often called "welfare capitalism," see, among others, Gerald Zahavi, *Workers, Managers, and Welfare*

"A LITTLE CHILD SHALL FEED THEM"

FIGURE 3. Reform spread as much through visual imagery as through the written word. This 1911 cartoon from *Life* illustrates the diminution of young workers in the construction of child labor. Arthur Young, *Life*, 1911. Courtesy Northern Illinois University.

The entrepreneur could, in the end, resist temptation. Just as often as reformer writers envisioned bloated businessmen, they saw factory owners as willingly complying with the letter and spirit of child labor laws.

Capitalism: The Shoeworkers and Tanners of Endicott Johnson, 1890–1950 (Urbana, 1988). Anyone interested in Cone himself can consult an interview by the Southern Oral History project at http://docsouth.unc.edu/sohp/C-0003/C-0003.html.

"There are numerous companies, presidents, and superintendents whose humanity in dealing with these conditions is unsurpassed," Aaron Hardy Ulm disclosed in the *North American Review*. "Many have enforced age limits outside and above the law." Far from being antagonists, mill owners sometimes aligned with the forces of good, as in the account of Columbia University's Holland Thompson. Owners and superintendents did "not want the children in the mills, but the pressure to admit them is steady and strong," Thompson maintained. Who did want the children in the mills then? "The blame," Thompson argued, "is put chiefly on the fathers, because they deserve it."[14]

So the temptations came in the form of parents who proffered their progeny at the factory gates. In fact, no image populated reform discourse as frequently as did the "lazy" parent, especially the "lazy father." Reform writers convinced themselves that derelict dads lived extravagantly, or at least ignorantly, off the backs of their broods. For some, the sins of the fathers resulted more from simple ignorance than any lack of parental morality. Illinoisan Francis H. McLean attributed child labor to "transplanted Old World ideals." Immigrant fathers recalled that they went to work at an early age, so why not their offspring? "To the Italian," she averred, "the boy of twelve is ripe for work." Leonora Beck Ellis advanced a similar proposition about the Southern hill folk who migrated to mill towns. "Accustomed in old rural life to keep children almost as busy as adults in planting and harvesting, they see slight reason for debarring youngsters from the new occupations," Ellis wrote in 1901. Like Ellis, Helen Todd captured an important dynamic in the lives of working families. She recounted the story of a Swedish immigrant father who brought his son to a Chicago woodworking plant. In her version of events, the man appeared indignant at her suggestion that having a twelve-year-old at work violated the law or its spirit. "There ain't no violation," the man declared. "That's my own boy, working here without pay, learning the business." All of these explanations for the presence of young workers intended to place blame on fathers, but only for their ignorance of proper roles in the modern household. In doing so, they inadvertently described the actual motivations for labor market participation by working families.[15]

[14] Aaron Hardy Ulm, "The Plea of the Child Laborer," *The North American Review*, June 1909, 898; Holland S. Thompson, "Life in a Southern Mill Town," *Political Science Quarterly* 15 (March 1900): 13. See also "The New South's Rare Opportunity," *Gunton's Magazine*, July 1902, 55; Ward Sanford, "Twentieth Century Herods," *Cosmopolitan*, July 1902, 350.

[15] "Child Labor in the United States – Discussion," *American Economic Association Proceedings*, Feb. 1906, 265; Ellis, "Child Operatives," 2644; Todd, "Why Children Work," 70.

Although reformers sometimes delved into the sociology of the working family, they more often relied on simple characterizations of fathers as lazy. The man who refused to work had been the stock-in-trade of moralistic reformers since the transition to wage labor began in the early modern era. Attempts to legislate steady habits notwithstanding, the menace of the able-bodied shirker lurked in the shadows of the Progressive age, now to be supported by the forced labor of the little ones. In 1891, Clare DeGraffenried brought the lazy father to a Southern setting in a classic piece of literary journalism, "The Georgia Cracker in the Cotton Mills." Armed with a pen and allied with a trusty sketch artist, DeGraffenried took aim. "Grouped about the single store of the village, lounging, whittling sticks, and sunning their big, lazy frames, sit a score of stalwart masculine figures, while their offspring and their womankind toil in the dusty mill," she wrote. DeGraffenried's image would be repeated remorselessly in reform discourse for decades. In 1909, Aaron Hardy Ulm found that "the littler tots are forced by idle fathers and indolent mothers into the factories and compelled to stay there." Time and victories for the child labor movement did little to temper the ire. Writing in 1917, Marion Delcomyn decried working fathers and mothers "who coin shameful dollars from the bodies and souls of their own flesh and blood." Not taken in by the new sociology, Delcomyn refused to blame child labor on the conditions in working households or the inequalities of industrial life. "Not the poverty of the family which makes children's earnings indispensable, but the greed and ignorance of the parents, is at the bottom of all child labor," she wrote. "And because of this labor of their children, the parents usually live in fairly comfortable circumstances."[16]

Evoking a standard character type from the antebellum era, the lazy father was often the drunken father. An overwrought Leonora Beck Ellis peered through the windows of the mill cottage and came away aghast at what she saw. "What of the homes – too numerous, alas! – where the drunken father, the debauched mother, can every day imbrute themselves the more deeply because custom and law sanction their own idleness

---

[16] Clare DeGraffenried, "The Georgia Cracker in the Cotton Mills," *Century Illustrated Magazine*, Feb. 1891, 484; Ulm, "Plea," 892; Marion Delcomyn, "Why Children Work," *Forum*, March 1917, 323–324. For more on the importance of home slackers in Progressive discourse, see Michael Willrich, *City of Courts: Socializing Justice in Progressive Era Chicago* (New York, 2003), Ch. 5. DeGraffenreid's piece provoked an angry response from Rebecca Latimer Felton and other prominent Southerners. Felton went on a speaking tour to debunk DeGraffenried's accusations. See LeeAnn Whites, *Gender Matters: Civil War, Reconstruction, and the Making of the New South* (New York, 2005), 128–149.

and their children's slavery?" the astonished lady wrote. The drunken dad popped up all over the country, not just in Southern mill towns. In 1904, the *New York Observer* declared that law must stop the "premature enfeeblement" of the boy who worked "to fill the beer mug of his cruel father." In an era where reformers carried the campaign for prohibition around the nation, connecting child labor to drink helped secure its power as a new language, linking it to a conventional wisdom decades, if not centuries, old.[17]

Southern reform writers sharpened the portrait of the imperfect patriarch to a singular inversion of gender roles: the male "dinner toter." Perhaps invoking the racialized meanings of "pan toting" by African American domestic servants, Southern writers described men who did little more than take meals to their working wives and children. These "cotton-mill hoboes" married weak-willed women and then forced them into the factories. "So numerous is this specimen of so-called 'man' that he has given rise to a brand-new term – 'dinner-toter' – which denotes the only useful thing he ever does, that is to carry the midday meal to his servile companion," Ulm wrote. *Gunton's Magazine* similarly noted families where fathers carried dinner pails, working only on odd days when they "tired of loafing." Child labor and educational reformer Charles Coon, of Wilson, North Carolina, pressed the dinner-toter image to the limits, conducting his own "study" of the matter. Not surprisingly, Coon confirmed his suspicions that "factory child labor always breeds the worthless parent, who lives off his children."[18]

In the gaze of reformers, these dinner-toting patriarchs knew and exercised their rights and power. As social commentators moved towards the notion of children's rights in the late nineteenth century, they confronted the long-standing concept of fatherly authority. Never as old or secure as tradition would have it, the prevailing idea that fathers possessed a property right in their children's labor both augured against the rapid articulation of children's rights and at the same time shored up the figure of the lazy father. An incident narrated in the textile industry trade paper, *The Dry Goods Economist*, portrayed the lazy but legally wise Southern father.

[17] Ellis, "Child Operatives," 2644; "The Salvability of the Child," *New York Observer*, April 21, 1904, 502.
[18] Ulm, "Plea," 893; "The New South's Rare Opportunity," *Gunton's Magazine*, July 1902, 55; Charles Coon Papers, Box 3, Folder 38, Southern Historical Collection, University of North Carolina-Chapel Hill. For a literary rendition of the dinner-toter tale, see "At the Factory Gate," *Life*, May 16, 1907, 694. McHugh, *Mill Family*, 47 notes the image in passing.

The narrator found a Southern husband loafing around the general store, bragging on how much he took in from the work his wife and children did in a nearby mill. The writer inquired why he did not go to work in the mills so at least his wife could remain home. Rebuffed with a "That's my business, sah," the author queried the man on what he would do if "his children should slip their cables and make for parts unknown." The proud father proclaimed that he would reclaim the miscreants and teach them "a lesson they'd never forget." He would be well within his rights. "The boys are mine till they're twenty-one and the girls till eighteen," the cracker parent declared, "and the law will uphold me in my rights."[19]

Such proclamations of parental power figured into how reformers explained their own failings. According to reform writers, working parents actively opposed pro-child legislation. For the cracker father, wrote Elbert Hubbard in 1902, "it is a question of 'rights, sah,' and he is the head of the family and you must not meddle – his honor is at stake." The alternative position swung the balance away from parental rights. Charlotte Perkins Gilman put the matter bluntly in 1906: "The family has no property rights in the child." In fact, Gilman argued, "The family has no claim on the child comparable to the child's claim on the family." While reformers certainly exaggerated the extent to which Southern working parents claimed an absolute right in their children's labor, such an inversion of power relations in the family put them squarely at odds with the slothful sires they excoriated.[20]

Charges of indolence flew mostly at the menfolk, but working mothers did not go unscathed. In an era where child-savers increasingly turned to "mother-blaming," women also took part of the censure for children who worked. Sometimes, they simply appeared as the hapless victims of a lazy father. In a conventional short story in *The Christian Observer*, Mary Grimes struggles to make ends meet, while her ne'er-do-well husband, William, lounges about the house and plots to enroll the children at the local mill instead of the local school. All is not lost, though, for sturdy Aunt Kate whisks into town, sternly lecturing William on his parental responsibilities and informing him that Ralph and Judith "are too bright

---

[19] As quoted in "Southern Protest Against Child Labor," *Outlook*, August 9, 1902, 907.

[20] Hubbard, "White Slavery in the South," 167; Thompson, "Life in a Southern Mill Town," 12; "Child Labor in the United States – Discussion," *American Economic Association Proceedings*, Feb. 1906, 260–262. On mother blaming, see Kathleen W. Jones, *Taming the Troublesome Child: American Families, Child Guidance, and the Limits of Psychiatric Authority* (Cambridge, 1999), Ch. 7.

FIGURE 4. Elbert Hubbard (1856–1915). Poet Elbert Hubbard joined the chorus of Progressive era writers who railed against child labor. He was less concerned about adults. Frances Benjamin Johnston, ca. 1890-ca. 1910. Library of Congress, Prints & Photographs Division, LC-USZ62–70337.

to be sacrificed on the altar of child labor." By the time Kate is finished, William is plowing a local farm, and Mary and the children, rid of their "Modern Millstone," are "too happy for words."[21]

Mary Grimes could do little to help herself. She needed a strong woman to reinvigorate her emasculated man. But other mothers appeared

---

[21] Mrs. F.M. Howard, "The Modern Millstone," *The Christian Observer*, June 3, 1908, 14–15.

as partners in crime, in cahoots with lazy fathers for the most selfish of reasons. Leonora Beck Ellis lumped women with men, conjuring "households of adults living in idleness upon the wages of their children, disorder and filth speeding after such shifting of duties." If shirking domestic duties presented part of the problem of working mothers, immodest public display subsidized by youngsters cried out as another. In addition to supplying swill for their dads, *The New York Observer* opined, children's wages helped "to deck out with a little more gaudy finery the gaunt figure of a neglectful mother." Such bad behavior started early on, as sweet mill girls turned into incipient bad mothers. "Go into the mills," an aroused Aaron Hardy Ulm beckoned, "and see them work in bare feet with their bodies half-clad, in order that they may wear badly fitting, but creased and starchy, store clothes on Sunday." To Ulm, inexpensive ready-mades indicated a certain cheapness of character as well. "Note the lack of modesty among the young women of this class," he did duly note, "their makeshift working costumes, their snuff-rubbing and expectorating habits, and their childish love of gaudy apparel for use on holidays." In the gaze of reformers such as Ulm, the gender and class inversions of mill mothers only added to the general picture of households in disarray. That children should be saved from such a fate was only obvious.[22]

All this luxury could be bought and paid for by young workers whose parents could slip between the cracks of the law. Ironically, while reform writers struggled to impose new rules, they frequently revealed that they were being broken. Alexander McKelway, a leading light in the National Child Labor Committee, bemoaned the fact that parents were "nearly always" on the side of the mills when it came to factory inspection. A Georgia correspondent to the *Ohio Farmer* affirmed McKelway's characterization, arguing that "parents do not hesitate to swear falsely about the ages of their children in order to put them to work in the mills." Indeed, reformers missed the mark only with regard to motivations, for working people did often seek to evade the law.[23]

In particular, reform writers honed in on the fact that parents and their children often acquired falsified age certificates and work permits. Helen Todd reported a Chicago girl who simply bought one from an older cousin after he passed sixteen and no longer needed it. "A bit of perjury in connection with certificates does the trick," wrote Marion Delcomyn. "And

[22] Ellis, "Child Operatives," 2642; "The Salvability of the Child," 502; Ulm, "Plea," 897.
[23] Max Harris Wilensky, "The Child Labor Situation," *Forum*, March 1917, 318; "Child Labor in the South," *Ohio Farmer*, Feb. 3, 1906, 121.

all for gain. Gain for parents, murderous injury to children." Immigrant parents, already under indictment for not grasping American customs of child-rearing, found themselves charged with perjury as well. Minnie J. Reynolds averred that immigrant parents in New York City resorted to "every trick and device to get the coveted 'working papers' for children under the legal age." When school officials tried to enforce child labor laws, they encountered "storms of abuse" in response. The same situation obtained in the mines, Francis Nichols revealed in *McClure's*, a leading reform magazine. Age certificates were "a criminal institution," because fathers and children alike simply lied about age, filling in blank papers with whatever age the law required.[24]

Lawbreaking and laziness went hand in hand, writing parents outside of respectability. As the *Southern Cultivator* put it, "parental affection" should govern the matter of child labor, but because it did not, it was "necessary to invoke the strong arm of the law in order to give the boy or girl a chance to become a man or a woman and not a mere human machine." Hence, working parents became the target, not the beneficiaries, of child labor reform. Avaricious mill owners played their part in the story, paving the road to perdition, but ultimately, parents drove the wagon. Between them and the helpless child stood an army of reformers ready to make their stand.[25]

A SMALL, YET VALIANT BAND

Elbert Hubbard, something of a poet, packed a 1902 piece on reform in the South with every available figure from the rapidly developing language of child labor. Cracker fathers quaff whiskey and talk politics at the general store, while "weazened pigimies" munch their lunch in dull silence until the foreman marches in to roust them out, "shaking the sleepers, shouting in their ears, and lifting them to their feet and in a few instances kicking the delinquents into wakefulness." Little could be done about this crying shame while "the cracker, the preacher, the overseer, the superintendent, the president, and the stockholders ... sink into the quicksands of hypocrisy." Against this coalition of the willing stood a "small, yet valiant band of men and women in the South, who are fighting this iniquity, to hold

[24] Todd, "Why Children Work," 78; Delcomyn, "Why Children Work," 324; Minnie J. Reynolds, "The 'American Children' of Foreign Parents," *Congregationalist and Christian World*, March 24, 1906, 427; Francis H. Nichols, "Children of the Coal Shadow," *McClure's Magazine*, Feb. 1906, 439.
[25] "Child Labor," *Southern Cultivator*, May 15, 1903, 3.

fast and not leave off in their work until the little captives are made free."
Braving ostracism and scorn, these soldiers for the good battled onward,
safe in the knowledge that "right will surely win."[26]

Hubbard's portrait underscores an important element of reform discourse. As reformers articulated the literary devices of the "child labor
problem," they simultaneously performed an act of self-definition, narrating their own identities as defenders of the good. In the end, the object
of their efforts was the passive child, unable to speak or act for him- or
herself, but reform writers arrayed themselves in front of other bastions as
well, albeit ones that ultimately depended on children for their existence.
Recalling the conventions of the antebellum era, reform writers defended
"the worker" from the cheap labor of children that depressed adult wages
and from the allure of tramping that early entry into the labor market
seemingly produced. At the same time, they looked to cleanse "the race,"
both in the eugenic sense and in the construction of "whiteness." Closely
linked to "race protection," they aimed to protect "the nation," greasing
the wheels of progress to keep pace with the "civilized world," overseeing
the next generation of fighting men, and ensuring that the possessors of
citizenship in the future would be fit to exercise it. Many of the elements
in this self-image had been around since the early nineteenth century, but
never before had so much depended on "the child" and her champions.

While much of reform discourse originated in middle-class studies and
parlors, labor leaders and their allies presented themselves as defenders
of labor rights in the face of degradation caused by the employment of
young people. Writing in 1906, American Federation of Labor President
Samuel Gompers affirmed that "the abolition of child labor would have
an influence to encourage the organization of wage-earners in those
industries." Legendary textile organizer Rose Schneiderman connected
child labor to strikebreaking as well as low wages. Narrating a successful organizing drive among capmakers in 1905, the young labor leader
reported that "the bosses intended gradually to get rid of us, employing
in our place child labor and raw immigrant girls who would work for
next to nothing."[27]

Replacing older workers with younger ones, as strikebreakers or
for simple economy, occupied the attention of voices outside the labor

[26] Hubbard, "White Slavery," 167–168, 178.
[27] Samuel Gompers, "Organized Labor's Attitude toward Child Labor," *Annals of the
American Academy of Political and Social Science*, March 1906, 79; Rose Schneiderman,
"A Capmaker's Story," *The Independent*, April 27, 1905, 937.

movement as well. Three decades before Schneiderman wrote, *Scribner's* had laid out the elemental economics of the market in youthful labor. "Children in many cases supply the places of more mature hands," the argument went, "and thus offer the employer an opportunity for gain not to be resisted as long as other manufacturers must compete with this cheap labor." Removing children from factories, reformers argued, would naturally lead to an increase in wages for adults, if only by forcing derelict parents into the labor market. A few went even further. Felix Adler, founding chairman of the National Child Labor Committee, tied the creation of labor rights for children to labor rights for all. The restriction of child labor, Adler argued, would force people to admit that adult workers could not be treated as a simple means of production. If young workers gained rights, he believed, so, too, would older ones. Though prominently placed, Adler's view also surpassed many of his colleagues. For them, child labor remained distinct from adult labor, and its elimination would, at most, increase wages.[28]

In fact, far from linking rights for children to labor rights for adults, some reformers resurrected the older bugbear of vagrancy, essentially arguing that workers had to be protected from their own childhoods. Reaching back to antebellum debates about paupers, Jane Addams first drew the connection between child labor and tramping in 1903. Young people "cannot stand up to the grind of factory life," Addams noted. Worn out while "still immature and undeveloped," they walked away from steady labor and toward the tramping life. Alexander McKelway put the matter more bluntly. "Statistics show that the army of tramps and paupers is mainly recruited from the ranks of children whose lives are embittered too early," McKelway wrote in 1907. In this vein, reform writers positioned themselves as defenders of labor, but not of laborers. Adult workers must be saved from childhoods that would unfit them for the burdens of wage work by showing them its face too early. Children must be useless when young so they could become useful when they came of age.[29]

Child labor writers positioned themselves between workers and their impediments, but they much more frequently spoke for "the race." That

[28] "Children Who Work," *Scribner's Monthly*, April 1871, 612; Ellis, "Child Operatives," 2644; "What Can Be Done About It?" *Gunton's Magazine*, Feb. 1900, 121; "Evils of Child Labor," *New York Observer and Chronicle*, March 2, 1905, 280.

[29] Jane Addams, "Child Labor and the Tramp," *Current Literature*, Dec. 1903, 741; Alexander McKelway, "The Child in the Midst," *New York Observer and Chronicle*, June 27, 1907, 835; Philip Davis, "Child Labor and Vagrancy," *The Chautauquan*, May 1908, 416–424.

laden term comprised two interconnected meanings. On the one hand, some writers bluntly stated their intentions to save "white" children from lagging behind their "colored" counterparts. On the other, they adopted the language of the incipient eugenics movement to protect "humanity" from "ignoramuses and imbeciles." As one historian of child labor has noted, "whiteness" lay at the heart of the child labor reform campaign in Alabama. Indeed, declarations of good intent towards the children of the Deep South surfaced often, especially during the first decade of the twentieth century. Irene Ashby MacFadyen, the American Federation of Labor's special agent in Alabama, frequently sounded the alarm about the evils of mill work for white children, conveying the sentiments of "Pitchfork" Ben Tillman and others that white children languished while black children got good educations in schools. That nothing could be further from the truth did not disturb MacFadyen and her associates. Such arguments touched a popular nerve. A correspondent to *Outlook* called for "the emancipation of the little white slaves of the South so that they may have an opportunity to live the normal child life that God intended they should." For reform writers, this new emancipation went beyond the borders of the South and the United States. Leonora Beck Ellis cast the movement in transatlantic terms. Child labor reform, she proclaimed, was a "movement to preserve Anglo-Saxon children, and the great countries they stand for, from premature blight and decay."[30]

Although Ellis envisioned "Anglo-Saxon children," her concern for "premature blight and decay" linked whiteness to larger arguments about "race suicide." By the first decade of the twentieth century, that sordid phrase flowed ebulliently from the mouths of middle-class progressives, from Teddy Roosevelt on up the evolutionary ladder. The "darker peoples," they worried, had embarked on a path way that would "breed" the "white race" out of existence. Tied to the language of the late nineteenth century imperial outburst, "race suicide" nonetheless became increasingly untethered from its explicitly racist moorings. Charlotte Perkins Gilman, who often blended feminism with racism, connected child labor to race diminution, throwing in a bit of class analysis for good measure. "Every higher race, in proportion to its own development, has an ever-growing longer period of immaturity," she maintained, "for in that prolonged

[30] Irene Ashby MacFadyen, "Child Labor in the South," *Current Literature*, July 1902, 77–79; Tully F. McCrea, "Child Labor in Factories," *Outlook*, Sep. 20, 1902, 184; Leonora Beck Ellis, "The Movement to Restrict Child Labor," *The Arena*, Oct. 1902, 378; Sallee, *Whiteness of Child Labor*; Stephen Kantrowitz, *Ben Tillman and the Reconstruction of White Supremacy* (Chapel Hill, 2000), 213.

period comes the growth, the development that elevates the race." Setting children to work too early forestalled this dynamic, leading to a "steady reduction in the value of the race" and "a constant replenishment of the lower classes with still lower types." While Gilman's version of the race suicide argument still invoked the notion of "higher races" and "lower classes," McKelway kept the genetic logic but jettisoned the explicit racialism. "Child labor results in race degeneracy," he boldly announced. Stunted young workers reproduced in their teens, "and the depreciation of the human stock is the inevitable result."[31]

As reformers spoke for the worker, and the race, they elevated the stakes of child labor reform and its vision of "the child" to heights unreached by their antebellum ancestors. Such lofty ends could not possibly be reached by young people themselves; they needed intervention by those older and wiser. To this powerful concoction of rhetoric, child labor reformers added a third object of protection: "the nation." Having invoked the vocabularies of "civilization" in talking about "race," writers turned their gaze to the state of "American civilization" and found a blot on the national character. As European nations restricted or outlawed work for young people, reformers fretted that the United States was falling behind. Comparisons with Britain abounded, but other nations also appeared to cast U.S. sins into relief. Francis McLean measured American progress on child labor against France and deemed the United States to be behind. With regard to the South in particular, *Gunton's Magazine* threw a particularly sharp barb. "The South should get in line with civilization, and be at least as humane and progressive as Russia," George Gunton pithily opined. Marion Delcomyn conjured a bit of Orientalism to prophesy the outcome of unregulated child labor. Relaying a story in which children in "unenlightened China" supposedly carried bricks up a hill for four cents a day, Delcomyn asked her shocked readers: "Are we, here in this enlightened land, coming to that?"[32]

Not only was America falling behind externally because of child labor, it was also falling apart inside. The connection between childrearing and

[31] "Child Labor in the United States – Discussion," *American Economic Association Proceedings*, Feb. 1906, 260–261; McKelway, "Child in the Midst," 835. See also "Coram Nobis," *The American Lawyer*, March 1907, 107; John A. Offord, "Help the Toiling Children," *New York Observer and Chronicle*, Nov. 14, 1907, 625; "Child Labor in the South," *Ohio Farmer*, Feb. 3, 1906, 121.
[32] "Child Labor in the United States – Discussion," *American Economic Association Proceedings*, Feb. 1906, 265; "Dodging the Child Labor Issue," *Gunton's Magazine*, March 1902, 247; Delcomyn, "Why Children Work," 328; Rodgers, *Atlantic Crossings*, 237–239.

citizenship had been strong since the early days of the Republic, and it remained so in the era after the Civil War. Elbridge Gerry, founder of the New York Society for the Prevention of Cruelty to Children, sounded this note early on. "From a political standpoint," he wrote in 1883, "the future status of the nation will depend largely on the proper physical and intellectual training of these children, yearly increasing in numbers, who before long will constitute the sovereign people of the Republic." Drawing upon such nuggets of conventional wisdom, child labor reformers raised the specter of a degraded citizenry and a declining Republic. Indiana Senator Albert J. Beveridge, sponsor of the first federal child labor bill, centered his remarks to the 1906 National Child Labor Committee (NCLC) convention on this element of the child labor question. "Any industrial system that robs American children of their rights is a crime against humanity and treason against liberty itself," he intoned. "A stream of poison is poured into American citizenship through the premature labor of children." Such degraded citizens would not protect the Republic in times of crisis, reformers feared, backing up their premonitions with statistics apparently demonstrating that young workers made bad soldiers.[33]

Whether menacing the worker, the race, or the nation, child labor threatened American lives and livelihoods. Against these dangers, reformers stood. By connecting their cause to such heightened aims, reformers wrote their own legitimacy, giving linguistic attacks on working families a level of authority they might otherwise have lacked. After all, there was a grain of truth in the words they placed in the mouths of lazy fathers. The law and the larger culture of patriarchy did, after all, recognize their rights and powers. By the late nineteenth century, debates about wage labor under capitalism had spread the belief that a wage capable of sustaining a family demarcated wage work from slavery. This notion of a family wage provided a way to indict those men who failed to provide it, but these charges always threatened to call wage-labor capitalism itself into question. Constructing their cause as critical to national survival itself, reformers positioned themselves as the new fathers, ready to protect the defenseless child toilers they took under their wings.[34]

[33] Elbridge T. Gerry, "Cruelty to Children," *North American Review*, July 1883, 68; J. Ellington McGhee, "National Child Labor Convention," *Zion's Herald*, Dec. 26, 1906, 1668; Ulm, "Plea," 896; McKelway, "Child in the Midst," 835; "Coram Nobis," *The American Lawyer*, March 1907, 107; Hoke Smith, "Child Labor and Illiteracy," *Christian Observer*, Sep. 7, 1904, 5.
[34] Amy Dru Stanley, *From Bondage to Contract: Wage Labor, Marriage, and the Market in the Age of Slave Emancipation* (New York, 1998), Ch. 4. On the persistence of the

LITTLE PRISONERS

All the objects that reformers sought to protect rested on a defense of "the child." This singular was and is important, for child labor reformers fashioned a language that reduced the wide and moving continuum of work for young people to a singular, powerful icon that people then and now understood as "child labor." Doing so was not without its difficulties. Middle-class writers and activists had worried about "delinquency" since the antebellum era. By the twentieth century, unruly boys and wayward girls still bedeviled the domestic longings of reform writers. Tracing troubled youth to premature labor helped to resolve the contradictions these non-angelic children posed, but thinking about work in a capitalist society raised prickly issues. Hard work had been the gospel of reform for decades, idleness the chief sin. To write an entire group of people outside of the capitalist duty to toil was no easy task. It required the drawing of lines. When should young people enter the world of work? How much work was too much? If not work, what? Play and school, reformers contended, should be where children spent most of their time, but how much of these could be considered enough? When did a young person cease to be a "child?" But more important, what made someone a child in the first place? At the center of reform discourse could be found the answer to that question. By definition, a child was a person who did not work.[35]

Young workers became, in reform language, "little sufferers." In part, this icon simply adopted the language of the poets and would-be poets of British factory agitation, but it also required painting pictures with words, with pen and ink, and with the new realism of photography. Writers occasionally depicted the violence that cut short the lives and limbs of young workers, but more often, the portraits of "little toilers" represented a different "deformed" body, a child beaten down by his surroundings. "Wizened" countenances replaced the cheerfulness of youth, a transfiguration that could be blamed on a dark and noisy environment. Chained to their machines, figuratively if not literally, these "little

---

family wage, see Alice Kessler-Harris, *In Pursuit of Equity: Women, Men, and the Quest for Economic Citizenship in Twentieth-Century America* (New York, 2001), esp. Ch. 1.

[35] Joseph M. Hawes, *Children in Urban Society: Juvenile Delinquency in Nineteenth-Century America* (New York, 1971); Jones, *Taming the Troublesome Child*, Chs. 5–6; Willrich, *City of Courts*, Ch. 7. On the longer history of these fears, see Paul Boyer, *Urban Masses and Moral Order in America, 1820–1920* (Cambridge, 978), esp. Ch. 7; and Karen Halttunen, *Confidence Men and Painted Women: A Study of Middle-class Culture in America, 1830–1870* (New Haven, 1986), Chs. 1–2.

prisoners" spoke when spoken to but otherwise remained silent. Their literary reticence mirrored their underlying passivity. As "receptors," in Edgar Gardner Murphy's words, children would increasingly be defined by what they could not do. Casting these inabilities in the language of rights heightened the stakes even more. These new incapacities put "little sufferers" on a collision course with the real young people who worked in mines and mills. Adherents of producer values had little truck for those who did not find something useful to do.

If children were supposed to be passive, some were all too active for their own good. Reform writers walked a fine line between blaming child labor for juvenile delinquency and allowing young people the agency that would undermine the image of the little sufferer. Working boys, in particular, presented a problem for anyone wanting to depict cherubs on the factory floor. Writing in 1885, John F. Crowell described a nine-year-old factory operative who "chewed tobacco vigorously." Aaron Hardy Ulm struck a similar note, depicting factories that produced vice in abundance. Innocent country boys encountered "a hardened class of youths whose ambition is solely to pattern themselves after the bad habits of their elders," he revealed. "To chew the most tobacco, to smoke the greatest number of cigarettes, to use most deftly the unprintable words of blasphemy and obscenity, are soon bound to be considered marks of superiority." Fun as this might sound, reformers were not laughing. As juvenile courts spread from Chicago and Denver outward, cleaning dirty mouths became a national obsession. Linking such bad behavior to child labor heightened the level of moral panic, but it also gave young people a voice, if one laced with naughty words.[36]

Naughty talk led to naughty games that should not be played by nice boys and girls. If tobacco and profanity were not bad enough, liquor, flirting, and sexual experimentation augmented the connection between factory labor and wayward youth. Expectoration bothered Connecticut clergyman John Crowell considerably, but the morals of young Southern factory operatives were downright "deplorable." Cursing religiosity, young operatives crowded close together, their "childish store of modesty" rapidly on the wane. Boys and girls as young as thirteen visited saloons after work, and intoxication was "no rarity among the girls

---

[36] John F. Crowell, "The Employment of Children," *Andover Review*, July 1885, 46; Ulm, "Plea," 895; William Macleod Raine, "How Denver Saved Her Juvenile Court," *The Arena*, July 1909, 403–414; Ben B. Lindsey, "Childhood and Morality," *Christian Observer*, Oct. 26, 1910, 7; David S. Tanenhaus, *Juvenile Justice in the Making* (New York, 2004).

even." Drink led naturally down the staircase of sin as these miscreants gave up to "the drift of passion from the years of early youth." Though Crowell observed the gender and sexual norms that had been part of rural Southern culture for decades, if not centuries, he was not alone in linking child labor and loose morals. Visiting a New York factory in 1903, Lillian Betts espied similar bad behavior. "Boys in short trousers, smoking, swearing, using vile language" engaged in a "coarse interchange of talk between the sexes." Not to be outdone, the girls joined in the fun. After eating their lunches, "girls not fully clothed" retired to the outdoors "for a breath of fresh air, hatless and coatless." More flirting followed. "So far as the interchange of jokes, conversation, a rough-and-tumble play, the sexes were equal," the stunned lady revealed. "The expletives used in conversation were the same." These lurid gender violations could shock, and perhaps titillate, but such tales sounded a little too much like the pages of *The Police Gazette*. Young workers in such accounts did not appear to be suffering unduly.[37]

Idle talk and stolen smokes led naturally to a life of crime. In pamphleteering for the NCLC, Alexander McKelway frequently featured the underworld of crime visited by night messenger boys. Running messages to brothels and gambling dens, these boys easily procured cocaine and opium for the agents of the reform organization (for what purpose, he did not disclose). Boys found the red-light district all too attractive. "The boys were much addicted to crap-shooting," McKelway revealed. "The glamour of the underworld, and the extra tips from its denizens" kept them from getting out. Worse still, these night riders exacerbated the South's race problem. The young African American who got the goods for NCLC agents in Macon, Georgia, boasted of his skills in conducting the drug trade at disorderly houses. "This negro boy was already the type of gambler and tough who brings so much trouble upon the community where he lives," McKelway warned.[38]

Hardened street toughs could be expected to go wrong, but innocent youngsters could end up in the same place if put to work too soon. In

---

[37] Crowell, "Employment of Children," 51; Lillian W. Betts, "Child Labor in Factories," *Outlook*, March 14, 1903, 638. Such fears would come to the fore after World War I, but they were present in child labor discourse well before that. On the youth revolt of the 1920s, see Paula S. Fass, *The Damned and the Beautiful: American Youth in the 1920s* (New York, 1979); and Mintz, *Huck's Raft*, Ch. 11.

[38] Alexander McKelway, *Child Labor in Georgia*, National Child Labor Committee Pamphlet No. 138, 18–19, TSLA; McKelway, *Child Labor in Tennessee*, National Child Labor Committee Pamphlet No. 150, 14–15, TSLA.

Lillian Betts's account, a twelve-year-old Russian immigrant boy went to work after his father coerced the local school to release him by lying about his age. A few months later, father and son returned to the school with a woeful tale of decline. The school principal found the lad to be drastically changed. "The boy who had left me a rosy, rollicking, happy, brilliant school-boy, stood before me a cowed, broken boy, looking like a sneak," the principal reported. The boy's handsome father had turned into "a gray-haired, broken man." What had gone wrong? "The father, in a tone vindictive and cruel, responded: 'He is a thief'." Having gone to work at a jeweler's illegally, the boy had begun to steal almost immediately. Caught in the act, he landed in jail, his father mortgaging their tenement to bail him out. Though back where he belonged, the boy was now three grades behind, and his prospects were dim. Betts's principal supplied the moral: "I think his mind is destroyed."[39]

Narratives of criminality and its attendant ills linked child labor to other reform movements in the Progressive era, particularly the drive for "juvenile justice." As many historians have noted, sentimental notions of innocence have always masked an adult uneasiness with children. Those fears have frequently surfaced in crusades against youthful crime, and the Progressive era child-labor reformers, connected organizationally and socially to these movements, naturally adapted the characters and plots of juvenile delinquency for their own storylines. While present, this motif never became dominant, perhaps because it afforded young people all too much power over their own lives. Betts's immigrant boy had reached the point of being irredeemable. McKelway's bike-riding miscreants enjoyed their work. Such children could not be reformulated, nor could they stir the heart. As writers constantly employed the device of asking readers to imagine the children as their own, a cocaine-dealing, crap-shooting, street tough was not what they had in mind.[40]

Children did not belong in the streets. This modern convention had been asserted by reform writers before the Civil War. Just as unquestionably, factory labor was off limits, but that certainty left open the question of whether young people should "work" at all and, if so, how they should

---

[39] Betts, "Child Labor in Factories," 4.
[40] For excellent summaries of the broader context of these fears, see Willrich, *City of Courts*, 212–217; and Hugh H. Cunningham, *Children and Childhood in Western Society Since 1500*, 2nd ed. (Harlow, 2005), 146–152. See also Hawes, *Children in Urban Society*; and Cat Nilan, "Hapless Innocence and Precocious Perversity in the Courtroom Melodrama: Representations of the Child Criminal in a Paris Legal Journal, 1830–1848," *Journal of Family History*, 22 (1997): 251–285.

do it. Old fears about sloth died slowly, and some writers fretted about what a generation of children raised in idleness would become. The specter of idleness raised another possible impediment to the "little sufferer" becoming common currency.

One of the clearest and most forceful statements of this challenge appeared in 1884, coming from the pen of Edward Everett Hale, by that time a respected writer best known for the patriotic short story, "The Man Without a Country." A living link to the antebellum era and indeed the Revolution, Hale reminisced about school and work in the pages of the *North American Review*, the leading journal of respectability at the time. "Fifty years ago it was understood that a boy or girl had many things to learn besides reading, writing, and arithmetic," Hale recalled. "A boy must know how to use his hands and his feet. ... He must know how to milk, how to plow, how to cradle oats, how to harness a horse, how to take off a wheel, and how to grease an axle." Hale sensed that this bygone agrarian era could be no more, but he wanted a practical system of half-time schools, with short terms that would allow boys and girls time to learn the ways of the world's work. No advocate of factory labor, Hale nonetheless worried about young lives cordoned off full-time in the schoolhouse. "Taking boys and girls out from the working-force of the world ... gives them to understand that they are the only creatures of God that have nothing to do with the world in which they live," Hale pointed out. Not doing for themselves, children never learned to do for others. Such a child "is almost annoyed if it is suggested that he is part of the working force." Invoking producer values that would have been familiar to Southern working people, Hale reminded gentle readers that the common weal required common work.[41]

Unusual by the time it appeared, Hale's view had faded to obscurity by the early twentieth century. Still, some reform journals continued to sound the alarm that the prohibition of child labor and the concomitant enforcement of compulsory schooling threatened to enervate future workers. A half-comic, half-serious piece in *Harper's Bazaar* chronicled the tribulations of middle-class mothers confronted with bored offspring who had nothing but time. In a middle-class household, such a predicament was not Junior's fault, of course. "It is the natural right of childhood to be doing something," the editors advised. "Failing everything else, he

[41] E.E. Hale, "Half-Time in Schools," *North American Review*, November 1884, 445, 448–449; Charles Royster, *The Destructive War: William Tecumseh Sherman, Stonewall Jackson, and the Americans* (New York, 1991), 148–149.

will do mischief." To avoid such a calamity, good mothers must serve up "healthy, helpful child labor" of just the right sort. Filthy lucre must not enter the picture, "otherwise joy in his work is soon lost in greed for money returns." In a more serious vein, *The Independent*, a reform journal that slowly shifted position against expanding child labor reform, argued in 1912 that "every child should be trained to take his place in the working world." Having read the work of kindergarten pioneer Friedrich Froebel, the magazine averred that "work and play are substantially one, and that a child old enough to play is old enough to work." Sounding much like Hale, the editors saw the need to "train the hands to helpfulness; that is, to express a desire to share the burdens of others." This directive extended to schools, which should be organized around "work, not play; both brain work and hand work."[42]

Such a sentiment would have aggravated Charlotte Perkins Gilman. Writing on "Child Labor in Schools" more than twenty years after Hale, Gilman reached much the same conclusion: that young people spent too much time at their studies. But her reasoning for this assessment indicates how much the language about school and work had changed in two decades. Time spent stooped over a desk produced the same debilitation as hours bent over a machine. "The result of this forced labor of the mind is precisely analogous to that of the body," Gilman maintained. "First, there is the direct personal suffering involved, the loss of pleasure, the pain of exhaustion, the danger of injury, weakened eyesight, overtaxed brain, the narrow chest and stooping shoulders, the deprivation of physical exercise as should have been allowed." Mental fatigue followed. Children forced to read books in school spurned reading for pleasure and enlightenment at home. Weak minds left the public open to the wiles of sensational journalists, religious revivalists, or any other "self-interested pleader for a specific cause." Like child labor in factories, child labor in schools undermined the Republic. The antidote lay in a Rousseauian "free exercise of natural faculties, the pursuit of knowledge for the love of it, the reverence for truth, the delight in feats of mental skill, and in all the daily wonders of an unfolding world of fact and law." Such could not be found in the quarters of Mr. Gradgrind. Instead, young people needed "plenty of wholesome, slowly eaten, well-digested food; plenty of merry outdoor exercise; plenty of calm, care-free sleep." For Gilman, unlike Hale, young people needed to be free from work, not free to work.[43]

[42] "Nothing to Do," *Harper's Bazaar*, June 1906, 572; "Child Labor Reform," *The Independent*, April 11, 1912, 803–804.
[43] Gilman, "Child Labor in Schools," *The Independent*, May 21, 1908, 1135–1140.

Few child labor reformers would have agreed that less desk time was needed. Child labor reform had been the counterpart of the drive for compulsory schooling since its inception, and schoolboys and school-girls remained central to reformers' narratives of childhood during the Progressive era. As with work itself, what seemed like an easy argument kept getting complicated by the actions of working people, and working children in particular. Clare DeGraffenried bemoaned the sorry state of education in Southern mill villages. "Schools were opened," she pointed out. "Not a single child could be enticed therein." Yankee principals had little better luck. John Crowell passed along the woes of a Connecticut administrator who "had to fight children and parents alike to keep pupils of the working classes in school after they had once acquired an elementary knowledge of the three R's." For some, the predilection to leave school was just a natural part of boyhood. Boys went to factories because "they love tools and mechanical appliances."[44]

While the factory might prove attractive to the mechanically inclined schoolboy, the schoolyard offered few pleasures. When Helen Todd conducted an informal survey of working children in Illinois, over 90 percent told her they would prefer work to school. If the answers Todd cited can be believed, they are quite revealing. Some of her respondents stressed the violence of city schools, others talked about racism, and a few just could not see the use. One Tillie Isakowsky summed it up: "School is de fiercest t'ing youse kin come up against. Factories ain't no cinch, but schools is worst." If Todd had ended her narrative there, young Tillie would have carried the day, but the story resolved with young Maria, who loved her teacher and threw her a farewell party when she had to leave the school.[45]

Assuredly, young people's time should be spent at school. More importantly, children should play. No image contrasted more with the notion of "little prisoners" in the mills than the rosy-cheeked child merrily at play. Work in factories stole these precious moments. Mill children lacked the "natural impulse to play," John Crowell reported. "They have lost that spontaneous buoyancy which belongs to the life of every child." Delcomyn detected "an artificial disdain of play" in mining and milling districts, so much so that young people displayed "an ostentatious impatience" with the idea. For McLean, the "play instinct" had not been

---

[44] DeGraffenried, "Georgia Cracker," 485; Crowell, "Employment of Children," 44; McGhee, "National Child Labor Convention," 1668; Holland, "Life in a Southern Mill Town," 8–9.
[45] Todd, "Why Children Work," 74, 78.

extinguished; it had just been channeled into factory work. "The work of a child, say between fourteen and sixteen, may often embody in it much undeveloped play-instinct," she noted.[46]

As play became the heart of childhood, its antithesis – work – took an increasingly adult cast. In part, reform writing only had to demonstrate that children did work, a task reformers took up with alacrity. Armed with satchels of statistics being pumped out by state labor bureaus, the U.S. Bureau of Labor Statistics, and eventually the Children's Bureau, reformers delineated labor market participation by young people in elaborate reports fashioned in the language of the emerging disciplines of social science. As their critics sometimes noted, statistical snapshots frequently conflated all young people who worked with the very young, but that was part of the power of the language. By the early years of the twentieth century, reform writers had established "two million" as a conventional number of "little conscripts" who toiled across the country. Senator Beveridge had helped shore up this notion by pointing to "two million child breadwinners" during his crusade for federal child labor regulation, but reform magazines such as *Cosmopolitan* upped the ante considerably. Replete with a disheveled ragamuffin drawn to gaze longingly at middle-class readers in their easy chairs, the magazine admonished its holiday readers in 1906: "When Your Children Romp Around the Christmas Tree, Think of Two Million Little Wage Slaves." Happy holidays aside, the two-million image became so prevalent that Owen R. Lovejoy, assistant secretary of the NCLC, had to remind his cohorts that those who threw around such numbers willy-nilly were "a menace to reform."[47]

The power of reform discourse to construct "little sufferers" did not arise solely, or even primarily, from statistical tabulations. Certainly,

---

[46] Crowell, "Employment of Children," 46; Delcomyn, "Why Children Work," 326.

[47] The publications of the American Economic Association provide a good example of statistical arguments about child labor. For examples, see Samuel McCune Lindsay, "Child Labor in the United States," *American Economic Association Publications*, Feb. 1907, 258; "The Employment of Women and Minors [in New York]," *American Economic Association Publications*, Nov. 1905, 144–167; "Child Labor [in Connecticut]," *American Economic Association Publications*, August 1907, 1–73; "Child Labor Must Be Swept Away," *Cosmopolitan*, Dec. 1, 1906, 233; Owen R. Lovejoy, "Child Labor and Family Disintegration," *The Independent*, Sept. 27, 1906, 748; "The Effects of Child Labor on National Life," *Outlook*, Feb. 2, 1907, 235. For other examples of causal references to the "two million" figure, see Edwin Markham, "The Smoke of Sacrifice," *Cosmopolitan*, Feb. 1907, 392; McKelway, "Child in the Midst," 835. For another contemporary criticism about statistics, see E.E. Pratt, "Child Labor: A Rational Statement," *The Arena*, June 1907, 613–619. On Children's Bureau studies, see Kriste Lindenmeyer, *"A Right to Childhood": The Children's Bureau and Child Welfare, 1912–1946* (Urbana, 1997), 113–115.

numbers mattered, but reform writers took as their main goal the task of "putting a face" on child labor. Fortunately for them, they did not have to work from whole cloth. European, and especially British, reform writing supplied a ready reserve of literary images on which authors could rely. One particular piece of writing stood out: Elizabeth Barrett Browning's poem, "The Cry of the Children." Appearing originally in 1843 as part of the drive that produced the Factory Acts in Britain, the poem's title and its sentimental stanzas would be repeated ceaselessly in child labor writing. A 1902 piece used Browning as something of a benchmark, playing with the title to chide the passive into action. "The Children Are Still Crying," *Zion's Herald* announced. Giving the British poet the power of a member of Parliament, the magazine reminded readers that "her thirteen stanzas did not fall upon listless or unresponsive people." Aroused by her call, Britain acted.

What had roused *John Bull*? Not rows and columns of numbers, but literary images of degradation. Melding Browning's verses with popular iconography created during the factory agitation, the magazine traced the outlines of the dominant image of child labor, attributing all to Browning. "Nearly sixty years ago her woman's heart was roused to indignation by the condition of the child-toilers," the editors recalled. "Chained to little wagons, they crawled on their hands and knees in foul, dank mines to haul their loads of coal to the foot of the shaft where the women workers waited to carry the coal in baskets up the dangerous ladders to the top." British factory children toiled as breadwinners amidst disease and dust, exposed to the whip and the "angry curses" of their bosses. Those "child victims" who survived this ordeal of "human cupidity and cruelty" grew up in "ignorance, vice, and deplorable degradation." Such passages worked because they drew upon a common language: dark, danger, disease, degradation, all images popularized by Browning's progressive verses. Reform writers would invoke these referents in countless books, pamphlets, and articles, whether they acknowledged "Mrs. Browning's" copyrights or not.[48]

---

[48] "The Children Are Still Crying," *Zion's Herald*, June 18, 1902, 773. For some other direct references to Browning, see W.W. Landrum, "Child Slavery in Georgia," *Christian Index*, Nov. 23, 1899, 3; John A. Offord, "Help the Toiling Children," *New York Observer and Chronicle*, Nov. 14, 1907, 625. At least one book on child poverty also took its title from Browning. See John Spargo, *The Bitter Cry of the Children*, (New York, 1906). The book was widely read and reviewed by reformers. For some reviews, see "The Cry of the Children," *Independent*, Feb. 22, 1906, 461; "The Bitter Cry of the Children," *Arena*, Feb. 1907, 205–211; "The Bitter Cry of the Children," *Congregationalist and Christian World*, April 28, 1906, 618.

In the character of the "little toilers" and their environs, numerous traits stood out. The dangers of exposure to machines appeared, though less frequently than might be expected, given the epidemic of industrial accidents that young workers endured. The noise of industrial settings figured prominently, as did the dark, whether the dinginess of poor lighting or the dusky walks to or from work. More importantly, the continual reference to size and physical appearance inscribed child labor with an easily recalled mental picture: child laborers were little. In an era only a generation removed from abolitionism, invocation of the chains of bondage empowered these images. Factories felt like prisons; their inmates imitated slaves.

In an era coming to define human identity around the body, mutilation and deadly blows to bodily integrity could capture the popular imagination. Indeed, reform writers occasionally described the aftermath of industrial accidents as part of the horrors of child labor. John Offord relayed the story of Sarah, a thirteen-year-old Philadelphia woolen mill operative whose arm was broken in several places after she slipped on a greasy floor and thrust the limb into a loom. Irene Ashby-MacFadyen disclosed that a Southern doctor she knew had "personally amputated more than a hundred babies' fingers mangled in the mill." Connecting such injuries to play, *Scribner's* reported mishaps that occurred in a New York twining factory. "A moment's forgetfulness, but one moment of yielding to the universal childish impulse to play, and the mischief is done," the author pointed out.[49]

If danger presented a particular peril on the factory floor, the din was omnipresent. To middle-class observers, unaccustomed to the noise of industrial machinery, the decibel level overwhelmed all. Visiting a cotton mill in 1917, John Sherwood stood aghast at the clamor of the weaving floor: "Here was an uproar that shattered – crashing, crashing, in measured beat, a vast mechanical bin [*sic*]; a vibration that shook from floor to rafter, as a hundred looms jerked and racked, tearing their frames to and fro." Since the first railroads (and before), the clang of industrial power had daunted the non-industrial classes and prompted them to wax poetic. Positioning "the child" in the face of this horrible force both dwarfed his own person and heightened his predicament.

[49] Offord, "Help the Toiling Children," 625; MacFadyen, "Child Labor in the South," *Current Literature*, July 1902, 78; "Children Who Work," 613–614; Sappol, *Traffic of Dead Bodies*, 9–12 and *passim*. The obvious counterexample is the work of Crystal Eastman. See Crystal Eastman, *Work Accidents and the Law*, The Pittsburgh Survey, Vol. 6, ed. Paul Underwood Kellogg (New York, 1910), esp. 22, 64, 88–89, 93.

Elbert Hubbard condensed the terrors of the factory to a fury of sound that consumed its young victims. "The noise and the constant looking at the flying wheels reduce nervous sensation in a few months to a minimum," Hubbard revealed, displaying the assault on his own senses and sensibilities. Such an atmosphere turned children into unfeeling drones. Imprisoned in the factory, even dreams departed the little toiler: "No more does he long for the green fields, the running streams, the freedom of the woods, and the companionship of all the wild, free things that run, climb, fly, swim, or burrow." Instead, the child laborer became "an automaton" incorporated into the general din of "the roaring machinery." Thankfully, memory and vitality faded. "Nature puts a short limit on torture by sending insensibility," Hubbard sighed. "If you suffer, thank God! – it is a sure sign you are alive." Such depictions literally rendered young workers voiceless. Benumbed by the howling of their motorized taskmasters, they could not think, much less speak. Unlike the unsettling street tough, this child could be saved without any interference on his part.[50]

As the clamor of the mill drowned out the cries of the children, darkness hid their sad figures. The scene at a tobacco factory could stand in for many others. In this "subterranean apartment" boys worked as stemmers, preparing the leaves in rough form for further processing. They toiled in partial darkness, an observer recounted, for only "a little light comes in from somewhere, enough for us to distinguish the utter dreariness of the scene." Children worked in the dark, but more distressing, they went to work in the dark. A century into advanced capitalism, it is hard to imagine a movement against night work, but child labor reformers campaigned vigorously against it. The sight of youngsters plodding to work in the gloom combined the dangers of the street with the decline of domesticity. "In midwinter, these little workers see the break of day as they trudge along the route to the mill or look from the windows of the room in which they work," Ulm wrote of young textile operatives. After work, "they hobble to their homes, often along badly kept streets, through almost total darkness." MacFadyen described a mill in Columbia, South Carolina, where young workers worked through the night "without a moment for rest or food or a single cessation of the maddening racket of the machinery, in an atmosphere unsanitary and clouded with humidity and lint." Night work and the darkness that accompanied it located

[50] John Sherwood, "The Cotton Mill," *Forum*, March 1917, 339–340; Hubbard, "White Slavery," 163–164.

young workers outside the middle-class household, with its well-lit parlors and mandatory bedtimes.[51]

Exposure to noise and dark, reformer writers concluded, diminished young people in stature as well as character. While obvious, the most common modifier applied to young workers was "little." In addition to "little sufferers," they were "little tots," "little toilers," "little prisoners," "little conscripts," "little slaves," and oddest of all, "wizened little pigmies." Engaging in a bit of hyperbole, Max Harris Wilensky claimed that Southern textile machinery had to be adapted to fit the pint-sized operatives who ran it. "Why the very machinery of our Southern cotton mill is adapted to child labor," he averred. "The spinning frame is built for a child of 12 to 14, so that an adult would have to stoop at the task." For Offord, child labor itself miniaturized its participants, leaving them stunted, sunken, and hollow. For Lillian Betts, young workers became so small as to almost disappear. "Such tiny little things," she lamented, "with bodies that looked as if they might be crushed in one's hands."[52]

Literary technology thus froze young workers in time, fixing their visages in early childhood even as their bodies and working lives matured. The photographs, drawings, and cartoons that accompanied reform writing drove this point home with visual force. The illustrators for *Life* magazine became particularly adept at this kind of iconography. In a 1913 *Life* cartoon, a wealthy businessman and an aristocrat dressed for the *ancien regime* dominate the view as they stand on the necks of suffering child laborers. In a small pen-and-ink illustration in the magazine a few months later, a babe in the one-piece shift of infanthood receives a pay packet from a disembodied paymaster's arm perched above the toddler. In a similar illustration, a fat cat businessman seated on a bag of money flogs two small boys with a whip in the shape of the dollar sign.[53]

Of all the visual representations of child labor, none had more impact, then or since, than those of Lewis Hine. The famous photographer first worked for *Survey* magazine, where his pictures lent visual power to child labor. Hired as the official photographer for the National Child Labor

---

[51] "Children Who Work," *Scribner's*, 612; Ulm, "Plea," 895; MacFadyen, "Child Labor in the South," 78. See also, "The New South's Rare Opportunity," *Gunton's Magazine*, 54; Holland, "Life in a Southern Mill Town," 11–12.

[52] Offord, "Help the Toiling Children," 626; Wilensky, "The Child Labor Situation," 320; Betts, "Child Labor in Factories," 639.

[53] Rodney Thompson cartoon, *Life*, April 10, 1913, 726; Illustration accompanying, "That Problematical Seventy-Five," *Life*, August 21, 1913, 319; Illustration accompanying, "Whereas and Therefore," *Life*, January 15, 1914, 101.

Committee in 1908, his images graced the pages of scores of NCLC pamphlets and countless magazine articles. Hine's work covered many types of industry and took many forms, but two types of images stand out. In one, a single young worker or a posed group stared accusingly at the reader. The other captured workers in action, often in shots composed to amplify the disparities in size. In one NCLC pamphlet, a young Tennessee operative in gingham, arms crossed, scowls at the reader on page one. On the next page appeared a classic Hine image. A young girl stands on a box to reach the work on a spinning frame, accompanied by the superfluous explanation: "Too small to reach her machine." Later in the tract, coupling boys strain against the weight of mine cars, while others pause from their work as "greasers." Foregrounded in the shot, heavy timbers accentuate the diminutive stature of these Tennessee miners. Perhaps the most classic Hine shot of all filled the cover of the NCLC's *Child Labor in Georgia*. In it, a Georgia doffer boy climbs onto a spinning frame to remove a spindle, while another lad stares at the view from behind him. "Some so small they could reach their work only by climbing up," reads the caption. While posed portraits conveyed numbers and general dishevelment, these "action" shots carried the narrative of little toilers who struggled with their duties.[54]

The unremitting representation of young workers as "little" incapacitated them while it simultaneously obscured the potentially rambunctious and uncontrollable rascals that other corners of the discourse produced. What the word modified mattered even more. Young workers were not simply small in stature, they were imprisoned and enslaved. John Sherwood, in a bit of self-referential irony, confirmed that to him textile mills resembled prisons not only because their regular rows of windows reminded one of Sing-Sing, but also because "the word 'prison-like' had been woven into my ideas by many social writings." Part of that weaving had been done by writers such as Hubbard, who in a singular bit of exaggeration, claimed that in the cotton mills "death sets the little prisoners free inside of four years." A cartoon in *Cosmopolitan* pictured a young girl chained to a spinning frame, looking longingly at her books and dolls abandoned in the bright, bird-filled skies outside. Likening the factory gates to prison walls further pacified the objects

---

[54] McKelway, *Child Labor in Tennessee*, 3; McKelway, *Child Labor in Georgia*, 1; Lindenmeyer, *"Right to Childhood,"* 113. Of course, photographic power also came from Jacob A. Riis's classic books *Children of the Poor* (1892), *Children of the Tenements* (1902), and *How the Other Half Lives* (1903).

of reform. Prisoners could be legitimately granted freedom only by agencies outside themselves.[55]

Prisons might confine the liberty of child laborers, but they represented a modern image, one that reformers in other venues proffered as the solution to, not the cause of, social ills. More common in the discourse was the equation of child labor with slavery. At times, these accounts resonated with racist fears, as authors bemoaned the onset of "white slavery" in the form of child labor. Frequently, however, the slavery trope shed its racialized overtones, reaching back instead to bound labor that predated the "peculiar institution." "Why ... should a labor baron be allowed to take scores of children, shut them in for long hours, dwarf them in body and stunt them in mind?" asked Edwin Markham. Certainly young people should work. "But the bondage and drudgery of these mill-children and factory-children are not work, but servitude that amounts almost to slavery." McKelway, as a central voice in the NCLC, made the argument in the abstract. "The slave is one who labors for another, with no choice as to whether he shall toil or not, with no rights to insist upon the conditions of employment ... and with no right to the rewards of his labor," McKelway declared. Men could fight for labor rights, "but the child can only submit. And so the child labor system of our modern industrial world has not been inaptly termed, 'child slavery'." As with the image of the little prisoner, child slavery incapacitated its victims, leaving them as wards of reformers and the state.[56]

In the dominant language of child labor, the ability of young persons to affect their own labor situations waned along with their physical powers. The troublesome child who chewed tobacco on the factory floor, fraternized saloons after hours, and flirted prematurely still loitered on the margins, but the "little sufferer" occupied the limelight. No doubt, reform writers described real conditions, at least as real as they could be to people who rarely set foot inside productive work spaces. The conditions of industrial life in the so-called Progressive era were horrible – for everybody. In those factories, however, a range of young people labored at a spectrum of tasks along a continuum of conditions. The power of the "little toiler" lay in the ability to reduce that variety to a single iconic figure so squarely at odds with prevailing middle-class expectations about growing up. Once

---

[55] Sherwood, "Cotton Mill," 339; Hubbard, "White Slavery," 162; Cartoon accompanying Ward Sanford, "Twentieth-Century Herods," *Cosmopolitan*, July 1902, 350.

[56] Markham, "Smoke of Sacrifice," 44; McKelway, "Child in the Midst," 835. See also Landrum, "Child Slavery in Georgia," 3; Ellis, "Child Operatives," 2639; Ellis, "Movement," 1; Hubbard, "White Slavery," 161; Wilensky, "Child Labor Situation," 320.

in place, this image of child labor split the child from his or her derelict parents. "Caring parents" would do all they could to avoid the calamities of the mine or mill. As Francis McLean put it in 1906, if children worked, it simply meant that "the parent or parents or other members of the family were not doing all they should and could do." More than a century later, McLean's view remains the conventional wisdom. In the early twentieth century, that was only starting to be the case. As knowledge of child labor grew, reform writers sought to inscribe young people with incapacity and vest them with the rights to maintain it.[57]

DIVINE RIGHTS

The portrait of child labor that reform writing articulated featured a small child helpless in the face of parental and industrial power. Such a feeble creature needed the assistance of valiant reformers, who knowingly took up its cause. If the images were not enough, narrators of child labor repeatedly made the point directly. Visiting canneries, Delcomyn observed "passive and uncomplaining children" who worked from early to late. These silent toilers could do nothing to voice their wrongs, much less to help right them. "They have no voice to speak their protest, even if they had the wisdom to see their wrongs," Edwin Markham cried. Markham and others like him constructed the mute child laborer, safely reticent in the face of industrial injustice. Never mind that such speechless toilers sometimes organized their own unions and fought for labor rights. They could be most energetically assisted if they were seen and not heard. "My plea is in defense of the innocent," Hubbard avowed. "I voice the cry of the child whose sob is drowned in the thunder of the whirring wheels."[58]

---

[57] "Child Labor in the United States – Discussion," *American Economic Association Proceedings*, Feb. 1906, 263. For historical treatments of "children's rights," see Hawes, *Children's Rights Movement*; and Lindenmeyer, *"A Right to Childhood."* Hawes suggests that children's rights advocates can be divided into "protectionists" and "liberationists" (x–xi). I would suggest most Progressive era writers would have taken issue with this characterization, believing instead that they were liberating children by protecting them. Hawes also argues that "the question of rights for children is a difficult one" because "children are less than fully autonomous." For the very young, this point is undoubtedly correct, but for all other young people, levels of autonomy depend on historically contingent, legal, and cultural outcomes. See Holly Brewer, *By Birth or Consent: Children, Law, and the Anglo-American Revolution in Authority* (Chapel Hill, 2005), and Ch. 4 below.

[58] Delcomyn, "Why Children Work," 325; Markham, "The Smoke of Sacrifice," 393; Hubbard, "White Slavery," 178. On the relatively unexplored topic of child unions and child involvement in unions, see Nichols, "Children of the Coal Shadow," 441; and John Mitchell, "The Mine Workers' Life and Aims," *Cosmopolitan*, Oct. 1901, 630;

Helplessness arose, reformers contended, because children lacked rights. "Children represent a helpless class, for they have no political influence," Offord emphasized. Adding in a bit of patriotic imagery, McKelway turned this helplessness into a "Declaration of Dependence" for child workers. "We declare ourselves helpless and dependent," he had the unnamed revolutionaries say. "We are and of right ought to be dependent; and ... we hereby present the appeal of our helplessness that we may be protected in the enjoyment of the rights of childhood." Unlike other groups excluded from rights-bearing citizenship, however, young people's deprivation appeared to be inevitable and natural. For Felix Adler, "child nature" contained "sacred possibilities ... which must not be infringed, human rights which must be respected." Those "sacred possibilities" represented the future and the past of humanity. Adler and others wrote as G. Stanley Hall worked out his theory of "recapitulation," which suggested that the entire evolutionary history of humans could be seen in the stages of child development. Hall's anti-modernist longings saturated his psychological theorizing, and reformers' understandings of children's rights aligned with these impulses. The innocent child represented the innocent human, as yet untouched by the travails of modernity. That "something" must remain unsullied. As W.W. Landrum, a Georgia clergyman saw it, the rights of childhood were intangible yet self-evident: "the right to be young and happy and to laugh and enjoy freedom from care." Then as now, the notion of children's rights expressed both a commitment to protect young people from powers not yet attained and a yearning for paradises impossible to regain.[59]

These modern-day Mrs. Brownings deployed the available figures of speech of the modern-day movement, but others told these parables in an older verse. Biblical imagery sanctified the child's helplessness and cast aspersions on the sinners. "Jesus called the little child and set him in the midst of them," the Reverend McKelway intoned. "The stronger will of man prevailed. So to-day the child is helpless." Ward Sanford invoked religious imagery as well, but of another sort. Southern industrialists

C.K. McFarland, "Crusade for Child Laborers: 'Mother' Jones and the March of the Mill Children," *Pennsylvania History* 38 (1971): 283–296; Hall et al., *Like a Family*, 104, 328.

[59] Offord, "Help the Toiling Children," 625; McKelway quoted in Hindman, *Child Labor*, 44; Adler quoted in "Evils of Child Labor," *New York Observer and Chronicle*, March 2, 1905, 280; Landrum, "Child Slavery in Georgia," 3. On Hall, recapitulation theory, and "child primitivism," see Bederman, *Manliness and Civilization*, 92–110. On anti-modernism, see Lears, *No Place of Grace*.

were "twentieth-century Herods" who were "turning the blood of these innocents into money." Innocence and incapacity combined to render the child passive in the face of daily life.[60]

Religious imagery imbued the cause with sacred overtones, and it melded closely with reformers' understanding of rights. Hence, reformers frequently located the font of children's rights not in the social contract, but in a higher place. "Do you think God intended childhood as a season of toil?" asked *Scribner's* in 1871. By the Progressive era, the answer was manifest. It was the "God-given right of every child to its period of normal physical, mental and moral development," Max Wilensky believed. Undoubtedly, assertions of rights in U.S. history have almost always carried religious justification somewhere along the way, and just as certainly, children's rights borrowed the language of possessive individualism crucial to modern, liberal capitalism. Nevertheless, the rights of childhood that arose with the movement against child labor represented something different than those concerning education or the right to be heard in custody battles. They spoke to the core of the human experience. They answered central questions about one's place in the social order. It should not be surprising, then, that a movement often led by religious men and women should cast those rights as divinely inspired.[61]

The clearest statement of the divine rights of children came from the pen of Alabama clergyman and NCLC founder Edgar Gardner Murphy. Until his early death in 1913, Murphy worked ceaselessly in his Alabama homeland, throughout the South, and around the nation in the cause of child labor abolitionism. Not unaware of the economic dislocations that underlay the burgeoning employment of young people, Murphy nonetheless insisted idleness was not the chief concern for Southern youngsters. Instead, he sketched a childhood of the hills and woods; of romps, rambles, and reveries; of careless freedom. "Hasn't a child of seven years got a right to be careless?" he asked. "What would the world be if all its little children were all careful, were all sold [*sic*] philosophers of possibilities, knew all the dangers of life and all emergencies?" This carelessness was no cause for concern, nothing to be squelched by virtuous labor in the mills. In fact, it formed the very core of the child. "What are the awful and portentous perils of depravity from which the mills would save children of tender years?" he inquired. "Perhaps a little mischief, a little sassy backtalk on the part of the girls, a little scuffling on the part of the boys,

---

[60] McKelway, "Child in the Midst," 835; Sanford, "Twentieth-Century Herods," 351.
[61] "Children Who Work," *Scribner's*, 610; Wilensky, "Child Labor Situation," 319.

a little wild-hearted, old-fashioned, human 'fun' (God bless their hearts), and perhaps a little of that incorrigible bumptiousness which is doubtless found as familiarly in the abode of the rich as in the abode of the poor." To this carefree existence, children had a "right."[62]

The right of young people to untroubled liberty was not passing fancy for Murphy. "We must remember," he told the people of Alabama in 1902, "that amongst the most distinctive rights of the little child is the divine right to do nothing." This sacred liberty outweighed any parental rights, especially "the right of the parent to shift the burdens of the bread-winner to the shoulders of his defenseless children." These lazy fathers inverted the normal happy home and "reverse[d] the function of the child, which is not productive, but receptive." Sensing the dangers of providing divine sanction for idleness, Murphy clearly delineated the rights of man and the rights of his progeny. "The man has a right to work, and the child has a right to be worked for," he clarified.[63]

Like McKelway's "Declaration of Dependence," Murphy's assertion of children's rights depended on the images of helplessness that child labor reformers had fashioned. Drowned out by the noise of the factory, benumbed by unremitting toil, taxed by lazy fathers, child workers could do nothing to help themselves, but that was as it should be. For reformers, children possessed an anti-right: the right to be dependent. Rights talk for child laborers, then, drew upon longstanding conceptions of inborn and inalienable liberties, but at the same time inverted them. Instead of the right, and even the duty, to enter the labor market, young people had a right to avoid it. Older people had the duty to ensure the young enjoyed that right.

The right to be "dependent" or "receptive" blended well with emergent notions of a feminized state that protected the vulnerable, responding to their needs and welfare. In some ways, this conception evoked much older conceptions about the legal disabilities of youth, but those ideas anchored

---

[62] Edgar Gardner Murphy, "Child Labor in the United States," Address delivered before the Society for Ethical Culture, March 20, 1904, Edgar Gardner Murphy Papers, Southern Historical Collection, University of North Carolina Library, n.p.; Edgar Gardner Murphy, *The Case Against Child Labor*, Alabama Child Labor Committee pamphlet, 1902, Rare Books Room, Wilson Library, University of North Carolina-Chapel Hill, 16–17.

[63] Murphy, *Case Against Child Labor*, 6; Murphy, "Child Labor in the United States." Hindman, *Child Labor*, 45, accepts McKelway and Murphy's vision. "By virtue of their very helplessness and dependence," he writes, "the children themselves were incapable of resorting to effective self-help, either individually or collectively." Conceding that these words would not have appeared in an earlier era, Hindman nonetheless concludes "Someone had to speak for the children." Ibid., 45.

young people in the domestic sphere's regime of family governance. The rights that reformers asserted for the young replaced older conceptions of a single domestic unit, with a conglomeration of rights-bearing individuals often fundamentally at odds with each other. That same dynamic had laid the basis for women's rights across the course of the nineteenth century, but in the case of women – adult women – rights implied increasing legal personhood. For young people (including young women), the "rights" of childhood affirmed an absence of legal status and invoked the power of the state to maintain it.[64]

Few of the working people we have met so far would have had kind words for the Reverends Murphy or McKelway when they stated their case. How often young workers and their families read or heard about child labor reform can only be guessed. Certainly, Southern newspapers carried regular stories and editorials on the question by the turn of the twentieth century, but no sources remain to give us an exact idea of whether working people read these pleas, or how they reacted to them if they did. Nonetheless, they could not ignore the vision of childhood and work that these literary messengers proffered. The divine right to do nothing directly challenged the producer values that organized the economic and social lives of working people. Certainly, some young workers and their families responded favorably to this change in folkways, particularly when schooling offered an economic advantage. As reformers frequently remarked, however, just as many resisted. It would take more than clever prose to move them. The truant officer supplied part of the persuasion, but another force for change came from the shop floor itself. As young workers and their families carried the ways of the countryside into town, the machines fought back.[65]

---

[64] Welke, *Recasting American Liberty*, 104–105, 112–116; Theda Skocpol, *Protecting Soldiers and Mothers: The Political Origins of Social Policy in the United States* (Cambridge, 1992), 43.

[65] A sense of how widespread newspaper coverage had become by the early twentieth century can be gained from Murphy, *Child Labor in the Southern Press* (Montgomery, 1902), Rare Books Room, Wilson Library, University of North Carolina-Chapel Hill.

3

Mashed to Pieces

My condition keeps me all tore up in mind and distressed, and I can not do a man's work any more. (Bruce Holt, 1918)

H.E. Kinder knew something was amiss when the coal tram he was riding failed to slow down where it normally did to let him hop off. By February 1910, the sixteen-year-old mine worker had been laboring in West Virginia's coal districts since before the age of fourteen, evading mine safety laws by moving around between mines when company officials learned his age. Now he was legal, but in trouble nonetheless. As the motor trip of coal cars sped up, he assessed his chances. "My object was to save myself," he recalled. "I knew the cars would wreck down there." H.E. had a pretty good idea of the fate that awaited him if he was not off the cars by the time they crashed. At best, he might be thrown out; at worst, the cars would knock down the timbers, collapsing the slate, and certainly snuffing out his life. "I knew, just knew it was get out there or get hurt on below, and I made for safety as soon as possible." His only chance was to jump for it. Springing from the cars, he aimed for the bank outside the tracks, but when his feet hit the loose rock, the impact swung him around and thrust his leg under the runaway tram. "When it jerked me back on the road and the cars began running over my leg, every time a car hit my leg it dragged me and dragged me on down to probably seven or eight feet below there, and then it began, the cars ... every car dragged me a piece further, they all run over me." As the last car echoed down the passageway, H.E. feared the worst for his injured leg and, shining his lamp downward, he saw what he expected. "It was just tore all to pieces, as I raised up, the

FIGURE 5. Braking a tram of coal cars required physical strength and considerable skill. Accidents in mines claimed the lives and limbs of many young workers. Lewis Hine, 1908. Library of Congress, Prints & Photographs Division, National Child Labor Committee Collection, LC-DIG-nclc-01075.

blood squashed out, and I heard some of the bones in my leg move and it made me deathly sick, and I hollered and laid back down."[1]

In the helter-skelter decades of American industrialization, the violent encounter between Kinder and Boomer Coal's tram cars quickly faded into statistics that numbered in the millions. For H.E., his family, and countless others like him, however, the aftermath of such calamities would prove as significant as the accidents themselves. Industrial violence wrenched the lives of working families, in the South and throughout the nation. Beyond the death, injuries, and subsequent suffering, the horrors of the shop floor tore at working people's vision of how young people would fit into industrial labor, presenting a challenge ultimately more significant than the rewards of middle-class childhood tendered by reformers. Violence and its effects evoked profound emotions, moving working people to seek ways of preventing it. Indeed, violent encounters with industrial machinery did not produce the shocked silence engendered by

[1] *Record in Kinder*, 42–48. On young workers and coal mining accidents, see Robert McIntosh, *Boys in the Pits: Child Labour in the Coal Mines* (Montreal, 2000), 153–156.

other sorts of modern cruelty. Instead, they led to extended conversations: at the dinner table, on the job site, during a trip to town, and, eventually, in court.

Above all, the search for meaning on the bloody ground of modern industry came from a sense of betrayal. Time and again, young workers and their families sought bargains that would keep young people away from danger. Time and again, employers broke their promises. As death piled upon death and injury upon injury, accidents moved working people, younger and older, to confront their employers in the courts, a place where they would meet ideas about childhood and work foreign to their own.[2]

THE MOMENT OF IMPACT

For young workers, their families, their co-workers, and their neighbors, an industrial accident was not simply an episode to be dutifully compiled. An accident had stages. It began with an invasion of the body, an event that might result in death, permanent disability, temporary loss of function, or recovery and rehabilitation. There followed a period of grief or adjustment, for survivors and for family members in all cases. How long that period lasted depended on the initial incidents, which varied widely. Industrial accidents ranged from life-ending mine cave-ins to the much less dramatic loss of a finger to a spinning frame. Anyone who has ever worked in industry knows that being injured all the time goes with the job. Most injuries are small and heal on their own. Bruises, scrapes, first- and second-degree burns, small cuts, even breaks or cracks in minor bones – all are simply taken as part of normal life, treated and endured outside of medical help and means of redress. After these relatively minor mishaps, though, are more serious injuries, those that do intervene in daily life, or in the case of young people, slice across the developmental process. We can start to come to terms with the violence of young workers' lives by looking first across this variety of incidents.[3]

---

[2] Ironically, writing the history of violence is a dangerous undertaking. For a rumination, see Rachel Hope Cleves, "On Writing the History of Violence," *Journal of the Early Republic*, 24 (2004): 642–665. For the classic statement on pain in human experience, see Eileen Scarry, *The Body in Pain: The Making and Unmaking of the World* (New York, 1987). My account here and below adds to a growing body of scholarship on accidents, law, and modernity. It does so by bringing the actual violence to the forefront, by concentrating on the experiences of young workers and their families, and later on by expanding our understanding of how the legal language of accident law played out in local communities and courts.

[3] Gerald Markowitz and David Rosner, *Dying for Work: Workers' Safety and Health in Twentieth-Century America*, ed. David Rosner and Gerald Markowitz (Bloomington,

Probably the most common type of accident for young workers involved injuries to their hands. Spinning frames, lap winders, breakers, finishers, and the other machinery found in textile mills figured in many such mishaps. Lint and other trash frequently clogged the gears of these machines, and while common practice and common sense suggested cleaning them while stopped, young workers often believed they were being ordered to clean the gears while running. Working at Gaffney Manufacturing in South Carolina, Georgie Morrow tried to clean a spinning frame while it was running after he believed the boss had assured him the gears were stopped. The result was fingers that were "mashed and lacerated and so torn off" that it became necessary to amputate all of them. Anna Barnes lost her fingers when she was moved to a new spinning frame different from the one she had been running. Anna later died of tetanus, but her father remembered the injury well. "The middle finger was torn out on the right hand and the other finger was crushed and a bruise on the top of the hand and a piece of the cog wheel was in her hand," Columbus Barnes reported. Georgie and Anna's accidents involved young workers doing their jobs, but injuries could also happen to young workers not directly employed at dangerous machines. Such was the case with Harry Starnes, who lost his right hand in a Mt. Holly, North Carolina, cotton mill in 1907 after attempting to pick cotton off a mechanical carder.[4]

Injuries to extremities occurred at an equally alarming pace in other small shops and factories. Woodworking shops became a common site for injuries to extremities, especially because of the age-segregated workplace. A molder, with its knives rotating at 3,000 to 6,000 revolutions per minute, promised to shred anything that got in its way. In addition, such machines were usually equipped with vacuums that carried the waste material to furnaces that helped run the plant, and if slightly out of order, they showered their operators with wood shavings and dust. Employed in a West Virginia woodworking plant in 1897, Charles L. Giebell lost all the fingers of his left hand to a molder when he slipped while trying to remove a shaving from his eye. Accidents also occurred when machines jammed. A molder in Kentucky mangled Earnest Jordan's

---

1987) and Id. *"Slaves of the Depression": Workers Letters About Life on the Job* (Ithaca, 1987); John Fabian Witt, *The Accidental Republic: Crippled Workingmen, Destitute Widows, and the Remaking of American Law* (Cambridge, 2004), Ch. 1.

[4] *Record in Morrow*, 244–245; *Record in Barnes*, 2; *Record in Starnes*, 14–15. See also *Muscogee Mfg. v. Butts*, 21 Ga. App. 558 (1918). A carder pulls the cotton fibers between metal combs, straightening them for spinning.

foot when he tried to dislodge a jammed piece of wood but found that he "was not stout enough."[5]

Sixteen-year-old A.B. Ensley's injuries offer a close look at the power of a woodworking machine. The brief moment that comprised the accident began when A.B. attempted to remove a splinter from the machine. A suction pipe placed to carry wood shavings to the plant's boiler room jerked A.B.'s hand into the rotating knives. Reacting instinctively, A.B. jerked his hand back out and fell into the arms of a fellow worker. "My hand is all cut up, send for the doctor," he screamed. "Don't let me bleed to death, you ought to have told me about those knives." Later, the young worker methodically detailed his injuries. "The palm of my hand was all cut out. The leaders were cut in-two in my little finger and the bone was cut out. Part of the bone cut out of my thumb. My two middle fingers were cut off close and my forefinger slightly," A.B. relayed. The mishap left him in incredible pain and manually disabled. "I suffered great agony with my hand," he recalled. "My little finger is no use to me at all." Such mishaps reshaped their victims in the blink of an eye. Like many textile accidents, these injuries were not life-threatening so long as the bleeding was stopped quickly and infection or tetanus did not develop.[6]

Extremity injuries could show up in the most unexpected of places, such as steam laundries. Commercial laundries offered girls and young women jobs that mirrored their domestic duties, but they concealed a hidden danger: the mangle. Essentially a huge steam iron, a mangle operated at extremely high temperatures. Sixteen-year-old Virginia Adams supplied this description of the ironically named "Hazen Annihilator" mangle: "[It] had great big rollers on it, it was under the steam, I don't know how the rollers go, remove the blanket some how or other, real long, you can put a big sheet in it." Asked about the temperature of Annihilator, Virginia laconically answered: "Hot enough to take the meat off my hand." When her right hand got caught by the mangle, "all the back [was] burned off, all the bones burned and crushed." As with other accidents, injuries could occur outside the regular course of work. The heat rising from a mangle at a Louisville, Kentucky, laundry on a chilly March morning in 1918 tempted Margaret Michaels to place her hands too close: "I was standing there, my hands were cold, ... and I put my fingers up there to get them warm." Someone called Margaret's name, and

[5] *Record in Giebell*, 519; *Record in Ritter Lumber Company*, 16.
[6] *Record in Ensley*, 17.

FIGURE 6. These young women are seated at a mangle, the center of operations in a steam laundry. Mangles could press clothes efficiently, but they could also strip the flesh from a girl's hand. Lewis Hine, 1917. Library of Congress, Prints & Photographs Division, National Child Labor Committee Collection, LC-DIG-nclc-05620.

when she turned to look, she thrust her hand into the mangle. The other girls saw what happened and jumped to the rescue, pulling on her arm to keep it from being sucked further into the rollers. They saved her life, but the damage had been done. Laundry accidents were perhaps the most common mishap for girls, outside of textile mills. As with other extremity injuries, they were rarely fatal.[7]

If injuries to hands and feet killed their victims infrequently, they nonetheless produced extreme pain and permanent disfigurement. In a similar vein, eye wounds could mutilate their victims while leaving them otherwise physically unaltered. Eye injuries could and did occur in just about any setting. William Whitelaw lost his sight to a piece of flying metal while working as an apprentice machinist. A similar mishap befell Ebbirt Ward in a North Carolina textile mill. Metal was not the only

---

[7] *Casperson v. Michaels*, 142 Ky. 314 (1911), 316; *Record in Sanitary Laundry Co.*, 5–6; *Record in Casperson*, 316. See also *Record in Ballard*, 36617; *Capital Laundry Co. v. McRoy*, 190 Ky. 440 (1921); *Evans v. Josephine Mills*, 119 Ga. 448 (1904), GA, 26289.

flying substance young workers had to avoid. At soft drink companies, which often employed younger boys in their bottling and packing sections, bottles frequently exploded, spraying their handlers with glass. Ellis Crosby's accident at a Waycross, Georgia, bottling plant was typical. In April 1918, ten-year-old Ellis had just recovered from a three-week bout with malaria when he took a job at D.L. Keen's plant. His mother, Lucinda Crosby, a nurse, thought he was selling papers, but soon found out differently when a driver from the company delivered an injured Ellis to the Crosby home. She called the family doctor and rushed the boy to the hospital. She feared the injury was dire: "The ball of his eye was split open and it was bleeding. The little black jelly that was in his eye ran out on my white waist on the way to the hospital." Lucinda Crosby knew, as did the doctors, that Ellis's sight was gone. They tried to save his eyeball, but it became inflamed and had to be removed several months later. Thinking back on the accident, Ellis remained unsure about its cause, unless perhaps "the gas exploded it." To Ellis, the mishap seemed totally a matter of chance. "I was inspecting bottles and had one in my hand, and went to put it in the box, and one or two or three of the bottles busted and I had my face over it like this (indicating) and they exploded and cut me in the face."[8]

While damage to hands, feet, and eyes could lead to permanent disability, those that affected the head, torso, or larger extremities proved much more serious. A simple list conveys only part of the sickening horror of these accidents of greater magnitude. Otis Fletcher Willis, eleven, slipped into the pulleys on a textile drawing machine, a fall that resulted in his left arm being pulled off, his right arm being severely mangled, and his body and head being badly beaten. Arthur Burnett, fourteen, fell into a beater in a textile mill, tearing off his left arm, cracking his skull, and gouging out his left eye. McKinley Lyons, fifteen, fell under a hand car on a railroad; the car crushed his skull, badly lacerated his face, and destroyed one eye. John Finley, thirteen, caught his leg between an elevator and the flooring, leading to the limb being "crushed off." Willie Bartley, seventeen, got caught under falling slate in a mine, leaving cuts to the face and head, a fractured leg, and fractured vertebrae. All five of these young workers survived their accidents, as did many of their companions. With their

---

[8] *Whitelaw v. Memphis and Charleston R.R. Co.*, 84 Tenn. 391 (1886), 392; *Ward v. Odell Manufacturing*, 123 N.C. 248 (1899), reheard 126 N.C. 946 (1900), 947; *Record in Keen*, Brief of Evidence, 2–3. See also *Roberts v. United Fuel Gas Company*, 84 W. Va. 368 (1919), 370; *Herbert v. Parham*, 86 S.C. 352 (1910), 354.

bodies partially intact, yet suffering in the aftermath, they were forced to rebuild their lives with what they had left.[9]

A different and particularly gruesome type of accident involved burns, especially of the full-body sort. Minor burns could heal, and even major burns to small parts of the body could mend, but some burn victims faced a fate unique to their situation: slow, torturous death. Such was the case of Charlie Wilson, an eighteen-year-old worker at Chess and Wymond, a barrel-making facility in Louisville, Kentucky. When Charlie reported for work on a November morning, the plant had been shut down for the night. Open water tanks, where barrels were softened before final shaping, had cooled down, allowing the water that had slopped out the previous day to freeze on the surrounding walkways. Charlie began his day's work, moving kegs in and out of the now-boiling bath. Oliver Collins, a co-worker, ran a wood lathe next to where Charlie was working. He saw Charlie put a keg in the vat and shove it to the other side with his foot. As Charlie "leaned over to shove the keg, his foot kind of slipped out and he fell in the vat. He kind of caught his left hand and turned over on the right side, and he went in the water all but his head and on the left hand side." They wrapped Charlie in cloth and brought him home to his mother, Samantha Arnett. When she opened the wrappings, she found that Charlie was "burnt to his hip on this side and was burnt clean up to this arm and up in the edge of his hair." Scalded over half of his body, Charley's "hair would slip off his head," his mother recalled. "You could take your finger and rub over it and it [was] just like you would scald a chicken." In fact, Samantha Arnett may have understated Charlie's injuries. J.P. Sonne, a neighbor of the Arnett's, described part of Charlie's body as "entirely burnt – the flesh was all off." Yet Charlie lived eleven months in this condition, as his mother, stepfather, family, and neighbors helplessly watched his slow decline.[10]

While Charlie Wilson's death was protracted, many injuries brought swift ends to young lives. Industrial violence reached a crescendo in accidents that simply destroyed the body, crushing its parts, or tearing them asunder. Young textile workers such as twelve-year-old Tom McDaniel plunged to their deaths in elevator shafts. William Gray Haynie fell onto the belt of a large pump engine at a construction site on the French Broad

---

[9] *Willis v. Cherokee Falls Mfg. Co.*, 72 S.C. 126 (1905); *Record in Burnett*, 14; *Louisville, Henderson & St. Louis Railway Company v. Lyons*, 155 Ky. 396 (1913), 9; *Record in Finley*, 2; *Record in Bartley*, 9–10.

[10] *Record in Wilson*, 2–16.

River in North Carolina. The force of the belt slammed him into a nearby wall with such force that "his skull was cracked, his leg broken, and he was mashed to pieces and died in four hours." On a hot July afternoon in 1914 in an embankment cut between Spartanburg, South Carolina, and Asheville, North Carolina, fifteen-year-old Bub Raines watched for trains. Bub had been sent out to flag down approaching engines in front of a construction team for the Southern Railway. The boy grew drowsy and went to sleep on or beside the road. When they found him, his body had been scattered two hundred feet down the tracks.[11]

Bub's ghastly demise captures the casual way that death dropped in on Southern working families. Bub's older brother, Lewis, had been working a ways down the track from where Bub was killed. To Lewis, Bub's death was an immediate reality, not news brought by the sheriff or a concerned neighbor. The integration of work, family, and death colored the experience of industrial violence. This melding appears clearly in the case of Ben Hodges, who got himself a job as a water boy at Savannah Kaolin Company, a clay processing plant near Gordon in central Georgia. Ben's actual age at the time of his employment in 1917 was uncertain. He might have been thirteen, or fifteen, or eleven, but most people agreed he was still "in knee trousers." Before 1915, the Hodges family had lived in the countryside as farmers. Back then, Ben had been a "small boy," but he was "big enough to chop cotton," according to his mother, Minnie Hodges. Even after Ben's death, Minnie beamed that on the farm Ben "worked the whole day. He could pick a hundred pounds heap of days." A black family working in the cotton, the Hodges clan was perhaps eaten out of farm and home by the boll weevil, or maybe they sought a better life in the city. In either case, 1916 found them in Gordon, where Kelley Hodges, Ben's father, "was the first one that bored a hole to start up the Savannah Kaolin Company." One of six children in the Hodges household, Ben joined his father at the plant about a year after the move, probably at about age eleven.[12]

Ben Hodges toted water and cleaned troughs at Savannah Kaolin off and on for two years without event, but an off-the-cuff order during a breakdown took him to a new place in the plant, and to his death. John Moore saw Ben's fatal encounter with a conveyor belt. Moore had been carting wheelbarrow loads of clay and had stopped to rest. He heard the boss man and another "colored fellow" tell Ben to mount

---

[11] *Record in McDaniel*, 63, 27, 29; *Record in Haynie*, 504; *Record in Raines*, 18.
[12] *Record in Hodges*, 13–15.

a scaffolding and replace the conveyor belt. Ben started to put the belt back on the pulley, but it caught him. "The belt taken him and wound him up and whipped him over a time or two," Moore remembered. By the time the men stopped the pulley, Ben was "hanging by his left arm and shoulder with his heels down. As to the condition of his feet, both of them was whipped off, frazzled rags, sorter like a beef steak or a person had an old piece of knife or something beat up. He was bleeding and bloody."

The men removed Ben, who was still alive, and went to tell the Hodges family what had transpired. Minnie Hodges was at home when they arrived. "On that morning when he got killed there come a white man along and told me, he says, Minnie your little boy has got killed," Hodges recollected. She headed over to Savannah Kaolin, arriving around noon. There she found Ben laid out on some blankets. Met by the plant supervisor, she viewed her broken son. "Mr. Woodward met me, I was crying and he says, don't cry so loud," she remembered. "When I got there he was lying there all mangled up, his legs was all torn off, that was Ben I am talking about, my little boy." The accident still clung to the machinery that had caused it. "I also see'd the shirt and belt hanging up there where they hadn't been long taken him down," she recalled. "It was up there where they cut him down at, up there on the shaft, and there was blood and flesh and bones lying around." Ben was injured at 11:30 in the morning; he died at 3:30 that afternoon, November 11, 1919.[13]

A LONG RECOVERY

The impact of industrial violence on the lives of young workers and their families came not only from the mishaps themselves but also in the period that followed. In cases of death, families had to deal with the costs of funerals, the loss of income, and the emotional impact of the death of a child. After the immediate shock abated, they faced the future. Would family life change with a member now gone? How they answered that question led to another. Would they seek compensation, either directly from an employer or in the courts? These were not simply material questions. The ways in which parents, siblings, and family members grieved

[13] Ibid., 16–17, 11. On race and accidents, see Barbara Young Welke, *Recasting American Liberty: Gender, Race, Law, and the Railroad Revolution, 1865–1920* (New York, 2001), 50–52, 62–63.

their loss and how employers responded to their grief figured into how and why working people sought redress.[14]

The death of a young family member jarred all families emotionally, but for many it also created an immediate financial burden. An economic crisis was particularly acute when older boys provided the primary income for households headed by single parents, especially older women. Russell G. Allen was nineteen when he died in a West Virginia coal mine, but he had been the main breadwinner for his family for some time by then. His father had abandoned his mother, Sabina, who struggled to keep the household running in the aftermath. "My husband left me over three years ago, and I went ahead and kept my children and made a living for them," Allen proudly stated. Crying while telling her story, she recounted how her husband had been gone three, going on four, years. Nobody knew anything about his whereabouts, and the family figured he was dead. In the wake of this family catastrophe, she ruefully admitted, Russell became her "main dependence for a living; all the support I had." Russell's death came as a bitter blow for Sabina, for he had both raised crops and worked for the cash that paid taxes and provided clothing for the family, giving her amounts as large as $25 to $30.[15]

The death of a young worker such as Russell Allen unsettled the family accounts. Certainly, these economic losses supplied part of the impetus for the suits that followed. Still, lost wages do not tell the whole story. The financial distress caused by the death of a young wage earner could be severe, but the emotional loss was equally exhausting of family resources. Historians in recent decades have come to question the view that divides families into those that value their younger members economically versus those that stress their priceless emotional value. Southern working families did both, as one might expect of average human beings. While there is scant evidence of the middle-class romantic ideal or the nineteenth-century cult of dying, working families loved their children nonetheless, and they mourned deeply at their loss. Time and again, parents and siblings reported being "all out of sorts" since an accidental death. The law took little formal notice of their grief, but their sorrow motivated their response to industrial violence in greater measure than did their diminished pocketbooks.[16]

[14] On American ways of death in this era, see Drew Gilpin Faust, *This Republic of Suffering: Death and the American Civil War* (New York, 2008).

[15] *Record in Allen*, 21, 30. See also *Record in Davis*, n.p.; *Record in Raines*, 16; *Record in Girvin*, 7.

[16] The classic statement of the "economic" valuation of children versus an "emotional" one is Viviana A. Zelizer, *Pricing the Priceless Child: The Changing Social Value of Children*

The death of a child was no less devastating for working people than
for the middle class. When Augustus Williams lost his boy, Eugene, in a
West Virginia coal mine, he was shaken. Having directed the body to his
brother-in-law's place, he tried to collect himself. "I went right on to the
shanty, and I couldn't wash, and it seemed like I was all out of my head
some way or another," he remembered. Calling for some hot water, he
washed up and went over to the home where his boy lay. "I asked the
doctor, 'Can I go and see my boy once more?' He says, 'No, you can't see
him any more'." Augustus had a close relationship with Gene. They had
been wandering around West Virginia's coal communities and picking up
work at various mines for some time before Gene's accident. As Augustus
put it, "my boy was working with me ... me and him was batching."
Right before the accident, Gene had asked his dad for leave to go get
some bread for supper. Augustus Williams was not a man who saw his
son in dollar signs.[17]

As draining as death might be, injuries that ended in serious and permanent disability were worse. Recoveries could be short or long, relatively easy or excruciating, simply expensive or financially catastrophic.
How recovery proceeded depended very much on the nature of medical care, something that changed dramatically during the period. In fact,
the increasing availability of antisepsis and anesthesia meant that workers who might have previously died from their injuries survived, only
to undergo a lengthy and painful recuperation process. Long recoveries
had a myriad of effects on working families. As opposed to one-time
funeral costs, long-term serious injury sent families a mounting pile of
doctor bills. Disability also reoriented regular rhythms of households as
the sufferer became the focal point of daily routines. Work routines, sleep
patterns, mealtimes, leisure activities, and other regular activities bent
to the new reality of a household member in recovery. Bandages had to
be changed, meals had to be fed, and soiled linens had to be removed.
Beyond the minutiae of caring for the victim, parents had to deal with the
emotional distress of someone struck down "in the vigor of youth." As
young workers slowly realized what had happened to them, they struggled to find new identities for a body no longer intact. In doing so, they
found nothing in the culture from which to draw strength. They were not

(New York, 1985). For a brief critique of this view, see Hugh Cunningham, *Children and
Childhood in Western Society Since 1500, Second Edition* (Harlow, 2005), 103–106. On
Southerners mourning the deaths of their children, see Edward Ayers, *The Promise of the
New South: Life after Reconstruction* (New York, 1992), 185–186.
[17] *Record in Williams*, 8–11.

the heroes of wars, Civil or Great. They were not the elderly, diminished in capacity but wise in years. In the idiom of their era, they had become "helpless cripples." For young men, in particular, they had lost the first marker of their manhood: physical strength.[18]

As young workers recovered, their convalescence disturbed household routines, especially sleep patterns. After Harry Starnes hurt his hand in a Mt. Holly, North Carolina, cotton mill, his mother tended him at home. "He kept me up day and night for about two months," she reported. If Harry got better in a few months, some cases dragged on and on. Mrs. A.R. Speer, mother of Hester, dealt with her daughter's ongoing reaction to the accident, even after her physical ills had healed. "Her nights are very restless," Mrs. Speer testified. "I don't think I ever had a good night's sleep since she was hurt. Sometimes she raises up in bed and sings. Sometimes she hollows and sometimes she puts out her arms just as though she was going to jump out of bed, and then sometimes she calls for somebody to sit by her." As Hester's postaccident behavior indicates, sleep disruption was not just a result of physical pain. Trauma had left its mark. After rail cars crushed Joe Ellington's foot, he also had trouble sleeping. "The suffering has been dreadful ever since," Joe stated. "[I] have not been able to sleep for the pains and anguish of body and mind."[19]

The extent to which recovery disrupted the lives of working families depended, of course, on the nature and severity of the injury, but it also hinged on the state of medical care. The speedier transit and communication available in urban-industrial environments increased the chances of stabilizing trauma quickly and certainly prevented patients from bleeding to death. By the early twentieth century, follow-up surgeries became more common and allowed injuries to mend. The widespread

---

[18] Many standard accounts of men and work focus on middle-class men or on such notions as craft identity. See E. Anthony Rotundo, *American Manhood: Transformations in Masculinity from the Revolution to the Modern Era* (New York, 1993), Chs. 8–9; and Michael Kimmel, *Manhood in America: A Cultural History* (New York, 1996), Ch. 3. Labor historians have more recently addressed the question of "rough masculinity" among working people. On working-class masculinity, see especially Steven Maynard, "Rough Work and Rugged Men: The Social Construction of Masculinity in Working-Class History" *Labour* 23 (1989): 159–169; Paul Michael "What We Want Is Good, Sober Men: Masculinity, Respectability, and Temperance in the Railroad Brotherhoods, c. 1870–1910" *Journal of Social History*, 26 (2002): 319–338; Gregory L. Kaster, "Labour's True Man: Organised Workingmen and the Language of Manliness in the USA, 1827–1877," *Gender & History*, 13 (2001): 24–64; Stephen Norwood, *Strikebreaking and Intimidation: Mercenaries and Masculinity in Twentieth-Century America* (Chapel Hill, 2002).
[19] *Record in Starnes*, 15; *Record in Atlanta Cotton Factory Co.*, 14; *Record in Ellington*, 4.

use of ether and morphine rendered such operations considerably more bearable than they would have been a half a century earlier. Southern medicine had reached a particularly peculiar stage by the turn of the twentieth century. Private hospitals spread throughout the region, but compared with other parts of the country, public hospitals lagged. The South had never seen the broad growth of the almshouse system of poor relief that gave rise to public hospitals in the North. In between the public and private spheres, larger industrial concerns maintained on-site infirmaries or kept doctors on call, as much to prepare for the inevitable lawsuits as to provide care. Still, these forms of institutional care were available only for workers lucky enough to be located near them. For many Southerners, health care meant a local, family doctor supplemented home care. Caring for an injured child at home called for a reliance on folk wisdom and a good dose of whatever remedy might be obtained from the family doctor, the druggist in town, or the general store down the road.[20]

If stabilization of injuries represented one side of the coin, treatment afterwards stamped the other. Infection could easily turn a wound into a life-threatening crisis, or at least make for a difficult recovery. After Myrtice Ransom lost her fingers in a Georgia candy plant, her stumps had to be dressed on a daily basis, but that was not the worst of it. "The stumps were infected and a lot of pus got in them, because the cut was made with a dirty instrument," her doctor reported. Tetanus, now easily preventable, created a special worry for parents and young workers. After being injured in a Georgia cotton mill, Anna Elizabeth Barnes fought a losing battle with the disease in April 1881. Born in 1866, Anna was a little past her fourteenth birthday when her hand slipped into the gears of a spinning frame on March 31. At first she seemed to do well, slowly recovering from the tearing blows that had left blood "pouring" from her hand. Her mother permitted her to leave the house, and she even visited the factory. But on April 11, she began to decline. By that time, Anna and the rest of the Barnes household had contracted the measles, and Anna's tribulations were compounded by the onset of her menses, which left her in a "nervous" condition. By the 13th, the attending doctor was certain that Anna had come down with tetanus as well, and a second opinion

---

[20] Paul Starr, *The Social Transformation of American Medicine* (New York, 1982); Charles E. Rosenberg, *The Care of Strangers: The Rise of America's Hospital System* (New York, 1987); Anne C. Loveland, *Southern Evangelicals and the Social Order, 1800–1860* (Baton Rouge, 1980).

confirmed the diagnosis. Over the next two weeks, her condition worsened. She began "frothing at the mouth and chewing her tongue." By the time she died on April 26, convulsions had contorted her body beyond help. "She was completely drawn back," her mother later told the court. "At the time of her death, Dr. Pendleton told me she would never have been straight if she had lived. She would never be any pleasure to me if she had lived."[21]

While tetanus and infection lay outside the control of parents and doctors, advances in medical treatment presented a brutal choice to young workers and their parents: whether to amputate a mangled extremity. Andy Giebell faced this decision when his younger brother, Charley, hurt his hand in a West Virginia woodworking plant. Both brothers worked in the factory. As Andy fed wood into a molder, Charley appeared. "He came running around by me and said 'My God, I am ruined,' and I threw off the belt and took him home," Andy recounted. To Andy, the situation looked grim: "His fingers looked like they had been run through a cog wheel, all tore to pieces." With their father dead, Andy apparently headed the Giebell household and communicated with the doctor who came to tend Charley. He hoped to preserve as much of Charley's hand as possible. "One of the fingers they went to cut off and I told the doctor to save what he could of it, and he said he didn't think he could do anything for the finger. I told him to try to save all he could of it," Andy remembered. "I guess he save[d] … the big end of it, – a kind of a stub."[22]

The Giebell brothers' story could be repeated over and over. Amputation, uncommon before the middle of the nineteenth century, became ordinary thereafter. Postbellum America in particular abounded with amputees, first from the Civil War and then from industrial accidents. Young Southern workers shared in this universal fate, and it is important to notice that amputation's impact lay not solely in the diminished capacity that followed, but in the loss of bodily integrity itself. Some amputations were indeed life-altering experiences. Jackson M. Ewing, thirteen, lost his right leg a few inches above the knee after it was crushed between coal cars in a West Virginia mine. In Tennessee, a pile of iron fencing fell on eleven-year-old Luther Green, resulting in amputation of his leg. While these surgeries clearly altered the lives of their victims forever, other amputations were less invasive. Ellen Gibbs worked at Tifton

---

[21] *Record in Ransom*, 11; *Record in Augusta Factory*, 3, 8–11, 26, 33–34, 52–53.
[22] *Giebell v. Collins Co.*, 54 W. Va. 518 (1904), WVSA, 150–3, 18–19, 24, 46.

Cotton Mills in Tifton, Georgia, in 1904. Nine years old at the time, she attempted to grease the travelers on a spinning frame and in doing so, her right forefinger ended up in the cogs, necessitating its amputation "just above the first joint." Eight-year-old Jimmie Taylor endured an almost identical injury and ensuing amputation after an accident at Bibb Manufacturing in Georgia. In fact, these smaller amputations figured prominently in actions by young workers for redress. A survey of the Mecklenburg County, North Carolina, county court records from 1900 to 1920 suggests that finger amputations typified suits brought by young workers.[23]

Young workers and their families were well aware of the social results of an amputation. This fact brought them into conflict with doctors, and they occasionally resisted doctors' attempts to remove mangled appendages, preferring to keep the body whole. When a Dr. Weisiger found Robert Jones injured in a Virginia cotton mill in October 1880, he figured the boy's arm would have to be removed. "My opinion was that the boy's arm was useless, and ought to be amputated," the doctor testified. "But the mother of the boy insisted that she would not have it done; and it is fortunate for him, as he has it now to give comliness [*sic*] to his body." Such moments presented young workers and their parents with a decision that had considerable consequences for recovery. Elbie Showalter and his family chose not to amputate immediately, prolonging the boy's pain in the aftermath, and only delaying the inevitable. Elbie found that his injured finger was "always sore ever since it was first fixed until it finally got so it very nearly come off itself, and I had to have it taken off."[24]

The spread of amputation as a medical treatment altered how young workers and their families dealt with injuries. In essence, amputation *created* a recovery period that had not been there before, at least not so frequently. The same could be said for internal medicine. While many accidents still brought sudden or slow death, changes in medicine allowed more and more patients to live, even after traumatic injuries. Nonetheless,

---

[23] *Ewing v. Lanark Fuel Co.*, 65 W. Va. 726 (1909), 727; *Record in Ornamental Iron and Wire Co.*, 3; *Gibbs v. Tifton Cotton Mills*, 15 Ga. App. 213 (1914), 214; *Record in Bibb Manufacturing Co.*, 1–3. See Mecklenburg Civil Action Papers, Mecklenburg County Records, NCSA, Boxes 39–62, North Carolina State Archives. On amputation generally, see Seth Koven, "Remembering and Dismemberment: Crippled Children, Wounded Soldiers, and the Great War in Britain," *American Historical Review* 99 (1994): 1167–1202. On amputation and masculinity, see Erin O'Connor, "'Fractions of Men': Engendering Amputation in Victorian Culture," *Comparative Studies in Society and History*, 39 (1997): 742–777.

[24] *Record in Jones*, 64; *Record in United States Leather Co.*, 46.

modern medicine could only go so far, as the story of Bruce Holt reveals. His tale of partial recovery, with his mother by his side, illuminates how dramatically industrial violence could reshape the lives of working families, both during a hospital stay and afterward.[25]

After the grooving machine crushed his intestines, Bruce lay unconscious for four weeks at Wesley Long Hospital in Greensboro, North Carolina. When he came to, he discovered that he had undergone a "very serious operation" in his abdomen and that he was "suffering greatly." The suffering continued. "I suffered all the time I was there; couldn't sleep at night; in mind I was all torn up on account of my condition," he recalled. But Bruce's anguish was not just mental. It came from the treatment. "They put me in water in a bath tub, and I remained there for fifteen weeks altogether," Bruce testified. "For eight weeks I stayed there day and night and was never taken out." Doctors treated Bruce in this fashion to contain the irritation around a discharge hole left in Bruce's abdomen after the operation. All of Bruce's digestive fluids exited his body through this incision. "This caused great discomfort and pain; acid discharges from the stomach just took off the meat and made a sore across there; nearabout ran me crazy sometimes," he lamented. Indeed, during the early days of his recovery, Bruce was literally wasting away. His weight declined from 170 pounds at the time of the accident to a mere 70 pounds after weeks in the water bath. His pain was unrelenting. Edna Beasley, a nurse at Wesley Long, watched as Bruce struggled to recover. "At first [he] begged for opiates or morphine," she reported, "but later [he] would turn and twist and suffer rather than take it; [he] preferred to endure the pain than run the risk of becoming a morphine fiend." This continual suffering took its toll. "Mentally he was almost like a crazy man at first," Beasley relayed.[26]

Bruce's trials did not end when he left Wesley Long. A second operation at Central Carolina Hospital in Sanford eventually repaired his damaged intestines as well as contemporary medicine allowed, but until then, the discharges continued. They became the central fact in Bruce's life. "All this time I could not associate with any one," he recalled. "[I] felt cramped when I was around where anyone was. I had to avoid association with people because of the bad odor from the discharge on my abdomen, from the excrement." Bruce had lost all control of his bowels, and doctors could not find a good way to deal with the discharge. At first, they installed a rubber

---

[25] O'Connor, "Engendering Amputation," 746–747.
[26] *Record in Holt*, 2, 8.

bag but then discontinued the treatment when it irritated Bruce's skin. Eventually, they simply covered the hole with a bandage and let the fluid drain into a small cup. This plan of treatment only complicated Bruce's life even more because he had to empty the cup every thirty minutes.[27]

Of course, Bruce did not suffer alone. His mother, Cora Carter, remained at his side during most of his ordeal. When she first came to him in the hospital, she found that her son "didn't know anybody, seemed as if he was paralyzed." Initially, Dr. Long told Cora that "the fatal blow had been struck; that he would not live twelve hours." Yet those twelve hours passed, and Bruce lived, and Cora stayed. "I was with him the whole time at Wesley Long Hospital, except five nights," she remembered. "I was with him day and night when it was necessary." As Bruce declined, Cora watched and listened. "He just suffered death; the only way he got any relief was by their giving him a hypodermic. He felt like he was going to die, and so expressed himself frequently; his mental condition was awful." Back at home after the weeks of hospital care, Cora had to deal with her son's continued physical and mental debility. His discharges meant that he avoided contact with others, leaving Cora to listen alone to Bruce's lamentations. She frequently heard Bruce say that he would "rather be dead than living in his condition."[28]

Adolescent workers such as Bruce Holt who endured lengthy and harrowing recoveries after serious bodily injuries were common, and they provide the clearest image of how recovery periods shaped the response of working people to industrial violence. Yet even if most young workers did not undergo an ordeal as lengthy or painful as Bruce's, they still had to face a period of adjustment after their injuries. During that time, they assessed their losses, connecting their accidents to the normal activities of growing up in the late nineteenth and early twentieth centuries. At times, play became a marker of how injury had affected a young worker's life. At age eleven, Betty Evans lost an arm in a mangle accident, and the injuries brought about a change in her normal childhood behavior. Not only did her injuries prevent her from working, they also affected her play habits. "[I] can't do anything," she declared. "[I] can do nothing but go to school and play with my dolls and can't hardly dress my dolls." Play changed for Conley Robinson as well. After swimming with local boys, he found he could not walk home, forcing his companions to cart him back on their bikes. Regular games were out as well. "I played

---

[27] Ibid., 2–3.
[28] Ibid., 5–6.

three games of leap frog and [my] stomach commenced hurting the night on the day I jumped, and papa had to take me to the bed and I haven't jumped since," Conley recalled.[29]

Young workers more typically understood their plights in relation to the ability to work. In the transitional economy of the New South, young workers looked to the farm as much as the factory when assessing what had happened to them. "I cannot work good with my finger off," Jimmie Taylor commented. "When I work cutting wood or hoeing and the wood part of the handle works against my knuckles and it hurts me." T.W. Craven surveyed his circumstances similarly: "I was raised on a farm. Cannot do much now. Cannot grasp anything now." W.H. Wynne, who had worked with his father as a carpenter before being hurt in a Georgia metal works, regretted his inability to use the common tools of that trade. Such comments underscore the importance of manual ability, even in, or perhaps especially in, an industrializing economy.[30]

Pain and diminished capacity could be psychological as well as physical. Injured workers often referred to their mental anguish. Ella Gibbs's lost finger gave her "mortification and worry." After a broken leg left Emanuel Hatcher "permanently lame," he suffered great "mental pain and mental worry." Conley Robinson's ruptured intestines left him "very nervous," according to his father. "He has been very nervous, most nervous child I ever saw and before this he wasn't nervous in any way that I could ever detect," C.M. Robinson observed. Conley's behavior in the wake of his accident suggests that his mental trauma was not simply the direct result of physical pain. The accident had left an adolescent boy without complete control of his bowels, reducing him to a condition of infancy. Perhaps to hide this fact from himself, he concealed his symptoms from his parents, only worsening his medical condition. "He suffers lots now, more than he did a month ago," his mother revealed. "For a while he would not tell us of it, be sick and maybe have to lie down sometimes until he got better and he would come home and wouldn't mention it at home, and the neighbors would come in and tell me Conley had had a bad spell."[31]

[29] *Record in Evans (Georgia)*, 2; *Record in Robinson*, 17, 19.
[30] *Record in Bibb Manufacturing Co.*, 12–13; *Record in Craven*, 21; *Record in Wynne*, 12.
[31] *Record in Gibbs*, 6; *Harbison-Walker Refractories Co. v. Hatcher*, 203 Ala. 588 (1920), 588; *Record in Robinson*, 25, 29.

BARGAINING FOR SAFETY

Faced with the ever-present threat of violence and the ongoing realities of victimization, young workers and their families sought to create meaning out of what had happened to them. They tried to figure out why injury or death had befallen them. Conceivably, Southern evangelical religion could have offered an answer, one focused on God's will, one that encouraged a kind of fatalism in the face of industrial violence. The religious revivals that swept over the South in the eighteenth and nineteenth centuries left many Southerners churched in evangelical meeting houses. There, they heard proclamations of God's providence that told them all events were His work. The need to explain the tribulations of the Confederacy only added to the genre. The Reverend Joel W. Tucker laid out a conventional proposition to his Fayetteville, North Carolina, flock during the dark days of 1862. "If the teaching of the Bible, and the revelation of the Christian religion be true, there is no such thing as fortune; there can be no accidents," Tucker preached. "Everything is of providence and under the control of God." A.M. Poindexter struck a more poetic note. "God garners the good of the wandering sparrow. God numbers the hairs of his people," he spoke in comforting tones. "Yes, God's hand is every where, and in every thing." Such sentiments were not confined to great affairs of state. When John Sehon wrote of his dear wife Annie's death in 1864, he knew his duty, even if he could not bring himself to perform it. "If I could but feel in my heart reconciled to such a manifestation of God's will," Sehon wrote, "... then I might realize the consolation said to be reserved for the Christian." This legacy of providential explanation provided working families with one possible source of meaning, one that would have ended their response to death and injury as funeral flowers and scars faded into memory. By the time the accident crisis appeared full-blown in the late nineteenth century, however, providence was under siege.[32]

Over the course of the nineteenth century, the cultural meanings Americans attached to accidents and violence changed dramatically.

---

[32] J.W. Tucker, *God's Providence in War*, (Fayetteville, 1862), 3; A.M. Poindexter, *God's providence a source of comfort and courage to Christians* (Raleigh, N.C., n.p., n.d., between 1861 and 1865), Rare Book Collection, University of North Carolina at Chapel Hill, 3–4; John Sehon to Annie M. Sehon, October 20, 1864, Kimball Family Papers, Southern Historical Collection, University of North Carolina-Chapel Hill; Michael Sappol, *A Traffic of Dead Bodies: Anatomy and Embedded Social Identity in Nineteenth-Century America* (Princeton, 2002), Ch. 1; Richard E. Beringer et al., *Why the South Lost the Civil War* (Athens, 1986), Ch. 14; Faust, *This Republic of Suffering*.

Identity increasingly departed the soul for the body. Medicine and its study of anatomy stripped away the body's mysteries, creating new conceptions of the self. Simultaneously, religious liberalism redefined the place of pain. No longer proof of God's plan, suffering now indicated something amiss, engendering what one historian has called "a universal entitlement to bodily integrity." Modern war and modern industry, however, undermined these visions of corporeal sanctity. The great conflagration that sundered the Union swept up its participants in a whirlwind of violence, one that they increasingly explained as outside their own control. As memories of the war dimmed, railroads replaced rifles, and the carnage continued. Crushing derailments and near misses at night crossings left many Americans to wonder about the vaunted individualism of their day. While legal minds searched for fault, others wondered if no one was to blame.[33]

For young workers in the South, industrial violence appeared neither as a crisis of modernity nor as a pre-modern manifestation of God's will. Rather, explanations grew from the shop floor and the place of children and youth on it. Workers reflected on the inherent dangers of industrial technology, investigated its defects, and proposed ways to make it safer. They also considered the ability of young people to operate in such an environment. Their explanations returned most often to the social relations of production. To be sure, accident litigations, with their requirement of proving "negligence," framed the story in this fashion. But workers' testimony reveals that they repeatedly sought to control the workplace in ways that would protect young workers and their particular vision of industrial childhood. Most often, this exertion of workplace control involved implicit or explicit agreements to confine young workers to spaces or duties that would be relatively safe. But prior agreements did not constitute their only efforts to bring order to a chaotic work environment. Young workers and their parents mapped the overlapping domains of authority that held sway on the shop floor. Blame rested on those who gave orders, but this dynamic was especially muddled in the case

---

[33] Sappol, *Traffic of Dead Bodies*, Ch. 2; Elizabeth B. Clark, "'The Sacred Rights of the Weak': Pain, Sympathy, and the Culture of Individual Rights in Antebellum America," *Journal of American History*, 82 (1995): 470–471; Charles Royster, *The Destructive War: William Tecumseh Sherman, Stonewall Jackson, and the Americans* (New York, 1991), 256 and *passim*; Welke, *Recasting American Liberty*, esp. 20, 38; Nan Goodman, *Shifting the Blame: Literature, Law, and the Theory of Accidents in Nineteenth-Century America* (Princeton, 1998). See also Karen Halttunen, "Humanitarianism and the Pornography of Pain in Anglo-American Culture," *American Historical Review*, 100 (1995): 303–334.

of younger children. The nature of youthful obedience lay at the heart of the disputes that violence incited. Hence, conflicts over children and young people injured or killed on the job raised central questions about industrial authority, questions that courts and industrialists believed they had adequately disposed of in the antebellum period.[34]

Undoubtedly, industrial work created inherent dangers, but those dangers threatened old and young alike. Young workers incurred only a part of the millions of workplace injuries that occurred during the period, though their incidence was higher than for older laborers. That greater rate of injury had more to do with relationships on the shop floor than with machines themselves. Nonetheless, we should not overlook the fact that mines, mills, railroads, and other industrialized work spaces *were* more dangerous than the agrarian world that preceded them. The physical conditions in nineteenth-century workplaces amplified that potential. Lighting was perhaps the biggest problem, but the cramped arrangement of machines; the presence of oil, lint, or other slippery substances; the cobbled-together nature of many machines on any given day all menaced workers. The scale and speed of industrial technology itself produced greater potential for death and injury.[35]

Certainly, life on the farm offered its own hazards. Domestic animals, in particular, imperiled anybody unfortunate enough to get in their way when they were in a bad mood. A mule could be just as devastating as a machine. Charles Turner, though hurt in a mine, conveyed just how much damage "an unusually vicious and dangerous mule" could do. "He kicked me in the face here, my nose was broken, my lips all cut across here, it broke this bone here and I think this bone here (indicating)," Turner recalled. The response of mules to the coming of capitalism remains an understudied topic, but it seems likely that this mule would have been just as dangerous on the farm. At least Will Hundley, an African American worker at the mine, thought so. "That was [a] mighty bad mule," he figured. "She was a dangerous mule for the men working her."[36]

[34] Christopher Tomlins, *Law, Labor and Ideology in the Early American Republic* (New York, 1993), 318–330; Witt, *Accidental Republic*, Ch. 1.

[35] Arthur F. McEvoy, "The Triangle Shirtwaist Factory Fire of 1911: Social Change, Industrial Accidents, and the Evolution of Common-Sense Causality," *Law & Social Inquiry*, 20 (1995): 621–651; Welke, *Recasting American Liberty*, 25. For a contemporary account of workplace deaths (but not injuries) to young people, see Crystal Eastman, *Work Accidents and the Law, The Pittsburgh Survey, vol. 6*, ed. Paul Underwood Kellogg (New York, 1910), 13.

[36] *Record in Turner*, 36, 71; Jason Hribal, "'Animals Are Part of the Working Class': A Challenge to Labor History," *Labor History*, 44 (2003): 435–453.

Agricultural mechanization only increased the chance for mishaps around the farm, as one Tennessee youngster discovered when he fell into the power mechanism of a threshing machine. A late-nineteenth century wheat thresher consisted of a ring of horses or mules that turned a gear-driven motor connected to the separator by lengthy belts. A driver controlled the team, while other men and boys pitched sheaves, collected grain, removed chaff, and stacked straw. Farmers often coop-erated in such activities, and such an interfamilial arrangement brought twelve-year-old Ed Williams into contact with a thresher in the sum-mer of 1899. Directed by his father to head over to Uncle Fin's place, the boy left home at 6:00 a.m., catching up with the men who started around 7:00. With the men needing water, he either was ordered to get it or he took the duty upon himself. Darting between the mules to give the driver a drink, Ed hopped up onto the platform of the power mechanism to avoid being hit as the levers came around. Expecting to land on a plank, he slipped (or was knocked) into a hole. As a result, Ed later recalled, his left leg was "mashed all to pieces and the doctors had to take it off."[37]

Young Williams's mishap indicates the risks that farm mechanization brought to the countryside, but it also illustrates how those dangers differed from the factory. For one thing, two mules could not com-pete with the power of a water wheel, steam engine, or electric motor. Witnesses to Ed's accident spent much time debating whether he could have gotten out of the way or not, trying to estimate how fast a horse could go at a walk. In addition to the particular rate of travel, the mules were under the direct control of a driver, as was the case in most farm machinery in that era. No mysterious force, horses and mules were known, if dangerous, characters. Most important, though, Ed's mishap took place in a web of social and economic relationships quite different from those that dominated the factory. While the threshing machine and accompanying machinery and animals were owned by W.A. Gobble, other local men and boys did the work. Albert Griffin, the driver who ran the teams, got paid two bushels of wheat per day for doing so. Ed's characterization of the operation was on the mark. "We was swapping work," he maintained. In other words, even mechanized farm work often remained within families, making it unlikely that young work-ers and their families would end up in the courts or come into contact with a language forged for industrial labor. With no authority lodged in

[37] *Record in Williams (Tennessee)*, 2–3, 5–8, 16–21, 25, 28.

bosses or owners, the dynamics that led to litigation did not appear in much of "farm labor."[38]

While farms could be dangerous places, young workers and their families envisioned the move from farm to factory as a distinct change in the safety of their work environments. Lon Dillon, sixteen, stressed that he was "raised on a farm" and "never was about a railroad" or "any public place at all to work" before he took a job at United States Coal and Coke in Alabama. A.B. Ensley told a similar tale: "Up to the time of the injury, I lived with my father and helped on the farm. I never had been about machinery." Young workers and their parents had good reason to be concerned about the move to town and industry. The dangers were multifaceted, but more important, the scale and speed of industrial production heightened the chances for injury. The knives that removed Ensley's hand revolved at 3,500 revolutions per minute. The velocity of industrial technology left workers with little time to react to unforeseen events. "When you felt the planer moving forward, why didn't you turn loose?" a lawyer asked Johnson Monroe. "I just caught hold to shake it and when I knowed anything my hand was cut off," the boy replied. Such incidents defied "common sense," and as these stories circulated, they underscored workers' intuition that the speed and scale of industrial labor was more threatening than life on the farm.[39]

Whether mechanization was inherently dangerous, of course, was not a simple question of physical conditions, scale, and speed. While a cotton mill beater did have to run at a certain velocity to work, the tempo of industrial life resulted from the demands of production. Working at Blackwell Durham Tobacco, Gaines Leathers tied tobacco sacks at the rate of one every two seconds on "the fast machines." Obviously, such machines did not have to work at that pace. More commonly, the demands of speed led to questionable decisions about making repairs with machines running. As safety requirements increased over the course of the late nineteenth and early twentieth centuries, such practices declined, but early in the process of industrialization they were common. Continuous-flow production placed those in charge in impossible positions. Such was the case with a Mr. Eastwood, a "second boss" at a Virginia textile mill in 1880. Eastwood ordered twelve-year-old Robert L. Jones to replace a broken belt without stopping the machinery because halting to make the repair

[38] Ibid., 21–22, 98–102, 105–106, 109.
[39] *Dillon v. United States Coal and Coke*, 75 W. Va. 666 (1915), 669; *Record in Ensley*, 16; *Record in Burnett*, 17; *Record in Standard Red Cedar Chest Co.*, 24.

would have necessitated shutting down about fifty looms "and the stoppage of fifty looms amounts to a great deal."[40]

Eastwood's choice reflects the interplay between the inherent dangers of industrialization and the social relations of production. The belt had to be fixed immediately, and while another adult worker was nearby, Eastwood believed he could not make himself heard over the din of the machinery. He knew it was dangerous to call upon Robert to replace the belt, but he "had no one else." In his view, his authority was limited to his room and the workers in it. With regard to other workers, "I could have asked, but I had no right to order," Eastwood concluded. Eastwood remained troubled, but he found reassurance from his superior: "On the next morning I was talking about it and said I was bothered about it and Mr. Robinson said he wanted the cloth and that it was my duty to do as I did."[41]

Such dramas of the shop floor occurred daily in industrial settings, and they called for a response by young workers and their families. While working people would eventually come to accept the notion that such events were the inevitable outcome of child labor, they clung stubbornly to the notion that the "causes" of industrial accidents could be found in the social relations of production. While the very young could easily be said to be incapable of understanding, older children and adolescents could learn to be careful, or at least that's what working families believed. That learning, however, could not come overnight. Young workers and their families realized as much and sought to organize the Southern workplace in ways that would be conducive to the seasoning process. These efforts to alter the physical and social geography of "child labor" underlay the conflicts that would lead workers and employers to the law. Such conflicts turned on the nature of industrial authority itself. For a young worker, who was the boss? Did they have to obey all adults, as they would outside the workplace? Were they responsible to parents or older siblings, or to community members? Or were they bound to follow the commands only of their immediate superior in the hierarchies of the job? Had they any will of their own? To understand the nature of industrial violence, then, we must turn away from the machines themselves and to the people who ran them.

In the language of the day, young workers were "green." The color and the word had been associated with youth and immaturity since at least

---

[40] *Record in Jones*, 71–75; *Record in Leathers*, 16. On changes in safety technology, see Mark Aldrich, *Safety First: Technology, Labor, and Business in the Building of American Work Safety, 1870–1939* (Baltimore, 1997).

[41] *Record in Leathers*, 16; *Record in Jones*, 71–75.

the late medieval period. The concept took on a special meaning in the rapid industrialization of the South. Mills and mines in Dixie overflowed with green hands, adult, youth, and child. Not everyone agreed that new workers were more likely to incur workplace injuries. J.H. Fleeman, a mine foreman, proclaimed that new workers were actually less likely to be hurt. "A new man at a position, whether he is young or old, generally gives better attention to his position than an older man at the position because as he grows older he grows more careless," Fleeman claimed. Most Southern workers would have disagreed. Being green was more than a simple matter of age. William Wrenn was in his late teens when he took a job at Alabama Steel and Wire, yet Thomas Harris, a machinist, considered William to be green. "After he came here to work he looked to be a green man to me," Harris said. J.F. Hancock, another worker at the plant, thought it might take as much as two years to get acquainted with the hoist that maimed William.[42]

Acclimation was not simply a matter of time, but also of place. At age thirteen, Perry Griffith already had a good idea of what being green meant. After insisting that "you can't learn everything about a mine in eighteen days," Perry made it clear that he meant a particular mine. "I was green about the place," he maintained. "I had trapped at the Gulf, but I had never been in that mine before." For Jim Harris, hurt at age thirteen in a Georgia textile plant, it was the move from the country itself. "I was green to the job you know," Jim declared two years later at age fifteen. "I had been raised on a farm and had been farming all the time until I went to work in the mills."[43]

The complex mixture of youth and experience captured in the moniker of a "green hand" figured centrally in the actions of young workers and their families in the Southern labor market, in their attempts to understand industrial violence to young people, and in their motivations for carrying their grievances to the law. Young workers and their families believed that they could control the terms of industrial life, and they realized that some jobs were inherently dangerous to young people. Their solution lay not in the abolition of child labor, but in the creation of safe places for young people to carry out their particular roles in production. If they came to call for an end to child labor and to acquiesce in its legal regulation, it is because they had lost the battle to change the

[42] *Oxford English Dictionary*, "green," entries 7, 8; "hand," entry 8; *Record in Wilkinson*, 72; *Alabama Steel & Wire Co. v. Wrenn*, 136 Ala. 475 (1902), 491.
[43] *Record in Griffith*, 56–57; *Record in Harris*, n.p.

industrial South into a place that accommodated young people. As such, they formed part of the long resolution to the conflict between workplace autonomy and worker safety.[44]

The prime vehicle for control of the workplace was individual bargaining for safety. When young workers and their parents negotiated with potential employers, they frequently sought agreements that would keep them out of harm's way. Walter Affleck and his brother, William, worked for Powhatan Lime, a quarry in Virginia under conditions they and their father believed were safe. "We had lived on the farm all the time, and we had never worked at no public work," Walter recollected. "Papa told Mr. Richards that he would like to get us a job like that, nailing barrels, that it would not be dangerous, that we did not know anything about dangerous work to put us at no place where it was dangerous." Assured that the job would entail no more than nailing, Walter and William soon discovered the value of Mr. Richards's word. First they loaded lime, then unloaded coal, and then went straight to work on the rock crusher. "I did not nail barrels more than half a dozen times while I was there," Walter insisted. When the boys told their father about the change of plans, he sent them back to Mr. Richards with instructions to inform him that what they were doing was "not the bargain, that we was not to work there."[45]

The Afflecks's story reveals bargaining for safety in detail, but examples of similar deals abound. Charles Burke, Sr., willingly let his eleven-year-old son Charley work as a trapper because "there was no motor power or electric cars for him to contend with and it was not dangerous like the place where he was hurt." John Ewing allowed his son to trap based on the assurances that there was "no danger in trapping." Alice Daniels believed the duties of her son, Charles, fifteen, would be confined to carrying water. After two to three weeks of bargaining with a hiring agent of the mine, she agreed. "I didn't want my boy to work where he could get hurt," she recalled. "He had never worked around public works and was not old enough to realize when he was in danger." G.W. Harris was firm on the limits for his son, Jim. "I never hired him to strip cards," the elder Harris insisted. "I didn't know it until he came home after he was hurt.

---

[44] David Montgomery, *Workers' Control in America: Studies in the History of Work, Technology, and Labor Struggles* (New York, 1980), 9–31. For coal miners and safety, see Walter Graebner, *Coal Mining Safety in the Progressive Period: The Political Economy of Reform* (Lexington, 1976), 112–139. On the broader conflict between worker agency and workplace safety, see Witt, *Accidental Republic*, 29–33; and Aldrich, *Safety First*.

[45] *Record in Powhatan Lime Co.*, 138, 145. The family name is spelled both Affleck and Afflick in the record.

He was raised on the farm." James Monroe thought his son, Johnson, was "simply picking up planks" but he still told the company not to put Johnson in dangerous spots. In addition, he warned his boys about working at Standard Red Cedar Chest Company. He had done nothing special, he said, "No more than to teach them like a father always teaches: Keep away from dangerous places."[46]

Avoiding danger so as to work in relative safety was a matter on the minds of young workers themselves as well. They most often expressed such thoughts by resistance to being moved to machines or work spaces that they believed to be more dangerous. Pearl McIntyre, fourteen, balked at being moved to a new machine at a Georgia printing facility. Pearl saw the matter simply: "I didn't want to work there because I was afraid." Similarly, Anna Barnes refused to work at a newer kind of spinning frame. In response, the second hand in the room "cursed after her and told her she had to go to work." Before Bruce Holt began work at the groover that caused his terrible injuries, he tried to keep his body out of harm's way. "I was firing the boiler, and the man who operated the grooving machine was out, and Mr. Stone put me to work on it," Bruce recalled. "I was scared I'd get my fingers cut, and told him so."[47]

The success of such efforts depended, of course, on employers. They would have to comply with bargains made with young workers or their families, and they would have to concede some measure of control to young workers on the shop floor. The legal regime that had grown since the antebellum period with regard to industrial accidents left them unlikely to cede much power to workers, especially younger ones. Company lawyers stated the upshot of this line of thinking bluntly in an early Virginia case. "We say that the master must be allowed to select and arrange the machinery according to the habits, customs, and usages of the business, whether the party to be employed about the machinery is an adult or a minor," they insisted. The assumption of control over the physical geography of the work space eventually became central to the conflicts between Southern working families and their employers, as workers continually pressed their case that something could have been done to prevent accidents. The uneasy resolution of this conflict in health

[46] *Record in Burke*, 155; *Record in Ewing*, 28; *Record in Daniels*, 22; *Record in Harris*, 9877, n.p; *Record in Standard Red Cedar Chest Co.*, 28. See also *Record in Ensley*, 14; *Record in Haynie*, 4; *Record in Stearns Coal & Lumber Co.*, 25–26; *Record in Skipper*, Complaint; *Marbury Lumber Co. v. Westbrook*, 121 Ala. 179 (1898), 179; *Leopard v. Laurens Cotton Mills*, 81 S.C. 15 (1908), 19.
[47] *Record in McIntyre*, 11; *Record in Augusta Factory*, 5; *Record in Holt*, 11.

and safety regulations took a long time, and here it is enough to notice that employers continued to operate on the assumption of relatively unbridled authority.[48]

These assertions of mastery applied especially to young workers. Their youth transformed them into industrial labor in its most pristine form, labor that was both highly commodified and easily controlled. In contrast, adults carried work identities that, while changeable over a worker's lifetime, acted as fixed markers on any given day. As we have seen, these identity markers produced a language of work that was both age- and gender-based. Some tasks were "boy's work," some "men's work. Whether young or old, "general help" had to do whatever was asked of it. Nevertheless, the situation was particularly acute for the young. With less life history to call upon and with the requirement to respect adult authority, they more easily came to be seen as jacks-of-all-trades. "I was underage, and whatever my father said to do on a job I did" is how one Georgia worker saw the matter. Especially for younger boys, the daily reality of work meant doing what they were told. To ten-year-old Johnnie Queen, his duty was simply "to mind the car driver and do whatever he told me."[49]

Minding others, as Johnnie Queen put it, characterized labor relations for young workers, yet lines of authority continually blurred, creating conflicts and undermining the edifice of industrial childhood being built by young workers and their families. Bargaining for safety called for the control of young working bodies from afar. Either employers must stand *in loco parentis*, or young workers themselves must obey the dictates of parents who often were not physically present. In theory, the hierarchical arrangement of most industrial workplaces could have made this dynamic function. Especially in textiles and other factories, authority resided in a series of bosses whose powers were set by factory rules and by the customs of the shop floor. Yet for young workers, these carefully crafted rules of the game constantly shifted. They did so in part because of the actions of older workers, many of whom assumed the prerogative to direct and discipline children based not on the posted regulations but simply on the fact that adults were older. All children should obey all adults, they believed. Others chose not to intervene, ceding authority, and hence, responsibility, to parents, family members, or to the appointed bosses.

---

[48] *Record in Lynchburg Cotton Mills*, 8.
[49] *Record in Eagle and Phenix Mills*, 63, 22; *Record in Queen*, 21; *Record in Byrd*, 62; *Record in Pelham Manufacturing Co.*, 66.

The nature of authority over young workers, however, was not simply a question of "who's the boss?" As in all hierarchical relationships, obedience could never become absolute. Underage workers had to acknowledge the legitimacy of those who wielded authority over them and choose to abide by it. For a growing young person, especially a growing boy, the accession of authority was always a moving target. In the nineteenth century, growing up entailed ceding less and less authority to adults while acquiring adult habits of independence. Outside the gates of mills and mines, contemporaries worried constantly about the "boy problem," but the workplace had its own "boy problem" as well as a "girl problem." The problem was that youth and industrial authority did not mix very well.[50]

Battling out the lines of authority both led to industrial violence and helped to explain it for young workers and their families. To imagine how this conflict arose and played out, we must first adjust our understanding of parental power. In agrarian or artisan households, control might be a contest of wills between young people and their elders, but (especially before the rise of social work in the twentieth century) few outside forces intervened. To be sure, the community set standards about *how* parental authority could be exercised, but it did not put itself in between parents and children. Before the rise of youthful wage labor, work outside the home maintained relatively clear lines of age-based governance. Apprenticeship contracts and indentures of service spelled out what masters could and could not do, even if they were honored more in the breach than in actuality. Such arrangements represented a formal transfer of authority and a literal creation of a new relationship *in loco parentis.* The willy-nilly fashion in which wage work for young people evolved meant that no such formal relationship materialized when a young worker hired to a mill, mine, shop, or factory. Theoretically, parents retained their power, but in reality, they did not. As "private legislators," employers possessed the power of masters, but without their responsibilities.[51]

Envisioned as a description of adult work, this evolution in the social relations of production is relatively clear. Adult workers had come to occupy a social position previously reserved for minors. But what of minors themselves? And of their parents? Fathers and mothers could no longer direct their children's work (if ever they had) without the reality

---

[50] Among the many insights of Eugene Genovese's classic *Roll, Jordan, Roll* is his discussion of the fable of absolute obedience. See *Roll, Jordan, Roll: The World the Slaves Made* (New York, 1974), 87–97. On growing up and independence, see Harvey Graff, *Conflicting Paths: Growing Up in America* (Cambridge, 1995), 7 and *passim.*

[51] Tomlins, *Law, Labor, and Ideology,* 365–367.

of the factory standing between them. In part, that meant the boss, but it also meant the physical geography of the workplace itself. A multistory textile mill or a mine that stretched for hundreds of yards in three dimensions was not the barnyard. Even if parents were present on the job, which they frequently were not, they might be laboring in a different location in the plant. Wherever they were, they were likely glued to their work, at least at places where machines ran in constant motion. Keeping track of young workers and making sure that they obeyed in such an environment required something quite different than it had before. If Southern industries relied on the family labor system, it was a new family, whose structures of governance were now quite up in the air, especially with regard to young workers, their social position, and their physical safety.[52]

All this is not to say that parents did not attempt to carry older assumptions about family life and adult authority into the industrial world. In fact, those assumptions did undergird their vision of how industrial life ought to work. Obviously, some working parents exercised authority directly over their children at the workplace, but usually they were in no position to do so. Consequently, they had to rely on the promises of strangers. Sometimes lingering notions of *in loco parentis* hovered over the process of bargaining for safety. When I.L. Affleck got work for Walter and William, he told their prospective employer that he "put them in his care." Such a deal evoked the old transfer of authority and responsibility bequeathed by apprenticeship and service. This language could also be used to induce reluctant parents into arrangements that they might otherwise have avoided. A West Virginia father permitted his sixteen-year-old son to remain at the mine that killed him based on such an assurance. The father had decided to leave the mine and take his son with him, but as he departed, he ran into the mine foreman, who asked him to leave the boy. "I seed him below Davy," he recollected, "and told him I was going home, and he asked me if the boy was going and I told him he wanted to go, and he said, 'I am scarce of men and if you will let him stay here I will take good care of the boy as if he was my own boy.'" With this promise in hand, he left his son working in the mine, warning him to stay away from "electric haulage."[53]

The transfer of authority in an industrial setting implied a relocation of responsibility, the obligation to keep young workers safe. But to whom that obligation had devolved was never certain. An actual owner,

[52] McEvoy, "Triangle Shirtwaist Fire," 629–630.
[53] *Record in Powhatan Lime Co.*, 166; *Record in Sprinkle*, 24–25.

"the master" according to the law, was either nonexistent in cases of corporate ownership or simply absent in instances of personal possession of larger firms. The "superintendent" could certainly not look after all youngsters in his care. Someone in the capacity of a "foreman" possessed somewhat clearer authority. T.F. Smith, who occupied such a position in a West Virginia mine, spoke of disciplining eleven-year-old trapper, Clarence Broyles, for "disobeying my orders – going on a haul where I told him not to go." The punishment was a two-day lay-off from work, something Clarence might have welcomed. A foreman's power might be straightforward, but they were not always the person in charge at any given moment. The boss might be the "second-hand" who had control of a particular room in a plant. Such was the position of Frank Thornburg, a second-hand at Melville Manufacturing in North Carolina, who meted out the "punishment" of extra sweeping to boys he caught fooling around with the high-pressure hose. In the end, from the point of view of young workers, the boss could be any adult who told them to do something. Another second-hand at a Virginia cotton mill noted that all employees had some power over younger workers, especially in matters of safety and machines. As he put it, "the hands have the right to keep them away if they see them playing with them."[54]

Still, the boss might be a family member. After all, the family labor system did bring groups of siblings into industrial workspaces. Yet the authority of an older brother or grandparent did not always hold. Harlie Daniels worked with an older brother who tried to look after him, warning him to stay off of a mine car because he was too small and could not hold the load. With their father at work elsewhere in the mine, Harlie paid his sibling little heed. "I didn't have control over the boy," his brother conceded. "He worked under the boss. If I had been his father I might have made him stay off." Sometimes problems of control could be intra-family. At age sixteen, Phil Waldron proved to be too much for just about anyone. Back and forth between the houses of his father, Guy Waldron, and his step-grandfather, H.S. Short, Phil also spent time in a boarding house. His mistress there, Bessie Peery, recalled this conversation with Phil. "I asked him why he didn't go home and go to school, that I thought he ought to be in school, and he said he and his father couldn't get along, his father was not good to him, and for that reason he wouldn't stay at home," she revealed. Beyond fights with Guy Waldron, school did not suit

---

[54] *Record in Swope*, 23; *Record in Robinson*, 36; *Record in Lynchburg Cotton Mills*, 83; Hall et al., *Like a Family*, 93–98; Tomlins, *Law, Labor, and Ideology*, 343.

Phil, who told Perry that whenever he went to school, "he was always so mean that he run the teacher away." His father became so riled with Phil that he threatened to send him to reform school, but the elder Waldron still seemed to think Phil should be working. His grandfather just wanted him out of the mines. If mine manager J.W. Baldwin is to be believed, the company was in the middle of a conflict between two men and a boy trying to become one. "Mr. Short intimated to me that he wanted the boy to go to school, and his father wanted him to work on," Baldwin maintained. "I kind of interpreted Mr. Short as meaning that if I got him away from there, it would relieve him of the burden; that he didn't want any friction with his father." Other community members corroborated the notion that Phil deferred to no one. At sixteen going on twenty-one, he was the "boy problem" writ small. His independent streak blurred obedience in the extreme, and it led to his death, when he defied everyone and decided to "work on the rock."[55]

If Phil Waldron's defiance of adult authority arose from his approaching adulthood, Jimmie Taylor's attempts to obey came from his meager years. What exactly happened in his case remains a mystery, with fellow workers telling starkly differing tales, but one reading is that Jimmie was playing at obeying. For Jimmie, who was eight when he lost his finger at the East Macon plant of Bibb Manufacturing in October 1891, the matter was simple. "I had to obey in the mill," Jimmie insisted four years later. "Mr. Hooks and Tom Couse; they ordered me to clean off the gear that morning is the reason I did it." Mr. Hooks saw things differently. "I never gave any order for the gear to be cleaned while it was running," James Hooks maintained. "You can't clean it while it is running because it runs too fast." Enter Henry Smith, the mine foreman, who had caught Jimmie playing with the machines and "got after him." He reported the boy to his father, Jesse, who promised to whip him. In addition, he claimed that when he threatened Jesse with firing the boy, "he begged me not to send him off." But Smith was not the only person in the mill who had gotten after Jimmie. B.F. Williams, a worker in the mill, had also surprised young Taylor "squatting down and playing with the twisting gear at the time he was hurt." Williams averred that he ordered Jimmie away from the gears, but that the boy replied "that it was none of my dam [sic] business as he knew what he was doing. ... I didn't believe I had a right to jerk him away from there after he made that expression, it really looked like he wanted to have his finger cut off." Yet this was not the first run-in

[55] *Record in Daniels*, 67; *Record in Waldron*, 49, 86, 98.

between Jimmie and Mr. Williams. "Williams's feelings are pretty bad towards me," Jesse Taylor revealed. "He took Jimmie by the hair of the head one day and slammed him against the floor and my little boy cut him across the thigh with a knife, and I told Williams if he did it again I would hurt him."[56]

Jimmie's accident illuminates the blurred lines of authority. The youngster knew he "had to obey in the mill," but exactly who deserved that obedience was an open question. All the other witnesses in the case deemed it absurd that an eight-year-old boy would be ordered to clean running gears. Although it is certainly possible that such was the case, it is just as likely that Jimmie imagined himself to be an older worker, dutifully following the orders of his bosses. In this imaginative world of authority, Williams, a fellow worker, could not legitimately claim power over the boy's body. If Jimmie imagined his relation to Williams as man to man, it truly was none of the latter's "dam business" what Jimmie was about. As an adult, it was the boy's right to tell a fellow worker possessing no real authority that "he knew what he was doing," and it was his prerogative to defend his adult identity with violence. But of course, Jimmie was not an adult. In the end, his father reasserted his parental powers over Williams, threatening violence for violence. Still, he had no such power over the true bosses of his son. To exercise any authority over them, he had to turn away from the shop floor and to the law.[57]

Disputes over authority based in age erupted in many different fashions, but their clearest form appeared in direct confrontations between bosses and young workers over issues of safety. To see how these conflicts arose and played out, we can return to the story of H.E. Kinder, the young mine worker we met at the outset. As H.E. lay bleeding and the cars rattled away, he had a pretty clear idea of what caused his mangled leg. While he eventually brought suit against Boomer Coal and Coke, his real antagonist was one Mr. Bostick, the mine boss. According to H.E., Bostick was a "habitual drinker," who was drunk on the day of the accident. Conflict between H.E. and Bostick about where and how H.E. should work had simmered for days, resulting in Bostick threatening to take away H.E.'s "turn" in the mine. For H.E., the threat of losing his turn forced him to act against his own wishes. "[I]f he had not used foul means against me, you might say starve me out – I had no way of providing a living except that. I had to take it," H.E. recalled. Pressed

[56] *Record in Bibb Manufacturing Co.*, 12, 17, 21, 26, 34.
[57] For a similar case, see *Record in Elk Cotton Mills*, 36.

on whether Bostick used force, H.E. remained firm: "That is force, he wouldn't allow me a turn."

Yet Bostick's power over H.E. was not simply economic. Some days earlier, the man had beaten H.E. "unmercifully and without cause." Now things were coming to a head. On the morning of the accident, H.E. decided to make a stand. "I made up my mind I had had so much trouble that morning, had cars off and one thing and another. I went out and told him, I says, 'Mr. Bostick, this is my last time.' I says 'I am not going back.'" Unmoved by H.E.'s courage, Bostick shot back a warning. "He told me 'you God damned little son of a bitch, if you don't get back in there and go to work, I am going to kick your God damned ass.'" H.E.'s clash with Bostick was unusual in its level of violence, but it was by no means unique. Other young workers reported being physically forced to do work they considered dangerous or onerous. The center of the conflict between Bostick and H.E. is captured in Bostick's language. As an adult talking to a child, he felt perfectly assured of his authority.[58]

The authority of men like Bostick over young workers such as H.E. Kinder arose with the coming of industrial society. While it echoed the powers of past masters – of servants, of apprentices – it was bounded by none of the paternalistic language or statutory oversight that formed those relationships. Bostick's power was closer to that of the slave master, or at least his right-hand man, the overseer. Yet unlike those legally grounded relationships of authority, the authority of the Bosticks of the world came and went, often on a daily basis. The labor regime that young Southern workers and their families entered in the late nineteenth century afforded no straight avenue for maintaining parental control. In turn, it opened new vistas for young workers, who now had to decide whom to obey and how to do it. For many Southern working families, these altered relations between adults and young people over the terms of youthful labor provided the best explanation when industrial violence befell young workers. Cora Magnus, the feisty and clearly agitated parent of thirteen-year-old Herbert, put the matter bluntly in a West Virginia courtroom. "They would tell me he was working there first rate," she told the assembled courtroom. "I told him not to go in and get on the cars but to carry water, and they would put him right back to work."[59]

---

[58] *Record in Kinder*, 51–52, 63. For another example of a case that turned on direct conflict, see *Record in McGowan*, 7.

[59] *Record in Magnus*, 19.

For Cora Magnus, Herbert's broken leg came from a breach of the trust she had placed in the hands of his employer. Like other working families, Cora and Herbert sought to repair the damage. Before the rise of workers' compensation and the modern welfare state, their main source of succor could be found in the halls of their local courthouse. There, they could recount their tales of death and mourning, of injury and recovery, of bargains sealed and bargains violated. In court, however, those stories could not be told entirely in their own dialect. Instead, working people had to learn how to speak the language of the law. Over the preceding century, the nation's jurists had been fashioning a script for youthful labor and its discontents. By the time Cora and Herbert came to court in the late 1910s, this legal lexicon had come to align with the disturbing vision of reformers: Young people were naturally unfit for industrial work.

4

Natural Impulses

Children, wherever they go, must be expected to act upon childish instincts and impulses. (Thomas McIntyre Cooley, 1884)

Walter Clark, member of the Supreme Court of North Carolina throughout the Progressive era, holds the distinction of being one of the few jurists in U.S. history to quote Elizabeth Barrett Browning (poorly) in a judicial opinion. Reviewing the cause of William Fitzgerald against the Alma Furniture Company in 1902, Clark turned to Browning's famous verses. Following a lengthy list of child labor statutes in the United States and around the world, Clark placed these stanzas: "The sob of the child in its helplessness/Curses deeper than the strong man in his wrath." Although garbling the lines, Clark captured the essence of Browning's reforming rhymes. This literary flourish epitomized the opinions Clark wrote over the three decades on the court, texts that imported much of the language reformers were busy articulating. In these texts, he decried "the inhumanity of shutting up these little prisoners eleven and one-half to twelve hours a day ... or depriving them of opportunity for education, or using the competition of their cheap wages to reduce those of maturer age." Speaking of Joe Pettit's death in a South Rocky Mount rail yard, Clark exclaimed: "This was truly 'the price of innocent blood'." Young Pettit was a "little sufferer" sent to his death by the "avarice" of the railroad. Invoking Pickett's charge, Clark noted that many brave Confederates had survived four years of war while Joe "was slain on the fourth day of his employment." Whether recalling an English poet or a Civil War general, Clark's penchant for the literary reflected his avocation as a historian and his fondness for reform. Corresponding with the likes of the American

Federation of Labor's Samuel Gompers and the National Child Labor Committee's Alexander McKelway, Clark moved in progressive circles. As a result, he used his position of increasing prominence on the North Carolina bench to aid those causes whenever he could.[1]

Pronouncements by Clark and his brethren on courts around the nation would have a profound influence on what would happen in the aftermath of the violence that young workers met on the job. Reformers had written one script for those events; jurists penned another. If all judges were as straightforward and transparent as Clark, revealing the plotlines of that story would be a simple process. "Law" could simply be said to reflect "society." Such was not the case. While reform writers spun their tales in a relatively condensed period starting in the late nineteenth century, the nation's courts had encountered young workers and their families from the beginning of the country's existence. Immediately after the break with Britain, those causes mostly involved bound apprenticeship. As the antebellum period wore on, judges considered more and more cases involving wage work by young people. At the same time, they talked about the mishaps that young people incurred, at first addressing those outside the workplace and then the ones that happened inside the factory gates. By the late nineteenth century, jurists had their hands full sorting out the violence that industrial society meted out to its young.[2]

Rules created in this long process defined the terms of youthful labor and governed the options for working people when they sought redress for their injuries, but law worked on a second level as well. By creating seemingly fixed categories and boundaries for disparate social practices, law laid the foundations for the cultural construct we now know as "child labor." It did so because the courts provided an authoritative forum where central questions about the social location of children and

---

[1] *Fitzgerald v. Alma Furniture Co.*, 131 N.C. 636 (1902), 644; *Ward v. Odell*, 126 N.C. 946 (1900), 948; *Pettit v. Atlantic Coastline Railroad Co.*, 156 N.C. 119 (1911), 137. For a biography of Clark, see Aubrey Lee Brooks, *Walter Clark, Fighting Judge* (Chapel Hill, 1944).

[2] Along with other scholars, I aim to bring age as a category of analysis to the study of law and society, particularly by turning our attention directly to the work experiences of young people and their interactions with legal constructs of childhood and youth in the legal process. Two of the best examples of the growing literature in this area are Holly Brewer, *By Birth or Consent: Children, Law, and the Anglo-American Revolution in Authority* (Chapel Hill, 2005); and Stephen Robertson, *Crimes against Children: Sexual Violence and Legal Culture in New York City, 1880–1960* (Chapel Hill, 2005). For an extended discussion of these matters, see James D. Schmidt, "The Ends of Innocence: Age as a Mode of Inquiry in Sociolegal Studies," *Law and Social Inquiry* 32(4) (Fall 2007): 1029–1057.

the cultural meaning of childhood under capitalism could be answered. The market revolution brought to the forefront new understandings of human agency. The central assumptions of a contract-driven society – self-ownership, consent, reciprocity – necessarily raised troubling questions when applied to young people. Did they own their own labor power and could they dispose of it as their own agents? Did young people possess a will of their own, one that would allow them to consent to a bargain? Could they appreciate the terms of a contract or the risks of a job? Ultimately, were children full participants in a market society or not?[3]

Reform writers had proffered one set of answers to these questions; the courts supplied a second language for talking about young people, work, and industrial violence, a lexicon intertwined with but distinct from the language of reform. That language depended very much on proceedings in the lower courts, on the campaigns of reformers, and on the reactions of industrialists, attorneys, and working people themselves. Other sources of cultural authority no doubt contributed to the vision of youthful labor as well. Just as working people sought meaning for industrial violence in court, for example, so, too, did they at the funerals of young people killed on the job. Moreover, the local legal process provided a medium by which this narrative language of the law entered the vocabularies of working people in their communities and in their local courts.[4]

---

[3] My argument here draws on an approach to legal history that sees the law as constitutive of social relations. For a brief and lucid introduction to this notion see Christopher L. Tomlins, "The Many Legalities of Colonization: A Manifesto of Destiny for Early American Legal History" in *The Many Legalities of Early America*, ed. Christopher L. Tomlins and Bruce H. Mann (Chapel Hill, 2002), 1–20, esp. 4–5. "In their Foucauldian sense, legalities are the symbols, signs, and instantiations of formal law's classificatory impulse, the outcomes of its specialized practices, and the products of its institutions," he argues. I think that understanding how this works out in actual practice requires keen attention to what Pierre Bourdieu labeled "the juridical field." Pierre Bourdieu, "The Force of Law: Toward a Sociology of the Juridical Field," *Hastings Law Journal* 38 (1987): 805–853. Judgments issued by courts serve as "performative utterances," Bourdieu wrote, and thus constitute "acts of naming or of instituting." "Law," he contended, "is the quintessential form of the symbolic power of naming that creates the things named, and creates social groups in particular." Bourdieu understood this process as essentially unidirectional and hegemonic, a point of view that is relatively suspect. Still, I think attention to the naming process of law is critical, especially with regard to children, who have subjectivities written on their bodies by any number of actors. A useful analog can be found in slavery. See especially Stephanie Camp, *Closer to Freedom: Enslaved Women and Everyday Resistance in the Plantation South* (Chapel Hill, 2004), esp. Ch. 1; and Walter Johnson, *Soul by Soul: Life Inside the Antebellum Slave Market* (Cambridge, 2000), Chs. 2, 5.

[4] In other words, I am not proposing a return to "functionalism" or related approaches to sociolegal studies, nor do I see the courts as supplying a straightforward force for the "legitimation" of norms pronounced by elites. Rather, my view of law and society aims to

While high courts could not and did not directly alter the practices of working people or their employers, formal law nonetheless articulated new conceptions of youthful labor. During the first half of the nineteenth century, judicial discourse increasingly imagined young people as capable of judging their interests and acting for themselves. This change in legal imagination, however, provoked new questions about young people's agency and prompted a return to limitations of their legal status based on a shared conception of young people's natural incapacities. After the Civil War, the judicial imagination of youth turned more and more to the idea of young people ruled by their "childish impulses."[5]

A PERSONAL TRUST

When the nineteenth century began, existing legal rules regarding young people augured against their circulation in the labor market. Early in the century, jurists explicitly recognized and affirmed this fact, but as time wore on, judges weakened these proscriptions and slowly authorized wage bargains made by young workers. High court decisions by themselves had limited influence over the actual conditions of labor, but they affirmed the broader workings of the emerging market by providing an authoritative legal language for wage labor by young people. Youthful work would increasingly be seen as a species of the wider conceptions of work in a capitalist society, where toiling for cash wages negotiated in the marketplace constituted "labor," while unwaged toil inside or outside of the domestic sphere did not. In other words, the concept of child labor could emerge only after jurists and others wrote young people into the wider conception of wage labor itself.[6]

This juridical shift was critical for the emergence of child labor as a cultural and legal construct because prevailing statutory and common

encompass all parts of the legal process as well as actors outside of the juridical field. The rest of that story plays out over the final chapters. For a critique of legitimation theory, see Alan Hyde, "The Concept of Legitimation in the Sociology of Law," *Wisconsin Law Review* 2 (1983): 379–426.

[5] In recent years, some legal historians generally have downplayed formal law as a subject of study. For an extreme version of this perspective, see Randolph Bergstrom, *Courting Danger: Injury and Law in New York City, 1870–1910* (Ithaca, 1992), 195–196. It is certainly unfruitful to argue about sociolegal change solely from a source-base of appellate cases, but the pronouncements of high court judges did carry cultural weight. Along with reformers, jurists helped articulate new conceptions of "child labor."

[6] On the distinctions between domestic and waged labor, see Jeanne Boydston, *Home and Work: Housework, Wages, and the Ideology of Labor in the Early Republic* (New York, 1990).

law principles in the early Republic restrained full participation by minors in a capitalist labor market. In the eighteenth century and before, most children's work outside the household constituted a form of bound labor, not free labor. Formal indentures, either for apprenticeships or for simple service, exchanged labor in return for support and education. Written and sealed, such agreements represented a bargain between a parent, usually a father, and a master, not between a child and an employer. Long-standing legal precedents, often referred to as the "privilege of infancy," prevented minors from making contracts for anything other than necessaries or education. The law of infancy in no way sheltered young people in the way that later protective legislation did, nor did it mean that young people never worked for wages. Rather, apprenticeship and the broader law of infancy marked youthful labor in bound relationships regulated by statute as the only sort that was normal and legitimate.[7]

By its nature, apprenticeship created legal and cultural barriers to wage work for young people, for it comprised part of the body of law that undergirded the legal incapacity of minors and prevented them from making valid contracts. As such, apprenticeship formed part of the larger web of hierarchical arrangements that defined social relations between nominally free persons in early America: husband-wife, parent-child, master-servant, town officials-paupers. Unlike the fictional equality that would accompany the rise of a market society, all of these relationships presupposed a superior and a subordinate party. Whether true in reality or not, all assumed a reciprocal exchange of protection and support for obedience and, usually, labor. In turn, all presumed a certain level of disability on the part of the inferior party, in part because of imagined natural incapacities, but also because inferior parties were under the legal control of another and hence were not full legal persons. All of this meant that children could not be seen as a party to a contract, that legally they could not be understood as free laborers.[8]

The legalities of apprenticeship clashed directly with evolving notions of contract in late-eighteenth- and early-nineteenth-century America. In an indenture of apprenticeship, the child was not a party, although his or her third-party consent to the bargain might be required. Rather, the

---

[7] On the nature of household authority, see Carole Shammas, *A History of Household Government in America* (Charlottesville, 2002), Chs. 1–4; and Christopher Tomlins, "Subordination, Authority, Law: Subjects in Labor History," *International and Working Class History* 67 (1995): 56–90.

[8] Shammas, *History of Household Government*, esp. Ch. 4; Tomlins, "Subordination," 65–73.

exchange occurred between parent and master; it represented a transfer of the rights of one superior party to another. The master acted *in
loco parentis*, providing education and support in return for the minor's
labor. Furthermore, the law assumed that this bargain took place in a
face-to-face society, where master and parent knew and trusted each
other. Both the assumptions and practices of such relationships contradicted the social and legal relations of a market society, ideas that were
inchoate in the early Republic but held increasing sway as the nineteenth
century progressed. Labor law presumed adults, usually men. Adopting
the assumptions of Lockean liberalism, as well as the gendered meanings of republican manhood, it envisioned contracting parties as equals,
people who owned their own bodies, who possessed full legal personhood, and who could assess the value of their labor and the terms of
their employment. The apprenticeship of minors, like slavery and servitude, lay grounded in starkly different principles. Moreover, unlike adult
dependents in early America who could eventually be imagined within
the framework of contract, children presented an insurmountable natural
barrier to its expansion. At some young age, infants must necessarily be
defined as outside the assumptions of contract, for their physical development truly incapacitates them from exercising judgment and consent-
ing to a bargain. As the courts grappled with the contradictions between
apprenticeship and contract, they slowly resolved these tensions by creating separate bodies of law for children who worked for education and
support under apprenticeships and those who worked solely for wages
under other kinds of contracts. By the end of this process, children working solely for wages – a relationship once legally and culturally circumscribed – had come to be accepted as normal.[9]

The emergence of youthful labor as a matter of contract ungoverned
by statute depended on the maintenance of strict definitions for apprenticeship and bound labor. The matter arose in the first place because
older definitions of apprenticeship were coming under considerable

---

[9] On apprenticeship generally in this period, the standard work is W.J. Rorabaugh, *The
Craft Apprentice: From Franklin to the Industrial Age* (New York, 1986). See also Mary
Ann Mason, *From Father's Property to Children's Rights: The History of Child Custody
in the United States* (New York, 1994), 30–39, 76–81. On the legal history of apprentice-
ship, see Michael Grossberg, *Governing the Hearth: Law and the Family in Nineteenth-
Century America* (Chapel Hill, 1985): 259–268; Holly Brewer, "Age of Reason?: Children,
Testimony, and Consent in Early America" in *Many Legalities*, 316–329. For a treatment
of pauper apprenticeship using economic analysis, see John E. Murray and Ruth Herndon,
"Markets for Children in Early America: A Political Economy of Pauper Apprenticeship,"
Journal of Economic History 62 (2002): 356–382.

strain. In the period following the Revolution, young workers, parents, and town officials had begun to make agreements that, while called apprenticeships, looked more and more like simple wage work for children. Such arrangements might contain no provisions for education in general or training in a specific craft. Masters and parents frequently tried to sell indentures to other parties. More and more young people ran away, often close to the end of their indentures when their value to their masters was on the rise. The litigants in these cases brought conflicting understandings of children's work to the courts, looking for resolution. On the one hand, some sought approval of new kinds of apprentice contracts, ones that would still be binding but which would avoid the strict regulations imposed by statute. Others contended that parents no longer possessed the power to bargain away their children's labor.[10]

Confronted with the conflicts that these shifting social relations produced, jurists held the line. Cases that tested the power of statutory definitions usually preserved customary understandings of apprenticeship as a subordinate relation that would educate young people for lives as economic producers and more generally would inculcate them with values leading to the acceptance of authority. The important 1793 Pennsylvania decision in *Respublica v. Keppele* began to limit the use of non-apprenticeship indentures. In other Northeastern forums, especially Massachusetts, jurists refused to allow the assumptions of contract and market relations to penetrate the logic of apprenticeship. While they affirmed the need for a minor's consent, they also maintained the notion that infants remained third parties without full legal capacity. Apprenticeship would remain a binding indenture that required education and support in return for labor. More importantly, it would be conceived as a personal trust between a parent and a master, not an exchange between an employer and a youthful free worker.[11]

One particular type of apprenticeship litigation – involving attempts to "assign" (that is, trade) indentures between masters – brought these

---

[10] Rorabaugh, *Craft Apprentice*, 50–53; *Smith v. Hubbard*, 11 Mass. 24 (1814); *Power v. Ware*, 19 Mass. 451 (1824), 456; *Butler v. Hubbard*, 22 Mass. 250 (1827), 254. See also *Reidell v. Congdon*, 33 Mass. 44 (1834).

[11] *Respublica v. Keppele*, 1 Yeates 273 (Penn. 1793); *Commonwealth v. Hamilton*, 6 Mass. 273 (1810); *Harper v. Gilbert*, 59 Mass. 417 (1850); *Lobdell v. Allen*, 75 Mass. 377 (1857). On children and consent, see Brewer, "Age of Reason?," esp. 316–321, 325; and *By Birth or Consent: Children, Law, and the Anglo-American Revolution in Authority* (Chapel Hill, 2005).

issues to the surface and compelled jurists to clarify the distinctions between apprenticeship and child labor. The implications of this seemingly technical debate were immense, for if indentures could be assigned, then a market in apprentices as bound laborers could exist. This was not an idle question of law, for in the mid-Atlantic region brokers carried out a lively trade in apprentices well into the nineteenth century. The courts sought to end this practice. To reach this conclusion, judges drew two important lines. One affirmed apprenticeship as a personal relationship between two households. The nature of the indentures being assigned and the arguments made in favor of these agreements forced judges to draw a second line, one that distinguished a valid apprenticeship from a mere contract to work. As such, children's labor outside apprenticeship would become a form of "free" labor to be judged by common-law rules of contract, while formal apprenticeship itself remained a form of "unfree" labor to be examined by statutory guidelines.[12]

Much of the law regarding apprenticeship arose in the state of Massachusetts, whose courts manufactured authority for much of the rest of the nation during the antebellum period. In one of the earliest assignment cases, *Hall v. Gardner* (1804), the Supreme Judicial Court established a guiding principle – that apprenticeship was "a mere personal trust" and therefore could not be traded away. Another assignment case a few years later illuminated competing visions of children's work, one that looked backward to the customary place for apprenticeship, but another that looked forward to the contract regime of the nineteenth century. The latter view was voiced by Joseph Story, who argued the case shortly before taking his seat on the U.S. Supreme Court. Story rested his argument on the notion that the utility and indeed the legitimacy of such apprenticeship arrangements were to be judged by the criteria of benefit to and consent from the minor. In keeping with his commitment to using the law to promote economic development, Story envisioned a new kind of apprenticeship, one much closer to contract, wherein minors could leave bound relationships and circulate more freely in the labor market.[13]

---

[12] For examples of trading apprentices and brokering, see *Commonwealth v. Kendig*, 1 Serg. & Rawle 366 (Pa. 1815); *Commonwealth v. Vanlear*, 1 Serg. & Rawle 248 (Pa., 1815).

[13] *Hall v. Gardner*, 1 Mass. 172 (1804); *Davis v. Coburn*, 8 Mass (7 Tyng) 299 (1811), 305. On the nature and uses of contract language, see Amy Dru Stanley, *From Bondage to Contract: Wage Labor, Marriage, and the Market in the Age of Slave Emancipation* (New York, 1998), Chs. 1–2. On Story, the law, and economic development, see R. Kent Newmeyer, *Supreme Court Justice Joseph Story: Statesman of the Old Republic* (Chapel Hill, 1985), 65, 115–154, 403 n128.

Story's plea fell on deaf ears, none deafer than those of aging Federalist Theodore Sedgwick, who penned the opinion. Increasingly embittered by the rise of democratic politics and culture, the sixty-five-year-old justice insisted that apprenticeship must remain a special relationship, neither a cheap form of child slavery, nor an unbounded species of free labor. Apprenticeships were made by "wise and prudent" parents who sought "moral qualities" in a prospective master. Envisioning the relationship in this manner made it fundamentally incompatible with a free market in youthful labor, for it said that more than a consensual exchange of labor for cash was involved. More importantly, it left bargaining power entirely with parents, denying the growing reality that minors were, in truth, becoming parties to labor contracts.[14]

The boundaries that the court was beginning to erect between apprenticeship and contract appear even more clearly in *Day v. Everett*, considered a year before *Davis v. Coburn*. The case presented directly the question of whether apprenticeship could be used to legitimate an arrangement that was more or less wage work. In July 1799, Levi Day bound his son to Aaron Everett for six years in return for a series of payments, the last of which remained unpaid at the time of the suit. Everett's attorney took a novel position. A proviso in the 1794 apprenticeship statute that stipulated all benefits must accrue directly to the minor, he argued, had all but outlawed fathers binding out their children for money.[15] Theophilus Parsons, who would later write a leading American treatise on contract law, used the opinion to clarify the growing distinction between apprenticeship and children's labor contracts. Parsons moved quickly to squelch the notion that the 1794 statute had taken away fathers' rights to sell their sons' labor to others for a fixed period. Rather, the 1794 act outlined the statutory constraints on both masters and apprentices. An apprentice was liable to corporal punishment, compulsory return, and discharge for "gross misbehavior." Conversely, the law also constrained masters, for it allowed apprentices to seek discharge for cruel treatment. Arrangements

---

[14] *Davis v. Coburn*, 305. On anti-slavery in New England, see Joanne Pope Melish, *Disowning Slavery: Gradual Emancipation and "Race" in New England, 1780–1860* (Ithaca, 1998), 68, 100–101. For biographical information on Sedgwick, see Richard E. Welch, Jr., *Theodore Sedgwick: A Political Portrait* (Middletown, 1965). Such a line of thinking could show up in the most unlikely of places, such as in the slave state of Kentucky. See *Shult v. Travis*, 2 Ky. 142 (1802); *Hudnut v. Bullock*, 10 Ky. 299 (1821); *Davenport v. Gentry's Administrator*, 48 Ky. 427 (1849).

[15] *Day v. Everett*, 7 Mass. 145 (1810), 146. For an extended discussion of this case, see Janet L. Dolgin, "Transforming Childhood: Apprenticeship in American Law," *New England Law Review* 31 (1997): 1132–1138.

that did not conform to the statute would be held valid, but, and here was the crux of the matter, parties could not avail themselves of its powers and limitations, a situation that "parents and guardians, as well as masters, ought duly to consider."[16]

Cited frequently in other states and enshrined by treatise writers as a leading case, *Day* helped validate a type of child labor becoming increasingly common in the first half of the nineteenth century. Numerous cases from elsewhere demonstrate that during the first few decades of the century children frequently worked in arrangements that were neither apprenticeships nor contracts but rather a hybrid of both. As with Levi Day's son, these young workers found themselves placed by parents into long-term arrangements, sometimes merely for cash, sometimes for training and support, sometimes for both. Parents, children, and employers often believed they had formed an apprenticeship, or at least some type of bound relationship, only to find that they had failed when the matter came to court after a dispute. With earlier understandings of children's work as their point of reference, such people thought that they had obligated both sides to abide by the long-standing customary and legal rights and restrictions. Cases such as *Day v. Everett* presented courts with the opportunity to broaden the authority of apprenticeship statutes beyond their increasingly irrelevant application to the arrangements people were actually making. Instead of allowing statutory or customary regulations of apprenticeship to apply in these cases, decisions such as *Day* cordoned off apprenticeship as a special form of child labor, one not likely to evolve with the market revolution.[17]

Taken together, the legal changes in apprenticeship marked an important turning point in the legal history of children's wage work. Responding to disputed arrangements that no longer fit eighteenth-century structures of domestic and labor law, the bench sought to protect those structures nonetheless. By preserving apprenticeship in its eighteenth-century form, the courts maintained the powers of masters and parents, and more importantly, confirmed the legal incapacity of

---

[16] *Day v. Everett*, 7 Mass. 145 (1810), 147–149.

[17] For examples of labor agreements in other states, see *Weeks v. Leighton*, 5 N.H. 343 (1831); *McCoy v. Huffman*, 8 Cow. (N.Y.) 84 (1827). In part, these developments help to explain the tortured history of apprenticeship in the wake of emancipation. The best in-depth treatment of the subject is Karin Zipf, *Labor of Innocents: Forced Apprenticeship in North Carolina, 1715–1919* (Baton Rouge, 2005). See also Laura Edwards, *Gendered Strife and Confusion: The Political Culture of Reconstruction* (Urbana, 1997), 43–44, 47–54; Barbara Jeanne Fields, *Slavery and Freedom on the Middle Ground: Maryland During the Nineteenth Century* (New Haven, 1985), 139–156.

minors. By drawing these legal lines, however, the courts created a new set of questions about how to treat the rest of children's work. Working parents and children continued to make labor agreements that did not conform to statutory or judicial rules. With apprenticeship set apart as a formal relationship, the legitimacy of other work arrangements had to be judged by common-law rules that governed adult wage work, not by older statutory regulations that had applied to minors. While the discourse of contract incorporated many of the tenets of household governance, the opposite occurred as well: It opened up previously unchallenged hierarchies to matters of will, consent, and reciprocity. For young people, it brought their customary status as natural and legal dependents into question.[18]

INDEPENDENT AGENTS

At the same time apprenticeship occupied the judicial imagination, the courts slowly worked out a set of contract rules for children's wage work. Doing so required resolution of a critical contradiction, both in the rules themselves and in the broader legalities of childhood and labor. On the one hand, custom and precedent granted fathers an absolute right to their children's wages and stipulated that minors themselves could not make binding contracts for anything more than support or education. Consequently, young people could not enter the labor market as their own agents unless they had been "emancipated" from the control of their fathers, or "given their time," in the parlance of the day. Bargains made by unemancipated minors were automatically void, or at least, voidable. On the other hand, developing labor law for adults held all labor contracts to be binding, authorizing employers to withhold wages from workers who quit without permission. This legal contradiction raised fundamental questions about the legitimacy of children's work outside apprenticeship and about the larger issue of rights and obligations of children in a capitalist society. By 1860, the courts had resolved the legal contradictions by fashioning two new rules about children's labor contracts. One allowed minors to break their agreements at will while holding their employers bound to their half of the bargain. A second precept, "implied emancipation" (or "implied assent"), supplied a fictional way around parental control of minors' earnings. In reaching this conclusion, the courts began

[18] Tomlins, "Subordination," 70–71.

to erode children's legal incapacity, increasingly envisioning young people as agents in a capitalist labor market.[19]

Like much of American labor law, legal changes for young workers in the early nineteenth century took place in the Northeast, once again in Massachusetts. Emancipating young people from household government was certainly not the intention of Bay State jurists. In the early Republic, the same court that policed the boundaries of apprenticeship upheld fathers' rights to their children's earnings as well. For the jurists of the early nineteenth century, the legitimacy of father's rights rested on reciprocity, but it was the organic reciprocity of the preindustrial household and its systems of authority. In 1825, for instance, Massachusetts Chief Justice Isaac Parker declared that children who left home to avoid parental discipline carried no credit with them, for if they did, "parental influence" would be greatly reduced and children might be inclined to withdraw from the "government" of their fathers.[20]

In the industrializing Northeast, fatherly governance increasingly grated against the workings of the region's developing market in labor. Youthful labor outside the home came to the forefront of public discussion with the emergence of textiles and railroads, but it did not commence in those typical industrial sites, nor was it confined to them. Labor historians have long known that the expansion of small-shop production constituted the first stage of "industrialization" in British North America and the United States. Moreover, historians who study the "transformation of the countryside" have outlined the ways in which the dissolution of the agrarian economy pushed generations of young people into towns and cities. There, they found work in places that increasingly practiced capitalist labor relations but that would not qualify as "industrial labor" by traditional definitions. While a good deal of lawmaking for young

[19] Stanley, *From Bondage to Contract*, esp. Ch. 5; Witt, "Rethinking the Nineteenth-Century Employment Contract, Again," 9–10; Brewer, *By Birth or Consent*, 264–271; Robert Steinfeld, *Coercion, Contract, and Free Labor in the Nineteenth Century* (New York, 2001), esp. Ch. 9.

[20] *Benson v. Remington*, 2 Mass. 113 (1804); *Angel v. McLellan*, 16 Mass. 28 (1819), 32. See also *Dawes v. Howard*, 4 Mass. 97 (1808). On mothers, see *Whipple v. Dow*, 2 Mass. 415 (1807). On stepfathers, see *Freto v. Brown*, 4 Mass. 675 (1808). On fathers's rights generally, see Grossberg, *Governing the Hearth*, Ch. 7; and Brewer, *By Birth or Consent*, Ch. 7. On growing concerns about young people circulating freely in urban society, see Karen Haltunnen, *Confidence Men and Painted Women: A Study in Middle-Class Culture* (New Haven, 1982), Chs. 1–2. On Parker, see Russell K. Osgood, "Isaac Parker: Republican Judge, Federalist Values" in *The History of the Law in Massachusetts: The Supreme Judicial Court 1691–1992* ed. Russell K. Osgood (Boston, 1992), 153–170.

people in the antebellum era involved farm labor, another good chunk involved these sorts of arrangements. That was especially true for the cases that articulated a free market for young workers. Moreover, some apprenticeship arrangements governed a type of youthful labor that was anything but a re-creation of the family model.[21]

The fluidity of youthful labor in the early nineteenth century is well illustrated by the northeastern whaling business. Boys and young men often enlisted for lengthy terms on ships without or with only partial consent of their parents. For instance, Robert Gray Smith, son of Pardon Smith, embarked on a whaling ship after having been apprenticed to a blacksmith. About nineteen years old at the time of the voyage, he appears to have undertaken the venture on his own volition. Fourteen-year-old John H. Vent, who sailed in June 1833 on the *Samuel Wright* with the consent of his mother but then jumped ship in Talcahuano, Mexico, somehow got home and sued for his wages. Merrick Wodell shipped from on the brig *Taunton* from Fall River without his father's consent and against his father's will. A boy "of vagrant habits," Merrick sometimes had found work in factories, but he "soon ran away and got into mischief." As a result, he had occasionally been in the almshouse and in the house of correction for larceny. Apparently, his mother signed him up on the *Taunton* not only for employment but also for punishment. Getting wind of the arrangement, Merrick's father, John, tried unsuccessfully to prevent the captain of the *Taunton* from taking Merrick to sea.[22]

All of these incidents involved considerable erosion in household governance. Increasingly common over the course of the early nineteenth century, such work arrangements compelled jurists to find new ways around the law of infancy. In *Nightingale v. Withington* (1818), Isaac Parker discovered for the first time what became a key part of the legal solution to the contradictions presented by children's labor bargains: implied emancipation. Generally, fathers' rights to their children's earnings rested on the obligation of support. "But," Parker declared, "where the father has discharged himself of the obligation to support the child, or has obliged the child to support himself, there is no principle but that of slavery,

[21] The literature on the transformation of the countryside is immense. For examples pertaining to Massachusetts, see Christopher Clark, *The Roots of Rural Capitalism: Western Massachusetts, 1780–1860* (Ithaca, 1990); and Daniel Vickers, *Farmers and Fishermen: Two Centuries of Work in Essex County, Massachusetts, 1630–1850* (Chapel Hill, 1994).

[22] *Manchester v. Smith*, 29 Mass. 113 (1831); *Randall v. Rotch*, 29 Mass. 110 (1831); *Nickerson v. Easton*, 29 Mass. 107 (1831); *Wodell v. Coggeshall*, 43 Mass. 89 (1840).

which will continue his right to receive the earnings of the child's labor."
In such a situation, he reasoned, the law would allow free labor for young
people. "Thus, if the father should refuse to support a son, should deny
him a home, and force him to labor abroad for his own living, or should
give or sell him his time, as is sometimes done in the country," he pointed
out, "the law will imply an emancipation of the son." The latter practice, giving or selling a son his time, was "certainly questionable, as to
any promise in consideration of it." Yet, the courts would allow minors
under such circumstances to make contracts directly for their own benefit. Clearly, the authority of fathers had its limits. If they did not live up
to their obligations, then their children might become free agents.[23]

Cited across the course of the nineteenth century, Parker's opinion in
Nightingale offered a way of understanding children's work when fatherly
obligations had broken down. Seven years later the court affirmed the
notion of implied parental assent under more normal circumstances.
Letting sons seek their own wages, Parker wrote in 1825, encouraged
youth and relieved fathers of the burden of support. When young men
sought work on their own and their fathers did not object, "an implied
assent" to sons keeping their earnings arose. In essence, Parker unwittingly
backed away from patriarchy, but he envisioned a father still firmly in
control, one who knew the situation and gave his implied consent. While
unintentional, Parker's opinions had started to break down the remaining
barriers to full legitimation of children bargaining for their own wages.[24]

Implied emancipation would eventually become an established doctrine that would legitimate labor market participation by young people,
but Parker and others reached this point by trying to reconcile young
men's propensity to "seek their fortunes in the world" with "the discipline
and restraint" of family governance. Implied emancipation presented an
elegant compromise that preserved the essential language of paternal
authority and children's legal incapacity – hence, the need for "emancipation" – even while it sanctioned social relations that undermined these
very assumptions. If implied emancipation envisioned minors as potential agents to contracts, the question still remained as to whether those
contracts bound them. In another opinion, Parker started to resolve this
question by declaring that minors were not bound by their agreements
and could leave at will.[25]

[23] *Nightingale v. Withington*, 15 Mass. 272 (1818), 274–275.
[24] *Whiting v. Earle*, 20 Mass. 201 (1825), 202.
[25] Ibid.; *Moses v. Stevens*, 19 Mass. 332 (1824). On patriarchy and the courts, see
Grossberg, *Governing the Hearth*, esp. 289–307; and Peter Bardaglio, *Reconstructing the*

Litigations in the early Republic sought to preserve parental authority and undergird a minor's legal incapacity, but in the end, they created a new set of rules and legalities about children's wage work. During the 1830s, the Massachusetts court under Chief Justice Lemuel Shaw affirmed the rules established by Parker and his brethren, but jettisoned their backward-looking vision of parental authority and child subordination. The Shaw court saw minors as legal persons, capable of making contracts for work in their own right. In an 1837 litigation involving George Corey, age thirteen, Shaw acknowledged the transformation of the New England countryside, noting "the ordinary case of young men under twenty-one coming in from the country seeking employment." Surveying the range of wage-bargaining practices, Shaw concluded that "the very offer of service" implied that a young person had parental consent to seek employment. In other words, employers could bargain directly with children on the implied assurance that good fathers had granted their consent. To this widening definition of parental assent, Shaw added a broadened definition of children's legal capacity. When a father gave permission to seek employment, his son "became, to a certain extent, independent, with a power to act in his own right, and then having performed services entitling him to compensation, he had a right to recover it in his own name to his own use." This conclusion represented a long journey from the notions of parental authority intoned by earlier justices and a considerable distance from the assumptions of formal apprenticeship as well. Children as young as thirteen could make their own contracts based on the implied assent of their fathers and be considered independent agents in the marketplace. By such resolutions of the law's contradictions, children's wage work achieved a new level of legal and cultural legitimacy.[26]

If children could make contracts for themselves and those agreements would be considered binding on employers for wages, it would seem to follow that such contracts would be binding on minors as to performance. A series of cases in New Hampshire and New York had brought the notion of children's ability to avoid labor contracts into question. Treatise writers struggled with this question as well. The eminent James Kent in his *Commentaries on American Law* described the issue as fraught with "much contradiction and confusion." Most courts and

---

Household: Families, Sex, and the Law in the Nineteenth-Century South (Chapel Hill, 1995).
[26] *Manchester v. Smith*, 29 Mass. 113 (1831), 115; *Corey v. Corey*, 36 Mass. 29 (1837). See Brewer, *By Birth or Consent*, 271–287 for a contrary view of children's labor contracts.

treatise authors settled this matter by leaving the question of whether a contract was binding or not up to young people themselves. Contracts such as that by John Vent were voidable "at the election of the infant," Justice Putnam wrote for the Massachusetts court in 1837. Employers should be aware of this basic fact. In short, Putnam declared, the owners "were to be bound; but the infant was to be at liberty to avoid the agreement."[27]

Over the course of the antebellum era, courts around the country followed the path opened by Massachusetts jurists. Lucius E. Chittenden, the editor for the second edition of Tapping Reeve's essential *Law of Baron and Femme*, put the matter bluntly in 1846. "The relation of parent and child is so far relaxed," he noted, that fathers may at any time relinquish their claims on children's wages. Looking to their eastern associates for guidance, a team of California lawyers at mid-century argued that "emancipation of the child, as it is called" could be "inferred from the slightest evidence." California's high court went even further a few years later. "The power of a father to emancipate his minor child cannot be questioned," Justice Shafter wrote in 1864. "The child is freed by emancipation from parental control; he can claim his earnings thereafter as against his father, and is in all respects his own man." The Superior Court of Delaware outlined how emancipation might take place in an 1868 opinion. It could be by abandonment of parental responsibility or by express agreement, or it might be "implied from the conduct and relations of the parties." If a father knowingly permitted his son to enter contracts and manage his own affairs, or even if he made no objection to such an arrangement, "the emancipation, or freedom of the son to labor for his own living, may be inferred," Justice Gilpin pointed out. Gilpin's vision of the way young workers entered the labor market covered most conceivable scenarios. Young people might work with or without the knowledge and support of their parents, but under all circumstances, they could manage their own affairs and obtain their own wages.[28]

By mid-century, then, a new legal regime for young workers had arrived. During the years since the close of the Revolutionary era, the

---

[27] *Vent v. Osgood*, 36 Mass. 572 (1837), 573; *Weeks v. Leighton*, 5 N.H. 343 (1831); James Kent, *Commentaries on American Law*, Volume II (New York, 1827), 192; Tapping Reeve, *The Law of Baron and Femme*, 2nd Ed., (Burlington, 1846), 250–255.

[28] Reeve, *Law of Baron and Femme*, 1846, 290, n2; *Swartz v. Hazlett*, 8 Cal. 118 (1857), 121; *Lackman v. Wood*, 25 Cal. 147 (1864), 151; *Farrell v. Farrell*, 8 Del. 633 (1868), 639; *The Etna*, 8 Fed. Cas. 803 (1838). For an extended discussion of these matters in case law at the end of the nineteenth century, see *Halliday v. Miller*, 29 W.Va. 424 (1887);

courts had found a solution to the conflict between labor law and the law of childhood by imagining contracts by children as having taken place after an implied emancipation or with the implied assent of parents and by allowing minors to break their contracts at will. In the process, jurists further freed children to circulate in the labor market. All of this is not to say that courts simply reflected developing capitalist social relations, or that they took an instrumentalist role in serving the needs of business. Instead, it is to argue that existing legal rules shaped these litigations, both in terms of the opinions of jurists and the behavior of the parties.[29]

The working people who built America certainly did not consult the voluminous production of the nation's courts, nor can it be said that elite opinion writing simply trickled down to the mines and mills. Still, the conditions of youthful labor did force the nation's jurists to address directly the place of young people in a capitalist society well before that concern became a burning issue for reformers. Over the decades before the Civil War, law writers repeatedly took up that question and articulated one vision of where young people belonged. In their imaginative constructions, young workers moved out of the statutory regimes of bound labor in households and into the market society of industrializing capitalism. This refashioning of the terms of youthful labor aligned well with the fluid nature of work actually being performed by young workers in the antebellum era, and it drew upon conceptions that working people themselves brought to legal tribunals. In the main, neither working people nor their employers consciously engaged in wage negotiations with a direct knowledge of the law in mind. Labor negotiations were a delicate dance, often based on cues that invoked legal categories but did not speak to them directly. This latter dynamic appeared even more frequently as the century progressed, as working families continued to insist upon an industrial regime that contained a safe place for young workers. Nonetheless, the words of elites did matter. Through a lengthy and uneven process, the judicial imagination of youthful labor reached

and *Watson v. Kemp*, 59 N.Y.S. 142 (1899). A series of opinions in New York had also helped establish the idea of implied emancipation. See *Burlingame v. Burlingame*, 7 Cow. 92 (1827); *McCoy v. Huffman*, 8 Cow. 84 (1827); and *Shute v. Dorr*, 5 Wend. 204 (1830). For later cases applying these rules in Massachusetts, see *Stiles v. Granville*, 60 Mass. 458 (1850); and *Abbott v. Converse*, 86 Mass. 530 (1862).

[29] On the relationship between legal rules and social change, see Steinfeld, *Coercion, Contract, and Free Labor in the Nineteenth Century*, 234; and Witt, "Rethinking the Nineteenth-Century Employment Contract, Again," 2–5. On instrumentalism and antebellum labor law, see Morton J. Horwitz, *The Transformation of American Law, 1780–1850* (Cambridge, 1977), 186–188.

working people. As we shall see later on, the primary conduits were lower court judges, attorneys, and the legal process itself.

Beyond the promulgation of rules, law helped to construct emerging notions of child labor by providing a language through which children's wage work outside the household could be imagined. That language envisioned young people as legal persons in a market society. Thirteen-year-old George Corey became an "independent agent." Fourteen-year-old John Vent acquired the ability to "judge for himself." Such characterizations of young people struck at the heart of older legal and cultural conventions about childhood and labor, constructs that constrained labor market participation by young people and imagined them as incapable of the acts of volition and consent that were coming to earmark "freedom." Judicial discourse helped remove those incapacities, but in doing so, antebellum jurists forced those who followed them to consider young people's capacity to judge the dangers of their newfound liberty.

CHILDISH INSTINCTS

In figuring out the place of children's work arrangements in capitalist society, jurists had followed the logical extension of contract thinking. To the extent that they could, given the weight of wisdom received from the eighteenth century, the courts had eased their young charges into the swelling stream of emancipation that rushed through the mid-nineteenth-century United States. While young workers might still be under the nominal control of their elders, that power was "much relaxed." At the same time, however, jurists confronted the problems associated with kids running at large. A growing population and an expanding transportation system brought young people into the streets, roads, and byways with inevitably tragic consequences. The accidents produced by encounters between travelers and children would dramatically alter the way the law understood young people, just as it reformulated liberty and liability for adults. Street and rail accidents frequently involved play, blending them with mishaps that occurred off-road. In particular, the merry-go-rounds provided by rail yard turntables sharpened the question of what could reasonably be expected of young people. Meant to turn around locomotives, these deadly yet attractive devices tempted youngsters to take a spin. The resulting tragedies produced an endless source of inspiration for jurists to talk about the natural inclinations of children. The answers to these questions created a counter to the youthful independence envisioned by jurists who discussed contracts. While law writers initially aligned young people and their parents with the notions of personal accountability that rang through contract thinking, they eventually concurred that "childish instincts and impulses" could not and should not be squelched.[30]

These ideas evolved from a seemingly arcane question in the law of negligence. If a driver struck a child in the road, who was to blame: the driver, the child, or the parents? With the very young, children themselves clearly could not be held responsible for their own actions. They were, in the pidgin of the law, *non sui juris*, not legal persons. If children themselves were not accountable for their actions, could those who injured them be held consistently at fault, and hence liable for damages? This, too, seemed dubious, for everyone knew that children could dart unexpectedly into the roadway. The initial solution, proffered by prominent New York jurist Esek Cowen in 1839 in the notorious *Hartfield v. Roper*, was to "impute" the faults of neglectful parents to their children. Thus began the bumpy travels of "imputed negligence," immediately maligned by other high courts, eventually excoriated by treatise writers, and finally spurned by most tribunals across the country. Most legal minds could not accept that the sins of the fathers could be visited upon the sons. Instead, they redefined the sons.[31]

The incident that triggered this line of thinking played out like a Currier and Ives print: a brisk winter afternoon; a cherubic youngster placidly contemplating the snow; a merry team trotting with a sleigh behind. Coming down a hill, the driver, his daughter, and their companion never saw two-year-old William Hartfield until they had passed over him. William sustained a severe break in his arm, leading to several months of painful recovery and mounting doctor bills. Who should bear the responsibility? Judge Cowen had a ready answer. While young William's accident was a "very serious misfortune," he pointed the finger directly at William's father, Gabriel. "A snow path in the public highway, is among the last places in this country to which such a small child should be allowed to resort, unattended by any one of suitable age and discretion," Cowen informed the Hartfield family. "It is the extreme of folly even to turn domestic animals upon the common highway. To allow small children to resort there alone, is a criminal neglect." True, children had a

---

[30] Barbara Young Welke, *Recasting American Liberty: Gender, Race, Law, and the Railroad Revolution, 1865–1920* (New York, 2001).

[31] *Hartfield v. Roper*, 21 Wend. 615 (N.Y., 1839); R. Perry Sentell, Jr., "Torts in Verse: The Foundational Cases," *Georgia Law Review* 39 (Summer 2005): 1257.

right to the road, but if accidents happened as a result of mischief, drivers could not be held responsible. The application of such ideas, devised for adults, "may be harsh when made to small children, as they are known to have no personal discretion, [and] common humanity is alive to their protection," Cowen conceded. Hence, he looked to the parents. Lacking discretion as well as legal identities, children naturally fell to the protection of others, and if that protection failed, those who neglected their duties could be held accountable. "The law has placed infants in the hands of vigilant and generally affectionate keepers, their own parents," Cowen intoned, "and if there be any legal responsibility in damages, it lies upon them."[32]

Cowen's position at once maintained older notions of parental authority and protection, and implicitly acknowledged the growing pressure to treat young people as legal actors. He did not simply accept the tendencies in the law of infancy to see all young people as *non sui juris*. Rather, he made the matter one of child development. "At the tender age of two or three years, and even more, the infant cannot personally exercise that degree of discretion, which becomes instinctive at an advanced age, and for which the law must make him responsible, through others," Cowen declared. The reason for this judicial sleight of hand was so "the doctrine of mutual care between the parties using the road" could be enforced. In other words, the law expected rational actors to come before the bench. Children as young as William manifestly were not that, so the law required an act of imagination to allow the promulgation of rules applicable with seeming equanimity to fictionally equal litigants. Much as Cowen wanted to exclude William Hartfield from legal personhood, the logic of the law pulled him in that direction.[33]

The strict line taken by Esek Cowen found some adherents in nineteenth-century courtrooms. New York and Massachusetts stuck to a line of thinking that placed responsibility for street and eventually railway accidents either on parents or on children themselves. By 1868, New York's Court of Appeals could maintain that the doctrine in *Hartfield* was settled law in New York, "notwithstanding a somewhat different rule" elsewhere. In the Bay State, the courts had followed a similar tack, sometimes resolving the contradictions for older children by holding them responsible. This latter position was best expressed by Walbridge A. Field in *Collins v. South Boston Railroad* (1886). Invoking the game of

---

[32] *Hartfield v. Roper*, 618–621.
[33] Ibid., 619.

chicken, Field acknowledged that a "spirit of recklessness or of mischief" might be found in all children, but he also pointed toward young people's "capacity of self-control, and their intelligence and ability to understand … danger." Hence, children could be expected to exercise a reasonable amount of care for their age and experience, a question to be determined as a matter of fact by juries. If children ran headlong into danger, Field declared, "they should take the risks." Young people should not be allowed "impunity" to "indulge" in dangerous conduct just because they were "often reckless and mischievous." Field's resolution of the problem of children in the streets took the logic of emancipation to its furthest extent and drew upon conventional wisdom at the same time. In essence, he was the perturbed father saying: "You should have known better."[34]

The hard line taken by the nation's two fonts of legal authority did not go unchallenged. In fact, by the time of the Civil War, the principles of parental responsibility announced in *Hartfield* had been rejected in many other states. As a result, a new judicial vision of childhood began to emerge, an ever-expansive redefinition of young people as unable to control their own actions. Such had not been the intention of the early reactions to Judge Cowen's austere sermonizing. When high courts in Vermont and New Hampshire considered similar incidents, they only needed to follow a leading English case, *Lynch v. Nurdin* (1841). There, the Queen's Bench had determined that children could only be expected to exercise the "ordinary care" that was ordinary for their ages. In practice, this apparently circular rule left determining what could be expected up to juries, men of the community seemingly more acquainted with the community members who stood before them. In an important 1850 opinion, Isaac Redfield spoke for the Vermont court in declaring the English solution superior to *Hartfield*. A year earlier, the New Hampshire court had similarly adopted *Lynch*, noting a rhetorical question that court after court would answer in the affirmative. For a child, "without judgment or discretion," Judge Church wrote, juries might consider "whether or not the acts done by him, were not rather the result of childish instinct, which the defendant might easily have foreseen." To say, as a matter of law, that children possessed no discretion might be going too far, but the law would not "require the same acts of caution and prudence in a child, as in a man." Taken together, these two New English cases became an effective roadblock to the spread of extreme

[34] *Mangam v. Brooklyn Railroad Co.*, 38 N.Y. 455 (1868), 457; *Collins v. South Boston Railroad*, 142 Mass. 301 (1886), 315.

accountability proposed by Cowen, and they opened the door to wider definitions of just how irresponsible children were.[35]

As more and more high courts came to oppose the notions in *Hartfield* and adopt the English way, judicial language about childhood became more expansive and expressive. The Supreme Court of Pennsylvania had the opportunity to comment on the subject in a set of litigations in 1858. Like their brethren elsewhere, they explicitly spurned Judge Cowen's exactions, but they went further in their discussion of what could be and could not be expected of youngsters. Penned by George Washington Woodward, the opinion in *Rauch v. Lloyd* respectfully disagreed with a lower court judge who had informed a jury that young children should be "kept under the eye and control" of their parents. Instead of this logic, based as it was on *Hartfield*, Woodward adopted the reflexive reasoning of his English and New English colleagues, concluding that "children are to be held responsible only for the discretion of children." Woodward could have stopped there, but he proceeded to discourse upon encounters between children and railroads. "Of what imprudence was this little boy guilty?" he asked. "Living beside the railroad he had become familiar with cars, and had probably lost much of that instinctive dread with which they are regarded at first." If so, the dangers of the rail yard would be "as likely to attract as to repel him." Beyond the lack of fear, however, Charles Rauch lacked elemental reason, and perhaps humanity. "Are transporters by railroad to be responsible for all the irrational animals that may get under their cars?" Woodward continued. "Certainly not. If sheep, or hogs, or children, incapable of reasoning, are permitted to wander in forbidden places," the railroads were not duty-bound to offer ironclad protection. Still, young Rauch could not be held to adult standards. "He acted like a child," Woodward declared, "and he is not to be judged as a man."[36]

Views such as Woodward's did more than simply establish standards of law in accident cases. They offered a vision of childhood in

---

[35] *Lynch v. Nurdin*, 1 Ad. & El. (n.s.) 29, [41 E.C.L. 422,]; *Robinson v. Cone*, 22 Vt. 213 (1850), 226; *Birge v. Gardener*, 19 Conn. 507 (1849), 512. For an early contemporary criticism, see "Contributory Negligence on the Part of an Infant," *The American Law Review* (1870): 405–416.

[36] *Rauch v. Lloyd and Hill*, 31 Pa. 358 (1858), 370–371. The other opinion is *Pennsylvania Railroad Co. v. Kelly*, 31 Pa. 372 (1858). In 1858, the Tennessee court also adopted the line proceeding from *Lynch v. Nurdin*. See *Whirley v. Whiteman*, 38 Tenn. 610 (1858). On the interconnections between children and animals, see Susan Pearson, "'The Rights of the Defenseless': Animals, Children, and Sentimental Liberalism in Nineteenth-Century America" (Ph.D. Dissertation, University of North Carolina-Chapel Hill, 2004), 42–93.

industrial society at odds with what came both before and after. This judicial language led in two directions. On the one hand, it diminished young people to impulsive actors, scarcely possessed of consciousness, much less rationality. On the other, it led towards a radical assertion of freedom: that children had a right to the streets that adults were bound to respect. A series of litigations between the late antebellum years and the close of the century announced and expanded this right, so at odds with the street-clearing exertions of the Children's Aid Society and other child savers.

This line of thinking also rejected assertions about parental responsibility, and not infrequently accounted for the real lives of working people in the country's burgeoning urban centers. In 1854, for instance, the Supreme Court of Illinois affirmed that children had a right to the streets, noting that laboring parents were "unable to employ nurses, who may keep a constant and vigilant eye momentarily upon their children." Hence, it could not be said that mothers whose children ended up in the streets were responsible for their injuries. By the late nineteenth century, children's right to the streets had reached spectacular heights in the judicial imagination, evincing the distance traveled from *Hartfield*'s austerity. Nowhere was this clearer than in an 1893 West Virginia litigation that echoed the theme of class offered by the Illinois court in 1857. "Children are not responsible for the choice of their parents nor the place or condition of their birth," Justice Dent wrote. If children could not find playgrounds elsewhere, Dent opined, the public byways belonged to them. "It is a right they have immemorially enjoyed, and should continue to enjoy as long as the public fails to provide them other free commons, where they can have the pure air, bright sunshine and sportive exercise so necessary to the healthful growth of their sensitive bodies," he concluded. While few jurists went as far as Dent, his image of children at public play encapsulated much of what his less effusive brethren had erected during the postbellum era. Before the playground movement safely penned youngsters in parks, the judiciary found a place for them in the streets, expanding the notion that "childish instincts" must be expected even in the roadways.[37]

---

[37] *Chicago v. Major*, 18 Ill. 349 (1857), 361; *Gibson v. Huntington*, 38 W.Va. 177 (1893), 179–180. For other opinions tending in this direction, see *Kerr v. Forgue*, 54 Ill. 482 (1870); *Moore v. Metropolitan Railroad Co.*, 2 Mackey 437 (D.C., 1883); *Kunz v. Troy*, 104 N.Y. 344 (1887); *Spengler v. Williams*, 67 Miss. 1 (1889); *Evers v. Philadelphia Traction Co.*, 176 Pa. 376 (1896); *Kreiner v. Straubmuller*, 30 Pa. Super. 609 (1906); and especially *Irvine v. Greenwood*, 89 S.C. 511 (1911), 523–524. This is certainly not to say

The nation's bench also discovered other locations for young folks to amuse themselves, particularly in rail yards. If street accident litigations sired the notion of childish instinct, the so-called turntable cases and the subsequent debates about "attractive nuisance" nurtured it. Here, authority came from the highest courts in the land. Originating in the small town of Blair, Nebraska, the case of Henry Stout and his parents against the Sioux City Railroad Company ushered in several decades of judicial contemplation about how much duty landowners owed to youngsters who might sneak in for some fun. Many of these cases, Henry Stout's included, concerned railroad turntables, machines meant to turn locomotives when they got to the end of the line. Groups of children made a habit of entering rail yards to play on the dangerous but inviting apparatus. Some would work the levers, while others jumped on for a ride. Inevitably, somebody's foot would get caught in the fasteners. Debilitating injury and sometimes death resulted. Henry Stout and his older companions had imitated their peers elsewhere, meeting at the road's depot in Blair on March 29, 1869. Someone in the group suggested heading for the turntable, even though the boys had been previously warned away from the device by the yardman. When it came Henry's turn to jump on, his six-year-old strength failed him. He caught his foot between the rail and the spinning table, cutting and crushing the appendage.[38]

When the Stout family's injury suit against the railroad came before Justice Dundy in the federal district court for Nebraska in 1872, he cast the matter directly against the duty of parental responsibility propounded by the New York and Massachusetts courts. Fathers had the duty to protect their offspring, Dundy acknowledged, but they could not be held accountable if children wandered off. Children could not be "tied up and confined as we confine our domestic animals," Dundy pointed out. "Most, if not all, of us who are at all conversant [*sic*] with human nature, and understand the difficulties growing out of the parental relation, know full well how easy it is for children six or eight years of age to escape the watchful care and vigilance of parents for the purpose of indulging in childlike

that courts relieved parents of all negligence. In cases of older children or clear parental neglect, the courts usually indemnified municipalities or common carriers. For example, see *Dowd v. Brooklyn Heights Railroad Co.*, 29 N.Y.S. 745 (1894); *Cauley v. East St. Louis Electric Street Railroad Co.*, 58 Ill. App. 151 (1894).

[38] *Railroad v. Stout*, 84 U.S. 657 (1874). For a detailed description of turntable accidents, see *Edgington v. Burlington, Cedar Rapids & Northern Railway Co.*, 116 Iowa 410 (1902), 411–416. The description of Henry's accident comes from the U.S. Circuit Court report of the case. See *Stout v. Sioux City & P.R. Co.*, 23 F. Cas. 183 (1872).

FIGURE 7. The legal minds who created the language of childish instincts frequently reviewed accidents involving railroad turntables such as this one from Petersburg, Virginia, ca. 1865. Andrew J. Russell. Library of Congress, Prints & Photographs Division, LC-DIG-ppmsca-08269.

amusements." Two years later, the U.S. Supreme Court agreed with Dundy. Justice Ward Hunt, known better for his opposition to women's suffrage, issued a workmanlike opinion that reviewed and approved the opinions in opposition to *Hartfield*, proclaiming confidently that "it is well settled that the conduct of an infant of tender years is not to be judged by the same rule which governs that of an adult." The railroad should have known and accounted for this legal and commonsense fact.[39]

Hunt's unexceptional opinion in an extraordinary case might have led nowhere, but turntable accidents had become so common that the results came before courts repeatedly. A year later the Supreme Court of Minnesota authorized a suit by seven-year-old Patrick Keffe, deploying the language that would become commonplace in the coming decades. In the court below, where the suit had been squelched, Patrick had been treated as "a mere trespasser, whose tender years and childish instincts

---

[39] *Stout v. Sioux City & P.R. Co.*, 23 F. Cas. 180 (1872), 182; *Railroad v. Stout*, 660, 662. Historians have devoted little attention to the turntable cases in specific and attractive nuisance in general. One of the few extended treatments is Peter Karsten, "Explaining the Fight over Attractive Nuisance Doctrine: A Kinder, Gentler Instrumentalism in the 'Age of Formalism'," *Law and History Review* 10 (1992): 45–92.

were no excuse for the commission of the trespass." Lumping children in with adults in this manner was something Justice Young was not willing to abide. Left unfastened and unguarded, the Milwaukee and St. Paul's turntable became "attractive, [and] presented to the natural instincts of young children a strong temptation; and such children, following, as they must be expected to follow, those natural instincts, were thus allured into a danger whose nature and extent they, being without judgment or discretion, could neither apprehend nor appreciate, and against which they could not protect themselves." Certainly, Young agreed, the road was "not required to make its land a safe play-ground for children," but following on *Lynch v. Nurdin* and the U.S. cases adopting it, the company must use "ordinary care" to protect children who might wander onto its lands.[40]

Together with *Stout*, the Minnesota court's opinion in *Keffe* sparked rounds of debate about turntables and countless other industrial settings where children played and got hurt. Some jurisdictions explicitly rejected the line of thinking that held companies responsible for young intruders, while others took up the assertion of duty proclaimed in Minnesota. Critically, however, both sides increasingly adopted the language of childish instinct that had been forged in the reactions to *Hartfield*. In fact, the Minnesota court had second thoughts by the late 1880s. In an opinion often cited by opponents of attractive nuisance, Justice Mitchell worried that this line of thinking had "undoubtedly gone too far." By making "childish instincts" the explanation for everything, the courts had created a rule of "indefinite and unbounded applicability." If some jurists were prone to laugh away boyish antics, Mitchell was not. "To the irrepressible spirit of curiosity and intermeddling of the average boy there is no limit to the objects which can be made attractive playthings," he intoned. If property owners had an unbounded duty to account for such behavior, "the duty of the protection of children would be charged upon every member of the community except the parents or the children themselves." Mitchell had no doubt that young people naturally obeyed their instincts; he simply had a different idea about how that fact should be confronted.[41]

---

[40] *Keffe v. Milwaukee & St. Paul Railway Co.*, 21 Minn. 207 (1875), 209–213.

[41] *Twist v. Winona & St. Peter Railroad Company*, 39 Minn. 164 (1888), 167. For an extended judicial review of the debate about turntables, see *Edgington v. Burlington, Cedar Rapids & Northern Railway Co.*, 116 Iowa 410 (1902). The turntable cases and the larger doctrine of attractive nuisance occupied the attention of law academics and treatise writers as well. Perhaps the most comprehensive review can be found in Seymour D. Thompson's massive, six-volume *Commentaries on the Law of Negligence* (Indianapolis, 1901). See Volume I: 932–963. See also Francis M. Burdick, *The Law of*

By the last quarter of the century, then, the debate that began with *Hartfield* had nearly played out. Some states stuck to some version of Cowen's severe formulation, but most had abandoned or modified it. Increasingly, the conventional wisdom maintained that children could not be expected to act like adults in dangerous situations. The Supreme Court of Illinois had made the point aphoristically in 1870: "The child is reckless and thoughtless; the man prudent and watchful." But no one stated the case more forcefully and with such influence as Thomas McIntyre Cooley, Chief Justice of the Michigan Supreme Court and author of highly influential treatises on *Constitutional Limitations* (1868) and *Torts* (1879). Reviewing a case in 1884 where a young boy had been injured by unguarded blasting caps, Cooley crystallized the developing line of thinking into one highly quotable rendition. "Children, wherever they go, must be expected to act upon childish instincts and impulses; and others who are chargeable with a duty of care and caution towards them must calculate upon this, and take precautions accordingly," Cooley wrote. "If they leave exposed to the observation of children anything which would be tempting to them, and which they in their immature judgment might naturally suppose they were at liberty to handle or play with, they should expect that liberty to be taken." Cooley's words fell on friendly ears among his judicial brethren. Cited repeatedly and given added weight by treatise writers, he had articulated briefly and authoritatively the view that others in the juridical field had helped to create.[42]

APPRECIATING THE DANGER

The developing juridical vision of young people controlled by instincts and impulses remained a separate line of thinking for several decades, but eventually it would come to inform and influence the way courts responded to industrial accidents involving young workers. As with contracts, the law of children's industrial accidents encountered categories established for workers presumed to be adults. Over the course of the antebellum period, courts had fashioned a series of rules governing the law of negligence as it applied to industrial accidents, rules that all but

---

Torts, 2nd ed. (Albany, 1908), 443–465; Irving Brown, "The Allurement of Children," *American Law Review* (1897): 891–905.

[42] *Kerr v. Forgue*, 54 Ill. 482 (1870), 484; *Powers v. Ware*, 53 Mich. 507 (1884), 515, 57 Mich. 107 (1885). For a garbled version of Cooley's assertion that indicates how it turned into conventional wisdom, see *Force v. Standard Silk Co.*, 160 F. 992 (1908), 1000–1001.

indemnified employers. For workers to win damages after an injury, they had to prove that the accident had not been their own fault, not the result of their own "contributory negligence." Workers had to establish that they had exercised "ordinary care," to show they had not been reckless in their own actions. Finally, plaintiffs had to demonstrate that the injury had not resulted from the carelessness of another worker, a notion that became known as the "fellow-servant rule." These concepts rested in part on the fictions of contract. Primary among these was that when laborers consented to work, either in the larger sense of the wage relation itself or in the narrower sense of following a command on the shop floor, they could be presumed to have knowingly "assumed the risks" involved in the job. These considerations all presumed a world of adult workers, versed in the nature of factory work, but more importantly, possessing all the imagined free will of fully formed persons. Injured young workers called these comforting notions into question. Was a twelve-year-old truly capable of understanding risks and exercising ordinary care?[43]

As with apprenticeship and contract, these issues arose initially in Massachusetts. The Massachusetts courts first considered the matter of an injured underage worker in 1851 and concluded that age had no place in the law of industrial accidents. Benjamin King, age seventeen, had been hurt while working for the Boston and Worcester Railroad Company. His work evinced the evolving nature of young people's labor in the antebellum period. An "apprentice" in the road's machine shop, he worked "with his father's consent." His employers clearly envisioned him as something less than a master in training, having reassigned him to be a fireman, his task at the time a faulty switching device caused his injuries. For Justice Fletcher, King's case presented few difficulties; King was simply a worker, not a child worker. "The fact that the plaintiff is a minor," Fletcher declared, "does not at all affect his legal rights." Because

[43] On changing conceptions of negligence and industrial accident law in the nineteenth century, see Horwitz, *Transformation of American Law*, 85–99; Christopher Tomlins, *Law, Labor and Ideology in the Early American Republic* (New York, 1993), 301–384; Bergstrom, *Courting Danger*; John Fabian Witt, *The Accidental Republic: Crippled Workingmen, Destitute Widows, and the Remaking of American Law* (Cambridge, 2004), 43–70; Welke, *Recasting American Liberty*. Law and economics scholars have debated how "effectively" or "efficiently" the "negligence liability system" functioned as a system of social insurance. See Price V. Fishback and Shawn Everett Kantor, *A Prelude to the Welfare State: The Origins of Workers' Compensation* (Chicago, 2000), Ch. 2. Lawrence Friedman and associates have studied the legal changes of accident law extensively over the years, starting with the classic Lawrence M. Friedman and Jack Landinsky, "Social Change and the Law of Industrial Accidents," *Columbia Law Review* 67 (1967): 50–82.

Benjamin entered the company's employ with his father's consent, he was "lawfully in their employment." Whether Fletcher meant to imply that the lack of parental consent would presuppose a different outcome is not clear, but parental consent freed Fletcher to render King the same as any other laborer. Benjamin "had the same rights against the defendants that any other person employed by them had, and no more," Fletcher maintained, "and the defendants were under the same liability to him which they were under to their other workmen, and no more." King had assumed the risks, and he must withstand the consequences.[44]

In some ways, *King* formed one of the last important minor's contract litigations as much as the first children's industrial accident case. The key issue for Fletcher appears to have been the "lawfulness" of Benjamin's employment. Such reasoning aligned with antebellum decisions by the Massachusetts court that fostered children's participation in the labor market. Fletcher's opinion also presaged the conclusions many courts would reach by the early years of the twentieth century – that the *unlawful* employment of children constituted negligence in and of itself. *King* demonstrates the distance the court had traveled from the eighteenth-century idea of childhood as a special, protected category. Having legitimated children's employment in general, Massachusetts's antebellum justices could now imagine underage workers within categories created for adults.

Whether because of *King* or other reasons, no industrial accident cases involving litigants identified as minors came before the Massachusetts Supreme Court for the next eighteen years, but in 1869, the court considered the claim of Elnathan Coombs against New Bedford Cordage Company. The case appears to have arisen for two reasons. First, the court had declared in *Cayzer v. Taylor* (1857) that employers had a duty to ensure at least a modicum of safety in the workplace. Second, the burgeoning growth of nonindustrial accident cases involving young people had begun to raise questions about whether children could be presumed to judge danger and hence whether they were owed special protection. The justices's decision in *Coombs*, that under certain circumstances companies must maintain a higher standard of care for young workers, ushered in a new era in labor law for young workers.[45]

Elnathan Coombs's story was typical. In August 1866, eight months after his thirteenth birthday, Elnathan applied for work with his father's

---

[44] *King v. Boston and Worcester Railroad Co.*, 63 Mass. 112 (1851), 112, 113.
[45] *Cayzer v. Taylor* 10 Gray 274 (1857); Witt, *Accidental Republic*, 51–63.

knowledge and consent at New Bedford Cordage, a ropewalk in the heart of the southeastern Massachusetts shipping industry. The overseer sent him to work with the seventeen-year-old James Davenport on a hemp-drawing machine, and told James to show Elnathan how the machine worked. Ten feet long, four feet high, and three feet wide, the hemp-drawing machines were "worked by two persons, and usually by boys, the work on them being considered 'boys' work'." Coombs worked out the day with Davenport and returned the next morning, only to find himself placed at a different hemp-drawing machine with a different boy named Manchester. As with James Davenport, Manchester was instructed to show Elnathan how things worked. Though Elnathan tried as best he could to follow instructions, his hand ended up in the gearing. When he pulled it out, it was "all ground up."[46]

Elnathan's accident ended up becoming an important test case in part because of the actions of his father, Asa Coombs. A shipwright, Asa visited the ropewalk a few months after the accident and concluded that the gears that crushed Elnathan's hand could easily have been covered with a wooden box, quickly constructed in a couple of hours for a cost of less than two dollars. This commonsense argument rooted in craft-based work culture formed one central part of Coombs's case against New Bedford, and it shows how working people themselves contributed to the legal imagination of child labor. Yet Asa Coombs's idea about child safety was not an argument the court was disposed to entertain. Noting that the state had no statute that required safety equipment, the justices simply dismissed Asa's request. Indeed, the question of protective equipment would remain off-limits in Massachusetts until the legislature passed the Employer's Liability Act of 1887. Nonetheless, the court recognized that Coombs's appeal presented, in the words of Justice E.R. Hoar, "an extremely interesting question."[47]

The "extremely interesting question" that caught Justice Hoar's attention was not simple protection from danger, but rather Elnathan's youth. The attorneys on both sides understood the importance of that question as well, and during two sessions of argument before the high court, they piled up authorities in an attempt to answer it. The company's lawyers were on firm ground. They only had to paint Elnathan within established principles of law, and his case would evaporate. His work was easy to do and easy to learn, and the danger was clearly apparent, they argued.

---

[46] *Coombs v. New Bedford Cordage Co.*, 102 Mass. 572 (1869).
[47] Ibid., 583. For more on workers' notions of protection, see Ch. 5.

Further, if the boy had "done his work properly he would not have hurt himself." The accident was "the immediate and exclusive result of the act of the plaintiff himself doing his work awkwardly and inattentively." In other words, the boy had not exercised ordinary care. Drawing on *King* and a line of Massachusetts case law adopting the principles of *Hartfield*, they maintained that Elanthan's minority did "not affect in any degree his legal rights or obligations."[48]

While the company's attorneys could easily rely on settled law, Coombs's lawyers had to establish that young people in the workplace were legally entitled to greater protection than adults. They had to characterize Elnathan's injury as belonging to a special category, no simple task given the general direction the courts had taken on industrial accidents. Drawing on English and American accident law, as well as the English Factory Acts, Coombs's attorneys argued directly that Elnathan's age should matter. As a "child only thirteen years old," the boy "could not be considered capable of appreciating the danger," they maintained. When the mill owners "took charge of this child, away from his natural protectors, the measure of care over him and for him was greater than would have been due from them for a person of full age." In short, they challenged the court to understand Elnathan Coombs not as a free agent in a world of contract but as a weaker party in need of protection. Like a master, employers stood *in loco parentis*, charged with the duties of protection adhering to a child's natural guardian.[49]

The justices realized the importance of the question presented by the case, and the lengthy opinions delivered by Justice Hoar on the first argument of the case and by Justice Horace Gray on the second delved into the central contradictions between childhood and free labor. Hoar firmly defended the received wisdom that if Elnathan Coombs had been an adult he could be presumed to have assumed the risks of his employment, and therefore, the mill would not be negligent. Nonetheless, if inexperience or lack of instruction had caused Coombs's injuries, the mill would be liable. Gray's opinion was even more straightforward. In the hearing of the case in the lower courts, Justice Wells had allowed recovery based on the boy's "youth, inexperience, and want of capacity" and the fact that these deficiencies might render him "manifestly incapable of understanding and

[48] Ibid. For the other personal injury cases, see *Holly v. Boston Gas Light Company*, 8 Gray 123 (Mass., 1857); *Wright v. Malden & Melrose Railroad Co.*, 4 Allen 283 (Mass., 1862); and *Callahan v. Bean*, 91 Mass. 401 (1864).
[49] Ibid.

appreciating the danger." This standard the court accepted, as Gray noted the circumstances of the case. Elnathan was less than fourteen, had been at work only a day when injured, and had never performed such work before. Clearly, his age combined with his inexperience required a higher standard of care.[50]

The decision in *Coombs* might appear to be a simple qualification to the law of negligence, but it opened the door to a further consideration of the natural and legal capacities of young people. Significantly, the court had not accepted the whole of Coombs's argument. They did not say that age alone caused Elnathan's want of capacity. Still, the court's authorization of a special standard of care provided a potential basis for injured young workers to get around the tightening standards for compensation being imposed on adults. In essence, the decision, like those in street accident and turntable cases, allowed litigants to argue over what constituted childhood. What age was so young that a worker could be considered "manifestly incapable of understanding"? Was the lack of comprehension a natural function of child development, or was it simply a product of varied life experiences? What precisely constituted a deficiency of knowledge to the point that a child worker could not perceive danger? On the other side of the coin, when had employers discharged their special responsibilities in cases such as Coombs's? Answering these questions rested on how the law understood children and child development. Did children have wills that, while needing to be broken, guided their decision-making, or was childhood a special stage of life during which young people could not be expected to act and react as adults would?[51]

In resolving these uncertainties, young workers and their families got an additional piece of ammunition from the U.S. Supreme Court. In the same term that the court initiated the turntable cases, it also considered *Railroad v. Fort*, a case arising from the Fort family's claims against Union Pacific Railroad. Originating in the same district that produced *Stout*, *Railroad v. Fort* served as a companion to the turntable case, giving the highest tribunal the chance to make a definitive statement about young people in industrial life. Unlike Henry Stout's case, however, the

---

[50] Ibid., 592.

[51] For general treatments of nineteenth-century ideas about children and their capacities, see Carl N. Degler, *At Odds: Women and the Family in America from the Revolution to the Present* (New York, 1980), 66–69, 86–110; Steven Mintz, *Huck's Raft: A History of American Childhood* (Cambridge, 2004), esp. Chs. 4 and 9; and Karen Sanchez-Eppler, *Dependent States: The Child's Part in Nineteenth-Century American Culture* (Chicago, 2005).

court had much less to draw upon and much more to overcome. The rules regarding industrial accidents had been firmly ensconced in the previous three decades, and the *King* decision had "settled" the fact that they applied to young workers. *Coombs* had not yet gained the traction it would achieve as a "leading case." Hence, the court hewed a more conservative line than it did in the turntable case. The fellow-servant rule did not apply to young Fort, but only because he had been moved away from the safer work agreed upon by his father and the company. To do less would "withdraw all protection from the subordinate employes [*sic*] of railroad corporations," Justice David Davis wrote. If the railroads were not "insurers of the lives and limbs of their employes," (a common catch-phrase in accident law), they did "impliedly engage that they will not expose them to the hazard of losing their lives, or suffering great bodily harm, when it is neither reasonable nor necessary to do so." Thus constrained, the opinion did less than it could have, and it did not touch off the immediate reaction produced by its companion *Stout*. As such, it demonstrated the uphill battle facing young workers who hoped to bring their injuries to court.[52]

Despite the suggestive language offered by *Coombs* and *Fort*, most courts throughout the 1870s and 1880s continued to apply rules made for adult workers to young people. In doing so, jurists developed three positions. One simply shored up the illusory consistency of law, agreeing with *King* that all people before the bench were to be treated the same. A second enunciated a practical concern: Young people needed to learn how to work and anything that prevented their employment was detrimental. A third position harkened back to notions of the responsible child that had developed in the wake of *Hartfield*. Young people, these jurists argued, could reasonably be expected to figure out what was dangerous and avoid it.

Standing before the U.S. Supreme Court in October 1873, Union Pacific's attorney in *Fort* thought he was reasonably safe by citing *King* and a couple of English decisions to argue that "it makes no difference that plaintiff's son was a minor, sixteen years of age." Indeed, courts around the country throughout the middle part of the century relied on *King's* authority to apply the fellow-servant rule to young workers. Many went a step further and read *Coombs* and like cases as upholding assumption of risk and contributory negligence. The same Minnesota court that poured oil on the turntable bonfire doused any notion that

---

[52] *Railroad v. Fort*, 84 U.S. 553 (1874), 558–559.

minors could expect special treatment when hurt at work instead of at play. Even though fourteen-year-old Charles Anderson had been hurt in a cotton mill after his employment had been shifted, the court concluded the case did not fall with the logic of *Fort*, because there, Union Pacific had not been "prudent." In any case, "there could be no greater wrong in putting such a minor to do a work accompanied with risk than in setting an adult to do it."[53]

Standing on settled law provided one way to hold the line. Arguing that change would hurt young workers and their families was another. The Arkansas court engaged in an extended version of this line of thinking in an 1882 case. The boy in question had found work in a Little Rock cotton mill. His employment, the court noted, came at "the urgent request, not only of the boy, but of his father, who was certainly aware of all the perils naturally appertaining to the work." Placed for the purpose of "learning a lucrative trade," the arrangement was "laudable on all sides." No one seemed motivated by selfish greed, and everyone knew machines were dangerous. "It would be a sad detriment to minors in preparing for future usefulness, if they should be precluded from all occupations requiring them to work with or near machinery," Justice Eakin declared. Parents desired the "future success and usefulness" of their sons, and "parental instincts" were to be trusted in such circumstances. While Eakin's views on the need for youthful employment put a cheerful face on the matter, the Texas court took a dimmer view. To establish a special standard for minors, the court averred, would place "undue restraint upon this important class of our citizens in obtaining the means of a legitimate livelihood, and would tend to promote idleness and consequent demoralization."[54]

The arguments that working families presented to the high courts led back to the central question of accountability in young people, leading some jurists at mid-century to stake out a third position, one that envisioned children as capable of discernment, unless very young. The Pennsylvania court issued one of the balder statements of this conclusion in 1879. After taking the opportunity to lecture Jacob Nagle's father

[53] 84 U.S. 553 (1874); *Anderson v. Morrison*, 22 Minn. 274 (1875), 276. For some examples of decisions applying adult rules to minors, see *Ohio and Mississippi Railroad Co. v. Hammersley*, 28 Ind. 371 (1867); *Gartland v. Toledo, Wabash and Western Railway Co.*, 67 Ill. 498 (1873); *Kelley v. Silver Spring Bleaching and Dyeing Co.*, 12 R.I. 112 (1878); *De Graff v. New York Central and Hudson River Railroad Co.*, 76 N.Y. 125 (1879); *Hickey v. Taaffe*, 105 N.Y. 26 (1887); *Beckham v. Hillier*, 47 N.J.L. 12 (1885).
[54] *Fones v. Phillips*, 39 Ark. 17 (1882), 24–25; *Houston and Great Northern Railroad Co. v. Miller*, 51 Tex. 270 (1879), 274.

on the wisdom of placing him at work in a rolling mill, Justice Paxson reviewed the options for deciding such troubling cases. "The law fixes no arbitrary period when the immunity of childhood ceases and the responsibilities of life begin," he conceded. "It would be irrational to hold that a man was responsible for his negligence at twenty-one years of age, and not responsible a day or a week prior thereto." The question could not be left up to juries because that would simply produce "a mere shifting standard, affected by the sympathies or prejudices" of the twelve good men. Reaching back to Blackstone and even Michael Dalton, Paxson drew upon notions of criminal responsibility to reason that anyone over fourteen could "discern between good and evil." Hence, it required "no strain to hold that at fourteen an infant is presumed to have sufficient capacity and understanding to be sensible of danger, and to have the power to avoid it." Hewing to standards that had existed since the early modern period, Paxson saw no reason to update the law for industrial life.[55]

If Paxson was willing to fall back on traditional lines of age, other jurists pushed the bar even lower, making increasingly younger people responsible for their actions on the shop floor. Justice Earl of the New York Court of Appeals issued a notorious version of this extreme standard of responsibility. Twelve-year-old Dennis Buckley's injuries resulted from "a mere accident," he declared. "He could see as well as anybody that if his fingers got into the cogs they would be crushed into pieces." To Earl, a special charge to protect young people from danger was absurd. "We think it is preposterous to say that it was the duty of the employer to warn him not to put his fingers in between the cogs," he propounded. "It might as well be required to warn a boy twelve years old, who was working about boiling water or a hot fire, not to put his hand into the water or the fire."[56]

The learned Earl found a counterpart on the Massachusetts court, where despite the opening in *Coombs*, the justices had been doing all they could to beat back the tide of youthful litigation. Considering the case of Charles Ciriack, also twelve, Justice Knowlton took up the question of how people come to know danger. Some dangers are obvious to everyone, Knowlton pointed out, and companies could rely on this fact.

---

[55] *Nagle v. Allegheny Valley Railroad Co.*, 88 Pa. 35 (1879), 49–50.
[56] *Buckley v. Gutta Percha and Rubber Manufacturing Co.*, 113 N.Y. 540 (1889), 543–545. Drawing on *Buckley*, Nan Goodman incorrectly argues that judges routinely refused to separate children and adults in accident cases. Nan Goodman, *Shifting the Blame: Literature, Law, and the Theory of Accidents in Nineteenth-Century America* (Princeton, 1998), 116–117.

When hiring a twelve-year-old of average intelligence, "an employer is not called upon to tell him that, if he holds his hand in the fire, it will be burned, or strikes it with a sharp instrument it will be cut, or thrusts it between the teeth of revolving cog-wheels in the gearing of a mill, it will be crushed." For Knowlton, grasping cause and effect in this manner arose from environmental learning, a process that started at birth. "From infancy through childhood, as well as in later life, we are all making observations and experiments with material substances," he noted, "and every person of ordinary faculties acquires knowledge at an early age of those familiar facts which force themselves on our attention through our senses." For Knowlton, children were not innocent and unaware; nor did he recognize stages of development. Children could be presumed to act in ways similar to adults.[57]

The crass statements of childhood accountability by Paxson, Earl, and Knowlton marked the crest of judicial thinking about young people's ability to appreciate danger. By the time they wrote, a change was underway, one that would open the law to young workers and their families. Starting around 1890 and peaking in the early years of the twentieth century, courts slowly stripped companies of the traditional defenses for industrial accidents that happed to underage laborers. In doing so, they set the stage for judicial interpretations of the statutory changes being wrought by reformers in the form of child labor laws. In the early twentieth century, court after court upheld the constitutionality of these enactments, but more importantly, a broad swath of jurists articulated a novel meaning: that child labor law was intended primarily to prevent workplace accidents. From that conclusion, they began to make illegal employment an actionable offense by itself, and in more advanced jurisdictions, evidence of negligence *per se*.

In altering the language of the law for young workers, some judges occasionally echoed reform discourse, but most did not. Instead, they found language and authority within the juridical field itself. In part, they built on the themes in *Coombs* that employers owed a particular duty to their young charges to explain fully the dangers of their employment and to keep them at places specified by their hiring. In doing so, they had help from treatise authors, who had extracted the carefully worded rulings in *Coombs* and similar cases to fashion broad rules about the care required of employers of the young. Most important, they imported the

[57] *Ciriack v. Merchants' Woolen Company*, 146 Mass. 182 (1888) and 151 Mass. 152 (1890), 156–157.

notions of childish instincts, pioneered in street accident and attractive nuisance cases, into industrial accident law. Searching for the reasons for the horrific scenes before them, they increasingly attributed accidents to the uncontrollable impulses of youth. As opinion built upon opinion and as statutory prohibition lent more authority, the age of impulsiveness slowly rose. By the end of the Progressive era, young adults were turning into children in the judicial gaze.

By around 1890, the trend in industrial accident law for young people had begun to change. During the preceding decades, some courts had read *Coombs* or *Fort* to create a special standard of care, but it was not until jurists began to apply the lessons of the turntable and similar cases that the judicial imagination of young workers moved. In some instances, the standard of special care for young workers blended with and helped create the questions that led to the language of incapacity. In 1890, the Wisconsin court adopted the more progressive reading of *Coombs*, and simultaneously rejected the idea that boys could appreciate danger. "It is not at all clear to our minds that a boy of about fourteen years, wholly inexperienced in the use of, or in working about, machinery, would clearly comprehend the dangers attendant upon the work he affirms he was directed to do," Justice Taylor wrote. Indeed, he continued, it was the "tendency to thoughtlessness on the part of a boy ... which makes it incumbent upon the experienced master to caution him when he puts him in a place of danger." Drawing explicitly on *Stout* and the treatises that had elevated it to a maxim, the Ohio court took a similar stance a year earlier. "Children constitute a class of persons of less discretion and judgment than adults," Justice Williams maintained. "Hence ordinarily prudent men, reasonably expect that children will exercise only the care and prudence of children."[58]

In a carefully crafted opinion issued in 1890, the Illinois court creatively spliced together the various lines of thinking about children and the dangers of industrial life that had emerged over the previous decades. To say that young workers must be instructed and warned so that they actually understand the danger was "just and humane," the court opined, drawing on a standard line from treatises. Beyond this, however, the Illinois justices began the process of importing the language born of the street and turntable cases into industrial accident law for young people. "To say that such a child takes the risk of his employment – that if he is

[58] *Neilon v. Marinette and Menominee Paper Co.*, 75 Wis. 579 (1890), 585; *Rolling Mill Co. v. Corrigan*, 46 Ohio St. 283 (1889), 289–290.

not willing to take the hazard of obeying the command he must refuse – is idle, if not cruel," Justice Wilkinson proclaimed. "By his inexperience he is unable to comprehend the risk; by his childish instincts he implicitly obeys." Here was Cooley's language transferred to a new setting. What had once applied to play, now applied to work.[59]

Views such as Wilkinson's did not cause a direct line of case law. Rather, they reflected a general movement in judicial language about young people. If anything can be said to have caused these changes in the narrow sense, it is treatise writing. A growing shelf of leather-bound tomes helped members of the juridical field come to terms with the unmanageable mass of tort law. For cases involving young people, the most influential were those by Francis Wharton, Thomas Shearman and Amasa Redfield, Charles Beach, Seymour Thompson, and Cooley himself. All of them took Esek Cowen's opinion in *Hartfield* to task, and most adopted some version of the progressive side of *Coombs*, albeit after noting the "well-settled" rule that minority did not matter. As jurists drew on these authorities to write their opinions, a self-referential process occurred (as it always does with treatise writing and the law generally). Subsequent editions of treatises cited opinions that grounded their legitimacy on previous versions of the same treatise. By the early twentieth century, law school texts and low-budget home law books participated in this process. Consequent of these countless printed pages, the juridical conversation about young people and industrial life moved to places unimagined in the antebellum period.[60]

During the course of these movements, the tendency of the lawyers and jurists to lose sight of the facts of a case and extract language suited to their needs opened the door to an ever-expanding scope for childish incapacity. The victims in street and turntable accidents fell easily within the notion of "tender years" widespread in the law and given new force by developments in divorce law. Justices Taylor, Williams, and Wilkinson, however, were not considering small children. Two were fourteen, the other twelve. While many jurists balked at the notion of attributing the actions of a boy or girl in their mid-teens to "impulses," the age of

---

[59] *Hinckley v. Horazdowsky*, 133 Ill. 359 (1890), 364.

[60] For the original editions of the treatises, see Thomas G. Shearman and Amasa A. Redfield, *A Treatise on the Law of Negligence* (New York, 1869); Francis Wharton, *A Treatise on the Law of Negligence* (Philadelphia, 1874), esp. 724–726; Thomas McIntyre Cooley, *A Treatise on the Law of Torts* (Chicago, 1879), esp. 553–555; Seymour Thompson, *The Law of Negligence* (St. Louis, 1880), esp. 977–979; Charles Fisk Beach, *A Treatise on the Law of Contributory Negligence* (New York, 1885), esp. 103–151.

childish incapacity continued to rise. By 1918, a Utah court could accept the notion that a sixteen-year-old should not be considered in the same light as an adult. "The rashness and imprudence of youth, however bright and intelligent, is proverbial," Justice Thurman wrote. An adult would stop to think twice before obeying a seemingly irrational order. A sixteen-year-old boy "would, ordinarily, be more easily perturbed and disconcerted." His actions could be explained by "the thoughtlessness incident to childhood."[61]

Thurman's conclusion depended on a language of childhood built up in the two decades following the shift that began around 1890. While some courts, most notably and ironically Massachusetts, held to a strict standard, jurists elsewhere expanded the language of youthful indiscretion. The California court issued what became a classic statement of this new judicial vision of young workers in an 1896 litigation involving young Patrick Foley. "Children are taught obedience," Justice Henshaw observed. "They are taught not to oppose their will and their judgment to those in authority over them." More importantly, judgment developed last of all the faculties. A child might acquire facts and retain knowledge, but judgment appeared only later in life. Using a commonsense example, Henshaw noted that children might be made to understand how guns worked, but no one would think that meant they should be given firearms as playthings. In short, accidents and childhood went hand in hand. "The very accidents of childhood come from thoughtlessness and carelessness, which are but other words for absence of judgment," Henshaw reasoned. Hence, the court concluded Patrick Foley could be expected to obey the irrational orders of his superiors that led him to danger. "It would be barbarous to hold [children] to the same accountability as is held the adult employee who is an independent free agent," Henshaw wrote. At fourteen-and-a-half, Patrick might not have appreciated being lumped in with six-year-old Henry Stout, but to Henshaw and many of his brethren, both were children.[62]

This line of thinking had momentous consequences for the law of industrial accidents. The defenses that lawyers and jurists had built up over the course of the nineteenth century presumed rational citizens, usually men. If children could only be held accountable to what was normal for children, and what was normal was "thoughtlessness," the elegant structure

---

[61] *Stam v. Ogden Packing & Provision Co.*, 53 Utah 248 (1918), 255; Grossberg, *Governing the Hearth*, 248–250.
[62] *Foley v. California Horseshoe Company*, 115 Cal. 184 (1896), 192.

of industrial accident law fell apart when applied to minors. In lengthy and relatively technical debates over contributory negligence, assumption of risk, and the fellow-servant rule, courts around the country began to limit their application to minors, or at least leave it up to juries. As a growing group of progressively minded judges came to the bench, their sensibilities recoiled at allowing doctrines developed for adults apply to the young. "The children without opportunity of education, without rest, their strength overtaxed, their perceptions blunted by fatigue, their intelligence dwarfed by their treadmill existence, are over-liable to accidents," wrote Walter Clark in 1900. "Can it be said that such little creatures, exposed to such dangers against their wills, are guilty of *contributory negligence,* the defense here set up? Does the law, justly interpreted, visit such liability upon little children?" More and more judges answered in the negative, or at least so constrained the rule as to make it unavailable as a defense. The same could be said for the other pat answers to plaintiff's petitions.[63]

These changes intertwined with and set the stage for how the courts would interpret the statutory alterations brought about by Progressive era child labor statutes. Although legal restrictions on the employment of children had been around since the early nineteenth century in some places, the period after the Civil War witnessed a new wave of activism that altered existing laws and enacted new ones, pushing the legal age of employment upwards and constraining where and when young people could legally be employed. The effectiveness of this movement has often been viewed through the skewed lens of federal law, where reforms found much less success than they did at the state level. Having failed one effort in 1906, congressional reformers succeeded in obtaining some limitations in the Keating-Owen Act of 1916. Opposed by the Southern Cotton Manufacturers' Association, the law was quickly overturned by the U.S. Supreme Court in *Hammer v. Dagenhart,* employing argumentation based on the restrictive reading of the commerce clause then in place. A similar push-pull dynamic at the federal level occurred a few years later when the high court declared another federal law unconstitutional in *Drexel v. Bailey Furniture.* Throughout the 1920s and 1930s,

---

[63] *Ward v. Odell,* 126 N.C. 946 (1900), 948. For summaries of these judicial developments as viewed from the courts, see *Force v. Standard Silk Co.,* 160 F. 992 (1908); *Berdos v. Tremont and Suffolk Mills,* 209 Mass. 489 (1911); and *Louisville, Henderson & St. Louis Railway Company v. Lyons,* 155 Ky. 396 (1913). These changes aligned with statutory limitations being enacted by legislators. Price and Kantor, *Prelude to the Welfare State,* 94–102.

reformers continued to push unsuccessfully for a federal constitutional amendment banning child labor. While these efforts failed, Congress did enact prohibitory legislation during the New Deal, culminating in the child labor provisions of the 1938 Fair Labor Standards Act (FLSA). By that time, national legislation merely placed a federal stamp of approval on conceptions of young workers developed elsewhere.[64]

Indeed, arguments about federal power produced little during the Progressive era because the real action occurred at the state level. There, statutory regulation of child labor proceeded with the help of the courts, rather than in defiance of them. Occasionally, business owners who were arrested in direct violation of such statutes challenged their constitutionality, especially after the U.S. Supreme Court's decision in *Lochner v. New York* brought progressive labor legislation into question. Jurists had a ready answer for these challenges, however. They simply pulled out their copies of Christopher Tiedeman's treatise and informed litigants that the "liberty of contract" did not apply to minors. In the case of child labor laws, Tiedeman had written, "there has never been, and never can be, any question as to their constitutionality. Minors are the wards of the nation, and even the control of them by parents is subject to the unlimited supervisory control of the state." Drawing on this language, Justice Brown of the North Carolina court felt safe to conclude that child labor laws were "founded upon the principle that the supreme right of the State to the guardianship of children controls the natural rights of the parent when the welfare of society or of the children themselves conflicts with parental rights." In the United States, he maintained, they had "never been successfully assailed."[65]

Upholding the right of factory inspectors and local police to make arrests and levy the paltry fines stipulated by legislatures represented a symbolic

---

[64] For a brief summary, see Joseph M. Hawes, *The Children's Rights Movement: A History of Advocacy and Protection* (Boston, 1991), 49–53. For an extended discussion of the FLSA, see Walter Trattner, *Crusade for the Children: A History of the National Child Labor Committee and Child Labor Reform in America* (Chicago, 1970), 203–209.

[65] *State v. Shorey*, 48 Ore. 396 (1906), 399; *Starnes v. Albion Manufacturing Co.*, 147 N.C. 556 (1908), 559. See also *New York v. Chelsea Jute Mills*, 88 N.Y.S. 1085 (1904); *In re Spencer*, 149 Cal. 396 (1906); *Inland Steel Company v. Yedinak*, 172 Ind. 423 (1909); *State v. Rose*, 125 La. 462 (1910). On treatises, see Christopher G. Tiedeman, *A Treatise on State and Federal Control of Persons and Property in the United States* (St. Louis, 1900). Ernst Freund had said much the same thing as Tiedeman and provided another source of ready authority. Ernst Freund, *The Police Power: Public Policy and Constitutional Rights* (Chicago, 1904). This section affirms the important and underrated argument of Urofsky. See Melvin I. Urofsky, "State Courts and Protective Legislation during the Progressive Era: A Reevaluation," *Journal of American History* (1985): 68–72.

victory for child labor reformers (even if they rarely acknowledged it), but judicial interpretation of child labor statutes created a meaning for these enactments only occasionally asserted by reform writers. Starting in the middle 1890s, courts began to make illegal employment into a right of action, and eventually in some jurisdictions into evidence of negligence *per se*. Along with changes in the rules of negligence itself, these legal developments allowed working people to take their causes before local juries on a regular basis with considerable hope of winning. As we shall see, they did so with alacrity and often walked away with huge awards or at least some amount of funds to cover doctor bills and lost wages.

In coming to these conclusions, some courts explicitly borrowed the language that reformers were simultaneously creating in the popular press. Recalling the past decades of industrial development in 1904, Justice Gest of the Illinois Court of Appeals attributed child labor to the desire for low wages and the poverty of parents. "The desire of poor parents to have the aid of their children and the cupidity of employers united to bring about practically a condition of servitude of such children," Gest wrote. "Their lives, limbs and health and their minds and morals were sacrificed for gain." Sounding very much like the latest issue of *McClure's* or *Cosmopolitan*, the Court of Appeal of California cast child labor within the caricatures of lazy parents served up by reform writers. "If employers will aid and abet heartless and mercenary parents in taking little children from the playground and schoolroom to place them in factories or mills where dangerous machinery is in operation," the justices maintained, "they can hardly expect courts to indulge in nice discrimination touching the quantum of care and caution to be expected of such children." Occasionally, jurists even acknowledged explicitly the public movement for child labor regulation. In considering the effect of West Virginia's 1909 statute regulating work by young people in coal mines, Justice Brannon accounted for the public eye. "While the whole country is crying out against the employment of children in coal mines, and our state has yielded to the strength of this cry, we are asked to emasculate its act and defeat its purpose," he wrote. The court would not abide such a turn of events.[66]

While it might appear that jurists simply reflected public sentiment, such a conclusion would be unwarranted. Certainly, the judicial

---

[66] *Struthers v. Illinois*, 116 Ill. App. 481 (1904), 484; *Fries v. American Lead Pencil Co.*, 2 Cal. App. 148 (1905), 153–154; *Norman v. Virginia-Pocahontas Coal Company*, 68 W. Va. 405 (1910), 414.

imagination of childhood mingled with the images offered by reform writers. Nevertheless, courts began the groundwork for the emerging interpretation of child labor law a decade before the founding of the National Child Labor Committee in 1905, and in doing so, they drew on ideas available for decades in the law. One of the earliest cases to consider the violation of a child labor statute took place in Tennessee and involved Johnnie Queen, the rambunctious ten-year-old we met earlier. In a simply worded opinion issued in 1895, the Tennessee court concluded that Queen's employment in violation of the state's 1881 factory act was "an action of negligence on the part of the defendant." Six years later, the court strengthened this view when it took up Luther Green's case against Ornamental Iron and Wire. Luther's "boyish heedlessness" had caused the iron fence panels to fall on him, but he would never have been there if he had not been illegally employed, the court concluded. Luther's "very employment is a violation of the statute, and every injury that results therefrom is actionable."[67]

These Tennessee decisions had offered a new way to interpret child labor laws, and within a few years courts around the country expanded this outlook. In an important set of decisions, New York justices announced what would quickly become the conventional wisdom: that legislatures had passed child labor laws primarily because of industrial accidents. The preceding century, Justice Haight wrote, had been "an age of invention." Much had been accomplished with machines, but "the practice of employing boys and girls in their operation had become extensive, with the result that injuries to them were of frequent occurrence." As a result, the legislature had seen fit to restrict their employment. In Haight's view, this act lent legitimacy to the line of thinking that had been developing in the courts. "The statute, in effect, declares that a child under the age specified presumably does not possess the judgment, discretion, care and caution necessary for the engagement in such a dangerous avocation," he concluded. In the Court of Appeals for Illinois, the justices reached much the same conclusion. The legislature had forbidden young children to work in mines because "immature children are liable not to understand the significance and importance of the regulations prescribed for the mine and the employees therein; they may thoughtlessly disobey orders, or expose themselves to peril, or do acts which would be careless in an adult," Justice Dibell wrote in 1903. "The company which violates this

---

[67] *Queen v. Dayton Coal and Iron*, 95 Tenn. 458 (1895), 464; *Ornamental Iron and Wire Co. v. Green.*, 108 Tenn. 161 (1901), 165–166.

statute ought not to be allowed to screen itself from liability because the child has been injured by reason of those childish traits which give rise to the statute." Such a notion had been a minor theme in reform writing, but it had never occupied center stage. Now, jurists increasingly assured themselves that when altering industrial accident law for young people they were following the intentions of state houses.[68]

As with accident law outside of statute, the tendency of these decisions was expansive, pushing the upper limits of what could be considered the age where young workers became responsible for their actions. In prohibiting work at dangerous machines for fourteen- to sixteen-year-olds, the New York Supreme Court declared in 1904, "the Legislature appreciated that children between those ages are apt to be thoughtless and absent-minded and to have their attention diverted from work." Such views, however, were not without their limits. "It may be presumed that the Legislature felt that children over 14 were capable of taking care of themselves in ordinary occupations," the Louisiana court concluded in 1918. Still, such late misgivings only indicated how much matters had changed from the early nineteenth century. By the end of World War I, courts debated how old a person must be in order to be considered "thoughtless," not whether children and teenagers acted on impulse in the first place.[69]

The apex of this line of thinking about child labor statutes came in states that declared illegal employment actionable negligence *per se*. This rule meant that the only thing young workers and their families had to prove was that the young person in question had been hired illegally. Given that working people often knowingly violated child labor statutes to gain employment, such cases presented a sticky issue for jurists, and some sounded the alarm against "fraudulent representations." Such cases, Alabama Justice Mayfield sarcastically declared, amended the state's child labor statute "to enable boys and their parents to defraud and bankrupt coal mine operators."[70]

Misgivings notwithstanding, a number of states either explicitly adopted the principle of automatic liability for illegal employment or simply took away all the defenses, creating the same outcome in the end.

[68] *Marino v. Lehmaier*, 173 N.Y. 530 (1903), 534; *Marquette Third Vein Coal Co. v. Dielie*, 110 Ill. App. 684 (1903), 689. For a summary of how the courts got to this point and an important case in its own right, see *Perry v. Tozer*, 90 Minn. 431 (1903).
[69] *Gallenkamp v. Garvin Machine Co.*, 91 A.D. 141 (N.Y., 1904), 145; *Flores v. Steeg Printing*, 142 La. 1068 (1918), 1073.
[70] *DeSoto Coal M. & Dev. Co. v. Hill*, 179 Ala. 186 (1912), 197–198.

When Walter Clark conjured the ghost of Elizabeth Barrett Browning in 1902, he had been somewhat tentative. With the "consensus of opinion in the entire civilized world" and "the maturer judgment to which mankind is tending," it might not have been wrong to conclude that illegal employment was "irrebuttable" negligence *per se*. When the Court of Appeals of Georgia reviewed the history of this idea in 1908, the justices sounded more confident, concluding that even before the passage of the state's 1906 child labor law, juries had been called upon to consider the "great wrong" of employing young children in places where their "natural indiscretions" put them in great danger. Sounding a lot like Thomas McIntyre Cooley, the state's highest court affirmed this view five years later. "The legislature must have known that little children might not have the caution and prudence of older persons, and might yield to childish impulses in dangerous places," Justice Lumpkin wrote.[71]

To avoid the thorny issue of declaring a regime of automatic compensation for accidents that occurred to underage workers, some courts simply removed all the possible answers. A 1913 Kentucky litigation illustrates this more graceful solution and provides one final example of the long road traveled from the early nineteenth century. McKinley Lyons, less than fifteen, had been thrown under the cars of the Louisville, Henderson, and St. Louis Railroad. Rejecting a settlement "so inadequate as to be fraudulent," McKinley and his family sued the railroad under Kentucky's statute prohibiting the employment of young people under sixteen in dangerous occupations. After a lengthy review of industrial accident law for young people in other states, Justice Carroll argued that the statute aimed "to save children from accidents that their own heedlessness or carelessness might bring about." State lawmakers had imposed fines to put teeth into this legislation, but, Carroll asserted, they had intended more. The "small penalty" of the statute did not negate "the rights of the child who should receive the fullest measure of compensation if injured while working in a forbidden employment." It was the child's "thoughtlessness," "immature judgment," and "youthful habits" that caused such accidents in the first place, Carroll reasoned. Hence, young workers themselves could bear none of the responsibility. In

---

[71] *Platt v. Southern Photo Material Co.*, 4 Ga. App. 159 (1908), 165; *Elk Cotton Mills v. Grant*, 140 Ga. 727 (1913), 731; *Fitzgerald v. Alma Furniture*, 131 N.C. 636 (1902), 643–644. For all the assertions that these rules were well settled, much debate continued. For a review, see *Norman v. Virginia-Pocahontas Coal Co.*, 68 W. Va. 405 (1910).

explicitly striking down the traditional defenses, Carroll was blunt: "The employer takes all the risk, the child none."[72]

Carroll's understanding of youthful labor represented an advanced position, but it built upon more than a hundred years of juridical dialogue about young people in industrial life. At the start of that century, stern Northeastern patriarchs had lashed down the evolution of apprenticeship and then unlocked the world of contract for young workers. Melding young workers with adults carried radical, and unpalatable, implications for the legal status of young people under capitalism. The logical outcome of independent agency became all too clear during early industrial accident litigations. Refashioning children as controlled by childish impulses quelled this uneasiness, emancipating young workers from the bonds of reason. As with reform writing, young workers and their families would likely have been insulted by these characterizations if had they heard them in casual conversation. The authority of judicial pronouncements lent these ideas a force that they did not otherwise possess. Still, this legal language of childhood incapacity would gain cultural traction only if working people learned to speak it. Their tutors were the local courts.

[72] *Louisville, Henderson, and St. Louis Railroad Co. v. Lyons*, 155 Ky. 396 (1913), 404–406.

5

An Injury to All

A little sum of money like that was nothing to me. It was my child's suffering that was something. (Mrs. A.W. Speers, 1882)

Sweating in a Virginia courtroom, James Monroe strove to get things straight about his boy, Johnson. Young Monroe had gone to work in Lynchburg, Virginia, when he was around fourteen. A decade earlier, Johnson's employment would have been within the bounds of the law. By November 1916, when he took his job, Virginia's 1914 child labor statute restricted his employment at workshops such as Standard Red Cedar Chest unless he was over sixteen. While knowledge of such divisions in the youth labor market eventually became common, young workers and their families had only begun to learn of them by the time of World War I. Denying that he had ever said Johnson was over sixteen, James Monroe revealed that the particularities of Virginia law escaped him. "Did you ever have any knowledge of the fact that if they were over fourteen and under sixteen they would have to have a certificate?" the family's attorney asked. "No, sir," the elder Monroe replied. "I thought anybody could work if they could get a job." Monroe's seemingly commonsense answer illuminates a critical transition in the legal culture of childhood, labor, and the law. By 1916, it was no longer true that "anybody could work if they could get a job." Unraveling how this legal precept turned into an unquestioned element of modern childhood requires attention to a wide range of interactions between law, society, and culture.[1]

---

[1] *Record in Standard Red Cedar Chest Co.*, 28.

This statutory intervention into the lives of working people radiated in numerous directions. First of all, it confronted working people's conceptions of age and time. In a time and place where size and capacity mattered more than calendar age, the legislative assertion of uniformity ran into contrary customs. The lack of a developed age consciousness stymied simple enforcement of child labor law on the part of both working people and their employers. In company offices, owners and superintendents sometimes openly thumbed their noses at new statutes, but more frequently, they made at least a modicum of effort to comply. By the second decade of the twentieth century, they had even more reason to toe the line in order to avoid liability. For young workers and their families, child labor reform often presented a difficult and baffling proposition. It confronted them with the prospect that their producer-oriented worldview was not only antiquated; it was also illegal. While some working people welcomed this momentous shift and acted in accordance, many more resisted. Young workers and their parents frequently lied about age to obtain employment, but just as often, they simply followed what they knew. If a young person had the capacity to labor, then they could and should. For folks who did not keep careful track of the next birthday, carrying on as they had done meant running afoul of a new set of principles about what children should and should not do.[2]

Young workers and their families evaded and outright broke the law when they sought work while underage, but their interaction with the new constructs of childhood enunciated by statute did not stop there. As Southern courts made it easier to pursue negligence cases against employers of child labor, young workers and their families increasingly won their claims for redress. As awards in these cases went up, they came to represent a penalty for the employment of underage labor far greater than the nominal fines set forth in the statutes. While the greatest import of child labor law lay in the production of cultural knowledge that these suits engendered, the economic force of litigation was not inconsequential, especially for smaller Southern firms. In other words, as

[2] For a similar understanding of child labor regulation as a cultural conflict, see I.A. Newby, *Plain Folk in the New South: Social Change and Cultural Resistance, 1880–1915* (Baton Rouge, 1989), 514–516. Newby suggests that reformers simply bowled over mill folk. Against the representatives of the "modern state," he argues, devices of resistance were "ineffectual." He leaves open the question why mill, or other, workers eventually succumbed to this power. On the one hand, I think this view underestimates resistance; on the other, I think it oversimplifies the ways in which law works. See also, William A. Link, *The Paradox of Southern Progressivism, 1880–1930* (Chapel Hill, 1992), 304–311.

statutory regulation of youthful employment filtered out into Southern communities, it had more influence than can be found in factory inspector reports or in reform discourse about the enforcement of child labor law. Indeed, far more important than simple compliance was the way in which Southern working families found a weapon in the law, one that could be used in their fight to secure a safe place for young people in industrial life. Laboring people took up that potential source of power because industrial violence broke the bonds of paternalism. Employers, they believed, could have done more, more to help them heal and more to prevent accidents in the first place. Community sanction undergirded this motive to confront the power of the boss, turning assertions about injuries to the one into claims of justice for the many.[3]

HOW OLD ARE YOU?

Like other legislation that created age segregation in the United States, child labor laws imposed an artificial construct – calendar age – onto

---

[3] For conventional statements about the lack of "enforcement," see Walter Trattner, *Crusade for the Children: A History of the National Child Labor Committee and Child Labor Reform in America* (Chicago, 1970), 30–31, 122, 263–263 n54, 265–266 n12; Hugh D. Hindman, *Child Labor: An American History* (Armonk, 2002), 62–63; and Steven Mintz, *Huck's Raft: A History of American Childhood* (Cambridge, 2004), 183. Certainly, factory inspectors and others charged with ensuring adherence to every letter of the law frequently failed to fulfill their duties. This apparent breakdown in state power will lead us to conclude that child labor laws had "little effect" only if we conceive of the law as an on-off switch, where "law" (especially statute) is meaningful to the extent it produces the anticipated results. Law, however, rarely functions in this fashion. Legal texts are assertions of the good; people act or do not act upon those assertions, wholly or partially. They may read those assertions through social contexts or cultural lenses that make the meaning of a particular statute into something quite different than the text produced in a statehouse. If people talk and act in ways influenced by new legal constructs, they give those constructs their power, slowly turning them into the temporary certainties of what is and what is not "law." In this sense, the pronouncements of authority in official legal texts are constitutive of culture, but only in ways that are apparent if we look at what people actually do with those pronouncements.

My understanding of law's power is informed by, among many others, Christopher Tomlins, *Law, Labor and Ideology in the Early American Republic* (New York, 1993), 19–34; Robert W. Gordon, "Critical Legal Histories," *Stanford Law Review* 36 (1984): 57–125; Hendrik Hartog, "Pigs and Positivism," *Wisconsin Law Review* 4 (2005): 899–935; Patricia Ewick and Susan S. Silbey, "An Account of Legal Consciousness," *New England Law Review* 26 (1992): 731–749; Patricia Ewick and Susan S. Silbey, *The Common Place of Law: Stories from Everyday Life* (Chicago, 1998); Arthur McEvoy, "A New Realism for Legal Studies," *Wisconsin Law Review* (2005): 433–453. The idea of the "force of law" has its conventional meanings, but I also mean to invoke the discussion of this question offered by Pierre Bourdieu in "The Force of Law: Toward a Sociology of the Juridical Field," *Hastings Law Journal* 38 (1987): 805–853.

a natural one: child development. Working people in the South had assessed the ability of young people to labor, either at home or at public work, by literally sizing them up. Now, they confronted a legal regime in which something that had previously mattered very little began to matter very much. For parents, that meant keeping precise track of when your children had been born, something new to many working families. For young workers themselves, it meant paying attention to what your elders told you about how old you were. It also meant adjusting to the notion that this number, rather than natural ability or gained experience, would determine whether you could perform expected roles in the family economy. In a pristine example of what James Scott calls "state simplification," child labor laws replaced "big enough to work" with "old enough to work." This transformation carried the potential for radical alterations in the social fabric of work in the South and across the Western industrial working class.[4]

The statutory regulation of youthful employment arose over the course of three decades in the New South in conjunction with a broad set of other legislative acts that both altered the working lives of young Southerners and influenced their responses to industrial violence. Perhaps most important were the school laws. By the turn of the century, the South was notorious for its lag with regard to public education. While Reconstruction-era legislatures had begun to build a system of public schools based on a Northern model, the Democratic, white-dominated statehouses of the post-Reconstruction period slashed budgets. As the end of the nineteenth century approached, these same governments burdened the South with Jim Crow schools that all but ensured public education in the South would remain sporadic. Nonetheless, school reformers, who were often child labor reformers as well, continued to push for publicly supported schooling and, more importantly, for school attendance laws. By the early twentieth century, truant officers, school administrators, and the occasional reform-minded teacher took on the task of seeing to it that children were in their desks. Official enforcement of compulsory attendance was sporadic at best, but as with child labor law, ordinary Southerners in local communities made meaning out of the law as given

---

[4] James C. Scott, *Seeing Like a State: How Certain Schemes to Improve the Human Condition Have Failed* (New Haven, 1999). For a good example of how Scott's work can be applied to law and society studies, see Karl Jacoby, *Crimes against Nature: Squatters, Poachers, Thieves, and the Hidden History of American Conservation* (Berkeley, 2001), 29, 142 and *passim*. On child labor law and age consciousness, see Howard Chudacoff, *How Old Are You? Age Consciousness in American Culture* (Princeton, 1989), 3–8, 87–91.

to them. For their part, Southern working families often resisted school laws, sometimes passively, sometimes violently, sometimes legally.[5]

If school laws constrained when and how young people entered into public work, statutes that altered liability law influenced the course of action they or their families might take in the event of death or injury on the job. Two types of statutes were particularly important: wrongful death acts and employer liability laws. Over the course of the nineteenth century, legislatures across the country changed a basic element of the common law, enabling suits for damages by the survivors of a person killed by an accident. Perhaps more important than wrongful death statutes, a host of legal enactments, usually called employer liability laws, cleared statehouses starting at mid-century. These statutes fundamentally altered the balance of power in personal injury suits by weakening or removing the fellow-servant rule and the doctrine of assumption of risk. In 1906, Congress passed a Federal Employers Liability Law, a fact that did not go unnoticed by Southern industrialists. These statutory shifts enhanced alterations already taking place in the courts, where jurists created a special corner of accident law for young people.[6]

The horrors of industrial life created what many have called an accident crisis, but legal changes helped to prompt an accompanying liability crisis. The response, for reasons still debated by historians, was state-based, workers' compensation legislation, which created another part of a web of law into which working people fit their lives. One of the intended effects of workers' compensation legislation was to curtail litigation by individual workers. Perhaps more importantly, workers' comp left the impression among working people that they could no longer sue under any circumstances. Marie Manning's guardian made this point directly

---

[5] John Fabian Witt, *The Accidental Republic: Crippled Workingmen, Destitute Widows, and the Remaking of American Law* (Cambridge, 2004), 53–54, 66–67, 88–89, 132–133. For Southern educational reform in the Progressive era, see James L. Leloudis, *Schooling the New South: Pedagogy, Self, and Society in North Carolina, 1880–1920* (Chapel Hill, 1996); and Cathy L. McHugh, *Mill Family: The Labor System in the Southern Cotton Textile Industry, 1880–1915* (New York, 1988), 57–70. On resistance to school laws, see I.A. Newby, *Plain Folk in the New South: Social Change and Cultural Resistance, 1880–1915* (Baton Rouge, 1989), 418–445. Resistance constituted a national trend. See Stephen Lassonde, *Learning to Forget: Schooling and Family Life in New Haven's Working Class, 1870–1940* (New Haven, 2005), esp. Chs. 2–3.

[6] For a brief of employer liability laws, see Price V. Fishback and Shawn Everett Kantor, *A Prelude to the Welfare State: The Origins of Workers' Compensation* (Chicago, 2000), 251–254. On wrongful death, see John Fabian Witt, "From Loss of Service to Loss of Support: The Wrongful Death Statutes, the Origins of Modern Tort Law, and the Making of the Nineteenth-Century Family," *Law and Social Inquiry* 25 (2000): 717–755.

to a Tennessee courtroom. "I refused to bring suit because I thought the compensation act would be all that Marie would get out of it," John Rogers disclosed. "It was my understanding that damage suits were knocked out by the compensation act." Before such perceptions became widespread and before a state apparatus arose to deal with industrial violence, the main place young workers and their families experienced the power of the state directly came through attempts to enforce child labor laws. Changing broad social practices via regulatory bureaucracies has never been an easy task, and in the New South, those who hoped to curtail child labor through direct force ran into nearly insurmountable obstacles.[7]

Although a broad range of statutory alterations influenced the shape of work for young Southerners, the mainstay of child labor law involved statutes that harnessed the labor market and young people's role in it to the calendar. For centuries, Western law had marked some calendar ages as more significant than others. Statutory regulation of apprenticeship had governed youthful employment by age, but birthdays had mattered more in the common law, where jurists and legal writers outlined such notions as the age of consent to marry. More importantly, calendar age had never been systematically applied across whole ranges of activity such as work, nor had it been backed by the apparatus of the modern state. As "undeveloped" as government machinery was in the New South, state governments nonetheless followed the patterns laid down by their cohorts elsewhere in the country. They sought the radical simplification of human activity, and their efforts presented Southern working people and their employers with a task they had not faced before: precise reckoning of birth dates and ages.[8]

As state governments and the press publicized the frequently changing regime of law surrounding youthful employment, Southern industrialists and their agents had to decide whether to follow the guidelines promulgated by statehouses. When Southern working families came to the mines, mills, and workshops of the region, a new ritual took place. No longer was it just a matter of whether a youngster could work with the family or whether she would make a "good hand." Now, company officials, if they chose, needed to find out exactly how old the prospective employee was.

---

[7] *Manning v. American Clothing Co.*, 147 Tenn. 274 (1922), TSLA, ET-954, 7. On the "state" in the U.S. South, see Richard Franklin Bensel, *Yankee Leviathan: The Origins of Central State Authority in America, 1859–1877* (New York, 1991), Ch. 7.

[8] Scott, *Seeing Like a State*; Holly Brewer, *By Birth or Consent: Children, Law, and the Anglo-American Revolution in Authority* (Chapel Hill, 2005), Ch. 8.

Robert Cherry, an overseer at Albion Manufacturing in North Carolina, described one of these encounters concerning young Harry Starnes and his brother, Fred. "When [his father] brought him in I asked him if the boys were twelve years old and he said they were," Cherry recalled. "I had been instructed by Mr. Downum to find out if they were twelve years old when they came in, and if they were not, they were not to work in the mill." To modern observers, Cherry's charge would seem easy to carry out. In the early-twentieth-century South, it was not.[9]

While many working Southern families celebrated birthdays with cakes and presents, many others simply did not know the exact ages of all their members. Reform writers sometimes commented on Southern mill hands' lack of knowledge about their own ages as a way to demonstrate the general ignorance produced by child labor. Irene Ashby-MacFadyen revealed a South Carolina mill where children did not know their own ages, while Clare DeGraffenried queried the older set. "'How old are you?' usually elicited a look of uncertainty," she reported. "'Now yer got me,' was the constant rejoinder." Here was one place that reform writers hit the target. Parents might not mark birthdays with precision, so young workers themselves frequently did not know their own precise ages either. Virginia Adams, a young woman hurt in a Louisville steam laundry, could only confirm that at the time she was hired, she was "going on sixteen," that her age was "as close to fifteen as it was to sixteen." Virginia's difficulties stemmed from how she came to know her own age. As an illiterate young woman, she had to rely on what her family told her, and that seemed to change from time to time. Her brother, W.L., described the lax approach the Adams clan took to age-keeping. Asked a seemingly simple question, W.L. supplied what to him was a seemingly simple answer. How did he know his own age? "Simply parents will naturally tell their children how old they are, give them some track of it," he replied. Had *his* parents done that? This presented more of a quandary. "I had my age changed too much, I don't really know myself what year I was born in," W.L. replied. Adams's experience was not unique. Working families throughout the New South did not place the emphasis on calendar age that the emergent middle-class culture of childhood expected of them.[10]

---

[9] *Record in Starnes*, 20.

[10] "Child Labor," *The Independent*, August 21, 1902, 2033; Clare DeGraffenried, "The Georgia Cracker in the Cotton Mills," *Century Illustrated Magazine*, Feb. 1891, 493; *Record in Sanitary Laundry Co.*, 52; *Record in Moore (Kentucky)*, 20, 23; Newby, *Plain Folk*, 505.

In part, inattention to calendar age came from inattention to the calendar itself. While the New South is often characterized as an industrializing society, many of its time rhythms resembled the Old South, where numbers on paper sometimes meant less than events in the agrarian or community cycle. James Harris reckoned his family's return to Union Cotton Mills by tying it to the crops. "We came back at laying-by time in July sometime," Harris reported. James Hauser placed his arrival at Forsyth Furniture in Winston-Salem as "in Fair Time, about 1911." Christmas also served as a significant marker of time, but even then, time was approximate. "I went there to live just before Christmas," Mrs. L.V. Miller recalled about her time in Winston-Salem. "I can't tell you the year. I ain't got that studied up." Community events might also serve as signposts. Gaines Leathers remembered the day of his accident as "the day Mr. Wash Duke died in May, 1905."[11]

A big man's death might serve as a meaningful signpost, but the collective memory of family events proved more useful. When Fitz Stanley's brother-in-law tried to figure out his age, the best he could do was remember where the family was living at the time he was born ("on Mr. Lemon's place") and that "the balance of his family [had] always spoken of his age to indicate that he would now be about 12 years old." In trying to get a handle on how old Virginia ("Bessie") Adams was, her aunt, Alfreda Farrell, sorted through the history of the Adams family. Bessie had been a "six months old baby" during a family visit in October 1900, Alfreda remembered. "They had been gone from there a year in 1901," she continued. "I also remember my sister's death in 1901, and they had been gone a year then." Badgered about how she could remember such past events easier than later ones, Alfreda had a ready answer. "Because I have something to make me remember," she retorted. "That trip and that removal to Indianapolis and the baby, the name-sake." Nettie Griffith told a similar tale in pegging the birth of her son, Perry, to July 1900. "Well, I went to Mr. Griffith's home in East Virginia, the first trip I ever made to

---

[11] *Record in Harris*, n.p.; *Record in Hauser*, 12, 13; *Record in Leathers*, 15. For another example of "fair time," see *Record in Jones*, 29. For examples of Christmas time, see *Record in Leathers*, 17; *Record in Starnes*, 16; *Record in Lynchburg Cotton Mills*, 67–68. Of course, everyone uses such expressions now and again, but in the context of the overall lack of attention paid to time by the people in my sample, I would contend that these markers indicate a fairly strong tendency towards a pre-modern conception of time. DeGraffenried (493) noted older folks whose main time markers were "'cotton-hoein', 'horg-killin', or 'tween craps'." For a contrary view, see Mark Smith, *Mastered by the Clock: Time, Slavery, and Freedom in the American South* (Chapel Hill, 1997), 154 and *passim*.

his home and I taken the baby with me – a little baby four months old,"
she remembered. Family events were not foolproof, and they could just
as easily blur the passage of time. "My recollection isn't good, I've had
so much trouble in my family," Charley Daniels revealed. What kind of
trouble? "Why, I had my wife shot down and –" he broke off.[12]

All of this is not to say that working families depended only on family memory. Many did record births and deaths in a relatively systematic
fashion. Alfreda Farrell had to rely on her memory, she revealed, because
family records that had once existed had been lost. Her father (Virginia
Adams's grandfather) had been keeping a family record. "It was just a
family record, pictures around it, was on a tablet of paper with lines,"
she reported. Willis Wynne talked about a similar family practice. "His
age was put down in a little book, a kind of memorandum," he said of
his son, W.H. "It may have been in a testament." The Starnes clan wrote
things down in a more permanent fashion. "I had the date of [Harry's]
birth written down in a book, but we lost it in the moving, but I have it
on a quilt," Georgia Starnes recalled. Quilting or other more permanent
and visible records helped because memo books were easily misplaced in
the frequent moves made by Southern working families. As B.E. Raines
put it, "I did know how old my daughter was when she got married until
I lost this book, but I can't keep up with things like that."[13]

Before the advent of birth certificates, family Bibles with pages ready-
made for family histories supplied the most reliable form of age-reckoning.
Mary Monroe, mother of Johnson, remembered the event of getting
her first, real family Bible. Before that, she had recorded her children's
names and birthdates on a blank sheet in the first small Bible she had
owned. When she got her family Bible, she had immediately transferred
her records, having her daughter-in-law carry out the task because "she
could write better." By the early twentieth century, such practices were
so standard that they were assumed to have taken place. "Where is the
family Bible – his name was in the family Bible, was it not?" a company
attorney demanded in a 1902 Virginia litigation. Family Bibles, however,
were no more reliable than any other kind of book, as Charles Burke, Sr.,
made clear. After his wife died, his children contacted their grandparents
for some of their mother's things that remained at her parents' home.

[12] *Record in Lynchburg Cotton Mills*, 50; *Record in Sanitary Laundry Co.*, 70–71; *Record in Griffith*, 75; *Record in Daniels*, 92.
[13] *Record in Sanitary Laundry Co.*, 42; *Record in Wynne*, 22; *Record in Starnes*, 16; *Record in Raines*, 16.

One of those was the family Bible containing all the ages of the family's children. Placed in storage at the depot in Davy, West Virginia, the precious family record and many of the family's other possessions perished when the depot went up in flames.[14]

In an era before the spread of consistent state birth registration, other signifiers had to serve as indicators of age. As in the labor market, size, physical appearance, clothing, and behavior mattered as much as calendar age. Knowing how much a boy or girl weighed or how high they stood told as much about where they were in their development as did the date of their last (or future) birthday. In trying to determine the age of Phil Waldron at the time of his death, Lonnie Lewis, a friend, served as a benchmark. "He was just as big as I was," Lonnie recalled. "Didn't lack but a little bit being as big as I was." In fact, both boys had been weighed on the same day, with Phil coming in at "around a hundred." For working people, attention to what someone actually weighed made more sense than age. Weight did indicate development better than calendar age, and Southern working families were quite aware of this fact. Twelve-year-old Tom McDaniel was described as "heavy," "stout," and "powerfully fat" at 110 pounds, while James Harris was "small," tipping the scales at around 85 pounds at around age fifteen.[15]

While weight and height could be accurately assessed, most people simply guessed how old someone was. A boy or girl might "look to be around thirteen." Without the simplification required by law, estimates were good enough. "At the time I hired the boy his appearance was that he ought to have been about fourteen or more," J.W. Dorse said of James Hauser. John McArthur, superintendent at Dayton Coal and Iron, sized up Johnnie Queen in a similar fashion. "From his appearance I took him to be about twelve years old," McArthur remembered. When Daniel Kendrick applied to the Fulton Company for employment, he was "a large mature looking boy" who "had every appearance of being more than 16 years of age." According to the company, Kendrick's appearance did not give "the slightest intimation or suspicion that he might be under 16 years of age."[16]

Judging a boy's or girl's age also could be done by social markers, such as how one dressed. In the New South, many working families still followed older customs of youthful attire, especially for boys. The

[14] *Record in Standard Red Cedar Chest Co.*, 24–26; *Record in Lynchburg Cotton Mills*, 65; *Record in Burke*, 65; *Record in Moore (Kentucky)*, 21.
[15] *Record in Waldron*, 75–76; *Record in McDaniel*, 39, 51, 63; *Record in Harris*, n.p. See also *Record in Standard Red Cedar Chest Co.*, 23–24; *Record in Ransom*, 8.
[16] *Record in Hauser*, 27; *Record in Queen*, 32; *Record in Fulton Co.*, 6.

youngest wore "dresses," then moved on to knee pants, and finally gained the status of a young man by pulling on trousers. Aged near eleven at the time of his death, for instance, Joe Pettit was described as "a knee pants boy." Because long pants marked a passage to adulthood, young workers themselves were keenly aware of what someone was wearing. Young Conley Robinson relied on clothing when trying to determine the age of the boy who burst his intestines with a high-pressure air hose. "Tom Carpenter is about my size," Robinson stated. "I don't know his age, but he wears knee pants and has got them on now." The necessities of work environments could obscure this important marker, however. Fourteen-year-old Arthur Burnett recalled how he wore short pants covered by overalls while he worked at Roanoke Mills. The same was true for Ben Hodges, the young African-American worker killed at a Georgia mineral plant. Ben's clothing was a matter of some debate. E. V. Toomer, superintendent when Ben was killed, was adamant that Ben's clothing showed him to be an older boy. "The boy dressed in long pants just like a man dresses, I never did see him in short pants, he wore overhauls [sic] all the time that I saw him," Toomer declared. Ben's mother, Minnie, maintained precisely the opposite. "Ben wore knee trousers," she insisted. "He didn't own any long pants, he wasn't old enough to wear them."[17]

Size, appearance, and clothing all served as ways of figuring out how far down the path toward adulthood a youngster had trod. Young people estimated each other, parents proudly marked their progeny's progress, and community members watched as the younger generation came of age. Birthdays mattered, but not as much as they would in decades to come. The fact that many rural schools remained ungraded, leaving older children at the same level of reader or speller as young ones only reinforced customary assumptions that age was a nebulous concept. When reforming legislators enacted statutory regulation of youthful employment, then, they did more than restrict or prohibit "child labor." In manner similar to the bureaucratization of "race" in the early twentieth century, child labor laws prescribed a whole new understanding of what it meant to be a child, one that elevated the numerical standard of calendar age over the more natural markers that had preceded this social and cultural regime. In doing so, they opened a broad fissure between "law" and "culture" and

---

[17] *Record in Pettit (1923)*, 20; *Record in Robinson*, 32; *Record in Burnett*, 14; *Record in Hodges*, 12, 25.

created a situation where "enforcement" of the statutory regime would be confusing at best. Evasion seemed likely.[18]

THE FORCE OF LAW

As with any legal change that originates in statute, the implementation of child labor law depended not so much on the effectiveness of state authorities as it did on the actions of the law's subjects. If Southern industrialists chose to ignore or evade the law completely, the conceptions of childhood enunciated by legal texts would be unlikely to achieve widespread authority. Similarly, if young workers and their families acted as if textual assertions of power did not exist, those declarations would lose the "force of law." For law to attain its constitutive power, someone had to act on a daily basis as if it mattered. Generally, the history of child labor reform has been written as if industrialists largely scoffed at the notion of state interference in their business practices. Certainly, many did, but the evidence from Southern courts suggests that the story is considerably more complex than that. It shows that workers evaded the law just as often, seeking employment in direct defiance of statute or out of simple ignorance. Companies, on the other hand, sometimes sought to follow the guidelines set forth by legislatures. As workers became aware of the power that new statutes and evolving case law had placed in their hands, Southern firms needed to make sure their workers passed the age tests written in state capitals.[19]

Once Southern courts had begun to define illegal employment as negligence *per se*, company officials had even greater motivation to plead their rectitude in obeying the legislature's dictates. Hence, court proceedings frequently contained sweeping statements of good intentions. Grady Loftin, of Standard Red Cedar Chest Company, declared that the company "had an iron clad rule not to employ anyone under fourteen

---

[18] For references to spellers and readers, see *Record in Ewing*, 49; *Record in Harris*, n.p. On the interplay between law and age norms and on the rising importance for birthdays, see Chudacoff, *How Old Are You?*, 82–91, 126–132. On law, culture, and environment, see Arthur F. McEvoy, "A Realism for Legal Studies," *Wisconsin Law Review* (2005): 434–435. On the bureaucratization of race, see Daniel J. Sharfstein, "The Secret History of Race in the United States," *Yale Law Journal* 112 (2003): 1507–1509.

[19] Hindman, *Child Labor*, 53–58. On one level, this point suggests that Bourdieu placed too much power in the mouths of judges, but it also suggests that "legal consciousness" occurs in numerous ways, most importantly as "cultural practice." Bourdieu, "Force of Law," esp. 838; Ewick and Silbey, "An Account of Legal Consciousness," 734–738, 741–743.

and required a certificate between the ages of fourteen and sixteen." A.P. Rhyne, the chief shareholder of Albion Manufacturing, claimed that after North Carolina passed its child labor laws, he immediately instructed his superintendent not to violate them. "Captain" H.H. Tift, a Georgia factory owner, also insisted that he gave his superintendent explicit orders to follow the law. "To my knowledge, he did not employ any children. I would not have allowed him to do it," Tift maintained. His superintendent had "positive instructions to obey strictly the child labor law" and was "not allowed to take any chance."[20]

Owners and company officials sometimes backed up these broad assertions with details of how they went about implementing state regulations. E.H. Lane elaborated on Standard Red Cedar Chest's response to Virginia's child labor law. "Previous to the time this law went into effect, I had only instructed our factory manager not to work boys of tender age," he maintained. "But after this law went into effect I got a couple of printed pamphlets from our attorneys at Charlottesville showing the law with regard to employing minors." Lane's concerns stemmed from more than the obligations of law-abiding citizenship. He impressed upon department heads to watch for underage workers because he feared the consequences. "I instructed them very particularly to watch this as we would be liable in case we employed anyone under the age limit," Lane disclosed. The company sent boys seeking employment to a notary, Lane continued, and it relied on the assistance of another local firm in drawing up age certificates. Lane's anxieties were not misplaced. In drafting the state's 1914 law, the state legislature had written the notion of negligence *per se* into the statute.[21]

News of new statutory requirements might reach company officials via fellow industrialists or the press, but company attorneys played a key role in communicating the new legal regime. J.W. Baldwin of Garland Coal supplied a lengthy description of a conversation with the firm's lawyer. "Mr. Taylor cautioned me, asked me if I was working any young fellows around the mines, and I told him we had some boys working there but didn't have anybody under sixteen," Baldwin recalled, "and he said you better be mighty careful, mighty careful, on account of the Federal Law, and he got the law and read it to me and that made me more apprehensive than ever." Baldwin claimed that as a result of this conversation

---

[20] *Record in Starnes*, 33; *Record in Standard Red Cedar Chest Co.*, 32; *Record in Talmage*, 29.
[21] *Record in Standard Red Cedar Chest Co.*, 54. See also *Record in Morrison*, 101.

he immediately fired Phil Waldron, who he suspected to be underage. Clearly, Baldwin offered his narrative for the purpose of exoneration, but it seems likely that he reported the matter accurately, for companies had every reason to be "mighty careful."[22]

Baldwin's termination of young Phil exemplified the most common response of firms to violations of child labor law. H.E. Kinder recalled being fired from a West Virginia mine for being underage. "I worked a few days at the Columbia and they stopped me from working because I wasn't old enough," Kinder noted. The threat of discharge might extend to family members as well. Lacking childcare, Willie McGowan's parents frequently brought the lad to work at Ivanhoe Manufacturing. In response, company officials repeatedly warned the boy off the premises and threatened his father, Aaron, with dismissal if the family persisted in bringing his boy along. The organization of work in many Southern mines made such situations even more likely. Like elsewhere, Southern miners often brought their young sons into the mines to help out. James W. Henry, a Kentucky mine foreman, recalled having a chat with Jonathan Preston about his sons, Arthur and Asa, informing him that the company had "a rule that we would not let little boys work in there." He had ordered young boys out of the mines if they were found without a work permit on the precept that "it was contrary to law to let a boy work."[23]

For all of their protestations, some companies clearly did openly and intentionally violate statutory regulation. A Georgia cotton mill operative confirmed common notions about noncompliance. J.C. Brown recalled that he had seen "a good many children" operate spinning frames in his day. "We have forty-eight machines at Fitzgerald, and most of them are operated by children, before the child labor law and since," Brown pointed out. In a similar vein, it appeared to be common knowledge that Louisville's Sanitary Laundry Company operated with underage girls, no matter how much the superintendent denied it. "I say positively, no, wasn't a girl in my employment who had not stated her age first as eighteen years," he insisted, even though it was easily demonstrated that company officials had been arrested and convicted under Kentucky's child labor statutes. Of course, the trick here, as it was in many cases, was that all the girls had "stated" that they were over eighteen. Plainly, some companies figured out that verbal compliance mattered most. A West

[22] *Record in Waldron,* 97.
[23] *Record in Kinder,* 56; *Record in McGowan,* 7; *Record in North-East Coal Co.,* 149, 152. See also *Record in Hauser,* 35.

Virginia miner supplied an example of how this worked when Charley Burke went looking for work at Garland Coal. "My brother asked [D.M. Woody, the superintendent] for a job and Mr. Woody asked how old he was and he told him that he was [eleven] years old, and Mr. Woody said he would have to make himself twelve," Ollie Phillips recalled. In a time without firm birth records, Charley carried out instructions.[24]

In many Southern workplaces, however, the social relations of the workplace lessened the need for outright fabrication. Subcontracting, in particular, clouded the issue. Edward Messmer, Jr., was only thirteen when his friend, Eric Lightfoot, asked him to come along and work at Bell and Coggeshall Company. When Edward lost his thumb and part of a finger to the gearing at the Kentucky box factory, the central question became whether Bell and Coggeshall had actually hired him, or whether he had worked for Charles Wommer, who did the work with materials they provided. Dare Lumber Company in North Carolina also had a relationship with its subcontractors that muddled the application of child labor laws. Willie Evans was only ten when his arm was "snatched off" by a wood lathe at Dare's Elizabeth City plant in 1911. By that point, Willie's employment was illegal under North Carolina law by a long stretch. Yet the company managed to obtain a non-suit and drag out the proceedings for years because Willie had literally been hired by its contractor, Tony Spruill. For his part, Spruill blithely admitted that that he employed several young boys in the lathe room and that he did not know their ages (and did not appear to care, either). "I had as many as three working there who looked to be from ten to fourteen years old," he frankly acknowledged. In his defense, he claimed that company officials only mildly suggested he not hire youngsters. He recalled a conversation with a company official who had said, "Tony, that boy is too little to be working in here," but he maintained he had not been ordered to fire anyone. He had only been directed not to hire "a boy that small." Such a direction fit easily into the prevailing customs of the labor market for young workers, where size and ability mattered more than age.[25]

Subcontracting confounded the seemingly easy task of simplification offered by statute. Mining presented a particularly complicated work environment in this regard. Phil Waldron again provides a particularly good case of a young worker bound to confound child labor regulation.

---

[24] *Record in Gibbs*, 9; *Record in Sanitary Laundry Co.*, 99; *Record in Burke*, 20. (The case record shows that Ollie Phillips was actually Charley Burke's brother-in-law.)

[25] *Record in Messmer*, 6, 144–146; *Record in Evans (North Carolina)*, 15–16, 20, 23–24.

Prior to his death, witnesses recalled, Phil had met with a mine inspector who inquired about his age. Phil told the man he was sixteen (probably a lie), but in the end that mattered little. When the company fired him (or he quit), Phil simply hooked up with a subcontractor, since he could get fifty cents more per shift anyhow.[26]

These kinds of arrangements, common knowledge among miners, could become quite opaque to the noninitiated. An exchange from a Tennessee courtroom revealed how difficult it became to tell who had hired whom. Did miners do their own propping of the rock? A few did, Luke Smith answered. "Wasn't you a miner?" Dayton Coal's attorney asked. No, Luke replied. The consternated lawyer continued. "You hired to Mr. Head and you were digging coal, what were you if you wasn't a miner?" Versed in the ways of the pits, Luke knew the lingo and the proper comeback. "I was digging coal all right, but when I speak of miner I mean I was not digging coal on check," he confidently stated. "They called us Company men." What this all meant, it finally became clear, was that Luke worked for daily wages directly for Dayton Coal and Iron, while the "miners" dug coal as contractors, getting paid by the ton. In this particular instance, Luke and his fellow young miners worked at "robbing the mines," digging out the rest of veins left by the actual colliers. Such work was particularly intermittent at Dayton Coal and Iron, where he worked, because it was primarily an iron company that only dug coal for the market when conditions warranted. Common all over mining country, such customary work relations frustrated attempts to impose regulatory order.[27]

Even in the seemingly less complicated world of cotton factories, the organization of work stymied straightforward application of law. In textile plants, overseers had charge of particular rooms, and they often did hiring themselves, applying their own standards of what constituted a suitable young worker. Jimmie Taylor was apparently eight when he told a whopper to a Georgia textile room overseer, claiming he was thirteen, going on fourteen. The man surely must have known Jimmie was not thirteen, but he had his own rules. "I didn't know whether he looked that old," L. Massey admitted. "I didn't care as long as he looked like it and did the work." After this blunt admission, though, he backpedaled. "I never hired anybody unless I got their age," Massey insisted, "and it had to be

[26] *Record in Waldron*, 77.

[27] *Record in Smith*, 16, 29, 82. See also *Record in Daniels*, 131; *Record in North-East Coal Co.*, 152; *Record in Moore (Kentucky)*, 21.

over 12 years old." Such personal rules operated in tandem with other
mill directions, official, semiofficial, and unofficial. One of the most common and most applicable to young workers was that everyone must stay
where they belonged. "That is the mill rules for every man to stay in his
own room," confirmed W.L. Jenkins, a company official from Georgia's
Eagle and Phenix Mills. Given that adult operatives often brought children to work with them, these regulations seemed to make sense within
the internal logic of the mill. In practice, however, they clouded exactly
who was working for whom.[28]

All of these common forms of work practice conflicted with statutory
regulation grounded upon caricatures of child labor that pitted tiny tots
against fat-cat industrialists. As we have seen, a great deal of youthful
employment occupied a gray area, where it was unclear whether a young
person was working for a company or not. Then as now, large swathes of
youthful employment fell outside of the industrial regime, and as a result,
questions arose about whether those types of work also fell outside the
purview of statute. As one lower-court Tennessee judge saw it, the state
legislature did not intend to "prevent a minor under fourteen years of age
from being employed in a small country town butcher shop where a little
sausage mill was operated. The butcher shop was not a large packing
house or mill or factory or workshop." Beyond the differences between
small town shops and large industrial concerns, boys who picked up odd
jobs blurred the meaning of child labor regulation. Even though statute
writers went to great lengths to stipulate what applied to what, the conditions of work made achieving precision a difficult undertaking. What was
one to do with someone such as Luther Green, who did not exactly go to
Ornamental Wire looking for work, but ended up doing some anyway?
How should a water-boy such as Earl Butner, who sometimes worked for
money and sometimes just hung out at Brown Brothers, be considered? If
Harry Starnes was just a "learner," was he a "child laborer"?[29]

In most states, the one-size-fits-all solution to these dilemmas came in
the form of work permits, certificates, or other documents that attested to
a youngster's age and right to seek employment. In the wake of these statutes, working families learned to perform a new ceremony of initiation
into the labor force, one often laden with hidden meanings and messages.
Charley Burke encountered these new rites when he sought work at Big

[28] *Record in Bibb Manufacturing Co.*, 29; *Record in Eagle and Phenix Mills*, 57, 60. See
also *Record in Elk Cotton Mills*, 33.
[29] *Record in Harrison*, statement of case, n.p.

Sandy Coal. He hunted down the superintendent and asked for a job. "He asked me if I would like a job and I told him yes, and he asked how old I was and I told him I was 11 years old," Burke remembered. "He said that I would have to go and see my father and have him sign me up."[30]

D.M. Woody seemed to be implying that Charley would need to lie about his age, but in other instances, the implications flowed in the other direction. J.W. Baldwin recounted a conversation with Phil Waldron's grandfather. "He said he wasn't certain but he thought he was over sixteen," Baldwin remembered. The mine boss told the man that "he would have to be certain about that" if Phil was going to work in the mines. H.S. Short, Phil's grandfather, offered a compromise. He would get Phil's father to sign a note to the effect that Phil was indeed sixteen, assuring Baldwin that "there will be no trouble about that." Communication seemed to be breaking down, as the men jockeyed about pieces of paper. "I told him if they would sign a permit for us to work the boy, and that he was that old, I would give him a place," Baldwin maintained. After the implementation of statutory regulation, a "permit" differed dramatically from a "note," but this critical distinction had not sunk in to Phil's granddaddy. As Short later revealed, he really just wanted wayward Phil working with him, where he could keep an eye on the boy, instead of having him run loose in the mine and the local community. He might have known Phil's "real" age, or he might not have. His motivations were different from Baldwin's or the law's.[31]

In both of these cases, proof of age took a form somewhere between formal law and social practice. As such, they evince the slow process through which knowledge of the law took hold. Accustomed to working in a relatively unconstrained labor market, working families met the law in diverse times and places. The bank boss at National Coal and Iron at Straight Creek, Kentucky, introduced Elliot Smith to the legal world. The elder Smith had taken his son, Bentley, to see if he could get some sort of work for him. When the boss told him it was a violation of the law, Elliot sent Bentley home, assuring the boss that he was "a law abiding man."[32]

Such encounters became ever murkier because, in formal texts and in practice, there were always exceptions to the rules. Jonathan Preston tried to find jobs for his boys, Asa and Arthur, at North-East Coal near Johnson City, Kentucky, but the superintendent told him that they were

---

[30] *Record in Burke*, 29.
[31] *Record in Waldron*, 91.
[32] *Record in Moore (Kentucky)*, 11.

too young (Asa was fifteen at the time). The matter did not end there, however, for the company instructed Mr. Preston in the legalities of mining. Jonathan Preston told what happened next. "They told me I must come to town and get the County Judge to give me an order; that my boys were too young to work in the mines," Preston disclosed. On this advice, he looked up the judge only to be met with an initial refusal. "He said he had no right to give me an order," the father admitted. Still, he persisted in his quest, calling on the language working people had used for decades to envision the place of young workers. "I told him I was not able to work, ... that my boys had a good safe job, and they would rather work there than anywhere, and I would be glad if he would issue the order." Preston's pleas convinced the local solon to produce the goods. The victorious father carried the precious work permit back to the mines, where he met up with Henry Lavier, the superintendent. "I told him I had an order, and he said 'send the boys back to work'," Preston recalled.[33]

Jonathan Preston's story supplies an excellent example of the interactions between working notions of youthful labor and the law in practice. As a disabled worker, Jonathan wanted the boys to contribute to the family, but he also wanted them to be out of harm's way. He obtained assurances from the mine that they would not let his boys work in a room, for he recognized that the miners were not supporting the slate properly. In seeking safe work for his boys, he did not seek to violate the law openly. Rather, he asked the local judge to bend it. As a respectable farmer with many relatives in Johnson County, Preston must have known his pleas were likely to succeed.[34]

If some working families learned about the legalities of child labor from their employers, others seemed to wish to teach the bosses a thing or two. The suggestion that her son, Perry, had obtained a work permit clearly agitated Nettie Griffith. Judge Saunders was asking the questions. "Well, now, when he went to work for the coal company over on the Gulf you and your husband both entered into a writing certifying to his age, didn't you?" Saunders drawled from the bench. "No, sir, we didn't," Nettie shot back. "There was no writing, no way. The mine foreman sent up to our house that evening and told Mr. Griffith and me, we was sitting on the porch – he said send the boy down the next morning – he wanted him to work; and he went to the mines." For all of Nettie Griffith's

---

[33] *Record in North-East Coal Co.*, 55–56 and *passim*.
[34] Ibid; Kentucky Manuscript Census, 1910, Roll T624–480. For a similar process in a different setting, see Jacoby, *Crimes against Nature*.

emphatic denials, it is also possible that the Griffith clan was not being entirely forthcoming. Like many young workers seeking a position, Perry Griffith might have fibbed about his age – not that Perry was not just as adamant. Didn't he tell the foreman he was fifteen? "I never spoke to the man," Perry countered. Didn't he admit to the doctor who treated him that he was that old? "No, sir, he never asked me nothing about my age," the boy said. Well, didn't his father tell the boss that he was fifteen? "He never done. I wasn't no fifteen. I ain't fourteen yet," Perry exclaimed.[35]

If Perry Griffith and his parents were lying, they were in good company. While Southern labor leaders and some working families might have welcomed the statutory regime that comprised child labor law, others resisted. Because hiring often occurred through family or community connections, the application of law became entangled in a web of other considerations. J.W. Dorse, who hired thirteen-year-old James Hauser to work at Forsyth Furniture, was the nephew of the boy's stepfather. When the family moved into Forsyth County, they contacted Dorse and asked him about a job for James, telling him that the boy was thirteen. Dorse "thought the required age at the time was fourteen," and he informed Sallie Hauser of this proscription. "She asked me to take him and work him and if anyone said anything about his age to tell them he was old enough to work," Dorse recalled. This brief moment sheds light on what child labor law meant on a daily basis. As a younger member of an extended family, Dorse was in no position to say, "No." Moreover, even though he had charge of hiring, he only "thought" he knew the law. Most importantly, Sallie Hauser presented him with a customary understanding of boys James's age: He was "old enough to work." For her, though, that still meant something different than calendar age. Instead, it described her son's physical ability and social position.[36]

The Hauser family's tale played out over and over in the New South, for people then, as now, did not simply "know what the law is" instantly or fully. Because child labor regulation, like most state regulatory activity, grew up in fits and starts, it was easy for young workers and their families to have notions about the legalities of youthful employment that were off the mark. What they knew depended on who they heard it from. Myrtice Ransom had worked in factories well before she knew she was not supposed to be there. "I did not know about this law preventing factories from hiring me. I didn't know it until Miss Allen [a neighbor]

---

[35] *Record in Griffith*, 72–73, 79–80.
[36] *Record in Hauser*, 25. On resistance, see Newby, *Plain Folk*, 509–514.

told me," Ransom reported. Anyway, Miss Allen had not really said that much about it either. "She said that I had to be sixteen, but she didn't explain about the law," Ransom continued. Myrtice got word of the law from a neighbor; others got it at work. O.R. Dent reported a conversation between the superintendent of Savannah Kaolin and Ben Hodges's father, Kelley. According to Dent, the talk went like this: "Well, they had some law which came into effect and maybe its [the?] president had had a talk with the superintendent about boys that was employed with us that was under sixteen years, that [we] would have to let them go." Dent's tale captures a typical layperson's response to a new statutory regime. For him, "some law" represented the vague doings of the state legislature. The effect, firing young workers, was immediate and clear; the cause remained somewhat of a mystery.[37]

Ignorance of the law could cut both ways, however. Companies could claim that it was up to workers to get a handle on what was permissible and what was required for young people to work. J.E. Crafton, superintendent of Miller Manufacturing, a Virginia woodworking plant, figured that working parents ought to know better. When Wilbur Loving's father brought him to the plant seeking work, Crafton presumed he was older than fourteen, so he made no inquiries about Wilbur's age. "I didn't ask him any questions because his father had worked around factories long enough to know the law." Besides, Crafton continued, Wilbur was "a well-grown boy," and Crafton "took him from his size" to be over fourteen. Like many others, Crafton simply applied the standards of youthful employment that had prevailed for decades. This customary practice combined with the fact that Wilbur's parents did not know the intricacies of the statutory regime, that the boy needed an age certificate to get a position. "I didn't know anything about it," his mother admitted. "He wanted to work."[38]

Crafton counted on Southern working families to be law-abiding citizens, and many of them shared that conviction. Johny Miller, a young operative at Brown Brothers Lumber, remembered how he and his family responded to the passage of North Carolina's statute that raised the age of work without a certificate to sixteen. "I do not want to tell nary [a] lie about it," Johny assured the court, but getting things straight was not so simple. "I worked there before the rule about being 16 and then the rule came and we looked up my age," Miller said. He then told the company

---

[37] *Record in Ransom*, 5–6; *Record in Hodges*, 31.
[38] *Record in Miller Mfg. Co.*, 74.

he was sixteen and promised to have his father file an affidavit to that effect. Later, the family discovered that Johny's "age was down wrong in the new bible" because they had discovered the old one, a sacred text that turned Johny into a lawbreaker. Like O.R. Dent, Johny Miller experienced the law as a somewhat vague and distant force that influenced his daily activities. "There was a rule came around" was his way of talking about child labor reform.[39]

On the other end of the spectrum, though, were young workers who lied, or at least dissembled, about their age. Virginia Adams exemplifies what a young person might do when she wanted work in the era of child labor law. Virginia was clearly a bit of a ham, joking around with her fellow employees at Sanitary Laundry about how she was going to quit work and get married. How old Virginia actually was depended on what day it was and to whom she was speaking. "One time we were talking about her age; she told us she was 18, and another time she told me, down in the starch room, that she was 17, and another time she told me she was 14," Mary Johnson remembered. At least one of her fellow employees claimed that she openly admitted lying to get the position. May Figg asserted that during a visit with Virginia in the hospital that the girl claimed she had told the foreman directly that she had turned eighteen. "She says 'If I told him the truth I wouldn't be here tonight [in the hospital].' 'But,' she says, 'I told a lie to get the job,'" Figg insisted.[40]

Like many young workers who sought work in a constrained market, it seems likely that Virginia Adams did not lie outright, at least in her own mind. She simply followed instructions she received from Lucille Overstreet, another young worker, on how to get a job. Here is her version of what Lucille Overstreet told her to do. "She and I were together one Sunday; she says, 'Virginia, you want a job?' I said sure," Virginia recollected. As the two girls talked about the prospects, Virginia brought up the problem of the law. "I says, 'I am not old enough, Lucille.' She says, 'I will get you a job.' I said all right." Lucille used her connections with George Settle, the foreman, to secure the position for Virginia. When Settle became suspicious about Virginia's age, he queried Overstreet. "I asked Lucille, 'Are you sure this girl is eighteen?' Lucille said, 'Why sure she is.' She says, 'Her sister told me she was.'" Settle might have been telling the truth about Lucille Overstreet's positive lying, but Lucille's version of the story seems more plausible. "I didn't tell her to say she

[39] Record in Butner, 21.
[40] Record in Sanitary Laundry Co., 125.

was that old," Lucille maintained. "I told her if she wanted to work, she would have to tell him she was older than fifteen. That's all I told her." In other words, Lucille Overstreet told Virginia Adams the legal truth.[41]

The stories of Virginia Adams, James Hauser, Perry Griffith, and other young workers illustrate the complications that arose when simplifying reformers laid a new template for youthful employment onto older notions of when, where, and under what conditions young people should engage in public work. For working people, "old enough to work" meant many things. It might be connected to calendar age, but it was much more than that. Size, ability, and the state of the family exchequer all played a part. While child labor statutes sometimes took account of variations in workplaces, they nonetheless reduced the marker of legitimacy to calendar age. Working people met this new legal and cultural construct with a variety of responses, many of which can be characterized as resistance. They did not so much oppose the law outright as much as they found ways around it. They made their own meanings, whether via the literal-mindedness of Virginia Adams or the pleas for exceptions to the rules that were mounted by Jonathan Preston for his boys. Confronted with a new, middle-class language of childhood, young workers and their families spoke haltingly at first. As time passed, they would learn its grammar more thoroughly.[42]

A WEAPON FOR WORKERS

If young workers and their families had met child labor law only in the workplace, their exposure to its constructs of proper childhood would have been limited to the constraints placed on youthful hiring. For the law to do its cultural work, it needed to appear to be neutral and universal. That was much more likely to happen in the courts than in a one-to-one encounter with an inquisitive foreman or even a factory or mine inspector. Statutes that constricted youthful employment, when combined with other statutory changes and the evolution of common law negligence rules, gave working people an avenue to that forum. The violence that young people incurred on the job provided a powerful impetus to go there. Law became a weapon in the hands of workers, but it was one that had to be handled carefully.[43]

---

[41] Ibid., 8, 86, 106.

[42] Newby, *Plain Folk*, 503–509; Ewick and Silbey, *Common Place of Law*.

[43] Bourdieu, "Force of Law," 845–847. In a manner of speaking, this point contradicts older understandings of the power of law in labor relations. See Tomlins, *Law, Labor,*

The more working people came to know that employing young children was illegal, the more they could use that to their advantage. Two striking illustrations of this advantage come from the case of the Starnes family against Albion Manufacturing. The first involves Zeb Kinley, a fellow worker at the mill. Kinley was not exactly a paragon of virtue, admitting that he had been indicted in mayor's court for cursing and for "pushing a crippled nigger down." Nonetheless, Kinley knew how to use the law to his advantage. J.S. Downum, the superintendent, who had previously had Kinley "indicted for a little affray" had now "put out a report" on the man for public drunkenness. In this tussle, child labor law became a way for Kinley to fire back at Downum. "He told me he had heard I was liable to put a report on him about working chaps under age, and I told him I had made a threat of it, and he says, 'Of course I know the chaps are not twelve years old, but I will pay you [back?] if you will prosecute me for working them under age.'" Less stark but more telling is what W.S. Starnes learned from the suit the family brought against Albion after young Harry lost his fingers. The family won a $3,000 judgment against the mill, which held up in the North Carolina Supreme Court in an important decision that helped establish the rule that illegal employment of children was negligence *per se*. After the accident, the elder Starnes had moved with most of the children to Charlotte, where about ten years later he appeared as a witness in another family's litigation against the cotton mill where their own youngster had gotten hurt.[44]

William Starnes's ongoing involvement in the courts should not be overly surprising, for working people evinced a healthy stamina when it came to dealing with industrial violence via the law. Joe Pettit's family, for instance, spent over a decade in the North Carolina courts, enduring his mother's death, his brother's World War I injuries, and two trips to the state's highest tribunal. James Harris and his family took even longer. After the boy was hurt at Union Cotton Mills in 1905, the Harris family did not even file suit until 1911 and then spent another eight years battling it out before the bench. By the time a second trial occurred in 1918,

and Ideology; and William E. Forbath, *Law and the Shaping of the American Labor Movement* (Cambridge, 1991). Both see law as constraining the actions of working people, and in the broad scheme, I would agree. As I argue below, the legalities of childhood that young workers met in the courts subtlety reshaped their identities. My point here is that on a more tangible level law authorized contests with employers that would not otherwise have occurred. For another view of injury suits as a weapon (of sorts) for litigants, see Bergstrom, *Courting Danger*, Ch. 7.

[44] *Record in Starnes*, 17; *Charley Stamey bnf JL DeLaney v. Fidelity Mfg. Co.*, Mecklenburg County Records, Mecklenburg Civil Action Papers, NCSA, Box 60.

James had turned twenty-eight, a fact that no doubt hurt his chances. While most suits took less time than this, they often involved multiple hearings, trials, and appeals that spread out over the course of a few years. Many families gave up, but the fact that many stuck it out demonstrates both their commitment to the cause and the allure of the law as a cudgel to wield against their employers.[45]

Another indication that working people learned how to use the law to their advantage comes from cases brought long after the fact. Ellen Gibbs's action against Tifton Cotton Mills in Tifton, Georgia, nicely illustrates this point. Relative to the horrors endured by her fellow workers in the industrializing South, Gibbs's injuries were minor. At age nine, she lost about half of a finger, "down to the second joint," when it became lodged in the gears of a spinning frame. Nonetheless, Gibbs saw the injury as serious. "When I do anything with that hand now, I just have to let that finger be out there like that (indicating)," she testified. "It gives me mortification and worry." A couple of years after the accident, Gibbs's fortunes went from bad to worse when her father died. The family removed to Fitzgerald, Georgia, where they lived "in the mills" (presumably meaning a company town). Perhaps because of the family's declining prospects, she and her brother-in-law brought suit in 1919, ten years after the injury. By that time, the proper forms for telling the story of injured young workers were well established, and the Gibbs family made sure to stress that she had been small for her age, that she had never been warned by anyone, and that the spinning frame was improperly protected. Nonsuited at the initial trial, the family took the case to the Georgia Court of Appeals. In overturning this ruling, the higher court acknowledged the fact that the injury had occurred before Georgia's 1906 child labor statute, so it could not be considered negligence *per se*. Still, Justice Wade took note of all markers that cast Ellen as a nine-year-old child, not a nineteen-year-old young woman. "The employer of a child of such tender years is held to a high degree of care in protecting the child from injury," he wrote.[46]

Whether the Gibbs family ever wrested any damages out of Tifton Cotton Mills is not recorded, but if they fared as well as their counterparts did by the second decade of the twentieth century, their chances looked good. As the law evolved, working families won more and more of their cases. A survey of the civil cases in Mecklenburg County, North Carolina, confirms this fact. In the twenty years between 1900 and 1920, scores

[45] *Record in Pettit, passim; Record in Harris*, n.p.
[46] *Record in Gibbs*, 6–9.

of personal injury cases came before the court, many of them involving young workers. Early on, working people often found themselves non-suited or on the losing side of a jury verdict. As the years progressed, the trend changed considerably. Workers began to win awards in the hundreds to low thousands of dollars. By the end of the period, out-of-court settlements or jury awards in favor of workers were the norm.

Workers had learned their lessons well. In a case similar to Ellen Gibbs's cause, Fred Graham won a five-hundred-dollar award for losing a finger in a spinning frame. Although he had been around fourteen at the time of the injury, Graham had turned twenty-one by the time he brought suit against Highland Park Manufacturing in 1920. By that date, workers at Highland had sued the company fourteen times over the preceding twenty years. Sometimes they lost, but often they won, usually an amount between 100 and 500 dollars. Irie Martin, however, had pried $2,500 out of the company in 1907. Martin's award was by no means extraordinary, for juries became increasingly generous as the period progressed. Awards of thousands and even tens of thousands of dollars became common, if not the norm. Harry Starnes ended up with $3,000; Charley Burke got $5,000; Wilbur Loving received $8,000. Juries in two West Virginia cases awarded $10,000. Both verdicts were immediately set aside by the trial judge, but the Supreme Court of Appeals of West Virginia reinstated one of the two awards.[47]

Given the rising amounts of awards, it is no small wonder that companies became increasingly fearful of litigation. John Ewing heard this sentiment voiced by Lanark Fuel when he went to see about his son, Jackson, working in their West Virginia mines. As the elder Ewing told the story, the company was keen to get his consent for Jackson to work on mechanized tram cars. David Lang, the mine boss, had said that if the mine "would get him killed or crippled, it would ruin us." D.L. Keen, owner of a Waycross, Georgia, bottling plant, expressed similar concerns, if not so hyperbolically. When he heard that Ellis Crosby and his mother were talking about suing over Ellis's lost eye, he looked to settle. "I did not want to go to court, because it is very expensive and I lose a good deal

[47] *Fred Graham v. Highland Park Mfg. Co.*, Mecklenburg County Records, Mecklenburg Civil Action Papers, NCSA, Box 62; *Irie Martin by his next friend, W.T. Martin v. Highland Park Mfg. Co.*, Mecklenburg County Records, Mecklenburg Civil Action Papers, NCSA, Box 49; *Starnes v. Albion Manufacturing*, 147 N.C. 556 (1908); *Burke v. Big Sandy Coal and Coke Co.*, 68 W. Va. 421 (1910); *Record in Miller Mfg. Co.*, 1; *Rhodes v. J.B.B. Coal Co.*, 79 W. Va. 71 (1916); *Mills v. Virginian Ry. Co.*, 85 W. Va. 729 (1920).

of time," Keen pointed out. For small companies such as Keen's, a "very expensive" lawsuit meant something.[48]

No example shows the real threat of litigation to small firms better than that of the Ricks family against Dixie Manufacturing Company, an Atlanta-based twine factory. James Rick's injuries at the plant were prototypical. He went to work there at age thirteen, evading Georgia's child labor law probably with the collusion of his older brother, Gordon, who either literally hired him or arranged for him to get work. While working at a carding machine in July 1918, James's left hand was "badly mangled," so much so as to render it "practically useless" for the rest of his life. James might have received compensation from the liability insurance that the company took out with London Guarantee and Accident Company, but the company's agent decided that by employing James illegally, Dixie Manufacturing had voided its coverage. This left the Ricks family with only the courts to turn to.[49]

Faced with the threat of a suit, the company sought to settle. How genuine these attempts were depends on whom one believes. S.B. Wright, the insurance agent, remembered company president T.J. Monroe saying that he did not feel "morally responsible" for the accident because Gordon Ricks had illegally helped his little brother get the job. Still, he was willing to help the family pay bills, dispense James's back wages, and "help him financially." In his own words, Monroe recalled a conversation with Gordon Ricks in which he urged the family to settle, but, he claimed, Gordon had maintained that his father was "hard-headed" and would not agree. Gordon Ricks heard a different story. He claimed Monroe had told him to tell his father that "'As far as him suing ... I can fight him as long as I can." If Monroe's actions are any indication, Gordon heard the straight truth.[50]

With the case pending, the company found a way out. In a financial and legal sleight of hand, Dixie Manufacturing executed a chattel mortgage to Dixie Paper and Box Company, another firm owned by Monroe, though apparently run on a daily basis by his brother. Dixie Paper and Box then promptly foreclosed on Dixie Manufacturing, leaving the company "hopelessly insolvent." By late 1919, the Ricks family had received a $5,000 award from a Fulton County jury, but there was no company left against which to press their claim. As they saw it, the mortgage was

[48] *Record in Ewing*, 44; *Record in Keen*, 25.
[49] *Record in Dixie Manufacturing Co.*, 1–3, 31.
[50] Ibid., 30–31, 45.

"false and fraudulent ... executed solely for the purpose of evading and defeating" their lawful demands. In an outcome that must have chagrined T.J. Monroe, a jury in Fulton County Superior Court agreed with the Ricks clan, finding the mortgage to be fraudulent. The Georgia Supreme Court agreed.[51]

What is more telling than the outcome of the case, however, is the way T.J. Monroe reacted to the suit. With two other ongoing accident claims against the company, he had real cause for concern. In addition, the company's fortunes had tumbled in the wake of the armistice ending World War I, when buyers reneged on contracts and the price of twine plummeted along with the general collapse of the cotton market. With the company capitalized at just under $11,000 and with thousands of dollars in outstanding debts, an award of $5,000 was a meaningful threat to solvency. W.P Lovett, the secretary and holder of the rest of the stock, recalled Monroe, worried that "if the boy sued us and got judgment, it would take up all the plant." In court, Monroe took great pains to explain the company's financial quandaries, trying to paint the mortgage to Dixie Box as "an actual, honest debt." Eventually though, he admitted that "we were going to take this mortgage to protect our interest in the Ricks case." Clearly, Monroe's motivations went beyond the financial. Whether he really ever told James's father that he "would never pay out a single dollar," his comments to Wright abjuring moral responsibility intermingled with his pecuniary concerns. As far as he figured, the Ricks family was just as much at fault as he was. "We didn't propose to just sit down and see them take away our mill from us when his brother was the one who placed him there contrary to our rule and practice of law," Monroe flatly declared. With his dander up, Monroe made, to put it kindly, errors of judgment.[52]

A CHARITABLE PROPOSITION

Perhaps the financial shenanigans of T.J. Monroe were unique, but they evince the potential power placed in the hands of workers by child labor statutes and accompanying changes elsewhere in the law. Large awards against small companies presented a far greater impetus to avoid employing young children than did the trifling fines doled out by factory inspectors or other local officials. Certainly, large corporations

[51] Ibid., 1–3.
[52] Ibid., 3, 35, 42–44

could shrug off such irritations, or at least, deal with them via insurance policies. Smaller companies had to go to court. Before workers' compensation law transformed these personal litigations, workers hoped for large awards and companies feared them. Contrary to what "tort reformers" now and then maintain, working people did not pursue this avenue out of avaricious designs to benefit from their misfortunes. Rather, they usually felt genuinely wronged by what their employers had done to them. As we have seen, young workers and their families believed they could find a safe place in the industrial world, a place where younger people could make an economic contribution without the constant fear of death or injury that pervaded adult labor. As we have also seen, employers repeatedly violated the trust working people placed in them. The courts offered an arena where this conflict over the heart and soul of working life could be carried out. Young workers and their families went to find justice. They often found it, but along the way, they also discovered a new way of thinking about young people and industrial life.

When injured workers confronted their employers in the courtroom, litigations turned into open contests about economic and social power. Industrial accident litigations surged in the late nineteenth century throughout the United States, but unlike the vast urban-industrial belt of the Northeast and Midwest, many Southern workers toiled in small towns, where the assumptions of corporate paternalism prevailed. They often expected their employers to exercise care, in a real, personal sense not just a formal, legal one. When those expectations went unmet, feelings were hurt, and families turned to the courts for redress. Young workers asked for compensation, but they also asked for justice and recognition of the wrongs they had incurred. The legal process meant they necessarily had to paint their employers as guilty parties. Many owners and their managers took such accusations personally, for throughout the period Southern industries largely remained local, and often, family affairs. To be sure, large companies controlled some elements of Southern industry, especially railroads and mining. Still, many Southern owners and managers worked and lived in the small and medium-sized communities where their industries were located. In many instances, they thought of themselves as good corporate stewards and sought to portray such images to the community when on the stand.[53]

---

[53] Witt, *Accidental Republic*, 22–29 on the incidence of accidents. For a contrary view, see Bergstrom, *Courting Danger*, 40–57.

Mills, mines, and other workplaces in the South fostered social relationships between workers, managers, and owners that have often been
described as paternalistic. Nowhere was this paternalism more apparent than in the case of younger workers who had been hurt on the job.
An injured youngster, especially one quite young, gave those in power
the opportunity to display their largesse. Especially earlier in the period,
company officials visited the homes of injured young workers, bearing
gifts. The superintendent of Old Dominion Cotton Mills offered Robert
Jones's father twenty-five dollars after an accident. He later described
the act as "sympathy," denying intimations that it had been done to seek
a settlement. Clarence Miller worked in the office of an Owensboro,
Kentucky, print shop where Mike Hatfield was hurt. His boss sent him to
the Hatfield house after the incident. "I went up to see how he was getting along," Miller recalled. "Mr. Adams [the publisher] told me to watch
after him, and to see that he didn't suffer for anything. I went up there and
took him some fruit, also to the hospital while he was there." Such visits
did run the risk of seeming like the company accepted responsibility, a
charge that officials denied. The secretary-treasurer of Lynchburg Cotton
Mills in Virginia affirmed that he did not "stop to inquire whether the
mill [was] liable or not." Rather his rule was "to take care of them."[54]

Displays of corporate munificence could reach extreme proportions, as
a case from North Carolina in the late 1910s illustrates. Earl Butner lost
his arm at Brown Brothers Lumber Company in 1918. Butner's accident
was not even rightly a work-related injury. While he had carried water
in the mill, he had entered the plant to get wood strips to build a garden
fence at home. Ward F. Brown, the company superintendent, detailed the
gifts he showered on Earl after the injury. He ordered the vice president of
the company to send the boy a suit of clothes, a pair of shoes, and some
other trifles. Beyond this, Brown offered to send Earl to school "and keep
him in school until he got a fair education, provided that the boy would
stay in school and do some good." Brown intended to pay all expenses but
also to receive a monthly report from the teacher about Earl's progress.
Brown insisted that his actions admitted no responsibility for the accident.
Rather, he "would help that boy the same as anybody else."[55]

[54] *Record in Jones*, 32; *Record in Hatfield*, 92; *Record in Lynchburg Cotton Mills*, 97. For
a review of the older literature on paternalism in the New South, see David L. Carlton,
"Paternalism and Southern Textile Labor: A Historiographical Review" in *Race, Class,
and Community in Southern Labor History*, Gary M. Fink and Merl E. Reed eds.
(Tuscaloosa, 1994), 17–26. See also Newby, *Plain Folk*, 262–272.
[55] *Record in Butner*, 25.

Brown's largesse was not met with humble gratitude by the Butner household, a source of some bitterness on Brown's part. It seems that Earl's dad thought it might be good to get the deal in writing, so he hired a lawyer to draw up a contract. The elder Butner also sought to negotiate, insisting that the local schools might not be good enough and eventually getting Brown to agree to pay for both summer and fall terms. And still he insisted on putting it all on paper. The increasingly miffed Brown replied that he would not spend any money on Earl unless he showed progress. At this point, negotiations broke down. Mr. Butner "did not say yes or no but turned around and sued me or the Company," Brown declared. "I have sent dozens of boys to school and we have never signed a contract about it."[56]

The conflict between Ward Brown and the Butner family begins to reveal the volatile mixture of injured bodies, hurt feelings, and indignant expectations that brewed in small working towns in the wake of an accident or death. As always, the one-sided power relationship hoped for by owners and managers only succeeded in raising expectations on the part of workers. Chief among these expectations was the belief that owners should pay medical expenses after an accident, a reasonable hope since companies did often pay the medical expenses of injured young workers. As the president of Sylvia Lumber and Manufacturing put it, "I paid the plaintiff's doctor bill of $65.00 because it was our custom to do so irrespective of who was in fault." Some companies went further, paying medical expenses plus wages or other benefits. For instance, The Augusta Factory in Georgia procured a free rail pass for Anna Barnes's mother in the wake of an accident that eventually claimed the girl's life.[57]

Young workers and their families wanted medical care, but they wanted something more. They anticipated that their employers would genuinely care about their injuries and aid them in their road to recovery. While it might seem odd to want to return to the site of a life-altering injury, many injured workers expected the company to give them a job after a period of recovery. Candys Talmage was hurt at a Georgia bottling plant in 1912, and after he recovered, his mother requested employment for him. H.H. Tift later admitted that he often gave jobs to injured workers, but that he decided on a case-by-case basis. "If a man was injured

---

[56] Ibid.
[57] *Record in Ensley*, 19; *Record in Augusta Factory*, 23. See also *Record in Fitzgerald*, 13; *Record in Hauser*, 36; *Record in Manning*, Statement of Case; *Record in Lynchburg Cotton Mills*, 97; *Record in Woodruff*, 10.

at the mill I felt like I was under obligations to him," Tift averred. "I did it many times, simply as a charitable proposition." Apparently, Candys proved not to be one of those times, a decision that landed the company in court. "I decided to bring this suit last summer," the boy recalled. "And the reason I did [is because] mama went to him for support, to Captain Tift. She asked to give me a job to help to support her, and Captain told her he did not have anything for her."[58]

As with medical expenses, providing employment in the wake of an accident created expectations on the part of working people. When those expectations went unfulfilled, workers felt mistreated. Ebbirt Ward's family summed up W.R. Odell as "heartless" after he failed to visit Ebbie in the hospital. While Odell's lawyers stressed his "benevolence and philanthropy" in giving the Ward family employment, the Ward family's attorney revealed that he had "neglected" to give Ebbie "any help or assistance while so suffering." Similarly, Ward Brown stood accused of not contributing to a "subscription" being taken up by workers to help Earl Butner. When Willie Bartley was hurt in a Kentucky coal mine cave-in, the company treated his wounds (poorly in his estimation) and paid for medical expenses via the company commissary. Proffering assistance with one hand, Elkhorn Coal extracted its pound of flesh with the other. After Willie's little brother, Elisha, went to work at the mine, the company withheld his wages to cover the medical assistance they had extended to Willie. Not satisfied with this exchange, the company then withheld the wages they owed Willie from before the accident. Willie got fed up. "They done me so mean I just left," he declared.[59]

The unstated expectations of paternalism fostered rounds of negotiation before matters ever became conflicted enough to end up in a courtroom. Visits to injured young people might be about hurt feelings, but they also probed culpability. When a boss or owner called upon an injured young worker at home, the power relations of industrial life met human suffering at the bedside. Such meetings spoke a language of blame and forgiveness steeped in the evangelical culture of the New South but also redolent with the central constructs of negligence law. Did an injured young worker forgive her boss? Did a disabled boy blame the company? While the inquiries might be caught up in the emotion of pain

---

[58] *Record in Talmage*, 21, 24, 28. On corporate paternalism and rising expectations, see Gerald Zahavi, "Negotiated Loyalty: Welfare Capitalism and the Showorkers of Endicott Johnson," *Journal of American History* 70 (1983): 602–620.

[59] *Record in Ward*, n.p.; *Record in Butner*, 25; *Record in Bartley*, 11–14, 22; Freeze, "Patriarchy Lost," 28–29.

and suffering, the answers could have momentous consequences at a later date. According to one side of the story in an early Georgia case, Anna Barnes sent for her boss, Wellington Carter, as she lay dying from tetanus after her hand was smashed in the cogs of a spinning frame. "I went over, and she told me I have always loved you as a boss, and don't blame you," Carter testified. "I said I would have done all I could to prevent it if I had known you were there." Anna Barnes passed away shortly after her alleged conversation with Carter; Mike Hatfield lived to recount a story of blame and absolution in court. Like many others, Hatfield repeatedly denied having "blamed himself" after a mishap. "Q. Did you say you didn't blame anybody but yourself? A. I told him I didn't blame anybody but Ed Pendelton [his boss]. Q. Did you say you didn't blame anybody but yourself? A. No sir; I dint' say anything of the kind."[60]

Taking the time to see an injured young worker at home or in the hospital enacted the expectations of corporate paternalism, but the more negligence law developed, the more post-accident interactions focused on the legal necessities of the inevitable lawsuit. Company doctors and lawyers sought to take statements as rapidly as possible. Crown Cotton Mills procured a statement from William McNally shortly after he was hurt by a stripping machine in 1904. During the interview, they got William to say that "the machinery was all right" and that he had been "having good luck" with the cards. He stipulated that he had worked at the mill for three weeks and that he "knew perfectly well how to do the work." Beyond knowledge of the machines themselves, McNally affirmed that he understood that "it wasn't safe to put my hand down there when the door was open, as Mr. Brown had cautioned me to look out for the doors being left down." Covering all bases, the company lawyers assisted William to conclude that "the fault was that of the stripper, who left the door down, and nothing else caused me to get hurt. He alone was to blame for it." In a few short sentences, the company established that 1) it exercised ordinary care in providing safe equipment; 2) Will was an experienced worker who could only have gotten injured due to his own negligence; and, for good measure, 3) a fellow worker might have been responsible (just in case the fellow-servant defense might prove useful). Clearly, Will was not aware that at the time he was saying things that would come back to haunt him.[61]

---

[60] *Record in Augusta Factory*, 29; *Record in Hatfield*, 107. See also *Record in Craven*, 22–28; *Record in Jones*, 52.

[61] *Record in Crown Cotton Mills*, n.p.; Welke, *Recasting American Liberty*, 107.

As Crown Cotton Mills's conversation with Will McNally suggests, owners and managers might hope for peaceful relations with an injured family, but they also looked to the future and the bottom line. As time progressed, post-accident visits frequently offered condolences and a valise of papers to sign. Some settlements proposed a straightforward pay-off, but such buyouts of liability sometimes agitated injured workers and their families more than they soothed them. Lucinda Crosby recalled a conversation with an attorney who offered her twenty-five dollars to defray the expenses incurred by her son's injury. "He said to me, 'Mr. Keen asked me to come over here and see you; he heard that you expected him to pay a part of Ellis' expenses, and would if it was not over $25.00,' and I said, 'Why, I am expecting Mr. Keen to pay part of Ellis' expenses and then some,' and he says, 'Well if you are not going to accept that, there is no use to say anything further.'" When the Atlanta Cotton Factory tried to pay Hester Speer's wages in compensation for her accident, her mother disdained their overtures. "A little sum of money like that was nothing to me," she said. "It was my child's suffering that was something." Injured young workers themselves underscored such sentiments. As H.E. Kinder put it, "no amount of money would compensate him for his suffering and loss."[62]

Worse still were settlement attempts that relied on chicanery. Companies who suspected they had been imposed upon regarding a young worker's age or experience were particularly keen to create the appearance of a settlement. William P. Toms, secretary of the Fulton Company, a Tennessee firm, believed that Daniel Kendrick was much older than he claimed. Hence, they decided to pay his weekly wages while he was in the hospital "with a view of making a fair and equitable compromise of any claim of damages which might be presented by the boy and his parents, to the extent of at least allowing him the value of the loss of time, doctors bills and hospital fees."[63]

While company representatives could be duplicitous, conniving, and underhanded, working families still wanted something for their loss, and they often initiated attempts. James Monroe, a Virginia father, paid a visit to company officials after his son, Johnson, lost a hand in a woodworking plant in Altavista. "I said Mr. Loftin, what are you going to do about the loss of this child's hand," he recalled. "He replied and said, 'If

---

[62] *Record in Keen*, 21; *Record in Atlanta Cotton Factory Co.*, 19; *Record in Kinder*, 55.
[63] *Record in Fulton Co.*, 10–11; *Record in Interstate Coal Co.*, 17–48. See also *Record in Hammack*, 44–45.

he had been working in the shop and something fell on him I might pay him something; but as it is I am not going to pay anything unless [I] get it out of the insurance.'" Similarly, Ebbirt Ward's mother paid several visits to W.R. Odell asking him what he was going to do about Ebby's accident.[64]

Thomas and Emma Jones engaged in lengthy negotiations with Old Dominion Cotton Mills after Robert Lee lost his arm. First, they visited Edward Graham, treasurer of the company, only to be told the matter had to go before the board. A few months passed with no action, so Emma took the liberty of writing Graham. Her missive prompted a visit from the company's attorney, who brought with him two ten-dollar gold pieces and a five-dollar coin along with "some papers about ½ a yard long," Thomas Jones recalled. Those papers presented Robert with what was variously described as a "gift" or "present" and passed along the company's well-wishes. "I sincerely hope that you are improving," Graham wrote, "and that you will soon be completely restored." Graham's sympathy must have struck Robert and his parents as a bit misplaced, seeing how his arm, while still attached, was so mangled as to be "utterly useless." Their chagrin reappeared in court when Thomas Jones was presented with the documentation of the settlement. Jones admitted that he did not read the papers at the time because he was angry. What about? "About the way I was treated," he replied. By the time the case came to court, his trust of Old Dominion had hit rock bottom. Asked whether these were indeed the papers the family had received, he remained suspicious. "These may be the papers, or they may be fixed up," he reckoned.[65]

NO PROTECTION

Thomas Jones's waning trust in Old Dominion signaled the breakdown of paternalism that freed Southern working families to confront their employers in the courts. In these contests, early cases often revolved around money. Families and young workers sought lost wages and medical expenses. While physical and mental suffering appeared, it did not carry the significance it would in the early twentieth century. As time passed, working people demanded more than monetary compensation. They came to court to find justice. Though speaking through attorneys, the pleadings of working people rang with calls for the courts to make

[64] *Record in Standard Red Cedar Chest Co.*, 29; *Record in Ward*, n.p.
[65] *Record in Jones*, 4, 86–88.

right the wrongs they had endured. Stearns Coal and Lumber had run their operations at night and used boys to do the work of men. "There is no other solution to this question, and who shall bear the blame?" asked the Tuggle family's lawyer. "Will it be a mere child, whose father had requested this company to keep him out of the mines, or, will this court hold the strong and powerful to account for this wrong?" Another Kentucky case begged the courts not to sanction corporate reckless-ness: "Why should it be in the power of the employer of human machines, for that is about all ordinary workmen now are, to release himself from the obligation of observing ordinary care for their safety? Why should such a temptation to the sordidness and cupidity of employers be held out to them by the courts?"[66]

Beyond the injustices done to individual young workers and their fam-ilies, industrial violence was a shared experience, and many suits became a response to the injuries of the community. In fact, the Southern courts presented a venue where the largely non-unionized Southern workforce could engage in collective struggles for power against their employers. In many cases, young workers and their families called upon other workers who had been injured in a similar fashion, creating litigations that spoke for local working people in general. Although the accident crisis of the Progressive era eventually led to aggregate solutions via insurance settle-ments and workers' compensation, most Southern court appearances by working people into the 1920s still took on the trappings of a community get-together. An increasing number of young workers and their families did encounter the law when it came to their house in the form of a settle-ment offer, but they more often met it in town at the courthouse.[67]

In court, workers recited for the public the conditions and relations of their workplaces. A few workers single-mindedly took the part of the company, becoming, in essence, legal scabs, but for most, the response to industrial violence reinforced their sense of themselves as workers. Whether working people defended their employers or not, their court appearances formalized and authorized conflicts over workplace safety and the social relations of production. Court battles involving injured

---

[66] *Record in Stearns Coal & Lumber Co.*, 25–26; *Record in Wilson*, 25. For an example of an early case that involved few claims for anything other than monetary compensation, see *Record in Woodruff*.

[67] On the development of modern tort principles from the accident crisis and the impor-tance of settlements, see Samuel Issacharoff and John Fabian Witt, "The Inevitability of Aggregate Settlement: An Institutional Account of American Tort Law," *Vanderbilt Law Review* (2004): 1573–1602.

workers (adult ones as well) became a kind of collective action by working people. They allowed the burgeoning Southern industrial workforce to carry out battles that they might have pursued via unions had they been more widely available. For young workers themselves, the force of the community sanctioned their claims. In most circumstances, they did not stand against employer power by themselves. Moreover, it meant that their trips into town on court day gained a sense of legitimacy that originated in their own communities. It was not just their word against the company's. Kinfolk, friends, and neighbors also believed that something more could have been done to protect young workers. As the community sanctioned the idea of bargaining for safety, working people gained the fortitude to seek redress.[68]

Time and again, litigations allowed workers to discuss their shared experience of violence, and they did so in an authoritative, public location. Talking about Bob's broken leg around the lunch table was one thing, but testifying under oath lent such tales a stamp of legitimacy that informal conversations could not attain. For one thing, it put workers in a position where they became experts, displaying knowledge and skill increasingly denied to them in the supposedly deskilled environment of industrial labor. Though just twenty-one, Kelley Hendricks had worked for Lynchburg Cotton Mills for ten years when he took the stand in Fitz Stanley's case against the company. Such experience put him in a position to offer a credible opinion on whether an open belt could have been guarded against mischievous, young boys. Workers who spoke as authoritative witnesses were quite unlike hired experts. They possessed connections to the case, often familial ones. While J.C. Brown spoke about cotton spinning based on eight years experience, he also revealed that he was the brother-in-law of Ellen Gibbs, who had lost her finger in the machinery. Though such family connections might be unusual, workers spoke from a position of knowledge born of daily experience. Their knowledge set them off from their non-working employers, a point attorneys sometimes sought to drive home. When the vice president of a Virginia woodworking plant tried to offer an opinion on the machinery, Wilbur Loving's counsel quickly pointed out the obvious: "He has never shown he was an operator of a saw or had any experience along that line. He is simply an

---

[68] As such, they were political struggles. Stephen Hahn, *A Nation under Our Feet: Black Political Struggles in the Rural South from Slavery to the Great Migration* (Cambridge, 2003), 3. To an extent, it could be said these litigations confirm Forbath's thesis, albeit in a very different way. Forbath, *Law and the Shaping of the American Labor Movement*.

THE GEORGIA CRACKER IN THE COTTON MILLS.

AROUND THE GROCERY.

FIGURE 8. Reformers such as Clare DeGraffenried saw lazy fathers lounging around the general store, but such local community institutions served as critical locations where law and community melded. "The Georgia Cracker in the Cotton Mills," a seminal piece of reform writing, appeared in 1891. *Century Illustrated Magazine*, 1891. Courtesy of Northern Illinois University.

executive head there." Such statements threw into relief the sides of the conflict. Workers knew what was going on; employers did not.[69]

Only select workers could speak as experts, but the courts provided a forum for all working people to verbalize the violence that permeated everyday life in the industrializing South. Litigation allowed working people to recall publicly the private conversations they had with employers

[69] *Record in Lynchburg Cotton Mills*, 59–61; *Record in Gibbs*, 8; *Record in Miller Mfg. Co.*, 103. See also *Record in Davis*, n.p.; *Record in Vinson*, 8–10.

about workplace safety. E.W. Owsley described his conversation with Dan Carger, the boss at Hambrick Keg Factory in West Virginia. "I just told him that the floor was powerful dirty, with splinters and shavings, and it would probably cause some of the boys to get hurt there," Owsley told the court. Benny Laverty had been one of those little boys, and his feet eventually slipped on the trashy floor, throwing his hand into an unprotected saw. W.M. Dillon, another worker at the plant, noted that the saw had not had any protection until after the boy got hurt. Together, Owsley, Laverty, and Dillon re-created the conditions of the workplace that all of the employees at Hambrick faced on a daily basis, and as a result, Benny Laverty's claim became more than an individual contest.[70]

Workers talked about their experiences in a shared culture that placed industrial violence at the forefront. As J.W. Smith put it: "None of the railroad officials or anybody else never told me how to couple cars but I knew there was danger in railroading. I knew lots of people to get hurt by the railroad." Speaking to the danger of coupling rail cars, West Virginia worker John Ewing relied on local knowledge of the danger. Circulating among other workers, he had "heard of boys getting their brains busted out or cut in two coupling." Car coupling, whether on the railroads or in mines, was one of the most dangerous of all jobs, but other workplaces witnessed frequent accidents, a fact well known by workers and emphasized by their attorneys. "How many men did you have with fingers cut off last year?" W.C. Oslin, foreman at Miller Manufacturing, was asked. "You had more than several, didn't you?"[71]

Usually this collective discussion of industrial violence occurred as part of the routine proceedings of an individual case, but sometimes young workers and their families more consciously engaged in something akin to a class action suit, more explicitly turning court days into collective actions about workplace safety. Gaines Leathers's case against Blackwell Durham Tobacco exemplified this approach. In addition to Gaines, the Leathers family rounded up several other boys who had been hurt tying tobacco sacks at the factory. Each dutifully took the stand, detailed the tying process, and displayed his stump to the jury. Fifteen-year-old Fletcher Vickers recalled the danger matter-of-factly. "You have three chances to tie," he noted. "If a boy gets his hand caught with the string and it goes under the table, it gets cut." Wallace Minor, fourteen, was

---

[70] *Record in Laverty*, 1–5, 32, 59. See also *Record in Acme Box Co.*, 15, 46.
[71] *Record in Atlanta and West Point Railroad Co.*, 22; *Record in Ewing*, 32; *Record in Miller Mfg. Co.*, 92–93.

pithier: "If your hand gets caught in a string and gets below the plate, it is good-bye finger." Each boy who told his tale helped build the larger point that the Leathers family was making. It was not just Gaines. Rather, "a number of boys and young men working at automatic packing machines have been seriously injured or maimed for life."[72]

While most did not go to the lengths of the Leathers clan, young workers and their families had a strong sense that something could have been done. Injured young workers recalled conversations that seemed to indicate that company officials had known of the danger and refused to do anything about it. Oliver Collins, a worker at Chess and Wymond's barrel factory where Charles Wilson was scalded to death, overheard the foreman tell the superintendent that an uncovered vat was dangerous and that they ought to have something over it. Jessie Scott got the word straight from the horse's mouth. "After I was hurt, Mr. George Wade, the Gen. Manager of the Josephine Mills, said to me, that the machine was dangerous, but he supposed that I had found it out by this time," Scott averred.[73]

An even more compelling sign of employer responsibility appeared when companies made quick repairs or installed safety equipment immediately after an accident. After Tom McDaniel fell to his death in an elevator shaft, workers at Lynchburg Cotton Mills replaced the lattice gate guarding the elevator almost immediately. "We put the gates down as quick as we could," George Daniel, a worker at the mill, testified. "They were afraid somebody else would fall down." Charley Giebell discovered that Collins Company had later installed a guard on the joiner that tore up his hand. "About three weeks after I got hurt, I came down to the mill and seen it on there, and my brother told me they put it on about two weeks after I got hurt," Giebell recalled. Such statements cast blame on the company. If such repairs could be done easily and quickly, why hadn't they been done sooner?[74]

Companies appeared even more heartless, and negligent, in the face of hideous accidents that could have been prevented by simple safety measures. Fifteen-year-old Ralph Girvin fell into a vat of boiling water at a Georgia woodworking plant. Later, fellow workers recalled the lack of attention to safety. "What protection, what guard or rope if any?" Blair Latham, a fellow young worker who witnessed the accident, was asked. "They ain't had nothing; they didn't have anything around it," he

---

[72] *Record in Leathers*, 7, 23–24.
[73] *Record in Wilson*, 10; *Record in Evans (Georgia)*, 13.
[74] *Record in McDaniel*, 25; *Record in Giebell*, 22.

replied. Ralph's dad confirmed this fact. "There was no rope, no protection, no guide line, no life line," a distraught Henry Girvin told the court. "Nothing to keep anyone from falling in there, not a thing in the wide world."[75]

The bottom line for young workers, their families, and their associates was that something ought to have been done. Either protective equipment was in disuse or disrepair, or it had never been installed as it should have been. After a shuttle from a loom took her eye, Leila Vinson learned that the guards that should have prevented the accident had been removed. Ellen Gibbs echoed Vinson's experience. Gibbs was nine when she lost her fingers in a Georgia textile mill. Coming to court some years later, she knew why she was there. "Those cogs that were not covered up like they ought to have been," she argued. J.P. Butler, the stepfather of a boy injured by falling into an elevator shaft, had a similar outlook. "There isn't anything about the elevator shaft to prevent a fence or guard being put across that opening," Butler suggested.[76]

In the face of such notions, companies often answered that workers' notions of commonsense protection were neither common nor sensible. A lengthy exchange from a Virginia textile case reveals the commitment of working people to their own notions of workplace safety and the lengths to which company lawyers would go to disparage them. Kelley Hendricks was convinced that the belt that injured Fitz Stanley could have been fenced off. Lynchburg Cotton Mills Company's attorney was not so sure. "How would you fence it?" he asked. "You could start from the floor and build up and run it as high as the boy that runs it to throw the belt off on the loose pulley; that could be done easily," Hendricks replied. Pressed again and again, Hendricks maintained that it would be "easy enough" to cover the belting. "Tell me how?" the attorney demanded. "Fence it in, just as any other thing would be done," Hendricks insisted. If all else failed, he affirmed, the company could make "a top to go over the machine." This exchange went on for several minutes, repeated with Fitz's brother, Gus, and continued the next day. Kelley and Gus stuck to their guns. Eventually, the company produced another worker to testify that such fencing would interfere with the operations of the machinery, but the point had been made. If Lynchburg Cotton Mills had taken obvious precautions, Fitz would still have his arm.[77]

---

[75] *Record in Girvin*, 14. See also *Record in Laverty*, 61–62.
[76] *Record in Vinson*, 2–4; *Record in Gibbs*, 8; *Record in Kendrick*, 51.
[77] *Record in Lynchburg Cotton Mills*, 93.

As this instance reveals, fellow workers sometimes took the position of the company. Still, in doing so, they also drew upon elements of the work culture of laboring people and thus contributed to the sense of industrial violence as a shared experience. As labor historians have pointed out, bosses in the industrializing South had often come up through the ranks. These men often took pride in their abilities as foremen. A coal mine foreman told Ben Wasson, a young collier in Tennessee, that "he had been working in mines for about 25 years and had never had any one hurt yet." Such men were likely to see accidents as the fault of workers themselves. John C. Bailey was in his seventies or eighties by the time he testified as a "practical machinist" in a Georgia courtroom. Having started out as an apprentice in the 1820s, he worked at several textile plants, and then served as superintendent of a company. He believed he knew the ways of the mill folk. Some of them just would not listen. "Most of the factories they stop the machine in cleaning it so as to avoid all danger, but there are some hard heads that don't do what they are told, and they take things in their own hands an attempt to clean them without stopping the machine," Bailey declared.[78]

The varying experiences workers brought to their perceptions of danger sometimes produced radically different assessments of the risks involved. Joe Coggins took the stand in Edward Moncrief's claim against Eagle and Phenix Mills, and related his run-in with a lap winder. Like Ed, he had gotten hurt on the machine shortly after he started running it. "This machine known as the lap-winder machine is a dangerous machine to operate," Coggins maintained. "Because when you get up there you are liable to get your fingers caught, and the lap turns all the time and gets your fingers in the rollers." J.W. Creech, an oiler and maintenance man (and an adult), begged to differ. To him, a lap winder was "a simple machine to operate," no more or less risky than any other piece of equipment in a cotton mill. "There is not any danger at all in this one when it is running, without you just go[ing] there and stick[ing] your hand in those rollers," Creech insisted. "That is all the way I see a man could get hurt on them."[79]

Coggins and Creech might differ about the hazards associated with a lap winder, but they shared a common point of reference. Creech did not deny that mill work was dangerous; he just could not see a lap winder as

[78] *Record in Smith* 37; *Record in Davis*, n.p.; Jacquelyn Down Hall et al., *Like a Family: The Making of a Southern Cotton Mill World* (Chapel Hill, 1987), 91–98.
[79] *Record in Eagle and Phenix Mills*, 41.

any more threatening than the next machine. These sorts of debates ran through most accident cases, and they reveal how complicated enforcement of law could be. The social justice sought by reformers depended to a great extent on how workers and their employers responded to those efforts. In some cases, both sides welcomed the change; in others, they fought back. In either case, the actual implementation of child labor law mattered less than did the avenue it gave working families into the courts. Statutory reform, and more importantly, the changes in the judicial imagination of childhood over the previous century had set the stage on which young workers and their families would seek justice. Moreover, the shared experience of violence meant that an industrial accident litigation became a community event, one in which other injured workers got the chance to tell their stories and one in which the community came together to discuss the meanings of life-ending or limb-shattering violence. Workers, parents, teachers, doctors, ministers, neighbors, and bosses all worked on this stage, but they did so with props supplied to them by the law. Their performances would put the constructs of childhood imagined by journalists and jurists into practice.

6

The Dawn of Child Labor

He acted like a child, and he is not to be judged as a man. (Pennsylvania Supreme Court, 1858)

"Go on and tell the jury how it happened – tell the truth." Fitz Stanley was in the witness box, responding carefully to a series of questions posed by his attorney. What made him stop at the lap winder? He didn't know. What made him play with the belts? He'd seen his companions do it. What happened when the belts hit him? "Knocked a hole in my head," the twelve-year-old Fitz responded. What happened at the hospital? "Took my arm off." In this series of staccato calls and responses, Stanley and his lawyer re-created scenes of industrial violence, a performance that no doubt reached its dramatic height when A.W. Nowlin instructed Fitz, "Now take off your coat and let the jury see where they took your arm off." Even if Fitz did not know what truth all this was driving at, Nowlin did. Had Fitz seen the boys playing with the belt before? Yes. Did he know it was harmful? No. Had anyone warned them? "No, sir."[1]

By the time Fitz and his extended family walked into a courtroom in 1902, reform writers and jurists had supplied a script for the injuries and amputation Fitz had endured. The language of that script said that injuries to young workers likely resulted from "childish impulses and instincts" given free rein in places children had no right to be. This explanation for

---

[1] *Record in Lynchburg Cotton Mills*, 43–49. On personal injury lawyers, see Randolph Bergstrom, *Courting Danger: Injury and Law in New York City, 1870–1910* (Ithaca, 1992), Ch. 4.

the lives and losses of young workers and their families collided with the desires of working people to bring youthful labor into the factories in ways that could be safely contained. The statutory restriction of child labor had begun to alter the ways working people understood "child labor," but many continued to resist. The encounter with violence on the shop floor brought working people into contact with new ideas of childhood in a setting where who said what mattered as much as who did what. Seeking recompense for their injuries, working families came to tell their stories, but they could not tell them entirely in their own words. Each trial presented the community with a miniature melodrama of child labor, offering a public setting for discussing events and making sense of them. Workers, neighbors, judge, and jury assembled to come to terms with the deaths and injuries young workers experienced on the job. How well the members of this troupe played their roles would influence both the literal outcome, in dollars and cents, and the cultural one, in the framing of new ways to understand the place of young people under industrial capitalism.[2]

These judicial morality plays invoked and evoked elements of the surrounding culture of industrializing America, although some were notably absent. In a Southern setting, the immigrant story rarely figured prominently. More importantly, while race weighed heavily on Southern reformers when they talked about child labor, it appeared only fleetingly in Southern courtrooms. This does not mean race was unimportant. The whiteness of the proceedings heightened the salience of gender, particularly masculinity. The prototypical courtroom drama involved a young, male worker on the cusp of coming of age, and it told a story of manhood lost and offered the hope for manhood regained.[3]

Still, young workers who came to court were not men and women in the eyes of the onlookers or in the view of the law. They were children,

---

[2] These stories form what Michael Grossberg calls the "ontological narrative" of "legal experience," wherein participants seek through their personal stories to make meaning out of events. Michael Grossberg, *A Judgment for Solomon: The d'Hauteville Case and Legal Experience in Antebellum America* (New York, 1996), xiv. For more on legal story-telling, see (among others) Norma Basch, *Framing American Divorce: From the Revolutionary Generation to the Victorians* (Berkeley, 1999), Ch. 6; and Hendrick Hartog, *Man and Wife in America: A History* (Cambridge, 2000), 1–7.

[3] On injury, gender, and law, see Barbara Young Welke, *Recasting American Liberty: Gender, Race, Law, and the Railroad Revolution, 1865–1920* (New York, 2001), esp. Ch. 2; John Fabian Witt, *The Accidental Republic: Crippled Workingmen, Destitute Widows, and the Remaking of American Law* (Cambridge, 2004), esp. Chs. 1, 5; and Jamie L. Bronstein, *Caught in the Machinery: Workplace Accidents and Injured Workers in Nineteenth-Century Britain* (Stanford, 2008), 86–89.

either in the flesh or remembered in death. Winning a case required narrating a story in which images of child labor took a central part. In court, many cultural and legal strands came together. Lawyers took care to present young accident victims to juries in ways that conformed to expectations about children and child labor, depicting dark scenes of frantic toil performed by laborers unversed in the ways of the factory. Young workers and their families drew upon prevailing imagery as well, increasingly fashioning their claims around good children who should have been in school. By the 1920s, working people and their legal representatives more consistently portrayed young workers through the lenses of middle-class childhood.

THE AVERAGE OF THE COMMUNITY

Telling stories in a courtroom lent them a power they did not have when recited elsewhere. Here, workers and community members met the formal law in the form of pronouncements from judges and direction by their attorneys. These actors served as conduits for the legal principles and cultural imagery worked out by jurists and reformers. Important as they were, judges and litigators found their influence constrained by juries. Jurors represented a wild card in the proceedings, vested with cultural and legal power, yet limited by the law as they received it from the mouths of the man behind the bench. All of these actors shaped the legal culture in which Southern working people would formulate meanings for industrial violence and the place of young workers in an industrial world.[4]

As the directors of courtroom dramas, attorneys on both sides served as crucial translators of legal precepts to the assembled community. As we shall see, plaintiffs's lawyers led their young and not-so-young actors toward particular versions of the legal script of childhood, not without considerable difficulty in some instances. Too much preparation might lead to charges of witness coaching, or a young worker might not remember rightly. On the other side of the conflict, company litigators perforce took the role of the heavy, slighting injuries or deflating tales of suffering. Questions real and rhetorical cast working people in poor light. "Is your job worth more than the life of your wife's grandson?" a coal company attorney inquired in a West Virginia litigation. Such affronts did

---

[4] For a similar investigation of children in the courts, see Stephen Robertson, *Crimes against Children: Sexual Violence and Legal Culture in New York City, 1880–1960* (Chapel Hill, 2005).

not overawe working people, but they sometimes led to uncomfortable encounters redolent of class and cultural conflict. "What makes you so uneasy while you are testifying?" asked Thacker Fuel's attorney. "I am not uneasy," replied a West Virginia miner. "Look at the jury," the lawyer commanded. "I would rather look at you," his subject retorted. "You are the prettiest." Interacting with attorneys on either side, working people learned to play with and within the language of the law. A West Virginia grandfather put his young charge's defiance in legal terms. H. Marshall had warned Frank not to take the motor trip into the mines, but, he disclosed, his grandson had "over-ruled my motion."[5]

Lawyers served as one critical junction between the precepts of the formal law and the realities of working people, but even more vital were lower court judges. While the law might present itself as unitary, the judges who occupied local benches by no means spoke with one voice. Some judges took their lines from the anti-child labor law forces. Judge Howard Van Epps of the City Court of Atlanta deployed common arguments made by Southern industrialists and opponents of child labor reform. Considering the case of W.H. Wynne, a young worker injured while using a tin shears for his own purposes, Epps bluntly told the jury that he would not allow a verdict for the plaintiff. In particular, he wanted to squelch the notion that employers had any duty to fence off dangerous machinery. "The rule would prohibit the employment of children in every factory in Georgia," Van Epps declaimed. "The employment of children in places where machinery is used is often a beneficence to the poor, whose circumstances cannot allow them to sustain their children in idleness or emply [employ] them at school."[6]

Other members of the bench followed the discourse of reformers and progressive jurists. Floyd Estill, a lower court judge in an important Tennessee case, reversed the logic of the defense, arguing that even if Luther Green had been playing with the wire panels that injured him, his case fell within the purview of the state's child labor laws. "I think the Legislature had in mind in passing this statute just such cases as this – to keep boys of tender years off such premises where they would be liable to be injured by iron fences and such things," Estill opined. E.W. Saunders of the Circuit Court for Lynchburg, Virginia, went further, invoking both

---

[5] *Record in Rhodes*, 132; *Record in Daniels*, 70. On the importance of plaintiffs's attorneys in a later period, see John Fabian Witt, *Patriots and Cosmopolitans: Hidden Histories of American Law* (Cambridge, 2007), 211–278.

[6] *Record in Wynne*, 7–8; Bergstrom, *Courting Danger*, 114–132.

the language of child labor reformers and accepting the arguments of working people about the ease of preventing harm. Throughout a lengthy opinion, Saunders contrasted the "little boys" in the case with the "big machines" in the mill. He accepted the line of argument coming from turntable cases that the "natural instincts" of children made them likely to be mischievous around machinery. Hence, the perils of the workplace must be explained to a child in a way "adequate to his childish understanding." Finally, if that did not suffice, employers could fence off dangerous machinery, just like working people continually argued they could. Without doubt, Saunders admitted, truly mischievous children might find a way to meddle with the machinery anyway, but this was the very reason they should be protected from mishaps caused by "their very youth and inexperience."[7]

Issued in 1903, Saunders's opinion presents one of the most forthright statements of reform discourse emanating from a lower court judge, but it stands in line with other lower court judges who transmitted the evolving discourse of child labor to Southern locales. It is important to note who, exactly, Saunders identified as a child. Fitz Stanley and his associates were between twelve and fourteen, the mushy age at the center of the child labor controversy. Drawing on the long line of thinking encapsulated by Cooley's famous aphorism about "childish instincts and impulses," judges such as Saunders helped redefine such young persons away from adulthood and into childhood, with its attendant "natural" incapacities. Obviously, Southern working people did not pick up *A Treatise on the Law of Torts* at their local bookseller, but they did hear what the elites of their communities told them from the bench. That they brought an ever-increasing number of cases suggests they took seriously what His Honor said. Such authoritative pronouncements offered young workers an avenue to compensatory justice, but at the price of a redefinition of working-class understandings of childhood and youth.

Judges spoke to litigants and attorneys, but above all they spoke to the assembled community in the jury box. Throughout U.S. history, juries have been praised and reviled as symbols of reason and unreason, democracy and corruption. In the famous turntable case, Justice Hunt issued an oft-repeated ode to juries. "Twelve men of the average of the community, comprising men of education and men of little education, men of learning and men whose learning consists only in what they have themselves

---

[7] *Record in Ornamental Iron and Wire Co.*, 51; *Record in Lynchburg Cotton Mills*, 26–32.

seen and heard, the merchant, the mechanic, the farmer, the laborer; these sit together, consult, apply their separate experience of the affairs of life to the facts proven," he wrote. Twelve heads were better than one, Hunt reasoned, and acting together they could draw "safer conclusions" than could a lone judge.[8]

Other high courts were not so sanguine. Justices frequently lectured their audiences about undue sympathy and prejudice. "The sympathies of the fathers and brothers who compose the jury, are always powerfully excited by the distressing circumstances of the case and the eloquent appeals of counsel," the Pennsylvania court had opined in 1891. "Wild verdicts are frequently rendered." Many Southern lawyers, and not a few judges, also found juries to be a problem. When Lynchburg Cotton Mills's attorneys set out to establish an employer's "right to control his own business," they found juries to be an impediment. They took the liberty to cite a lengthy critique of juries from another Pennsylvania litigation. Except for making wills, Justice Mitchell had written, "there is nothing which a jury is more apt to think it can do better … than to say how another man's business ought to have been managed, and nothing in which juries should be held more strictly and unflinchingly within their proper province." The ruling, Lynchburg's litigators contended, provided a valuable lesson that could not be ignored. Employers must remain free from the constraints of the community imposed via jury trials.[9]

In fact, from the perspective of those who wanted "efficient" or "modern" law, juries were a problem. In smaller towns especially, jurors might be related to litigants. At the very least, many people in court knew each other and had multiple associations outside the courtroom. In such settings, expecting impartiality was virtually absurd. More importantly, as fellow community members and sometimes fellow workers, jurors often acted on shared community understandings of justice as much as on the central precepts of accident law. A North Carolina jury found a young worker guilty of contributory negligence, a finding that should have stopped the case, yet awarded him $700 in damages. Such outcomes evinced a desire to both find the truth and to dispense some kind of assistance. Out of step with the doctrines of negligence law, these were just the sort of outcomes that corporate attorneys feared.[10]

---

[8] *Railroad v. Stout*, 84 U.S. 657 (1874), 664.

[9] *Pennsylvania Railroad Co. v. Kelly*, 31 Pa. 372 (1858), 379; *Record in McDaniel*, Brief for Defendant in Error, 8, citing *Kehler v. Schwenk*, 144 Pa. 348 (1891), 358.

[10] *Record in Pressly*, 19. It could be said that the jury was following the doctrine of "comparative negligence." See *Glover v. Gray*, 9 Ill. App. 329 (1881).

As a result, judges and attorneys sought to rein in the latitude juries claimed. Judges repeatedly warned juries that they could not award damages for pain and suffering. The judge's charge in the case of Bub Raines typified these perorations. Perhaps because the accident was so gruesome, with Bub's body strewn hundreds of feet down the tracks, the judge took special pains to dampen any idea of damages for pain and suffering on the part of the boy's family. "You cannot give anything as a balm to anyone," Judge James L. Webb intoned. Just to be clear, the learned judge reminded the jury that they would not "undertake to give the equivalent of the value of human life," and by no means could they "punish the railroad company."[11]

Restrictions on awards that would soothe grief aligned with available, though contested, doctrines in negligence law, but judges frequently went beyond law on the books, taking it upon themselves to comment directly about the power relations of the case. Judges repeatedly told juries not to be influenced by the fact that the case pitted a "poor boy" against a "rich corporation." Judge O.H. Guion of the Halifax, North Carolina Superior Court made the point plainly to a jury considering the cause of Arthur Burnett, the fourteen-year-old orphan horribly mangled by a textile mill beater. Jurors, he instructed, should not be "controlled by any personal or collective sympathy" for Arthur due to his age, his "position in life," or his "maimed condition." Invoking the standard rhetoric of classical legal thought, Thomas Shaw put the matter simply in another North Carolina litigation. Jurors were to consider the case "as if it was between a man and a man and do what is right and do your duty conscientiously and honestly."[12]

In issuing such statements, lower court judges simply performed their prescribed role in the legal culture. But the fact that what they were doing was normal does not diminish its significance. As these examples demonstrate, Southern courtrooms of the late nineteenth and early twentieth centuries provided a venue for the discussion of economic power. As juries increasingly sided with working people, awarding ever-larger damages, such conflicts took on more and more salience. Nothing threw the issues into starker relief than a young worker with a broken body confronting his former employer and his retainers. These proceedings went forward

---

[11] *Record in Raines*, 50, 52.
[12] *Record in Burnett*, 34; *Record in Ward*, Judge's Charge, n.p. See also *Record in Ensley*, 44; *Sparks v. Maeschal*, 217 Ky. 235 (1926), 243. For an example of anticorporate sentiment elsewhere, see *Englund v. Mississippi Valley Traction Co.*, 139 Ill. App. 572 (1908), 578–579.

with a central tension. On the one hand, injured young workers sought to perform their pain and win over the jury. On the other, they and everyone else in the court swore to get to the bottom of things.[13]

As progressive justice sought to restrain the role of juries in the late nineteenth and early twentieth centuries, the twelve good men looked to retain their traditional functions. Over the preceding centuries, the jury had evolved from a body of community members intimately associated with the case towards the more modern idea of impartiality. Moreover, the legal community had increasingly severed the roles of judges and juries, leaving judges to expound the "law" and juries to determine the "facts." Such fictions rested centrally on the anonymity of urban life. In Atlanta or Richmond, imagining the jury as an impartial fact-finding body might approach being true, but in the country courthouses that dotted the rural South, jurors took a role more in keeping with their early modern progenitors than with the dragooned auditors of today's court proceedings. In either case, the jury embodied the central institutional assumption of Western justice – that a court could find the "truth" hidden in the welter of hazy memories, shrewd exaggerations, and downright fibs that constituted the "evidence."[14]

In seeking the whole truth, courts in the South ran into something peculiarly Southern. The South has often been described as a land of storytellers, and the late nineteenth century marked the emergence of this regional identity in a literary genre know as local color writing. Authors such as Joel Chandler Harris made a career out of adapting (to put it charitably) the voice and narrative thread of stories passed down by generations of working folk in the South, particularly African Americans. In a more original vein, Mark Twain helped cement the region as a place where people loved to tell a good story, and the best stories always had a bit of bull in them. If images of overall-clad men spinning yarns around the cracker barrel are overblown, Southerners nonetheless brought to court a culture steeped in narrative traditions increasingly at odds with the modernizing forces of Progressive era law.[15]

---

[13] Bourdieu, "Force of Law," 846–847; Tomlins, "A Manifesto of Destiny," 4.
[14] On juries, see Kermit Hall, *The Magic Mirror: Law in American History* (New York, 1989), 107–108; Bergstrom, *Courting Danger*, 133–143; Gail Williams O'Brien, *The Color of the Law: Race, Violence, and Justice in the Post-World War II South* (Chapel Hill, 1999), 235–255.
[15] Edward Ayers, *The Promise of the New South: Life after Reconstruction* (New York, 1992), 339–372; John Mayfield, "Being Shifty in a New Country: Southern Humor and the Masculine Ideal" in *Southern Manhood: Perspectives on Masculinity in the New Old South* ed. Craig Thompson and Lorri Glover (Athens, 2004), 113–135; Nan Goodman,

At the same time, however, Southerners carried with them an evangelical and honorific culture that valorized personal honesty and public rectitude. While honor and its manifestations have been contested subjects in the history of the region, Southerners who came to court took pride in "knowing what they were talking about," and they took umbrage at implications that they were lying. In doing so, they also drew upon the region's evangelical culture, especially its conflicted tenets on oath-taking and witnessing. Southern pulpits expounded the imperative to tell the truth, to be upright yet humble in dealings with neighbors, to be above reproach in the public eye. As with storytelling traditions, these injunctions clashed with the need for advocacy in a winner-take-all courtroom.[16]

Sometimes the actors in Southern courtroom dramas addressed the matter of truth-telling directly. Invoking the words of Sunday morning, a Georgia cotton mill operative confirmed that he had "never been approached by anybody to get me to swear falsely in this case." A linguistically challenged West Virginia man put it this way: "I want an indistinct understanding. I want to be straight, gentlemen." Time and again, working people volunteered their intentions in this manner, insisting that they knew what was going on. Challenged to say whether he was "perfectly certain" and threatened with a rebuttal witness, Thomas Grubbs pointed out how he could be so clear about the actions of Tom McDaniel's behavior in a Virginia cotton mill. "I was standing right there," Grubbs declared, "and I know what I am talking about."[17]

Establishing one's own veracity mattered so much because it related intimately to one's character and reputation in the community. Being a gifted storyteller was one thing; being known as a liar was quite another. Moreover, neighborly relations depended upon maintaining public appearances of trust in character. As the supreme test of that trust, words spoken under oath carried potentially explosive results for life outside the courtroom. As in any legal proceeding, witnesses repeatedly faced a choice about whether to identify fellow workers or community members as trustworthy and truthful. The question "Do you know what his character and general reputation where he lives is for truth and veracity?"

Shifting the Blame: Literature, Law, and the Theory of Accidents in Nineteenth-Century America (Princeton, 1998), 65–97.

[16] Bertram Wyatt-Brown, *Southern Honor: Ethics and Behavior in the Old South* (New York, 1982); Kenneth S. Greenberg, *Honor and Slavery*, (Princeton, 1996); Ayers, *Promise of the New South*, 169–173.

[17] *Record in Elk Cotton Mills*, 38; *Record in Waldron*, 53; *Record in McDaniel*, 64.

carried enormous implications outside the courtroom in a culture still shot through with notions of personal honor, especially for its menfolk.

Someone like Thomas Grubbs could proclaim that he knew what he was talking about, but in the end, his veracity depended upon his neighbors. Grubbs could not have been too pleased when Roy Ferguson recalled hearing people say that Grubbs was "the biggest liar in the state." Calling Grubbs a liar in a formal, public setting was risky business, however. In a male culture where honor and fistfights were virtually synonymous, one had to watch what one said. Asked to affirm the notion that Grubbs was the "biggest liar in the state," J.L. Page backpedaled. "If I said it – I might have said it through a joke sometimes, but I didn't mean any harm," Page admitted. Such character assassinations were not limited to adult men. One person after the next stood up to impugn the reputation of David Salzman, a teenager central to a Georgia case. Besides being a "loafer" who had already run afoul of the law, folks in Waycross found his reputation so bad that they would "not believe him on his oath."[18]

Downright lying was not so common as accusations and counteraccusations that involved rewards for telling the story a particular way. Working people and their attorneys repeatedly raised the notion that fellow workers who testified for their bosses had something to gain. J.C. Carter, an employee of Elk Cotton Mills, denied that he was "a regular witness for the company" and that he was "looking for a better job" on account of the case. Flossie Saxon, a young worker at High Shoals Manufacturing, exemplified the multiple rewards that might come from creative veracity. On the one hand, she denied asking for a raise in pay for helping out the bosses, though she admitted that her father had gotten the job previously occupied by the stepfather of Jim Kendrick, the plaintiff. On the other hand, she boldly accused J.P. Butler (said stepfather) of trying to bribe her. "Mr. Butler approached me and talked to me about this case soon after it occurred," Saxon revealed. "He told me one Sunday evening at his house if I would just swear that Jimmie fell through the elevator hole and not swear anything else and if I didn't come out better by it he would buy me the finest silk dress there was in Madison."[19]

In all likelihood, Flossie Saxon was fibbing, perhaps on all counts, but her yarns illuminate the complex dialogue that the culture of the court

---

[18] *Record in McDaniel*, 71; *Record in Keen*, 23; Ted Ownby, *Subduing Satan: Religion, Recreation, and Manhood in the Rural South, 1865–1920* (Chapel Hill, 1990), 53–54.
[19] *Record in Elk Cotton Mills*, 38; *Record in Kendrick*, 65–66, 71–72.

created when melded with the assumptions participants brought along. Community expectations about righteousness ran counter to practices then becoming increasingly common in the modern courtroom. Chief among these was coaching of witnesses, a charge made all the more salient when children testified. Children on the stand frequently faced charges that they were just saying what some adult told them to say. "My mother didn't tell me what to testify in this case," Ellis Crosby insisted. "She didn't say anything, just told me to go to see Parks and Reed," the family's attorneys. Robert Jones, a teenaged plaintiff in a Virginia litigation, rebuffed allegations of coaching in a similar fashion: "Nobody has been talking to me about this case since the last trial (telling me what to say)."[20]

As time progressed, matters became ever more muddled as company attorneys rushed to collect statements, witnesses, and physical evidence with the expectation of an eventual suit. In a time and place where many potential witnesses were illiterate, a written statement represented a powerful tool in the hands of company officials or lawyers. Officials for Crown Cotton Mills in Georgia took the next logical step, preparing statements beforehand. W.K. Moore, an official for the company, revealed that the firm's lawyer, a "Colonel" McCamy had talked casually with Will Nelms and then handed Moore a statement for the man to sign. "I went to him with a statement about it and witnessed his signature to that statement," Moore reported. "He signed it, he made his mark." While Moore relied on counsel, other managers took matters directly into their own hands. Trying to discern Charley Grant's actual age, L.F. Kelly, superintendent of Elk Cotton Mills, hit the road. "I made a trip over to Clinton about this case and we got what we were after," Kelly acknowledged.[21]

If company officials tried to be cagey, they also discovered that workers could outfox them. J.H. Cyphers just did not perform as expected when talking about Phil Waldron's death at Garland Coal. Sure, the company had taken his deposition, Cyphers said, but they had not asked him to remember what they wanted now. Percy Dick, a West Virginia collier, was even more cantankerous when asked to remember what he had said in a statement. "Didn't you come into Mr. O'Toole's office up there and in the presence of his stenographer and several other gentlemen make a statement about how this accident occurred?" he was asked. "Probably I might have," he responded. "A man is liable to say anything. I wasn't

[20] *Record in Keen*, 9; *Record in Jones*, 41. See also *Record in Eagle and Phenix Mills*, 32.
[21] *Record in Crown Cotton Mills*, n.p.; *Record in Elk Cotton Mills*, 34.

summoned there." Agitated by Dick's impertinent reply, U.S. Coal and
Coke's attorney refused to drop the matter. "You don't tell the truth
except when you are under oath?" he parried. "So far as I know," the
miner drawled. "I wasn't sworn." As Dick's comments indicate, oathtak-
ing could cut both ways. Something was only true if said under oath, and
when that magic moment actually occurred was never clear. Fooling with
a company attorney only added to the fun.[22]

The answers to simple questions grew even murkier as cases spread
over days, months, and in some cases, years. As accident litigations
sought ironclad proof of causation, they asked witnesses to recall details
that seemed meaningless at the time. Kate Carter knew she had seen Tom
McDaniel playing around the elevator at Lynchburg Cotton Mills, but,
of course, she thought nothing of it until he plunged to his death. "I
wouldn't have thought of it again I guess unless he had been killed,"
she pointed out. Such is the nature of human memory, and that memory
clouded under the stress of the courtroom. Lucille Overstreet, a witness
in a Kentucky case, expressed her frustration at the confusion created by
the trial. Yes, Virginia Adams had told Lucille her age, but now, she could
not be sure about what she had said. "There have been so many things
told about her age, I don't know her age," Overstreet admitted. "I don't
know if she knew her age." Cora Magnus begged a badgering company
attorney to lay off so she could get things sorted out about when her
many children were born. "I can remember the days they was born if you
just didn't bother me. Leave me alone," Magnus spat back after a lengthy
line of questions. "You got me bothered now, and I don't know whether
I have got it straightened out or not now."[23]

Ultimately, the bedrock fictions of the legal system, that truth could
be found, broke down into a myriad of competing stories about what
had actually happened. Narratives and counternarratives spilled across
the doorways that supposedly separated the "legal" world of the court
from everything else. Violent accidents provided a source of conversation among workers, something to talk about on lunch breaks, with relations, or at the store. Those conversations then reverberated to the halls
of justice. In short, the "courts" did not occupy a cultural space separate
from the "community." Litigants, witnesses, attorneys, judges, jurors – all

---

[22] *Record in Hairston,* 51.
[23] *Record in McDaniel,* 47; *Record in Sanitary Laundry Co.,* 104; *Record in Magnus,* 22.
It could be contended, perhaps, that these instances exemplify a gendered dimension to
testimony, and certainly women told stories differently. But for similar examples from
men, see *Record in Waldron,* 87; *Record in Crown Cotton Mills,* n.p.

formed part of a local (and vocal) legal process that made meaning for youthful labor and industrial violence.[24]

VIOLENCE ON TRIAL

For all the confusion that time and trouble caused to their memories, Southern working families came to court with a desire to talk about the miseries that had befallen them. Cora Magnus might have been "bothered" on the witness stand, but she knew why she was there. When asked the relatively simple question of whether her son, Herbert, could walk after his accident, the feisty West Virginia mother snapped her answer. "No, indeed, he couldn't walk," Magnus responded. "See a boy walk on one leg? He couldn't hop, let alone walk, and hold that leg up." Throughout her time on the stand, Cora interrupted the proceedings to interject her voice, insisting that she had the right to tell things her way.[25]

Young workers themselves were no less ardent in their efforts to get across the pain and suffering they endured. "I suffered near about death," Arthur Burnett testified. "I thought I was going to die." Even long after the accident, his head ached all the time, he told the court. "I see fire at times coming out of my eyes." Similarly, Bruce Holt recounted bouts of depression and thoughts of suicide. "I couldn't sleep at night," he recalled. "In [my] mind I was all torn up on account of my condition." Bruce's condition was indeed horrible, and the nature of a civil lawsuit for damages required him and young workers like him to re-enact the violence of their injuries for the assembled court. In cases of death, kinfolk, fellow workers, and community members did that duty in their stead. As a result, their claims for damages became something more than a simple (or not so simple) search for who was to blame. Rather, they provided the only consistent public forum in which workers and their families could discuss the chilling truths of industrial life.[26]

The courts provided the stage on which a tableau of horror unfolded. In this arena, workers and their attorneys re-created the details of their accidents: the scene, the sounds, the blood and broken bones. Sometimes that meant literally reconstructing the shop floor before the bench. Sometimes it entailed dramatic tales of rescue or hopeless feelings when

---

[24] For more examples of the overlap between court and community, see *Record in Atlanta Cotton Factory Co.*, 99; *Record in Augusta Factory*, 43; *Record in Davis*, n.p.; *Record in McDaniel*, 80–81; *Record in Talmage*, 23.

[25] *Record in Magnus*, 18.

[26] Record in Burnett, 14; *Record in Holt*, 11.

nothing could be done. Frequently, it involved performing the loss of bodily integrity by removing the glass eye, revealing the scarred torso, or holding up the armless sleeve. These dramas of violence brought the brutalities of industrialization into the open. Each time an injured young worker or a grieving family came to court, they had to work through memories probably best left buried. Each time, the story was similar. An irreparable loss had occurred; monetary compensation could only ease the pain, not repair the damage. The legal process reopened old wounds for all to see, but more importantly, it slowly forced Southern working families to rethink the place of young workers in industrial society. As horror story piled upon horror story, a moral to the tale became clearer. Maybe a mine or factory was not just like the farm. Maybe young bodies and machines were inherently incompatible. Maybe contracting out of danger was not possible after all.

While some mishaps to young workers involved such raw elements as a sheet of slate, most deaths and injuries came at the hands of machines. Hence, part of performing violence meant bringing the culprit into the courtroom through meticulous verbal depiction, revealing photographs, or actual reconstruction. In addition to a picture, Arthur Burnett described the beater that shattered his body as "a great big thing" with a lid weighing 150 pounds, a full 60 pounds more than he weighed at the time of the accident. "The Beater is something with teeth like a railroad spike sticking off of them," he continued, "and they run so fast you can't hardly see them." Time and again young workers supplied such descriptions, but if words were not enough, actual machinery, or a model, arrived in court. Sometimes even competing models sat before the bench, each side begging to be judged correctly. Jim Kendrick's stepfather, J.P. Butler, built his own model of the elevator at High Shoals Manufacturing, only to have its accuracy disputed by the company's president. If models would not do, operatives disassembled whole machines and put them back together. This process allowed young workers such as Pearl McIntyre to finger their assailants in court. "I have seen that machine before," McIntyre said, "(pointing to a machine in the corner of the Court room, said to have been the one by which she was hurt). I have worked on that machine, or one just like it."[27]

Having a firm grasp on what a machine looked liked, getting a sense of its power, coming to grips with its terrible potential – all these lent an

---

[27] *Record in Burnett*, 16–17; *Record in Kendrick*, 56, 87; *Record in McIntyre*, 7; *Record in Jones*, 51. See also *Record in Davis*, n.p.; *Record in Wynne*, 10.

air of authenticity to the retelling of violent encounters with technology. Occasionally witnesses told of dramatic rescues, carried out in the nick of time to save a life if not a limb. In one of the more daring of such incidents, operatives rushed to the aid of thirteen-year-old Robert Jones when he became tangled up in the belts of a loom at Old Dominion Cotton Mills in Manchester, Virginia. Mrs. E. Jones, Robert's first cousin, heard him scream. "I turned around and saw Robert caught up in the machinery among the shafting and belts," Jones recalled. "Miss Vaughn and I ran to him and caught him by his legs and held him until the machinery could be stopped." They had prevented Robert's death, but he had not emerged unscathed. "I was caught under my arm and all the flesh torn off to the bone," Robert later told the court.[28]

As with Fitz Stanley, Robert Jones's graphic description of his injury typified the opening stages of each case that young workers and their families brought. In personal injury suits, injured young laborers took the stand to describe their accidents and the aftermath. When they had not survived, family members and fellow workers told tales of terror in their absences. In many cases, these narratives played out in a series of questions by plaintiffs's attorneys, but just as often, litigants were asked simply to "tell what happened." In a few cases, young workers actually showed the court what happened. With a box-folding machine sitting in a Georgia courtroom, Pearl McIntyre placed her finger in the apparatus up to the point where it had been taken off. More often, though, workers recounted their accidents through their words. Sam Honaker's story of his mishap in a West Virginia mine was typical. "I was sitting on the rim of the car with my feet sitting on the bumpers," he remembered. "The trip was going in pretty fast and I did not have much of a light on my head ... and I saw the cars when I was about as far as from here to there (indicating the Jury box)." Having set the scene, Sam narrated the action. "I jumped back and threw my left foot into the car and started to throw my right on in and it slipped off the bumper," he told the court. "I was not fast enough and the car mashed my foot." Time and again, juries heard such descriptions of the dangers of mines and mills. In these tales, the particular hazards of industrial work for young people became manifest.[29]

While we should not dwell upon the violence, it is important to realize that auditors in Southern courtrooms heard more than just relatively

---

[28] *Record in Jones*, 42, 61.
[29] *Record in McIntyre*, 15; *Record in Honaker*, 18.

sterile descriptions of how things went wrong. Rather, the legal process forced them to confront elemental fears about the loss of bodily
integrity. These fears could only have been heightened in a culture with
no significant tradition of bodily mutilation for decorative, religious,
or other legitimating purposes. Indeed, the only widespread practice
of mutilation in the New South came in the horrific rituals of torture
and dismemberment that sometimes accompanied lynching. At the same
time, Civil War veterans provided a common counterpoint to industrial
dismemberment. In short, the New South provided a cultural environment that heightened the significance of bodily loss. Connected to the
mechanisms of racial control or memories of the Lost Cause, the loss
of bodily integrity suggested not only a physical decline in power, but a
moral one as well.[30]

Young workers who took the stand supplied the most poignant images
of violence, talking about their pain, describing the brutality that caused
it, and demonstrating the disabilities that followed. When young workers
appeared, one of their tasks involved displaying bodies that were no longer whole. Attorneys almost universally had living plaintiffs reveal their
wounds. Young workers held up stumps, removed glass eyes, peeled back
clothing to display scars, and hobbled across the room to portray their
difficulty in walking. Charley Burke, for instance, told a West Virginia
jury about his injured foot. "When I walk it gives out on me and if I step
on the side of a little gravel to throw my foot over it hurts me," Burke
said, arising from his seat to limp across to the jury box. Such performances made injuries real for the assembled court, and their recurrence
drove home the dangers of industrial life for young workers over and
over again.[31]

Demonstrating injury was necessary for the legal process of a negligence suit, but young workers did more than prove their diminished
capacity. Beyond disability, they re-enacted their pain and suffering. Leila
Vinson recalled incurring "intense pain and suffering" after a shuttle
guard hit her in the eye, but her account of what happened made things

[30] Fitzhugh Brundage, *Lynching in the New South: Georgia and Virginia, 1880–1930*
(Urbana, 1993); Drew Gilpin Faust, *This Republic of Suffering: Death and the American
Civil War* (New York, 2008); Elizabeth B. Clark, "'The Sacred Rights of the Weak': Pain,
Sympathy, and the Culture of Individual Rights in Antebellum America," *Journal of
American History* 82 (1995): 463–493; Erin O'Connor, "'Fractions of Men': Engendering
Amputation in Victorian Culture," *Comparative Studies in Society and History* 39
(1997): 742–777.
[31] *Record in Burke*, 34.

FIGURE 9. Giles Newsom lost his fingers in a North Carolina textile plant in 1912. Displaying such mangled extremities provided a climactic moment in court proceedings. Lewis Hine, 1912. Library of Congress, Prints & Photographs Division, National Child Labor Committee Collection, LC-USZ62-20093.

even clearer. "The shuttle flew out and hit my head in two places on that side and went across the ball of the eye and hit the nose," she told the court. Similarly, Willie Bartley's account of his accident left little to the imagination. "[The slate] hit me in the back, knocked me down, hit me in the back of the head and splattered me out, and this leg went under this leg," Willie recounted. "It busted me in here and knocked me down against the coal and cut this piece of my face." C.M. Trivett, another victim of a slate fall, told his story of suffering by referring to other sources of pain his auditors could understand. After the circulation returned to his legs, the pain became unbearable. It was like this: "You would have my toes in a cane mill and grind them up and take a sledge hammer and lay my limbs on something and then hammer them," Trivett testified. "That kept up for seventeen days."[32]

If young workers did not supply the gory details, fellow laborers or family members did. As might be expected, blood and dismemberment dominated these narratives. Jason Daniels told about how he found his younger brother Harlie. "Why, when I got to him two or three fellows had

[32] *Record in Vinson*, 4; *Record in Bartley*, 9; *Record in Interstate Coal Co.*, 14.

him, holding him up, and he was bleeding," Jason said. "There was blood all down his overall." Etta Cushon talked about fourteen-year-old Anna Barnes, whose hand became lodged in the cogs of a spinning frame. "I seen her hand in the machinery. She was crying out that if they did not take her hand out it would kill her," Cushon related. "I took hold of her left hand and told her to hush, they were coming. Her hand was all mashed up: the blood was pouring from it." In some scenes, pouring blood gave way to even worse terrors. S.B. Creasman was the first man to reach the site where a locomotive had barreled over Bub Raines. He methodically described what he saw. "I reached the railroad track a good piece south of the place where the boy was killed; the first thing I saw was his head and shoulders; they were lying beside the railroad track; the next thing I saw was his body from here down (indicating); the next thing I saw was a leg; the next thing was another leg," Creasman told the shocked community. So far as he could tell, Bub's body was scattered "a hundred yards or more," but who could say. Asked if he measured the distance, an agitated Creasman responded, "Of course, I never measured it."[33]

Still, blood was not the only horror, or even the worst. A particularly gut-wrenching tale came from Ralph Girvin's accident at Georgia Veneer and Package Company. Ralph plunged up to his neck into a vat of boiling water. Remarkably, he actually survived the accident for a few days. As his father Henry put it, "it seemed like the whole body was perfectly dead; but his brain was perfect; it seemed like he had his perfect mind. From that position down, his body was terribly scalded. Most awful." Henry Girvin had not seen his son fall, but Blair Latham, another boy employed at the woodworking company, had. He talked about what happened when they got to Ralph. "He was in the water, and held his hands up and screamed, and the Price boy taken hold of him, and the skin peeled off his arms," Latham recalled. "At the time Ralph was pulled out of the vat I did not hear him say anything he just screamed." The incident shattered Latham's confidence. "It hurt me so bad seeing how he was scalded and hurt that I just couldn't do a thing," he declared, telling how he walked off the job and never came back for fear of ending up like Ralph. E.R. Johnson, another worker at the plant, had a similar reaction. Both he and Latham insisted that Ralph had been ordered to the vats against his will. In the immediate aftermath of the fall, Ralph had screamed "'Oh my God, I didn't want to go out there,'" Johnson

---

[33] *Record in Daniels*, 57; *Record in Augusta Factory*, 13; *Record in Raines*, printed record, 18, typescript, 26.

maintained. It was more than he could stand. "It got a little the best of me, and I walked off," he recalled.[34]

The post-accident reactions of workers such as Latham and Johnson reveal how industrial violence was not confined to young workers and their families. Horrible accidents were community affairs, and this collective experience played out anew when cases came to court. Like S.B. Creasman, fellow workers often had to deal with body parts left after accidents, and they brought their stories to court, forming part of the larger chorus of voices that worked through the meanings of industrial violence. J.L. Young, for instance, removed pieces of Charley Giebell's fingers from the cog wheels of a molder. "I took them out of the machine and took them and buried them," Young recalled. Workers such as Young seem to have been fascinated rather than repulsed by scenes of dismemberment. Lawrence Campbell detailed his immediate actions after Elbie Showalter's run-in with a leatherworking machine. "When I got to the scrub room someone met me near the center of the scrub room and says, 'Elbie Showalter has got his hand cut off.'" Drawn to the violence, Campbell made his way to the room where Elbie's accident happened. There he found another worker "standing there with a part of the flesh off his hand." The scene moved Campbell to insert himself further into the events of the day by handling the flesh. "I looked at it," he acknowledged. "I taken it and looked at it." Handling the body in this manner incorporated fellow workers into the violence. They touched it; they felt the weight of it; they bathed in its blood. When they revealed these contacts in court, violence became real once more.[35]

Contact with sites of violence was not limited to fellow workers, however. Then as now, accident sites provided a source of fascination. When Tom McDaniel plummeted to his death at Lynchburg Cotton Mills, local folk wandered into the mill all weekend to view the site. "They would come in and walk right up to it and look down the hole," one company official put it. Another company man explained their motivations: "They were full of curiosity and wanted to see the place where the boy was found." This incident repeated itself in the courtroom, where company officials had to defend their decision to fence off the elevator from the public, when it had been unprotected at the time of Tom's death. If the public came to view the location of Tom's death out of morbid curiosity, Clarence Miller took matters a step further, using Joe Pettit's

[34] *Record in Girvin*, 3, 10, 11, 14–15.
[35] *Record in Giebell*, 58; *Record in Showalter*, 65.

dismemberment in a North Carolina rail yard as an object lesson for his own brood. Miller and a friend went down to where it happened and looked around. "We saw blood on the rails and a piece of bone, shiver of bone about this size and a piece of black stocking," he noted. "I took it and wrapped it up in paper and carried it home to be a warning to my children."[36]

Clarence Miller's literal transportation of Joe Pettit's body highlights the ways in which industrial violence radiated into Southern working communities. It also shows how these stories came full circle, as memory returned them to the present tense in a court of law. One final story illustrates clearly how the post-accident experience of violence touched lives beyond those of the young worker who had been injured or killed. J.P. Sonne lived next door to the Wilson family in Louisville, Kentucky, and he took it upon himself to help out in the wake of Charley Wilson's dreadful fall into a vat at Chess and Wymond's barrel factory. Sonne saw Charley many times during the eleven months he suffered before death. He witnessed Charley's leg, burnt to a stub, and he saw his body laid out in death. Still, some things he could not stomach. Charley's mother wanted to show him more. "She wanted to show me the arm but I didn't want to see it," Sonne admitted. "There was a stench in the room from the effects of the burn." In fact, he could not stand to be in the Wilson household for long periods. "I went up there one evening when they were dressing the wound in his leg," Sonne recalled. "One of his legs was burnt to his thigh, and she had that dressing on it, and I stayed there a few minutes and it made me sick to see it, so I had to go."[37]

J.P. Sonne could not stand to be around Charley for long as he lay in agony, but he did stick with the family after the young worker's death, becoming the administrator of the family's suit against Chess and Wymond. Sonne's response to Charley Wilson's torments fittingly demonstrates the collective nature of industrial violence in Southern working communities. More importantly, his retelling of those actions and reactions in court illustrates how the creation of meaning in a legal setting was also a collective process of cultural production. As other historians have shown, law did not simply emanate from above. Rather, judges, attorneys, jurymen, litigants, witnesses, and the assembled audience all took part in a community investigation of the violence done to young

---

[36] *Record in McDaniel*, 52–56. See also *Record in Craven*, 23; *Record in Miller Mfg. Co.*, 85; *Record in Pettit (1923)*, 25.
[37] *Record in Wilson*, 2.

workers. While certainly not the only lens through which working people viewed the place of young people in industrial life, courtroom performances of violence provided a setting both authoritative and dramatic. People were likely to remember and talk about the pain, mortification, and disability. They could relay what they heard about the daring escapes or unfortunate slips. The proceedings lent a reality to the work of young people, one that repeatedly portrayed that work as inherently fraught with difficulties.[38]

Still, litigants' tales of violence by themselves could not have built the legal and social construct of child labor. For all of the importance imparted by "law from below," the larger legal and cultural context supplied the final element that transformed courtroom proceedings into sources of cultural authority. The story that emerged from Southern courtrooms was one that downplayed race and ethnicity and emphasized gender, particularly Southern white masculinity. In the end, what mattered most was the discourse of childhood. As young workers, their families, and their neighbors talked about industrial violence, they drew upon figures of speech from the lexicon of child labor reform, and more importantly, from the formal law itself. As such, the court became a place where they learned to speak the language of middle-class childhood, a set of symbols in which child labor was coming to have a settled and widely accepted meaning.

A POWERFUL SILENCE

If the Southern dialect of child labor was "white," it was also male and native. Cases in other parts of the country frequently involved immigrants, and less often, girls. In contrast, Southern courtrooms almost never hosted immigrant families, and only occasionally entertained the families of workers who were female or of African descent. As a result, the assembled community considered the cases of young workers who were as culturally normative as possible. The relative dearth of cases involving immigrants, African Americans, or girls of either group narrowed the range of experiences that courts considered, making it all the more likely they would draw on the unitary discourse of "the child" that had been asserted by reform writers and jurists. That language did not declare a set of expected behaviors for a series of fragmented social

[38] For a recent statement about legal change from below, see Robertson, *Crimes against Children*, 234–235. For the classic version, see William E. Forbath, Hendrick Hartog, and Martha Minow, "Legal Histories from Below," *Wisconsin Law Review* (1985): 759–766. With regard to injury cases, see Bergstrom, *Courting Danger*, 8–9 and *passim*.

groups. Then as now, the language of childhood turned a blind eye to other social locations, collapsing all to the undifferentiated mass of "the child" and "children."[39]

The history of the late nineteenth and early twentieth century United States (as opposed to "the South") often centers on the rapidly growing swell of immigrants from southern and eastern Europe. Whereas earlier generations of newcomers had hailed from the northern and western parts of the continent, new arrivals came from Italy, Russia, and the numerous lands in the Austro-Hungarian Empire. Frequently settling in ethnic enclaves in the nation's growing cities, they provided labor for the massive industrial expansion of the period. Many of these workers were in their twenties, teens, or younger. Important as the immigrant experience is to U.S. history in this period, it does not figure prominently in the history of the South, or in the story of young workers there. One remarkable case from West Virginia, however, does allow us to see some of the ways in which the immigrant experience differed, and it serves as a counterpoint to the largely white, male, native-born profile of most young workers in the region's courts. *Shaw v. Hazel-Atlas Co.* illustrates the obvious but important point that fluency in English mattered, both at work and in court. Less obvious but more importantly, it demonstrates how conflicts over ethnic and religious identity could color litigations involving immigrant workers in ways unlikely among the native-born.[40]

Malky Shaw arrived in Bellaire, West Virginia by way of Baltimore and Bremen. Born in Kiev, she and two sisters departed for the United States in 1907, leaving another sister in Bremen for lack of a ticket. With their father dead, their mother, Razeal (Rosie), followed some time later, perhaps with the deserted sister in tow. Malky, sixteen, worked for a time at Enterprise Enamel, a dish-making company, but when work got scarce she took the typical route for immigrant girls, securing a place as domestic help for Alexander Emmerman in Wheeling. The position at the Emmermans proved fortunate for Malky and her sisters, Rachel and Annie, for Mr. Emmerman helped them gain employment at Hazel-Atlas. Malky's luck only went so far, however. After working at a cap trimmer for a few days, the blade struck her hand, cleanly amputating two of her fingers.[41]

---

[39] On the raced dimensions of this discourse, see Shelley Sallee, *The Whiteness of Child Labor Reform in the New South* (Athens, 2004).

[40] For an introduction to Progressive era immigration, see John Bodnar, *The Transplanted: A History of Immigrants in Urban America* (Bloomington, 1987).

[41] *Record in Shaw*, 54, 61, 66, 77–79.

When Malky's injury came to a Wheeling courtroom, the cause turned on a typical question: Had she been warned of the danger? Answering that question depended on the abilities of the concerned parties to understand and speak English. Malky and many other witnesses in the case spoke through an interpreter. One participant, Annie Miller, served both functions, telling her own part of the tale and relaying the stories of others in English. Long lines of questioning probed the extent of Malky's English and the meaning of words in Yiddish versus English. All of this mattered because of Malky's interactions with Percy Steinecke, the manager charged with teaching her how to use the machines and warning her of the danger. Although Steinecke refused to admit that he "scolded" her about her work, Malky recalled angry interactions with the man, confrontations that grew out of her lack of the language. On the stand, Malky struggled to relate this story to an all-English–speaking jury. She maintained that Percy "scolded" her and ordered her to fix a machine. What had he said, exactly? Allowed to talk directly to Malky, the translator produced this response: "She didn't understand him, but his face showed that he was angry and she had to fix it herself. That is the way she answered."[42]

Such exchanges were common during the trial, and they illuminate how immigrant cases differed. On the margins of the South geographically and socially, Malky's trial suggests that a multiethnic courtroom might have altered the outcomes. Still, the lack of understanding between the girl and her boss reflects more than just language barriers. In fact, Steinecke treated her like bosses treated their young workers, with impatience and contempt. As such, her narrative fit those of her native-born comrades.[43]

Malky Shaw's case illustrates the salience of language barriers, but it says something about larger cultural boundaries as well. Determining if Malky had been warned also depended upon what litigants recalled about her relationship with Daniel Magilavey, another young worker who testified in the case. Company officials insisted that even if Malky had not understood Percy Steinecke, she had been warned by Dan, a fact he confirmed on the stand. "I told her not to use her fingers and to use a stick instead of her fingers," Magilavey reported. Malky saw things differently, but one thing she was sure about: Magilavey's real name was

---

[42] Ibid., 72, 97, 161.
[43] For similar patterns of abuse, see *Record in Ewing*, 42; *Record in Sanitary Laundry Co.*, 96.

Maglovitch. He was a Russian Jew who hid his own identity, she argued, and sister Rachel insisted that he repeatedly warned them not to reveal his religious and ethnic identity if they went to the factory seeking work. In response to repeated questioning about his name, Dan maintained the right to take whatever name he chose. "It makes no difference what the right name is," he declared. Magilavey was "my name here at the factory, is the way I call it."[44]

Dan Maglovitch's insistence on his right to be called whatever he wanted fits with what historians of Jewish immigration have repeatedly noticed, that young immigrants often took the lead in "Americanization," serving as cultural mediators for their parents and older siblings. Dan's interactions with the Shaw sisters reveal a slightly different part of that familiar story – conflict between young immigrant workers. Dan was likely younger than Malky and her sisters. They referred to him as "little Dan." That someone younger than themselves would deny a common heritage outside the family home must have been particularly grating. The girls had a keen sense of being "green," the immigrant term for new and inexperienced, and they had witnessed Dan operate in green environments. "At home they are all green and they can't talk English and he had to talk their language," Rachel Shaw recalled. Immigrants such as the Shaw family depended on people like Dan to negotiate the new and potentially unfriendly world of American factory work, but such negotiations did not always go smoothly.[45]

Such immigrant families were relatively rare in the New South, leaving the region in a peculiar relationship to the burgeoning industrial North, which depended upon newly arrived labor to feed its machines. In states north of the Mason-Dixon, young workers who appeared in court were just as likely to be foreign-born as not, just as likely to have arrived recently as not, and just as likely not to speak English, the language of the legal process in the United States. While European immigrants typified workers young and old in the North, African-American workers were relatively uncommon, at least compared with the South. One might expect, then, that court proceedings in the latter region would frequently involve black workers and that race would be at the forefront of the discourse. Such was not the case. Whether because poverty, fear of

---

[44] Ibid, 170, 225–238, 244.

[45] Ibid, 232; Steven Mintz, *Huck's Raft: A History of American Childhood* (Cambridge, 2004), 200–212; Stephen Lassonde, *Learning to Forget: Schooling and Family Life in New Haven's Working Class, 1870–1940* (New Haven, 2005).

white power, or a lower rate of death and injury consequent from being excluded from industrial jobs, young black workers brought few cases. In those they did bring, racialized language or imagery rarely played any part. The paucity of African-American cases does not mean that race was unimportant in the construction of the legalities of child labor in the South. Because cases involving young black workers often went forward in much the same fashion as those with injured young white employees, the cultural and legal construct of child labor became more unified and powerful.[46]

Often, cases proceeded with little mention of race. In a Tennessee coal mining litigation, the plaintiff and many of the witnesses were black, but this fact was revealed only by passing references to race. Consider the following exchange, where an attorney asked mine foreman W.R. Pressnell about his opinion of Luke Smith, who had been injured in a cave-in. "Q. Do you regard an 18-year-old colored boy as an expert miner? A. I do not know how old he was. He was about the best one I had. Q. Had you ever given him any room? A. No sir, because he made me a good hand and I wanted to keep him." As a witness for Dayton Coal and Iron, Pressnell had every reason to play up Luke Smith's skill, but that's precisely the point. The legal conventions that structured his description smoothed out the racialized edges.[47]

Simple racial stereotypes sometimes did enter the courtroom discussion, but rarely did they stand at the forefront or influence the general tenor of the conversation. A defense attorney in a West Virginia case called upon the notion that blacks in the South did not keep track of age or time as a rule, noting that the plaintiff in the action was "of a class of negroes whose age would not be and was not a matter of definite knowledge among his neighbors." A more extended deployment of racial stereotypes occurred when the Hodges family brought suit against Savannah Kaolin after young Ben had been slashed to pieces by a conveyor. The company's attorneys tried to make an issue out of the fact that Ben wore his shirt loose, averring that black workers' "sleeves are always more or less hanging down when they are working." The racial etiquette of the New South also appeared in a much more subtle way in this particular case. When Kelley Hodges, Ben's dad, testified about how Ben got hired, he recalled a company official estimating the boy's age at between

---

[46] Poverty was not the barrier we might think it was. Poor litigants could sue as paupers after signing an affidavit that verified their inability to pay court costs.

[47] *Record in Smith*, 80.

nineteen and twenty, far above what it really was. "I didn't say anything," Kelley Hodges recalled. "I didn't dispute his word."[48]

Disputing the word of white authorities was exactly what African-American families did if they sued in the wake of death or injury to a young worker. The power disparities that such cases brought to the surface might help explain why African Americans appeared in Southern courtrooms so infrequently. A singular case from Louisville, Kentucky, illustrates what could happen when the lines of racial interaction in the Jim Crow South were crossed. On one side of the dispute stood Mary Hunter, a single black mother of little means who came to Louisville by way of Clark Street in Atlanta. On the other stood Ed Corrigan, a wealthy thoroughbred breeder from the heart of Kentucky's horse country. In the middle stood Rich Hunter, Mary's high-spirited ten-year-old son. About the only thing certain was that Rich had broken his leg while riding one of Mr. Corrigan's horses around the stable at the Jockey Club on the outskirts of Lexington.[49]

As Mary (and sometimes Rich) told the story, the boy was a typical youngster, going to school, helping around the house, and fortifying the family account books by selling newspapers after school. She had always kept good track of Rich, but then one day in the fall of 1907, he did not come home from school as expected. She searched high and low but could not find him. Later, she learned that he had gone to stay with the Corrigans at their abode in Louisville, where he was cutting kindling and doing other odd jobs. She knew nothing of his being at the race track until she read about his accident in the newspaper. When Rich took the stand, he reiterated the fact that he had a fairly close relationship with Ed Corrigan. The man had gone to see his mother about his work, giving him money to go to the theater during the visit.[50]

Ed Corrigan found this tale to be fanciful at best. He had never seen Rich before the trial, he avowed. He had not employed him, had not consented to have him around the stables, had not allowed him on his horses, and had certainly not given him fifteen cents to go to the theater. He heard of Rich's accident during a trip to New Orleans, when he received a letter from Mary Hunter's attorney demanding a settlement. A string of witnesses in Corrigan's employ then unfolded a very different

---

[48] *Record in Norman*, 11; *Record in Hodges*, 29, 41.

[49] *Record in Corrigan, passim.*

[50] Ibid, 1–46, quotation on 7. On growing up African American and male in the Jim Crow South, see Jennifer Ritterhouse, *Growing Up Jim Crow: How Black and White Children Learned Race* (Chapel Hill, 2006), esp. 191–196.

characterization of the Hunter household and of Rich's actions. Rich, it turned out, was a "bad boy" prone to fighting with other boys. He was frequently in conflict with his mother, who could not control him and had asked Joe Drake to take him off her hands. When Mary ran Rich out of her home, he ran first to Drake, who had transported him to Junius (June) Collins, an African-American trainer in Corrigan's employ. June Collins decided to make a project of Rich. "I took him as my own, to try to make something of the boy – for himself and me too," Collins disclosed. He put the boy up in his room at the track, letting him eat at the segregated table with the few other blacks who worked there. He had placed Rich on the horse that threw him, a colt, by the way, who had always shown a quiet disposition.[51]

By the end of the testimony, Ed Corrigan and his attorneys must have been quite certain of victory. They seemed to have established that June Collins had acted on his own and that Corrigan had no knowledge or involvement whatsoever. Even though the case involved a glaring dispute of power that trampled on customary lines of race and class, Corrigan's lawyers had established his lack of liability with little reference to either. They must have been quite shocked, then, when the jury returned a verdict of $750 for the Hunter household.[52]

With the racial wall breached, Corrigan deployed the big guns. In his petition for a new trial, which the Court of Appeals of Kentucky eventually granted on purely legal grounds, Corrigan gathered a posse of character assassins and sent them after Rich and Mary. Their affidavits deployed a powerful mixture of racial, class, and gender language that had been largely absent from the trial. Along with others, Gus Ferling summoned the customary language of the South's racial culture, describing Rich as "very saucy and impudent." Ferling revealed that Rich fought constantly with neighborhood boys, a fact confirmed by Eddie Clark, a self-described "white boy" from the vicinity. Gertie Gill maintained that Rich had drawn a razor on one of her children and beaned another one with a brick. Nannie Bohanon reported that Rich had broken into the local armory and been pursued by the police. Josie Green claimed to have seen Rich strike his mother with a club. Ada Wade relayed that Rich "played truant from school very often and spent his time out in the alley." All in all, Rich was "a very bad boy and hard to manage."

[51] Ibid, 46–97, quotation on 78.
[52] Here and following from *Record in Corrigan*, affidavits, no page numbers.

If Rich was bad, Mary was worse. Several affiants confirmed that she had tried to have Rich placed in the local reform school and that she had initiated the efforts to get him a place at the track. But beyond Mary's general lack of truthfulness, she appeared as a bad mother. Father Felten, of the Catholic school where Rich had briefly attended, had offered to clothe and feed Rich and his little sister, but Mary never replied. Bertha Preston, the boy's teacher at the Jim Crow public school, had sent notes about Rich's absences with the same result. Gertie Gill averred that if neighbors tried to say anything to Mary about Rich's behavior, "she would curse and abuse them." Nannie Bohanon went so far as to claim that Mary had tried to kill Rich, throwing him down so hard on his head as to render him unconscious for two hours.

To top it all off, the assembled crowd accused Mary Hunter of being a whore. Morton Brown, who lived in the same rooming house as the Hunters, dubbed it a house of ill-fame, "constantly visited by men who do not live there at all hours of the day and night." Maggie Anderson confirmed Brown's suspicions. She had known Mary way back in Atlanta and could say without reservation that she was "a common prostitute and tough character and very foul in her language." Just to liven up this characterization a bit, Gertie Gill threw in that Mary was "a very tough character and lives with a negro called Red Smoot."

Whether fact or fiction, these multiple blows to Mary and Rich's reputations were gratuitous. Corrigan's attorneys *were* on very stable legal grounds in their appeal. Rather than being necessary to the case, the affidavits sent a very strong message about messing around with a powerful white landowner. As such, *Corrigan v. Hunter* reveals the ways in which race was a silent but powerful presence in the legalities of child labor. Like Kelley Hodges, young black workers and their families knew the possible consequences if they "disputed" the words of white employers. If crossing the class line was a brave act for young white workers, breaching the wall of Jim Crow was doubly courageous. The fact that few African-American families undertook the challenge does not mean they willingly accepted their lot as injured workers, but it does mean that the courts remained largely white. This situation at the ground level confirmed and entrenched the "whiteness of child labor." At the end of the day, the legal and cultural constructs of child labor emanating from Southern courtrooms would be about boys who were white.[53]

[53] For insight into challenging Jim Crow in everyday life, see, among others, Tera Hunter, *To 'Joy My Freedom: Southern Black Women's Lives and Labors after the Civil War*

UNMAKING THE MAN

When incidents of industrial violence involving young workers came to Southern courtrooms, race and ethnicity were conspicuous by their relative silence. Such was not the case with gender. The dramas that unfolded before Southern judges and juries followed a script heavily laden with gendered imagery. Because the vast majority of litigations involved young, white, male workers on the cusp of manhood, Southern masculinity both informed and was formed by the dialogue of the courtroom. Young women were not absent from these proceedings, but the relative paucity of their cases meant that the courts did not serve as a center for cultural articulation in the same way they did for men and boys. Accident cases also revealed assumptions about adults, especially fathers, but the focus remained on the young men and boys who brought the vast majority of litigations. For them, a day in court offered both the chance to recount a story of lost manhood and the promise of restitution. At the heart of that story was capacity, to perform work and to perform as men.

If boys and young men formed the majority of industrial violence victims and litigants, girls and young women did bring their causes to the law as well. With a much smaller number of instances, any conclusions about their courtroom performances must be tentative at best. Certainly, some instances of language specific to girlhood and womanhood did appear. A witness in a Georgia case bluntly declared that "girls are more timid than boys." Girls also appeared frequently as shrinking violets who either ran away from accidents or fainted at the sight of blood. Girls might also be portrayed as particularly vulnerable. One early Georgia case involved several young girls who had been left alone in an Atlanta cotton factory early into Sunday morning, a point repeatedly stressed by an attorney while examining the superintendent of the firm. "You say that these little ones were kept there generally until three o'clock every Saturday night," he noted. "Was it necessary to do that?" Clearly the question was meant to suggest a lack of concern, but the implied wrongdoing had as much to do with youth, and the fact that it was Sunday, as it did with the fact the workers were girls.[54]

(Cambridge, 1997); Glenda Gilmore, *Gender and Jim Crow: Women and the Politics of White Supremacy in North Carolina, 1896–1920* (Chapel Hill, 1996); and Stephen Hahn, *A Nation under Our Feet: Black Political Struggles in the Rural South from Slavery to the Great Migration* (Cambridge, 2003), 451–464.

[54] *Record in McIntyre*, 14; *Record in Atlanta Cotton Factory Co.*, 39, 75, 79. On fainting or running away, see *Record in Evans (Georgia)*, 2; *Record in McIntyre*, 13; *Record in Sanitary Laundry Co.*, 100.

Cases involving girls also differed in how they marked capacity and incapacity. Although it probably hurt her cause by revealing a knowledge of knives, Myrtice Ransom proudly proclaimed her capacities in the kitchen. "Sure I know how to cook," Myrtice exclaimed, "and I know how to make bread and prepare steak and cut bacon with a knife." Instances specific to girlhood could also indicate incapacity. Ransom also employed gendered language in describing her loss. "It has affected me in my music and sewing," she pointed out. "I can't sew with my hand and can't do any work in the house where I have to use my hand." Similarly, Betty Evans bemoaned the fact that she could not work after her accident. All she could do was go to school and play with her dolls.[55]

As was usually the case in the nineteenth century, however, girlhood and womanhood were marked by physical attributes as much as by capacity or behavioral traits. In one Georgia case, for instance, the onset of menses measured whether the injured young worker could be seen as a child or not. In another, the lack of menstruation served as a marker of possible, undetected internal injuries. The doctor who treated Myrtice Ransom seemed to rely entirely on physical attributes in assessing her stage of life. When her fingers were mangled in a Georgia candy factory, she was twelve and qualified as a child. "At that time she was only a child," T.F. Guffin concluded, "and I was surprised to know that she had been at work." Two and a half years later, as Myrtice approached her fifteenth birthday, she weighed in at 169 pounds. She had become, in Dr. Guffin's estimation, "a strong, healthy woman." Perhaps his view had changed because Myrtice had since married (and possibly been abandoned), but his view fit with the general characterization of injured girls in Southern courtrooms, one that noticed their behavior but linked adulthood primarily to physical development.[56]

Girls and young women who appeared in court did so in an environment more likely to maintain existing gender conventions than confront them. The legal forms of personal injury and wrongful death suits further entrenched those norms. Measures of damages often turned on earning capacity, a matter much more easily calculated for boys and men who could be expected to undertake a lifetime of wage work. Arthur Burnett's lawyer deployed the customary language, noting his client's decreased earning capacity and inability to "follow his desired calling." A lower

[55] *Record in Ransom*, 4, 6.
[56] *Record in Augusta Factory*, 33; *Record in Atlanta Cotton Factory Co.*, 15, 26; *Record in Ransom*, 12, 13.

court judge in a Virginia case similarly instructed the jury that they could take impairment of earning capacity into consideration when calculating an award for Fitz Stanley. Such customary predictions of monetary loss could not be made so easily in the case of women and girls. Perhaps this kept them out of the courts, but in any case, it altered the gendered course of the story, pushing it towards an emphasis on masculinity.[57]

Girls played less of a role in courtroom conversations, then, if only because their narratives did not reach a critical mass for change. Boys and young men, however, appeared in Southern courtrooms over and over again, and they often framed their claims in ways that both invoked prevailing gender norms and at the same time undermined them. On the one hand, they claimed capacity and independence as young men, but as injured young workers their stories necessarily invoked incapacity and dependence, characteristics associated both with women and children. As we shall see momentarily, the legalities of child labor sanctioned the latter approach while discouraging the former.

Casting their losses in gendered terms, young male workers spoke in an environment that interrogated manhood from another vector as well – fatherhood. Prevailing wisdom, if not actual precedent, located authority in fathers, yet it also charged them with responsibility over their progeny. The vehemence exhibited by Southern working parents when contracting for safety served to solidify the father as protector-provider in cultural and legal discourse. Further, the ubiquitous image of the "lazy father" in child labor reform meant that litigations often focused on what fathers could and could not do or what they had and had not done for their offspring.

The right of fathers to wages sometimes clashed openly with intimations of laziness, as in this exchange from an early Georgia case: "Q. You mean when your son worked as a workman you would take all his wages and only give him a quarter or a half dollar at a time? A. I did sir, and I think I had the right to do it, and I think he will state it. Q. We won't discuss rights." Not only did Joseph Woodruff stand accused of profiting from his son's wages, he also admitted that he had furnished the teenaged Will Woodruff with tobacco and whisky. If Woodruff was a bad father for lack of provision, Charles Burke, Sr., failed to protect. "You were

---

[57] *Record in Burnett,* 5; *Record in Lynchburg Cotton Mills,* 6. On men, women, and earnings in this era, see Amy Dru Stanley, *From Bondage to Contract: Wage Labor, Marriage, and the Market in the Age of Slave Emancipation* (New York, 1998), Chs.4–5. Thanks to Melissa Hayes and Michael Spires for discussions on this point.

willing to allow your boy to work in the coal mines as a trapper when he wasn't quite 11 years old?" a company attorney asked Burke. Only because the place Charley went to work had no motors or electricity, the elder Burke answered. This exchange showed the latent danger in the approach Southern families took to public work. Contracting for safety offered a way around industrial violence, but a way that undermined a powerful element of the gendered authority of fathers.[58]

A large part of male authority drew upon the notion, half-true and half-fictional, half-customary and half-legal, that men acted independently. As we have seen, boys and young men often played out these roles when entering the labor market, frequently seeking work and taking jobs without parental oversight. These "independent" actions became important later on, for they spoke to the question of whether litigants controlled their own destinies and, hence, could reasonably be expected to act as responsible, risk-avoiding men. As a result, signs of independent manhood peppered the proceedings. Phil Waldron exemplified the in-between nature of teenaged boys. Bessie Peery kept a company boarding house where Phil stayed on one of his occasional bouts of domestic truancy, so she was well placed to observe Phil's behavior. Phil ate his dinner "with the men folks," Peery acknowledged. Still, she also noted how he played with her twelve-year-old son, but only "when there were no larger boys around." On the matter of independence, Phil had much in common with Bub Raines, the North Carolina boy who had left home at thirteen to live with relatives. By fifteen, he had held a job long enough that he "did his own trading."[59]

Phil and Bub represented the common experience of many of their cohorts. Gender conventions prompted teenagers to act as adults, but the law still considered them to be "infants." This peculiar ambiguity colored courtroom narrations, creating an unresolved tension that leaned towards reliance on the discourse of child labor. It was much safer, tactically speaking, to portray young workers in ways that stressed their childish dependence more than their manly independence, no matter how much their actual behavior contradicted such characterizations. Of course, doing so was much easier in the case of Phil and Bub. Both were dead, so they were not around to muck up the story.

Assertions of autonomy clouded the construction of young male workers in ways that could be sorted out only through hints such as eating with the menfolk, but the central gendered question in most industrial

---

[58] *Record in Woodruff*, 17–18; *Record in Burke*, 15. See also *Record in Mills*, 75.
[59] *Record in Waldron*, 88; *Record in Raines*, 23. For a good example of an older boy acting independently, see *Record in Interstate Coal Co.*, 48.

violence proceedings involved skill and capacity, something much more tangible and demonstrable. Young workers went to court seeking some means to continue their lives with bodies no longer fit for industrial work. Simultaneously, young men and boys also sought restitution for the manhood they had forfeited. In telling their stories, they often cast their incapacities in gendered terms. Before the accident, he "could do almost any kind of work," Conley Robinson told a North Carolina jury, echoing a sentiment put more or less plainly by many of his fellows. The legal language of industrial violence called on young workers to talk about abilities and disabilities, but such descriptions resonated with the central tenets of Southern working manhood as well. In a transitional economy where Southern folks migrated back and forth between farms and factories, young workers often measured their loss of capacity in agricultural terms, such as hoeing, plowing, wood chopping, or any sort of "heavy work."[60]

Incapacity for manual trades presented further evidence of diminished powers. J.W. Smith could not "couple cars at all," ruling out continued work at that particular railroading task. He could not work as a sign painter, his chosen trade before the accident. Altogether his prospects seemed bleak. "I have got no trade I can work at," Smith concluded. "I have got no sure way of making anything at all." Similarly, fourteen-year-old W.H. Wynne described how his injured hand prevented him from working with his father, a house builder. "I used to nail shingles and help him tote lumber," Wynne recalled. "I cannot hold a hammer steady at all now. It slips from my hand." In the world of work, hands meant everything. It mattered that one was left-handed, if that was the hand that was hurt. Whether it was agricultural or industrial work, manhood could be measured by the ability to wield tools.[61]

Rather than separating out one kind of skill from another, young male workers usually invoked a variety of disabilities, all of which entailed the loss of manhood. After losing the better part of his hand to a molder, A.B. Ensley talked of life in the aftermath. "I am incapacitated from doing any kind of work, lumber work or writing, anything I could do," he said. "I can't farm or railroad or join the army." Arthur Burnett told of his fate in a similar fashion. Recovered as best he could, a distraught Arthur described his life and prospects. His economic prospects weighed heavily on his fevered mind. "I can't get any work to do now," he said. "I can't

---

[60] *Record in Bibb Manufacturing Co.*, 12–13; *Record in Moore*, 6; *Record in Beck*, 3; *Record in Atlanta and West Point Railroad Co.*, 23.

[61] *Record in Atlanta and West Point Railroad Co.*, 23; *Record in Wynne*, 12; *Record in Beck*, 3.

do much of anything." He tried to clerk, but he could not wrap bundles with one hand. Work on the farm was out because who could "plow and drive with one hand"? Laboring in shops was no more likely. Being disabled brought more than economic hardship. "I feel somewhat embarrassed in a crowd that somebody is talking about my one arm and eye," he revealed. "[I] am inconvenienced in not being able to cut up my own food, or tie my tie, or can't do anything hardly." Certainly, these two young men would have had a great deal of pain and mortification no matter what the setting or circumstances, but the ways in which they told their stories are revealing. Plowing, joining the army, tying a tie – all were signs of being a Southern working man. A jury could not restore a lost limb or mangled face, but it could offer some restoration of dignity.[62]

Embarrassment, mortification, and mental suffering accompanied the loss of capacity that came in the wake of debilitating accidents. In a time and place where men were supposed to take pride in soldiering onward in the face of pain, injury took a heavy mental toll. Beyond the physical suffering, young workers talked again and again of being "nervous." Conley Robinson's mother told of how he had become a "nervous boy" in the wake of his accident, hiding his "bad spells" from his parents. Jim Kendrick's plummet down an elevator shaft at High Shoals Manufacturing gave "his whole system ... a fearful whack which made him extremely nervous for four months." While girls and young women used this language as well, it was particularly salient for young male workers. In the gendered lexicon of the day, women and girls were supposed to be "nervous." Men were not. At age seventeen, T.W. Craven's mind returned over and over to his lost hand. "I studied about my hand and suffered in body and mind," he recalled. Such worries were not unfounded, a point noted poignantly in Jimmie Taylor's case against Bibb Manufacturing. His injury was "a permanent one, and ... he will have to go through life maimed, and will always have to suffer the mortification and annoyance that such disfiguration will bring him."[63]

COUNTRY LADS AND SCHOOL BOYS

As teenagers came into court to demonstrate their incipient manhood, they encountered a legal and cultural environment that augured badly

---

[62] *Record in Ensley*, 18; *Record in Burnett*, 14–15.

[63] *Record in Robinson*, 25; *Record in Kendrick*, 3; *Record in Craven*, 21; *Record in Bibb Manufacturing Co*, 2–3. For examples of "nervous" girls, see *Record in Atlanta Cotton Factory Co.*, 20; *Record in Augusta Factory*, 11; *Record in Gibbs*, 6.

for their ultimate success. The context created over the previous several decades by jurists and reformers meant that winning compensation and securing justice required telling the story in a certain fashion. The most successful line of attack lay in the demonstration of an inherent inability to comprehend the danger of machines, the likelihood of violence, and the general risks of the workplace. Moreover, to win over the hearts of jurors, portrayals that evoked the innocence of youth offered much more chance of success than those that demonstrated knowledge, skill, and foresight. Drawing upon the prevailing constructs of child labor afforded a greater chance of success, even if the "child" involved was old enough to marry or serve in the military. The ultimate influence of the courts on young Southern workers lay in the law's authorizing power. In court, young workers fashioned and refashioned their identities by interacting with the language of child labor. Their attorneys served as conduits of that language, reformulating the experiences of working people in ways that made sense, legally and culturally, to the assembled court. It is in this manner, not simply via the direct means of enforcement, that law began to change the meaning of public work for young people.[64]

Working people and the attorneys who argued their cases had many legal means at their disposal, but as in all litigation, many of their more formidable weapons were cultural. Oftentimes, young workers appeared as affable bumpkins, fresh off the farm. Z.L. Powell's description of his work history could have stood in for many of his cohorts. "Before I moved to Darlington I lived in Stanton, S.C. and worked on my father's farm, I had never done any cotton mill work," Powell stated. Other young workers followed suit. "Before going to work with the Cedar Chest Company, had you ever had experience with machinery of any kind?" Johnson Monroe's attorney asked. "No, Sir," the fourteen-year-old worker answered. "I had worked on a farm."[65]

Such replies, especially when spoken at the court in town, invoked the notion that youngsters from the country knew little about the rigors of industrial work. Whether by design or natural inclination, their testimony often affirmed this convention. Jackson Ewing fielded the usual question about where he resided before being injured at Lanark Fuel with the usual confusion. He lived "out in the country." How far was that? For instance,

---

[64] In *Crimes against Children*, Robertson argues for a similar process. I would agree, other than to suggest that we should give more attention to what high courts assert to be "the law."

[65] *Record in Pelham Manufacturing Co.*, 72; *Record in Standard Red Cedar Chest Co.*, 15.

how far from the railroad? "I don't know," he replied. "A good piece." John Ewing, Jackson's father, sustained the notion that his folk were, to put it bluntly, hillbillies. He admitted that Jackson was illiterate at the time of the accident. "I draw idea he might spell a little spelling in the spelling book, I don't know for certain," the elder Ewing drawled. "He might have spelled a little from the first reader." In brief, Jackson was a country lad. "He had been raised back in the mountain on a little farm," John Ewing attested.[66]

Characterizing young workers as farm kids who were wet behind the ears blended easily into portrayals that stressed their inexperience in industrial settings. Certainly, young workers often did lack experience, but on the stand they and their family members faced the task of depicting them as completely untested. Given that nearly all of them had grown up in working homes, whether agricultural or industrial, this legal requirement called for some creative storytelling. Time and again, young workers talked about themselves as green to the job. "I was a green man when I first went there. I learnt there," Wilbur Loving said of his position as a take-away boy at Miller Manufacturing, a Richmond, Virginia, woodworking plant. Wilbur was pretty clearly new to all industrial work, but many others had been in and out of mills since they were little. This fact could lead to considerable debate, as it did in determining the abilities of Joe Coggins, a Georgia cotton mill operative. "Coggins was a perfectly green man, just started the day before," one worker testified, only to be flatly contradicted by another. "He wasn't a green boy," the second man said. "He had been working in the mill a long time." Such disputes arose because many boys had frequented factories their whole lives. At age ten, William Fitzgerald detailed his experience with industrial work. "I had never been in a factory to stay any time, but had been in furniture factories several times, but had not examined the machines," he noted. The intermittent nature of work blurred what counted as experience even further. As sixteen-year-old T.W. Craven outlined his work history on the witness stand, it became clear that he had worked at many jobs for short periods. Starting at around age thirteen, he worked for five textile mills and "four or five different saw mills" in addition to working on farms. For boys such as Craven, coming off as inexperienced was a tough sell.[67]

While demonstrating a farm kid's lack of knowledge and skill for industrial work might do well to establish inexperience, evoking child labor

---

[66] *Record in Ewing*, 23, 51.
[67] *Record in Miller Mfg. Co.*, 95; *Record in Eagle and Phenix Mills*, 55, 61; *Record in Fitzgerald*, 10; *Record in Craven*, 21. See also *Record in Ensley*, 16; *Record in Rhodes*, 72; *Record in Smith*, 78; *Record in Crown Cotton Mills*, n.p.

afforded a convention with far wider appeal. Earlier in the period before the rise of reform writing, the practice of employing women and children sometimes appeared as a defense. In a Georgia case from the early 1880s, the superintendent of an Atlanta cotton mill blithely admitted that his firm employed women and children because they could not afford adult male workers. "We would have to pay them higher wages and they could not do as well as children," George B. Harris maintained. "There is some work that the children can do better than grown people." By the beginning of the twentieth century, however, such images had become a weapon for injured young workers. As a result, working people directly called upon the critique of child labor that had been developed by the labor movement. Wesley Howard, who testified on behalf of injured young worker Ed Moncrief, painted Eagle and Phenix Mills as a cynical abuser of child labor. The mill endangered younger children such as Ed by putting them to work on a lap-winder, commonly considered a man's job, but they also tried "to get the smaller chaps to run it with as little wages as they can get." Similarly, an admission that young boys almost universally performed take-away duties at a Virginia woodworking firm prompted a rhetorical insertion by Wilbur Loving's attorney. "Is that done to get cheap labor?" he asked. An operative at Alma Furniture in High Point, North Carolina, confirmed these general notions about tail boys. "Boys are employed to do this work because they are cheaper than men," H.B. Crouch noted.[68]

Although working people occasionally sounded like unionists on the stand, they and their lawyers much more frequently conjured up general images of child labor consonant with those articulated by middle-class reformers. No doubt, Southern mines, mills, and shops *were* noisy and dark, and these images appeared again and again when working people sought to sketch their workplaces. For those who had never been in a mine, Ben Cary conveyed the total lack of light. "It is dark – if you haven't got a light you can't see nothing – can't see your hand if you haven't got a light," Cary explained. In detailing how his injury occurred, Arthur Burnett described the noise of a cotton factory: "I was at the machine but the other machines were running round me and making such a noise I could not tell whether this machine was running or not."[69]

These pictures of clatter and gloom subtly invoked the images that reformers had established over the preceding decades. If the moral was

---

[68] *Record in Atlanta Cotton Factory Co.*, 80; *Record in Eagle and Phenix Mills*, 22; *Record in Miller Mfg. Co.*, 98; *Record in Fitzgerald*, 15.
[69] *Record in Ewing*, 60; *Record in Burnett*, 15.

not clear, sometimes it had to be laid out directly. "The point we make is this," Wilbur Loving's counsel said. "Would you allow a boy to go there and undertake to fool with a thing he could not even see, it is so dark there, without first having given him definite and positive instructions so as to expose the danger?" By the late teens, when Loving's case came to court, these words called upon powerful texts. The insertion of "so dark in there" conjured images that jurymen had seen or read in the press. Whether it was actually dark or not did not matter so much as did the alignment of Wilbur's actual working conditions with the conventional wisdom of child labor.[70]

Among the most widely disseminated of images in the entire discourse of child labor reform was Lewis Hine's photograph of a bobbin boy stretching to reach a spindle, and working people's narratives evoked similar characterizations of young workers. While young workers them- selves might inadvertently speak to their own capacities, legal narration envisioned them as "little toilers," a characterization that had to over- come the fact that the actual boy sitting in court was often not so little any more. Jackson Ewing "had growed right smart since he was hurt," miner Ben Cary admitted. "He was a lot smaller than he is now." Since this disjoint was normal, witnesses and attorneys had to instantiate the "little boy" who existed at the time of the accident. This could be accom- plished straightforwardly, as when J.P Butler repeatedly referred to his thirteen-year-old stepson as a "little boy." Other terms might stand in for "little boy," as in the case of eleven-year-old mine trapper Charley Burke, who heard himself described as "a beardless boy," "a little fellow," and "a very small boy." Common markers from daily life might also construct a young worker as a little toiler for jurymen. For instance, Sallie Pettit recalled her son Joe's pant size as No. 12, when he was killed, "number eleven all the time before." The best strategy combined obvious physical markers with signs drawn from the wider discourse. Fred Platt, who lost his fingers to a press at Southern Photo Material Company, appeared as a "mere boy" of thirteen who was "very small and immature for his age." Fred was "put to work at a machine very dangerous in its character – a work, to do which, he had to stand upon a stool – and a work that should only be done by a person of more mature age, experience, and discretion." Standing on a stool to reach the work called upon a common thread in the discourse of child labor. Fred Platt fit the mold of a little toiler.[71]

---

[70] *Record in Miller Mfg. Co.,* 77–78.
[71] *Record in Ewing,* 72; *Record in Kendrick,* 51, 96; *Record in Burke,* 121; *Record in Pettit (1911),* 9; *Record in Platt,* 2.

Once established, the little toiler image offered plenty of ammunition. As litigators have known for ages, the best questions are often rhetorical, such as the one posed by Luther Green's attorney: "Now then, you tell this jury that this little boy was lifting up these heavy iron panels and pulling them over against him that way?" The answer was obvious. No "little boy" could have done what fellow workers claimed Luther had been doing. He could not have pulled the panels down on himself because little boys could not do that. The McDaniel family's attorney employed a similar tactic after discovering that Lynchburg Cotton Mills had guarded an elevator shaft only after Tom McDaniel's fatal fall. "So you thought it best to protect the general public and put that poor elevator boy in a hole?" he asked.[72]

Being crass might be the best tack, but in other instances, the tropes of child labor appeared only in lengthy exchanges meant to activate cultural referents. Twelve-year-old Fitz Stanley's attorney knew how to go about this process with aplomb. He established that upwards of 200 small children worked at Lynchburg Cotton Mills, a fact he had Fitz himself verify. When Fitz became confused, saying only four others worked in the bagging room, he was directed towards the picture of the whole mill, and he relayed that many boys and girls no bigger than him worked there. Apart from numbers, however, Fitz recounted the general situation of the mill in terms that had nothing to do with how he got injured or whether the company was liable. Lengthy portions of the trial were given over to lines of questioning such as this one. How long did it take for the bobbins to fill? "I think an hour." They had to be watched the whole time? "Yes, sir." How many frames did he have to attend? "Two, me and another boy." How many bobbins did each frame have? Wasn't it a good many? "No sir, I don't know; I never did count them." What time did he go to work in the morning? At six. "Was it as early as that? Was it half past six or six?" "It was half past six." What might appear as innocuous fact-based testimony communicated powerful images to the court. The point was that young Fitz went to work early and worked hard with other small children at a demanding task. Negligence law required that none of this be established, but the cultural environment of child labor did. Turning Fitz Stanley into a "little toiler" enhanced the chances for a big award, a fact evinced by the eventual judgment of $5,000.[73]

Descriptions of factory conditions and depictions of the physical limitations of youth only went so far. These more or less tangible indicators of

---

[72] *Record in Ornamental Iron and Wire Co.*, 40; *Record in McDaniel*, 54.
[73] *Record in Lynchburg Cotton Mills*, 43, 47, 54.

danger could be dismissed or disproved, especially if the young worker in question had grown in the time since the accident or if the company had cleaned up its act. More attractive was innocence, the broad construct that melded religious, legal, and physical attributes into one incredibly powerful marker of childhood. The more the story could be told as one of natural incapacity, the more the chances of success increased. Jurors might not understand the ins and outs of negligence law, but they did know what a sweet, little boy was. The fact that young Southern workers rarely fit into this iconography mattered less than did their momentary ability to don its mantle.

When young workers (especially the youngest of them) took the stand, they did not always stick to the script, something that put attorneys in a bit of a quandary. Young Ellis Crosby, for instance, eventually acknowledged that he did know that a bottling plant was a dangerous place to be. "There was a boy working there and he got his thumb caught under a belt and bottles bust there all the time, and he got a piece of glass in his thumb too," Ellis recalled. William Fitzgerald estimated the risks of a woodworking plant in a similar fashion. "It was a pretty dangerous place where I was working as the timber would come out and push you backwards if you did not look," Fitzgerald testified. Admissions such as these were damaging enough, but putting on a brave face was even worse. Charley Grant refused to stick to the script when it came to the pain of his injuries. "Yes sir, my injuries hurt of a night, but my hand does not hurt now unless I hurt it in some way," Grant declared. "My hand is not so easy to hurt."[74]

Such contradictory narratives often crept in because of the time gap between an accident and its retelling in court. Jesse Beck, a Georgia cotton mill worker, provides a particularly clear illustration of this point. By age ten, Beck had worked in several Georgia cotton mills, including The Standard, where his hand was "mashed all to pieces." Three years later, when Jesse told his story in a Polk County courtroom, he declined to play the simple-minded little boy and sought to draw clear lines between what he knew then and what he knew now. Did he know the machine that hurt him was dangerous? Not at the time, he replied. Well, did he not know that machines were dangerous in general? Of course he did. "Any of them will hurt me if I stick my hand in them when they are running," Jesse declared. "That window out there is dangerous if I go and jump out of it. I guess it is if I hit the ground." How, then, could he know something

[74] *Record in Keen*, 7; *Record in Fitzgerald*, 12; *Record in Elk Cotton Mills*, 30.

was dangerous now, when he did not on the day of his injury? Jesse was clear-headed on this subject. "Because I am old enough to know it now," he confidently proclaimed.[75]

Boys such as Jesse longed to demonstrate that they were no longer children, but the cultural and legal necessities of their causes meant that such assertions of incipient manhood undermined the narrative thread necessary to prevail. While sometimes young people told the story in unhelpful ways, more often the narrative proceeded with the necessary demonstrations of childishness. Legal necessities and cultural imagery came together in lines of argument and questioning that established incapacity. A wide variety of markers entered the courtroom discourse, all of which signaled the inherent divide between childhood and adulthood. For instance, young children might appear unaware of their legal capacity. Ebbirt Ward's attorney explained the delay after the eight-year-old's accident in this fashion. Ebbirt was "a boy of tender years [who] did not know his rights," he argued. "If he had been a man he would have brought his suit earlier, but being a child of tender years he did not know his rights." Statements such as this, that set children off so clearly from adults, were unusual. More commonly, conventional phrases that applied to children demonstrated incapacity. These included the notion that children could not understand instruction even when it was supplied, that they easily forgot what was told to them, that they possessed a "natural impulse to obey," and that they were naturally awkward around machinery.[76]

The incapacity of young workers could be demonstrated easily by putting them in front of a jury so long as they were available for that duty, but in wrongful death cases, parents and fellow workers had to play this part. Ralph Girvin's father Henry struggled to show that his dead son had been incapable of appreciating the risks of industrial work. Asked to tell the jury about Ralph's "age and ability," Henry Girvin could only say that Ralph was fairly normal. Ralph possessed "about the judgment any usual boy would have at his age" and he had "childish ways." Sometimes Ralph forgot to do what Henry told him; sometimes he remembered. The elder Girvin found the task difficult because Ralph had been fifteen at the time of his death. No one really expected a fifteen-year-old worker to be "childish," but it was true that he "didn't have ways like a man." In other settings, Henry would have undoubtedly called his son a "young man,"

[75] *Record in Beck*, 4.
[76] *Record in Ward*, n.p.; *Record in Fitzgerald*, 18; *Record in Lynchburg Cotton Mills*, 31; *Record in Hatfield*, Plaintiff's Brief, n.p.; *Record in Ensley*, 14; *Record in Rhodes*, 127.

worthy of respect and responsibility. His attempt to get something out of Georgia Veneer in return for Ralph's ghastly demise meant that his young man had to become his child.[77]

By the early twentieth century, stock phrases that captured childish incapacity could be found on any good shelf of treatises, but courtroom portrayals of childhood went beyond those suggested by prevailing doctrine. Crying, a marker of childhood in nineteenth-century culture, often came to the foreground when younger workers took the stand. Injured young workers were children who could be expected to cry. "After the little girl was hurt I carried her to the office, her finger was in pretty bad condition, just torn near up," a fellow worker told the court when detailing the aftermath of Ellen Gibbs's accident. "She was in misery and crying." Re-creating this scene was particularly important in Gibb's case because the young woman sitting at the plaintiff's table was nineteen at the time of the trial, but such descriptions appeared in regular proceedings as well. "When I got to the boy he was standing about three feet from the corner of the machine with his hand hanging down crying," textile worker J.A. Johnson said about Charley Grant.[78]

If children cried, they also played. Showing that a boy played set him off from the (supposedly) serious behavior of adulthood. As a result plaintiffs's attorneys drove home this attribute of childishness with force. Speaking of William Gray Haynie, killed by the belts of a pump at a North Carolina construction site, the family's attorney pressed the point that "he was inclined to be mischievous and playful." An affirmative response was not enough. The lawyer established that William was indeed "very playful ... like boys would be, just a boy ... full of boyish play ... full of life and play." Such portraits aimed to show that boys would be boys, that they could not possibly be expected to pay attention. "I have to keep after all of the boys, you know how boys are, they are idlesome," Tom Couch, a second hand at Bibb Manufacturing, confirmed.[79]

Pranks and horseplay showed that boys were naturally "idlesome" but as the period proceeded, a newer portrait of childishness arose – the good boy who went out of his way to please. Good boys might be good workers in the fashion that B.E. Raines recalled his departed son, Bub. "He was a good boy to work," B.E. remembered. Martha Hatfield cast her son, Mike, in a similar light. "He never missed a day from the time he

---

[77] *Record in Girvin,* 3.
[78] *Record in Gibbs,* 3; *Record in Elk Cotton Mills,* 45.
[79] *Record in Haynie,* 17; *Record in Bibb Manufacturing Co.,* 23.

first commenced to learn until he was hurt," she declared. Still, working was only part of the picture. Ben Hodges appeared in death as the quintessential good boy. By the early twenties, when the Hodges family went to court, the language was well-honed. Sixteen-year-old Ben had been "a quick and energetic boy, ready and willing to work and an unusually trustworthy and workable boy for his age as compared with others of his age and circumstances." I.L. Affleck doted even more on his son, William. "He always done what I told him, he always obeyed me and was a good boy," the elder Affleck stated. With the exception of Mike Hatfield, all of these young workers had perished in their accidents, so they remained fixed in their parents's minds as children, whose memories clearly grew fonder over time. Nonetheless, the more the good-boy characterization appeared, the more it enforced the notion that young workers were children.[80]

Of course, it was much easier to turn a child into an angel once they had gone to heaven. If they were still on the earthly plane, they had to be shown to be sweetly disposed. One sure sign was whether they cussed or not. Defense attorneys were often at pains to show that kids were ill-tempered and foul-mouthed. Earl Butner repeatedly found himself accused of using profanity around the employees at Brown Brothers Lumber. Young plaintiffs had to make sure they did not appear as little ruffians. Jimmie Taylor flatly denied that he told an older supervisor that it was "none of his damn business" when asked why he was playing with a machine. Even the brattiest of kids could be turned into charming helpmeets if need be. Hard as it might be to believe, the hard-slugging Rich Hunter appeared as a paragon of goodness in his mother's eyes. "He could bring up water for me, he could go and get groceries for me, he could go out and do almost anything," Mary Hunter doted. "He had all his limbs, he had his strength." Rich was a particularly hard sell, being poor, black, and plainly not a very good boy.[81]

Nowhere was the good-boy narrative more prominent than in the 1926 court proceedings surrounding the death of Armon Hammack. After hearing his dad talk about some construction work going on at Hope Natural Gas's Cornwell Station near Charleston, West Virginia, fifteen-year-old Armon defied his parents and took employment there, hoping to save up money for "a business course." It was not the first time he had disobeyed.

---

[80] *Record in Raines*, 13; *Record in Hatfield*, 28; *Record in Hodges*, 3; *Record in Powhatan Lime Co.*, 164.
[81] *Record in Butner*, 34; *Record in Bibb Manufacturing Co.*, 33; *Record in Corrigan*, 7.

While visiting his older sister in Michigan, he "stole away" to take a job on a dairy farm. Armon's precocity faded into a cherubic aura when his cause came to court. Tyre M. Doran swore that Armon was "mighty kind" and that he would do "just about anything that came to hand." He was such a good boy that he did not even have to be given chores. "He just took hold of anything free gratis," Doran reported. If asked to scrub the porch, "he would just take right hold and scrub like a hired girl if necessary." His mother fondly recalled how he would help out when she was ill. In such situations, "he would always say 'Mother, you stay in bed and I will get supper.'" Perhaps the Hammacks aspired to a middle-class household. Indeed, H.P. Hammack described himself as a "merchant," a moniker that rested on his "interest" in a pool hall, but his spouse got closer to the truth. "We are not wealthy people at all," she acknowledged. Coming after the law and its language had been sufficiently worked out, the Hammack family's story centered on the boy's "unusual goodness," a fact that made his death "a distressing loss" to parents "who were simply wrapped up in him."[82]

Good boys helped their folks, and good boys stayed in school. By the early twentieth century, public education had begun to catch hold in the South. Country lads were becoming school boys. Characterizing a young worker as such became a useful tactic for establishing incapacity. William Fitzgerald told the story of how he approached the boss at Alma Furniture and asked for work. "I hired for three weeks and told the foreman I was a school boy," Fitzgerald stated. A.B. Ensley had worked on the farm, but until sixteen, most of his time had been spent at school. C.M. Trivett relayed how he "just went to school" after being placed in an orphanage after his father's death. These self-descriptions helped identify young Southerners more as untested and less as worldly wise, more as green and less as experienced, more as children and less as workers.[83]

In fact, school became a marker of difference and the lack of worth. As an older producer culture faded and a new consumerist one took hold, Southern parents sought to grapple with the changes that the younger generation would see. As they told their tales in court, they worked toward a conclusion on what that future would hold. Some parents set school apart from work as something of little value. A.S. Craven made the point baldly. T.W. had been "an industrious, energetic boy" before he lost his fingers, but since then he was "not worth anything." What was a father to do? "I sent him to school since he was injured," A.S. noted. Other parents saw things differently. A.L Mills sent his son, James Allen,

---

[82] *Record in Hammack,* 45–46, 61, 85, 131, 137.
[83] *Record in Fitzgerald,* 10; *Record in Ensley,* 16; *Record in Interstate Coal Co.,* 48.

FIGURE 10. Most of these youngsters are focused on their teacher. Schools such as this one in Marey, West Virginia, around 1921 constituted the proper place for children in the age of child labor. Lewis Hine, 1921. Library of Congress, Prints & Photographs Division, National Child Labor Committee Collection, LC-DIG-nclc-04354.

to school starting at age six. Unlike the elder Craven, Mills saw benefits that would accrue. "He had education enough to keep my accounts and do my business for me, what I needed done," Mills pointed out. "I haven't had any education at all myself."[84]

Indeed, schooling became ever more important to establishing the illegitimacy of young workers's labor and demonstrating their natural incapacities. Banner Morrison's claims against Smith-Pocahontas Coal stemmed from injuries he received with braking cars in their mines near Caloric, West Virginia. Banner, or "Bona" as he appeared in the record, had trod a familiar path to the working world and its perils. At fourteen or fifteen, he had flown from his Virginia home, landing on the doorstep of his cousins in Caloric. When he applied to Smith-Pocahontas for work, he claimed to be eighteen. The company took him in, but told him he would need a work certificate shortly. Having procured one with the help of his relations, Banner continued to work in the mine, first as a trapper and then as brakeman. A "green" hand at the job of stopping coal cars,

[84] *Record in Craven*, 76.

he landed underneath one within thirty minutes of undertaking the new task. In the wake of his injuries, he told the court his story, recounting the horrors of passing blood in his urine, losing control of his bowels, and drawing up in epileptic seizures caused by a spinal injury. He endured the indignity of removing his trousers to show the jury his "rupture." His father recounted how Banner's mother had to tend to him "just the same as she did his little brothers."[85]

Family and medical testimony easily demonstrated Banner's debilitated state, but by the time the trial commenced in December 1919, school had become a key marker of the incapacities of youth. Within the first few minutes of the proceedings, Banner's lawyer led him toward an image that the jurymen might have seen in the magazines. Were the schools in session when he went to the mines? Yes, they were. Was there a school in Caloric that he could have attended? Yes, there was. Was that school in session and conveniently located? It was. "A cousin of mine that was staying at the same house was going to school," Banner affirmed. "I could see all the rest of the children up there playing and sometimes I would go by there going to my work of an evening." A good portion of the trial then demonstrated that the school was indeed there and that Banner had, in fact, worked for the mine illegally. When it all ended a few months later, the jury awarded Banner 8,000 dollars in damages.[86]

By the time Banner Morrison won his case against Smith-Pocahontas, the West Virginia coal fields teetered on the brink of the Mine Wars of 1920–1921. The Supreme Court of Appeals of West Virginia entertained the company's efforts to overturn the award twice during those tumultuous years and twice rebuffed the coal operators. As Banner grew older during the decades of the Great Depression and beyond, the illegality and illegitimacy of his work at Smith-Pocahontas would grow clearer until child labor entered the lexicon as an unquestioned social injustice.[87]

By the dawn of the New Deal era, most of the cultural work had been completed. Reformer writers had done their part, and jurists had done even more to place wage work for young people such as Banner outside the bounds of respectability. Those efforts were by no means insignificant, but they would have faltered without the movements of working people

---

[85] *Record in Morrison*, 28, 31, 41, 47, 101.

[86] Ibid., 1, 20, 51–63, 76–77.

[87] *Morrison v. Smith-Pocahontas Coal*, 88 W. Va. 158 (1921); David Alan Corbin, *Life, Work, and Rebellion in the Coal Fields: The Southern West Virginia Miners 1880–1922* (Urbana, 1981); Joseph M. Hawes, *The Children's Rights Movement: A History of Advocacy and Protection* (Boston, 1991), 39–53.

in long-forgotten places such as Caloric, West Virginia. Young workers and their families had entered the industrial era believing that producer values and machine technology could be reconciled. Perhaps they could have been, but bargains meant to protect young workers melted away in the fires of industrial labor relations. Horrific violence erupted from this breach of trust. Seeking to rebuild their lives and make meaning of what had happened to their bodies, young workers and their families traveled to Southern courtrooms. There, they found a script suited to their needs but not of their own making. Haltingly, they learned its language, a middling tongue that cast injuries to the young as the natural result of childish instincts. Safety, it said, could not be purchased at any price; loss of life and limb could be avoided only by removing young workers from perilous places and putting them in school where they belonged. The age of child labor had arrived.

Epilogue

Get Up and Play

The adult laborer cannot be regarded as a mere tool; ... in him, as in the child, there is something sacred, certain rights that we must not violate. (Felix Adler, 1905)

In the summer of 2006 near my home in northwest Illinois, two teenagers crashed the all-terrain-vehicle they were riding. The boys, aged fifteen and thirteen, had been helping a neighbor put up hay. Whether they had actually been in his employ was uncertain, but the boys' parents brought a wrongful death suit against the farmer, seeking $50,000 in damages. The suit asserted that the boys had been driving the vehicle with the consent of their possible employer, who should have known that ATVs were "notoriously dangerous vehicles." In addition to questions about the legality of employment, the case turned on long-standing conceptions about young people in industrial society. Everyone knew, the family's attorney declared, "not to trust minors with dangerous instruments." Indeed, all-terrain-vehicles had come to represent an early twenty-first century analogue of the railroad turntable, an attractive but powerful tool of both work and play. "Riding ATVs can be fun, provide a means of physical fitness, give parents and youth an opportunity for quality family time, and provide a means of accomplishing work," a Pennsylvania State University report noted in 2005. The problem, the report dryly continued, was that "ATVs can be dangerous." With thousands of injuries and scores of deaths every year, the all-terrain-vehicle epitomized a continuing conundrum of modern life: Young people and machines do not get along very well.[1]

[1] "Families Sue Over ATV Deaths," *Freeport Journal-Standard*, June 17, 2008; Dennis J. Murphy and William C. Harshman, "ATVs and Youth: Matching Children and Vehicles,"

What we know about that matter comes to us within a language forged by the interactions of law, industrial violence, and youthful labor that occurred a century ago. As capitalism swept over the United States, it raised fundamental questions about the place of young people in industrial society. Initially, it appeared that the market revolution would be no respecter of age, but by the turn of the twentieth century, a critical crossroads appeared. By word and deed, working people offered one path, a route that would combine labor and learning by ensuring a safe place for younger people in modern workplaces. Middle-class reform writers blazed another trail, one that proposed to solve the puzzle by excluding young people below a certain age from industrial employment. This radical simplification of human life eventually became conventional wisdom in the United States. That outcome depended vitally on the movements of working people in the courts. Their vision of industrial childhood depended on the good faith of their employers, a confidence that capitalist labor relations for young people was unlikely to support. The wrenching deaths and injuries that came from the shop floor led young workers and their families to seek justice. In the process, they often received compensation for their losses, but they also performed an imperative part in the fabrication of common knowledge. Initially, many resisted the assumptions of child labor, but eventually, they learned to speak its vernacular. As the folkways of the United States and the Western industrial world evolved into universals during the twentieth century, young people around the world gained divine rights.[2]

Back in the United States, however, older people had begun to worry that youngsters were taking Edgar Gardner Murphy's declarations a little too seriously. After decades of progress on children's health, government agencies, the corporate media, and average parents noticed an alarming phenomenon: the rapid growth of childhood obesity. Linked to poor diet and social factors such as two-parent wage-work, observers also pegged youthful inactivity as one of the culprits. "Use of computers and video games, along with television viewing, often occupy a large percentage of

Pennsylvania State University, College of Agricultural Sciences, August 2005 accessed at http://www.cdc.gov/nasd/docs/d001801-d001900/d001829/d001829.pdf August 24, 2008.
[2] For interesting discussions of Westernization and human rights, see Jerry Mander and John Cavanagh, *Alternatives to Economic Globalization* (San Francisco, 2002). For an excellent case study of how westernization changes basic outlooks, see Helena Nordberg-Hodge's work on the Ladahk summarized in "The Pressure to Modernize and Globalize" in *The Case Against Economic Globalization*, Jerry Mander and John Cavanagh, eds. (Berkeley, 1997), 34–35.

children's leisure time and potentially influence levels of physical activity for children as well as for adults," the authors of an influential study wrote in 2005. With no apparent irony, the study offered an unintentional indictment of modernity itself. "Many of the social and cultural characteristics that the U.S. population has accepted as a normal way of life may collectively contribute to the growing levels of childhood obesity," the authors mildly concluded. The epidemic called for a response, and the U.S. Department of Health and Human Services sprang into action, putting up a website and mounting a television advertising campaign. In the latter, sports stars urged children to "get up and play an hour a day," doling out the web address where children could go to find "fun play ideas" but warning kids: "just don't stay too long." Once there, visitors could click their way through a series of images that presented the popular cartoon characters from the movie *Shrek* dispensing instructions for calisthenics. After some mouse movements, a free *Shrek* screen saver awaited.[3]

If middle-class parents and government officials fretted over youthful inactivity at home, they agonized about children working abroad. By the 1990s, child labor again occupied the view of activists in the United States and around the planet as economic globalization resurrected old demons. Tragic fires at toy factories in Thailand and China highlighted the incongruity of young workers in developing nations manufacturing playthings for kids in the West. Echoing sentiments of a century's duration, a Christmas 2002 headline pricked readers's sensibilities with the obvious contradictions. "Young Workers Toil to Churn out Santa's Toys," it read.[4]

The heavy-handedness was not required by the early twenty-first century, for the notion of children's rights had been on the international agenda for years by that point. In 1989, the United Nations began the process that led to the U.N. Convention on the Rights of the Child. As the UN Children's Fund described the project, "world leaders decided that children needed a special convention just for them because people under 18 years old often need special care and protection that adults do not." Creating a biting irony when the U.S. government refused to sign the document, the convention harkened back to ideas worked out

---

[3] Committee on Prevention of Obesity in Children and Youth, Food and Nutrition Board, Board on Health Promotion and Disease Prevention, Institute of Medicine of the National Academies, *Preventing Childhood Obesity: Health in the Balance*, Jeffrey P. Koplan, Catharyn T. Liverman, and Vivica I. Kraak, eds. (Washington, 2005), 2; http://smallstep.gov/kids/flash/index.html accessed August 24, 2008.

[4] Antoaneta Bezlova, "Young Workers Toil to Churn out Santa's Toys" http://www.commondreams.org/headlines02/1223-01.htm accessed August 24, 2008.

in the United States and elsewhere in the West during the early twentieth century. Unless stipulated by law, the agreement declared, "a child means every human being below the age of eighteen years." Importing the language of progressive reform, the convention's article on child labor outlined "the right of the child to be protected from economic exploitation and from performing any work that is likely to be hazardous or to interfere with the child's education, or to be harmful to the child's health or physical, mental, spiritual, moral or social development." The child labor provision flowed naturally from the article that appeared before it, one that captured the heart and soul of childhood as written by the progressives. Parties to the convention agreed to recognize "the right of the child to rest and leisure, to engage in play and recreational activities appropriate to the age of the child."[5]

The U.N. Convention on the Rights of the Child encapsulated much of what children's rights advocates had been saying for years. Touching on issues such as health, free speech, and disabilities, the document served as a précis of thinking about "the child" in modern society. With its fixed calendar age of eighteen, it incorporated the simplifying process that child labor and other laws had initiated. Aiming for the broadest possible applications, United Nations Children's Fund (UNICEF) explained the convention as falling within "the human rights framework." When world leaders met in 1989, the organization pointed out, they "wanted to make sure that the world recognized that children have human rights too." As such, they invoked a central paradox that has plagued modern thinking about young people for at least the last century.[6]

The crux of that paradox is the conflict between Enlightenment-tinged conceptions of the rights-bearing individual and the necessarily messy progress of child development. Assertions of rights assume the capacity to reason and the ability to act as an independent agent to secure and protect one's own natural rights. Unlike most versions of rights-talk, discussions of children's rights rest on the opposite presumption, that rights are something that the older and wiser give to children who are naturally incapacitated from being their own political agents. This paternalist ethos works perfectly well for the very young, but as young people mature, it becomes tenuous. Seven-year-olds are not seventeen-year-olds, a natural

---

[5] UNICEF, Convention on the Rights of the Child, http://www.unicef.org/crc/ accessed August 24, 2008; United Nations Convention on the Rights of the Child, preamble, Articles 30–31.

[6] UNICEF, Convention on the Rights of the Child, http://www.unicef.org/crc/ accessed August 24, 2008.

fact upon which most people can agree. Nonetheless, the troubling implications of that fact disappear into the singularity of "the child." That notation recalls a time when reformers talked about other social "problems" in the singular: The Woman, The Laborer, The Negro. Modern thought has shed those insulting reductions for most social groups, but it has retained them for young people. Indeed, the UN convention raises the singularity of "the child" to a universal truth.[7]

Talking about human rights and children's rights in this context becomes fraught with difficulties. Progressive era writers sensed as much, and some had a simple solution: ignore adults. "For the adult who accepts life in the mills I have not a word to say," Elbert Hubbard wrote in 1902. "It is his own business." Crass as always, Hubbard hinted at separations to come. With young people removed from industrial work, the dangers of the shop floor seemed less horrible. This line of thought undergirded the adult-child binary that would define modern thinking about growing up, even as consumer capitalism fragmented identities in ever-expanding webs of market segmentation.[8]

Still, this outcome was not a foregone conclusion at the dawn of the twentieth century. Some had foreseen a different path. Unusual for his time, educational pioneer Felix Adler had placed children's rights and labor rights for adults within the same general framework. "The adult laborer cannot be regarded as a mere tool," he told the National Child Labor Committee in 1905, "In him, as in the child, there is something sacred, certain rights that we must not violate." Unlike conceptions that see children's rights as a special place, Adler's view foreshadowed a more thorough vision of human rights, one that refused to accept the adult-child bifurcation. An early twenty-first century symposium on children's law echoed this outlook, noting the need to help young people become "meaningful participants" in human communities. The "correct moral question," the authors asserted, was "whether children will be treated like *people* (not whether they will be treated like *adults*, the usual benchmark.)"[9]

[7] Holly Brewer, *By Birth or Consent: Children, Law, and the Anglo-American Revolution in Authority* (Chapel Hill, 2005), 342–343, 347–352; Linda Kerber, "The Meanings of Citizenship" *Journal of American History* 84 (1997): 833–854; James H. Kettner, *The Development of American Citizenship, 1608–1870* (Chapel Hill, 1978); Susan Pearson, "'The Rights of the Defenseless:' Animals, Children, and Sentimental Liberalism in Nineteenth-Century America" (Ph.D. Dissertation, University of North Carolina-Chapel Hill, 2004), 261–264.

[8] Elbert Hubbard, "White Slavery in the South" *The Philistine*, May 1902, 147.

[9] Lizabeth Cohen, *A Consumer's Republic: The Politics of Consumption in Postwar America* (New York, 2003), esp. 320–322; Adler quoted in "Evils of Child Labor," *New*

While Americans bemoaned the erosion of childhood at the turn of the twenty-first century, the cultural authority of the adult-child binary remained strong. Nonetheless, this language did not go completely uncontested. As working people had done a century earlier, young people and their families sometimes resisted, even if they were met with the conventional responses. In the summer of 2000, the town of Snowmass Village, Colorado, witnessed a minor reprise of the Progressive era battles over child labor when six youngsters between the ages of nine and fourteen worked illegally at a local grocery store. "Most parents do not question their children's participation in myriad extracurricular activities, like music lessons, sports and clubs that often take two, three or even four hours a day," said one of their fathers. "Doesn't working a few hours a week in a job also have educational value? By giving kids some extra money, doesn't it instill a sense of self-confidence and independence?" One of the young people involved in the incident also sounded notions about work and independence that could have been heard in a turn-of-the-century courtroom. "I was not working in a sweatshop," he pointed out. "I liked the experience of showing up on time and working with friends and not having to ask my parents for $50." His mother added that the job gave him "an unbelievable pride in his work. He felt like a hero and bought gifts for the family with his earnings." These activities ran squarely into the prevailing wisdom about child labor. A Denver labor lawyer, asked to comment about the case, put the matter in language anyone could understand: "Children should be learning the lessons of childhood, not adulthood."[10]

The most consistent resistance to those lessons appeared within religious groups, particularly the Amish. As the rural economy that supported that peaceable folk declined, they turned increasingly to light manufacturing, particularly woodworking. Treading the footsteps of their unrelated Appalachian kin, they brought young people into workshops, only to be met by the principles and language of child labor. As before, a contest of law and culture ensued. Amish families and their political allies fought for exemptions from state and federal child labor laws, contending that

York Observer and Chronicle, March 2, 1905, 280; Gary B. Melton, and Brian L. Wilcox, "Children's Law: Toward a New Realism," *Law and Human Behavior* 25 (2001): 6, emphasis in original.

[10] Gerald Zelizer, "Younger kids deserve chances to work" *USA Today*, July 20, 2000. By the late twentieth century, raft of cultural critics took aim at modern childhood. Among the most widely read was Neil Postman, *The Disappearance of Childhood* (New York, 1982).

the part-time work that teenagers did in Amish shops constituted a protected element of their cultural and religious heritage. Their supporters argued that outside observers did not "appreciate the value of children's socialization and orientation right on the job." Instead of a diminution of children's rights, work in shops was "an incubator for Amish values and culture." Labor advocates saw the matter differently. "We should certainly respect and tolerate religious and cultural beliefs that date from centuries ago, but it would be irresponsible and dangerous to begin to tolerate 17th- and 18th-century practices with respect to child labor," declared John R. Fraser, a labor department official during the Clinton administration.[11]

As for Amish people themselves, work for young people sprang from a decidedly alternative vision of childhood and labor. Young people, especially boys, should learn obedience and a trade, one Amish father told *The New York Times*. "If we couldn't put our boys to work and they didn't do nothing until they were 18, they'd be absolutely worthless." Marked by appearance as decidedly premodern, the Amish represented no real threat to the cultural power of child labor. Their views on young people and work were not likely to be taken any more seriously than their views on war and peace. Whether they should be remains an open question.[12]

[11] "Foes of Idle Hands, Amish Seek an Exemption from a Child Labor Law," *New York Times*, October 18, 2003. See also "Amish Toil Against Child Labor Laws," *International Herald Tribune*, November 13, 1998; "Amish Child Labor Bill Has Few Foes," *Washington Post*, April 2, 1999; "The U.S. Department of Labor Wants to Protect All Children" *Washington Times*, December 5, 1998. For a non-Amish example, see "Sect's Way of Teaching Faces Child-Labor Laws" *New York Times*, June 29, 1986.

[12] "Foes of Idle Hands, Amish Seek an Exemption from a Child Labor Law," *New York Times*, October 18, 2003.

Note on Sources

The main archival foundation for this study is approximately 100 litigations involving young workers hurt or killed in industrial accidents in six Southern states between the 1880s and the 1920s. As I note in the prologue, I chose to examine the states that roughly constitute the Appalachian South. I hoped to include South Carolina and Alabama in the group, but the South Carolina records have been destroyed and the Alabama records were unavailable at the time I completed the research. All of these records are located at state government archives across the region. I actually examined scores more cases than the ones used in the text, but for the most part, those records provided no more than initial pleadings or final dispositions. I chose to concentrate on those cases for which relatively complete records survived. These can be broken into two categories. Those from Kentucky, Tennessee, Virginia, and West Virginia supply substantial or complete records of the case, including pleadings, transcripts, judges's charges, briefs, and drafts of high court opinions. In these, transcripts are verbatim, with questions, answers, stricken testimony, and nonverbal clues such as "laughter" or "crying." The transcripts from Georgia and North Carolina follow a frustrating practice of removing the questions and turning attorneys's language into positive statements by the witnesses. As a result, these cases sometimes record the actual words of litigants and sometimes record words placed in their mouths by lawyers. I have tried to use such sources with care, and I have included an analysis of this practice as part of the story later in the book.

Throughout the text, I have used shortened citations for archival records following the form: "*Record in Appellate Plaintiff*." The full citations below employ archive-specific methods of identification. In Georgia, Kentucky, North Carolina, and Virginia, that means case number. After 1909, the North Carolina records have a new series of numbers that list the North Carolina Supreme Court term and then a case number. In Tennessee and West Virginia, it means archival box number. The list uses the following abbreviations:

GA – Georgia Archives, Morrow, Georgia

KDLA – Kentucky Department for Libraries and Archives, Frankfort, Kentucky

LV – The Library of Virginia, Richmond, Virginia

NCSA – North Carolina State Archives, Raleigh, North Carolina

TSLA – Tennessee State Library and Archives, Nashville, Tennessee

WVSA – West Virginia State Archives, Charleston, West Virginia

Archival Case List

Acme Box Co. v. Bascom, 119 Tenn. 537 (1907), TSLA, ET-370.

Allen v. Linger, 78 W. Va. 277 (1916), WVSA, 233–17.

Atlanta and West Point Railroad Co. v. Smith, 94 Ga. 107 (1894), GA, 18584.

Atlanta Cotton Factory Co. v. Speer, 69 Ga. 137 (1882), GA, 11827.

Augusta Factory v. Barnes, 72 Ga. 217 (1884), GA, 13079.

Ballard v. Louisville & Nashville R.R. Co., 128 Ky. 826 (1908), KDLA, 36617.

Bartley v. Elkhorn Cons. Coal and Coke Co., 151 Ky. 830 (1913), KDLA, 41377.

Beck v. Standard Cotton Mills, 1 Ga. App. 278 (1907), GA, 104.

Bibb Manufacturing Co. v. Taylor, 95 Ga. 615 (1894), GA, 18941.

Burke v. Big Sandy Coal and Coke Co., 68 W. Va. 421 (1910), WVSA, 76–6.

Burnett v. Roanoke Mills, 152 N.C. 35 (1910), NCSA, Spring 1910–51.

Butner v. Brown Brothers Lumber Co., 180 N.C. 612 (1920), NCSA, Fall 1920–508; Fall 1921–516.

Byrd v. Sabine Collieries, 92 W. Va. 347 (1923), WVSA, 393–1.

Casperson v. Michels, 142 Ky. 314 (1911), KDLA, 39423.

Corrigan v. Hunter, 139 Ky. 315 (1909), KDLA, 38886.

Craven v. Worth Mfg. Co., 151 N.C. 352 (1909), NCSA, Fall 1909–354.

Crown Cotton Mills v. McNally, 127 Ga. 404 (1907), GA, 28936 ALSO 123 Ga. 35.

Daniels v. Thacker Fuel Co., 79 W. Va. 255 (1916), WVSA, 285–19.

Davis v. Augusta Factory, 92 Ga. 712 (1893), GA, 17988.

Dixie Manufacturing Co. v. Ricks, 153 Ga. 364 (1922), GA, 2760.

Eagle and Phenix Mills v. Moncrief, 17 Ga. App. 10 (1915), GA, 5975.

Elk Cotton Mills v. Grant, 140 Ga. 727 (1913), GA, 33560.

Ellington v. Beaver Dam Lumber Co., 93 Ga. 53 (1893), GA, 18069.

Ensley v. Sylvia Lumber and Manufacturing Co., 165 N.C. 687 (1914), NCSA, Fall 1914–633.

Evans v. Dare Lumber Co., 174 N.C. 31 (1917), NCSA, Fall 1917–19.

Evans v. Josephine Mills, 119 Ga. 448 (1904), GA, 26289.

Ewing v. Lanark Fuel Co., 65 W. Va. 726 (1909), WVSA, 158–3.

Finley v. Acme Kitchen Furniture, 119 Tenn. 698 (1907), TSLA, ET-1354.

Fitzgerald v. Alma Furniture Co., 131 N.C. 636 (1902), NCSA, 20859.

Fulton Co. v. Massachusetts Bonding and Insurance Co., 138 Tenn. 278 (1917), TSLA, ET-1098.

Gibbs v. Tifton Cotton Mills, 15 Ga. App. 213 (1914), GA, 5571.

Giebell v. Collins Co., 54 W. Va. 518 (1904), WVSA, 150–3.

Girvin v. Georgia Veneer and Package Co., 140 Ga. 405 (1913), GA, 34605.

Griffith v. American Coal Co., 78 W. Va. 34 (1916), WVSA, 264–6.

Hairston v. U.S. Coal and Coke, 66 W. Va. 324 (1909), WVSA, 499–8.

Hammack v. Hope Natural Gas Co., 104 W. Va. 344 (1927), WVSA, 186–16.

Harris v. Union Cotton Mills, 23 Ga. App. 299 (1919), GA, 9877.

Harrison v. Rascoe, 139 Tenn. 511 (1917), TSLA, MT-2154.

Hatfield v. Adams, 123 Ky. 428 (1906), KDLA, 34581.

Hauser v. Forsyth Furniture Co., 174 N.C. 463 (1917), NCSA, Fall 1917–360.

Haynie v. North Carolina Electric Power Co., 157 N.C. 503 (1911), NCSA, Fall 1911–559.

Hendrix v. Cotton Mills, 138 N.C. 169 (1905), NCSA, 22096.

Hodges v. Savannah Kaolin Co., 28 Ga. App. 406 (1922), GA, 12799.

Holt v. Oval Oak Manufacturing Co., 177 N.C. 170 (1919), NCSA, 1919–101.

Honaker v. Consolidated Coal, 71 W. Va. 177 (1912), WVSA, 396–14.

Interstate Coal Co. v. Trivett, 155 Ky. 795 (1913), KDLA, 41484.

Jones v. Old Dominion Cotton Mills, 82 Va. 140 (1886), LV, 2792.

Keen v. Crosby, 25 Ga. App. 595 (1920), GA, 10785.

Kendrick v. High Shoals Manufacturing Co., 21 Ga. App. 315 (1917), GA, 8470.

Kinder v. Boomer Coal and Coke, 82 W. Va. 32 (1918), WVSA, 289–16.

King v. Flooding, 18 Ga. App. 280 (1916), GA, 6722, 6723.

Laverty v. Hambrick, 61 W. Va. 28 (1907), WVSA, 256–7.

Leathers v. Blackwell Durham Tobacco Co., 144 N.C. 330 (1907), NCSA, 22923.

Louisville and Nashville R.R. Co., v. Vincent, 116 Tenn. 317 (1905), TSLA, MT-1730.

Lynchburg Cotton Mills v. Stanley, 102 Va. 590 (1904), LV, 3235.

Magnus v. Proctor-Eagle Coal Co., 87 W. Va. 718 (1921), WVSA, 430–13.

Manning v. American Clothing Co., 147 Tenn. 274 (1922), TSLA, ET-954.

May & Co. v. Smith, 92 Ga. 95 (1893), GA, 16692.

McDaniel v. Lynchburg Cotton Mill Co., 99 Va. 146 (1901), LV, 2361.

McGowan v. Ivanhoe Manufacturing Co., 167 N.C. 82 (1911), NCSA, Fall 1911–146.

McIntyre v. Empire Printing Co., 103 Ga. 288 (1898), GA, 21299.

Messmer v. Bell & Coggeshall Co., 133 Ky. 19 (1909), KDLA, 37600.

Miller Mfg. Co. v. Loving, 125 Va. 255 (1919), VL, 6037.

Mills v. Virginian Ry. Co., 85 W. Va. 729 (1920), WVSA, 468–18.

Moore v. Dublin Cotton Mills, 127 Ga. 609 (1907), GA, 29163.

Moore v. National Coal and Iron, 135 Ky. 671 (1909), KDLA, 37604.

Morrison v. Smith-Pocahontas Coal, 88 W. Va. 158 (1921), WVSA, 468–15.

Newton v. Cooper, 13 Ga. App. 458 (1913), GA, 5024.

Norman v. Virginia Pocahontas Coal Co., 68 W. Va. 405 (1909), WVSA, 423–19.

North-East Coal Co. v. Preston, 132 Ky. 262 (1909), KDLA, 37604.

Ornamental Iron and Wire Co. v. Green, 108 Tenn. 161 (1901), TSLA, ET-1483.

Pelham Manufacturing Co. v. Powell, 6 Ga. App. 308 (1909), GA, 1636.

Pettit v. Atlantic Coastline Railroad Co., 156 N.C. 119 (1911), NCSA, Fall 1911–139; 186 N.C. 9 (1923), Fall 1923–60.

Platt v. Southern Photo Material Co., 4 Ga. App. 159 (1908), GA, 1008.

Powhatan Lime Co. v. Affleck, 115 Va. 643 (1913), LV, 1957-A.

Pressly v. Yarn Mills, 138 N.C. 410 (1905), NCSA, 21, 983.

Queen v. Dayton Coal and Iron Co., 95 Tenn. 458 (1895), TSLA, ET-1593.

Raines v. Southern Railway Co., 169 N.C. 294 (1915), NCSA, Fall 1915–546, Fall 1915–551. Raines was heard twice in the fall of 1915, hence the two records.

Ransom v. Nunnally Co., 26 Ga. App. 222 (1921), GA, 11609.

Ritter Lumber Co. v. Jordan, 138 Ky. 522 (1910), KDLA, 38886.

Roberts v. Southern Railway, 141 Tenn. 95 (1918), TSLA, ET-1114.

Roberts v. United Fuel Gas Co., 84 W. Va. 368, WVSA, 284–8.

Robinson v. Melville Manufacturing Co., 165 N.C. 495 (1914), NCSA, Spring 1914–488.

Rolin v. Tobacco Co., 141 N.C. 300 (1906), NCSA, 22454.

Rhodes v. J.B.B. Coal Co., 79 W. Va. 71 (1916), WVSA, 305–2.

Sanitary Laundry Co. v. Adams, 183 Ky. 39 (1919), KDLA, 46532.

Shaw v. Hazel-Atlas Co., 70 W. Va. 676 (1912), WVSA, 245–9.

Skipper v. Southern Cotton Oil Co., 120 Ga. 940 (1904), GA, 27076.

Smith v. Dayton Coal and Iron Co., 115 Tenn. 543 (1905), TSLA, ET-1428.

Sprinkle v. Big Sandy Coal Co., 72 W. Va. 358 (1913), WVSA, 016–15.

Standard Red Cedar Chest Co. v. Monroe, 125 Va. 442, LV, 6180.

Starnes v. Albion Manufacturing, 147 N.C. 556 (1908), NCSA, 23313.

Stearns Coal & Lumber Co. v. Tuggle, 156 Ky. 714 (1914), KDLA, 42255.

Swope v. Keystone Coal and Coke, 78 W. Va. 517 (1916), WVSA, 472–27.

Talmage v. Tift, 25 Ga. App. 639 (1920), GA, 10901.

Turner v. Richmond and Rappahannock River Railway Co., 121 Va. 194 (1917), LV, 5577.

United States Leather Co. v. Showalter, 113 Va. 479 (1912), LV, 1943-A.

Vinson v. Willingham Cotton Mills, 2 Ga. App. 53 (1907), GA, 233, 234.

Waldron v. Garland Pocahontas Coal Co., 89 W. Va. 426 (1921), WVSA, 375–12.

Ward v. Odell Manufacturing Co., 123 N.C. 248, 126 N.C. 946 (1902), NCSA, 19944.

Whitelaw v. Memphis and Charleston R.R. Co., 84 Tenn. 391 (1886), TSLA, WT-275.

Wilkinson v. K. & H. Coal and Coke, 64 W. Va. 93 (1908), WVSA, 40–4.

Williams v. Gobble, 106 Tenn. 367 (1900), TSLA, MT-1597.

Williams v. Belmont Coal and Coke, 55 W. Va. 84 (1904), WVSA, 105–6.

Wilson v. Chess & Wymond Co., 117 Ky. 567 (1904), KDLA, 32338.

Wilson v. Valley Improvement Co., 69 W. Va. 778 (1911), WVSA, 379–1.

Woodruff v. Alabama Great Southern Railroad, 75 Ga. 47 (1885), GA, 13921.

Wynne v. Conklin, 86 Ga. 40 (1890), GA, 16405.

Index

Wynne, W.H., 25, 35, 100,
172, 210, 239
Wynne, Willis, 25

young workers: and age structured
workplace, 17–19; and appropriating tools, 35; and consumerism,
17; and daycare, 7; and doffing
and sweeping, 19; and pride in
skills, 30; and vulgarity, 37, 249;

as general help, 21,
110; as trappers, 20–21; as
waterboys and tailboys,
19–20; desire to be
productive, 31
Young, Arthur, 49
Young, J.L., 225
Young, Justice, 143

Zion's Herald, 71

For EU product safety concerns, contact us at Calle de José Abascal, 56–1°,
28003 Madrid, Spain or eugpsr@cambridge.org.

www.ingramcontent.com/pod-product-compliance
Ingram Content Group UK Ltd.
Pitfield, Milton Keynes, MK11 3LW, UK
UKHW010032140625
459647UK00012BA/1340

* 9 7 8 0 5 2 1 1 5 5 0 5 2 *